Reading Joshua as Christian Scripture

Journal of Theological Interpretation Supplements
MURRAY RAE
University of Otago, New Zealand
Editor-in-Chief

1. Thomas Holsinger-Friesen, *Irenaeus and Genesis: A Study of Competition in Early Christian Hermeneutics*
2. Douglas S. Earl, *Reading Joshua as Christian Scripture*

Reading Joshua as
Christian Scripture

Douglas S. Earl

Winona Lake, Indiana
Eisenbrauns
2010

Copyright © 2010 Eisenbrauns
All rights reserved.

Printed in the United States of America

www.eisenbrauns.com

Library of Congress Cataloging-in-Publication Data

Earl, Douglas S.
  Reading Joshua as Christian scripture / Douglas S. Earl.
    p. cm. — (Journal of theological interpretation supplements ; 2)
  Includes bibliographical references and index.
  ISBN 978-1-57506-701-8 (pbk. : alk. paper)
  1. Bible. O.T. Joshua—Criticism, interpretation, etc.   I. Title.
  BS1295.52.E27   2010
  222′.206—dc22
                                                                2009053663

The paper used in this publication meets the minimum requirements of the American National Standard for Information Sciences—Permanence of Paper for Printed Library Materials, ANSI Z39.48-1984.♾™

For my parents, Bryan and Gillian

Contents

Preface   x

Abbreviations   xi

Section I
An Introduction to the Hermeneutics of Reading Joshua as Christian Scripture

1: Reading Joshua as Christian Scripture?	2
Introduction—a Sketch of the Problem	2
Cultural Memory	4
The Old Testament in the Christian Tradition	7
The Nature of Scripture and how we Learn to Speak of God	12
2: Learning to Speak of God Through Myth— Approaching Joshua as Myth	14
An Introduction to Myth	14
Ideological, Sociological and Political Approaches to Myth	20
Psychological Approaches to Myth	22
Existential and Symbolic Approaches to Myth	27
Structuralist Approaches to Myth	39
Reading Joshua with Mythical Perspectives	46
3: The Hermeneutics of Reading Joshua as Christian Scripture	49
The Hermeneutics of Texts	50
The Significance of Testimony	57
The Life of Symbols	64
Summary	69

SECTION II
MAKING JOSHUA INTELLIGIBLE AS DISCOURSE: STARTING TO READ WELL

4: JOSHUA AS PART OF TRADITION(S)	72
Deuteronom(ist)ic Affinities in Joshua	80
Priestly Affinities in Joshua	81
A Summary of the Deuteronomistic and Priestly Affinities in Joshua	85
The Significance of the Deuteronom(ist)ic and Priestly Affinities in Joshua	86
5: THE GENRE OF JOSHUA—CODES OF PRODUCTION AND USE OF LITERARY CONVENTIONS	89
Similarities Between Joshua and ANE Conquest Accounts	89
Differences Between Joshua and ANE Conquest Accounts	92
Summary	93
6: UNDERSTANDING THE SIGNIFICANCE OF חרם	94
Re-examining the 'Priestly-like' Approaches to חרם in the Non-priestly Literature	96
A Mythical Approach to the Deuteronomistic חרם	105
Conclusions	112

SECTION III
READING JOSHUA

7: THE TEXT OF JOSHUA	114
Differences in the Textual Witnesses to Joshua	114
The Significance of the Choice of Text for Christian Reading	118
Summary	119

8: READING JOSHUA	120
Joshua 1	120
Joshua 2	124
Joshua 3-4	127
Joshua 5:1-12	133
Joshua 5:13-15	139
Joshua 6	140
Joshua 7:1-8:29	148
Joshua 8:30-35	155
Joshua 9-10	157
Joshua 11-12	166
Joshua 13-21	170
Joshua 22	178
Joshua 23	183
Joshua 24	189
9: DRAWING IT ALL TOGETHER: READING JOSHUA AS CHRISTIAN SCRIPTURE TODAY	197
Joshua—Challenging and Constructing Identity	197
Appropriating Joshua—the Development and Use of its Symbols and Mythemes	203
Appropriating Joshua—its Development and Use as an Act of Discourse as Myth	212
The Context and Use of Joshua	233
Conclusion	236
BIBLIOGRAPHY	241
INDEX OF SUBJECTS AND AUTHORS	255
INDEX OF SCRIPTURE	265

Preface

This book is a slightly revised version of my PhD thesis, 'Reading Joshua as Christian Scripture' submitted to Durham University in 2008. It represents a reflection on the pressing question of what it means to read the Old Testament faithfully as Christian Scripture today in the context of the church but in the light of historical and ethical criticism.

This book is the result of a journey which has been guided by a number of people to whom I owe much gratitude. First and foremost, my PhD supervisor, Prof R.W.L. Moberly has been instrumental in shaping this work. I have also benefited from many conversations with others, especially in the realm of anthropology. In particular I would like to thank Prof Douglas Davies for helping find my bearings in the interface between anthropology and theology, Prof Robert Segal for helping me to understand concepts of myth, and Prof Seth Kunin for introducing me to neo-structuralism. Many others at Durham, both staff and students, have helped to shape my thinking for this book, especially Dr Chris Insole, Dr Marcus Pound and Dr Stuart Weeks. Prior to Durham Dr John Colwell, Dr Martin Selman and Dr Stephen Wright at Spurgeon's College, and Dr Stephen Dray and Steve King at Moorlands College were instrumental in preparing my thinking for this research project. Outside the academic context over these years the fellowship of the Sutcliff Baptist Church in Olney has provided much support for which I and my family are most grateful. This project has been partly funded by the Arts and Humanities Research Council, whose support I am most grateful for.

I am most grateful to Dr Murray Rae, the series editor, for accepting my thesis for publication in the *Journal of Theological Interpretation Supplement Series*, and for his assistance in seeing it through into print. I would also like to express my gratitude to my examiners, Profs E.F. Davis and C.T.R Hayward, and the two readers at Eisenbrauns, for suggestions to improve the thesis for publication, the majority of which I have endeavored to incorporate.

Finally, as always my family has provided vital support and encouragement in seeing this work through to completion, and so I must express my warm gratitude to Rachel my wife and our children Sophie, Daniel, Sarah, Peter, Hannah, Matthew and Chloe.

ABBREVIATIONS

AB	The Anchor Bible
ABD	D.N Freedman (ed.), *The Anchor Bible Dictionary* (New York: Doubleday, 6 vols., 1992)
ACA	K. Lawson Younger Jr., *Ancient Conquest Accounts: A Study in Ancient Near Eastern and Biblical History Writing* (JSOTSup 98; Sheffield: JSOT Press, 1990)
ACCS	J.R. Franke (ed.), *Ancient Christian Commentary on Scripture, Old Testament IV: Joshua, Judges, Ruth, 1-2 Samuel* (Downers Grove: IVP, 2005)
ACW	Ancient Christian Writers
Adv. Haer.	Irenaeus, *Adversus Haereses,* in *ANF* 1
ANE	Ancient Near East(ern)
ANEP	J.B. Pritchard (ed.), *The Ancient Near East in Pictures relating to the Old Testament* (Princeton: Princeton University Press, 2nd ed. with supplement: 1969)
ANET	J.B. Pritchard (ed.), *Ancient Near Eastern Texts Relating to the Old Testament* 3rd ed. with supplement (Princeton, Princeton University Press, 1969)
ANF	A. Roberts and J. Donaldson (eds.), *Ante-Nicene Fathers* (Buffalo: Christian Literature, 10 vols., 1885-1896, Reprint: Peabody: Hendrickson, 1994)
ARM	*Archives Roylaes de Mari*
ATR	*Anglican Theological Review*
AUSS	*Andrews University Seminary Studies*
BETL	Bibliotheca Ephemeridum Theologicarum Lovanisensium
BHS	K. Elliger and W. Rudolph (eds.) *Biblia Hebraica Stuttgartensia* (Stuttgart: Deutcsche Bibelgesellschaft, 4th ed. 1990)
Bib Or	*Bibliotheca Orientalis*
BZ	*Biblische Zeitschrift*
BZAW	Beiheft zur Zeitschrift für die Alttestamentliche Wissenschaft
CAD	A.L. Oppenheim, *et al.,* (eds.), *The Assyrian Dictionary of the Oriental Institute of the University of Chicago* (Chicago: The Oriental Institute, 1956-)

CBQ	*Catholic Biblical Quarterly*
CD	K. Barth, *Church Dogmatics* (London: T&T Clark, 15 vols., paperback ed. 2004)
CoS	W.W. Hallo and K.L. Younger Jr. (eds.), *The Context of Scripture* (Leiden: Brill, 3 vols. 2003)
D	Deuteronomist
DH	Deuteronomistic History/Historian
Dtn	Deuteronomy / deuteronomic
DtrG/H	Deuteronomistic History
DJD	*Discoveries in the Judean Desert*
DtrN	Nomist redaction of DtrG/H
DtrP	Prophetic redaction of DtrG/H
EJ	C. Roth and G. Wigoder (eds.), *Encyclopaedia Judaica* (Jerusalem: Encyclopaedia Judaica, 16 vols., 1971-1972)
FC	Fathers of the Church
FRLANT	Forschungen zur Religion und Literatur des Alten und Neuen Testaments
H	H source
HALOT	L.Koehler and W.Baumgartner, *The Hebrew and Aramaic Lexicon of the Old Testament* (Leiden: Brill, rev. ed. 1994-2000)
HAT	Handbuch zum Alten Testament
Hom. Josh.	Origen, *Homilies on Joshua,* trans. B. J. Bruce, ed. C. White (FC 105; Washington: The Catholic University of America Press, 2002)
Inst.	*Calvin: Institutes of the Christian Religion,* trans. F.L. Battles (The Library of Christian Classics 20; Philadelphia: The Westminster Press, 2 vols., 1960)
JAOS	*Journal of the American Oriental Society*
JBL	*Journal of Biblical Literature*
JCS	*Journal of Cuneiform Studies*
JSOT	*Journal for the Study of the Old Testament*
JSOTSup	Journal for the Study of the Old Testament Supplement Series
JSS	*Journal of Semitic Studies*
KBo	*Keilschrifttexte aus Boghazköi*
K_D	D-Komposition
K_P	P-Komposition
KRI	K. Kitchen, *Ramesside Inscriptions, Historical and Biographical* (Oxford, 1969-)
KTU	M. Dietrich, *et al.,* (eds.), *Keilalphabetischen Texte aus Ugarit einschliesslich der keilalphabetischen Text ausserhalb Ugarits.* Teil 1 *Transkription* (AOAT 24/1; Kevelaer: Butzon & Bercker 1976)

Life of Moses	Gregory of Nyssa, *The Life of Moses*, trans. E. Ferguson and A.J. Malherbe (The Classics of Western Spirituality; New York: Paulist Press, 1978)
LEC	Library of Early Christianity
LXX	Septuagint
LXX^A	Greek text of the Old Testament, Codex Alexandrinus
LXX^B	Greek text of the Old Testament, Codex Vaticanus
MDOG	*Mitteilungen der Deutschen Orient-Gesellschaft*
MI	Mesha Inscription
MT	Masoretic Text
NIDOTTE	W.A. VanGemeren (ed.), *New International Dictionary of Old Testament Theology & Exegesis* (Carlisle: Paternoster, 5 vols., 1997)
NAS	New American Standard Version
NET	New English Translation
NIV	New International Version
NJB	New Jerusalem Bible
NKJ	New King James
NLT	New Living Translation
NPNF	P. Schaff, *et al.*, (eds.), *A Select Library of the Nicene and Post-Nicene Fathers of the Christian Church* (Buffalo: Christian Literature, 2 series, 14 vols. each, 1887-1894, Reprint: Peabody: Hendrickson, 1994)
NRSV	New Revised Standard Version
OG	Old Greek recension of the Septuagint
OTL	The Old Testament Library
P	Priestly source / writer
P^g	*Priestergrundschrift*
PTMS	The Pittsburgh Theological Monograph Series
Quest. Josh.	Theodoret of Cyrus, 'Questions on Joshua' in *The Questions on the Octateuch*, trans. R.C. Hill (LEC 2; Washington, The Catholic University of America Press, 2007), 260-307
RedD	Deuteronomistic redaction of Joshua
RedP	Priestly Redaction of Joshua
RS	Ras Shamra field numbers
SJOT	*Scandinavian Journal of the Old Testament*
ST	T. Gilby (ed.), *Summa Theologiae,* Latin text and English Translation (Blackfriars ed.; London: Eyre & Spottiswoode, 60 vols., 1964-1974)
TDOT	G. Botterweck and H. Ringgren (eds), *Theological Dictionary of the Old Testament* (Grand Rapids, 1977-)
TOTC	Tyndale Old Testament Commentaries

Th R	*Theologische Rundschau*
VT	*Vetus Testamentum*
VTSup	Supplements to *Vetus Testamentum*
WBC	Word Biblical Commentary
WMANT	Wissenschaftliche Monographien zum Alten und Neuen Testament
ZAW	*Zeitschrift für die Alttestamentliche Wissenschaft*

SECTION I

AN INTRODUCTION TO THE HERMENEUTICS OF READING JOSHUA AS CHRISTIAN SCRIPTURE

In chapter 1 I shall sketch some of the contemporary issues relating to the interpretation of Joshua before considering how in fact the Old Testament has been read traditionally by Christians. This sketch leads into a discussion of recent anthropological approaches to myth in chapter 2 as a way of considering, in phenomenonological terms, how a renewed frame of reference might be constructed for illuminating Joshua and its use. This then requires questions of 'revelation' and of the 'good use' of texts to be addressed in chapter 3, where the material developed in chapter 2 is integrated into a proposal for the faithful appropriation of a text such as Joshua in the Christian tradition.

1. READING JOSHUA AS CHRISTIAN SCRIPTURE?

Introduction—a Sketch of the Problem

Throughout the church's history the Bible has been revered and understood to be trustworthy and true, being the inspired self-revelation of God to humanity.[1] This understanding of the nature of Scripture has often led to the privileging of its 'divine nature', with its 'human nature' sometimes being obscured and eclipsed within the church.

However, the rise of historical criticism drew attention to Scripture's very 'human' aspects, causing a re-evaluation of the nature of the material, which, coupled with the rise of historical consciousness and other trends in modernity in the nineteenth-twentieth centuries led to 'a great uncertainty of faith'. Scripture could no longer be assumed to be 'trustworthy and true' in a straightforward sense.[2] This was exacerbated by archaeological discoveries, such as the discovery of the ruins of Jericho. Whilst this discovery was initially taken as a confirmation of the veracity of the biblical material in Joshua, this evidence was subsequently interpreted by Kathleen Kenyon as demonstrating Joshua's lack of veracity—the 'historical Jericho' had fallen centuries before the alleged fall of the 'biblical Jericho'.[3] Parts of the Bible, such as Joshua, were understood to be inaccurate historically which then undermined their 'truth' and authority.[4]

A further challenge arose in the late twentieth century via rising ethical consciousness; a lack of 'ethical veracity' in texts such as Joshua highlighted again the 'human nature' of Scripture and called its trustworthiness and truth

---

[1] Cf. 2 Tim 3:16.
[2] Cf. *CD* III/I, 82.
[3] See T.A. Holland and E. Netzer, 'Jericho (place)', in *ABD,* 3.723-40, and J. J. Bimson, *Redating the Exodus and Conquest* (Sheffield: The Almond Press, rev. ed. 1981), 43ff for helpful summaries of the excavations at Jericho. Whilst I think that the work of John Bimson, and Peter James *et al., (Centuries of Darkness* (London: Pimlico, 1992)) offers a serious challenge to the reconstruction of Israel's early history, work that does not appear to have been engaged with properly, I shall be arguing that Joshua's significance does not lie in its historical veracity. Therefore I shall leave the question of 'what happened' open as I think that this is genuinely difficult.
[4] See e.g. G.W. Ramsey, 'If Jericho was not Razed, is our Faith in Vain?' in *The Quest for the Historical Israel: Reconstructing Israel's Early History,* (London: SCM, 1982), 107-24 for a basic discussion of some of the issues.

into question again at about the time when questions of historical veracity were becoming less important than they seemed several decades earlier. With the publication of works such as R.A. Warrior's essay on the problematic nature of conquest narratives in the Old Testament, and Joshua in particular, where he highlights the use made of motifs from such narratives by Puritan emigrants to America to legitimate genocide,[5] coupled with a rising global awareness of the atrocities of genocide, another blow to Joshua occurred that made it yet more difficult to assert that Joshua is in any sense 'trustworthy and true' or 'useful for teaching' as the word of God.[6] By the close of the twentieth century the perception of the 'human nature' of the Bible had, generally speaking, eclipsed that of its 'divine nature'.

These historical and ethical issues have raised more sharply the basic hermeneutical difficulty for Christian readers of the Old Testament, which is precisely that Joshua is an *Old* Testament book that is read and used in the context of the *New* Covenant. Historical and ethical issues aside, how does an Old Testament book continue to find significance in a Christian context *theologically* speaking?

Thus there are three basic issues that sharply raise the question of whether an Old Testament text, of which Joshua is a parade example, is able to find any enduring significance, in a positive sense, in the contemporary Christian context. First, a theological question: can, and if so how, does an Old Testament text continue to find significance in a Christian context? Secondly, a historical question: can a foundational 'history-like' narrative that appears to lack historical veracity, even when broadly construed, be seen as trustworthy and true in any sense? Thirdly, an ethical question: can an ethically problematic text such as Joshua continue to find Christian significance? Indeed, a student of Ellen Davis asked her if there was any biblical text that one should actually 'reject',[7] and it seems that Joshua might be a prime candidate. How might one discern whether or not Joshua does in fact have any continuing significance, positively speaking, today? Can one wholeheartedly read Joshua *as Christian Scripture?*

I propose to investigate two areas of research, a sociological one and a historical one, and consider them in theological perspective, in order to provide an opportunity to pause for reflection and for reconfiguration of the problem before dealing with the specific difficulties that the theological, historical and ethical questions raise.

---

[5] R.A. Warrior, 'Canaanites, Cowboys and Indians: Deliverance, Conquest, and Liberation Theology Today' in D. Jobling, *et al.*, (eds.), *The Postmodern Bible Reader* (Oxford: Blackwell, 2001), 188-94.

[6] However, I think that the citation and use of Joshua in the legitimation of genocide or religiously backed militarism is in fact rare.

[7] E.F. Davis, 'Critical Traditioning: Seeking an Inner Biblical Hermeneutic' in *ATR* 82.4 (2000): 733-51.

Cultural Memory

The first area to be explored is that of 'cultural memory', a recent field of research in social anthropology. 'Cultural memory' is a phrase coined by Jan Assmann in his development of Maurice Halbwachs work on memory in societies, and is a concept that he studies in the context of Ancient Israel amongst others.[8] Independently of Assmann, Danièle Hervieu-Léger has also developed Halbwachs work in relation to religion in modern societies using the concept of 'chain of memory'.[9]

John Rogerson offers a helpful summary of cultural memory as developed by Assmann, before applying it to the Old Testament, a point that I will return to. He comments,

> Corporate or cultural memory stretches back much further than individual memory. It can be located or perpetuated in ceremonies or customs or religious practices. While it depends on specialist individuals such as priests or scribes or the tellers of epics it embodies the interests of social groups, not individuals. Insofar as it is concerned with the past, it deals not with what modern scholars would call factual history, but with remembered history—a way of recalling the past which can change with the changing needs and situations of a given social group. This remembered history exists not because there is an interest in the past as such, but because the remembering enables a group to understand itself in the present and to generate hopes for the future.[10]

Importantly, Assmann contrasts cultural memory with communicative memory and collective, bonding memory (as he terms them) because cultural memory 'includes the noninstrumentalisable, heretical, subversive and disowned',[11] and suggests that it is 'complex, pluralistic, and labyrinthine; it encompasses a quantity of bonding memories and group identities that differ in time and place and draws its dynamism from these tensions and contradictions.'[12]

Danièle Hervieu-Léger argues that for religion to endure in the modern world it needs to have deep roots in traditions, through a 'chain of memory' in which 'individual believers become part of a community that links past, present

---

[8] J. Assmann, *Religion and Cultural Memory* (Stanford: Stanford UP, ET: 2006).

[9] D. Hervieu-Léger, *Religion as a Chain of Memory* (New Brunswick: Rutgers UP, ET: 2000).

[10] J.W. Rogerson, 'Towards a Communicative Theology of the Old Testament', in J.G. McConville and K. Möller (eds.), *Reading the Law: Studies in Honour of Gordon J. Wenham* (London: T&T Clark, 2007), 283-96, here 294. See also P.R. Davies, *Memories of Ancient Israel: An Introduction to Biblical History—Ancient and Modern* (Louisville: WJKP, 2008) for discussion of cultural memory in relation to the Old Testament. He suggests that cultural memory is formed by 'stories about the past shared by people who affirm a common identity, and who use stories to reinforce that identity' (12).

[11] Assman, *Religion*, 27.

[12] Ibid., 29.

and future members'. She argues that religion 'may be perceived as a shared understanding with a collective memory that enables it to draw from the well of its past for nourishment in the increasingly secular present.'[13] Interestingly, she argues that,

> [T]he modern secular societies of the West have not, as is commonly assumed, outgrown or found secular substitutes for religious traditions; nor are they more "rational" than past societies. Rather, modern societies have become "amnesiacs," no longer able to maintain the chain of memory that binds them to their religious pasts. Ironically, however, even as the modern world is destroying and losing touch with its traditional religious bases, it is also creating the need for a spiritual life and is thus opening up a space that only religion can fill.[14]

She develops her hypothesis using contemporary French society, noting that the uncertainties created by the removal of the presence of memory in society

> shows itself in a particularly acute form in the search for identity to which modern society is ill-suited to respond, lacking as it does the essential resource for identity of a memory held in common. ... The ever-increasing dislocation of this imaginative grasp ... forces society continually to reconstruct itself in new forms so as to ensure continuity for both the group and the individual. But without there being an organized and integrated social memory such reconstruction takes place in an entirely fragmentary way.[15]

Hervieu-Léger concludes that 'the religious reference to a chain of belief affords the means of symbolically resolving the loss of meaning that follows from heightened tension between the unrestrained globalization of social phenomena and the extreme fragmentation of individual experience,'[16] suggesting that, 'What clearly emerges here is the ambivalent character of religion in modernity, in which the traditional religions can only hold their own by tentatively exploiting the symbolic resources at their disposal in order to reconstruct a continuing line of belief for which the common experience of individual believers provides no support.'[17]

Taking Assmann and Hervieu-Léger together, an awareness of cultural memory is suggestive in three ways. First, granted the symbolic resources that

---

[13] Hervieu-Léger, *Religion,* from the cover.

[14] Ibid., from the cover; cf. viii-ix. Indeed, she defines religion as 'a particular form of belief and one that specifically implies reference to the authority of a tradition' (4).

[15] Ibid., 142. She illustrates this phenomenon via the current French passion for genealogy, historical novels, French Heritage days, the taste for antiques and for traditional crafts, concluding that 'the passion commonly felt for everything concerned with the celebration of roots may be seen as the converse of the intensely felt sense of the loss of collective memory' (142).

[16] Ibid., 166.

[17] Ibid., 176.

Joshua *has* provided throughout the history of the church—such as the evocation of crossing the Jordan in baptism, the collapsing walls of Jericho signifying the fall of 'the world' in all its negative aspects, the 'salvation' of Rahab prefiguring Christian salvation and the promise of the land being fulfilled as anticipating heavenly inheritance—even if these now have a somewhat problematic nature, to seek to excise them from the tradition is likely to be a mistake which might contribute to the 'collapse' or fragmentation of the Christian tradition with the loss of a distinctive Christian identity. Communities are 'historically' constituted with traditional roots, and their identities are not sustained 'from nowhere'. Secondly, material such as Joshua has provided the basis for our 'God talk', where, for example, the Old Testament materials provided the basis for the narration of Jesus' identity in the gospels, and thus for our understanding of Jesus. However, thirdly, whilst Hervieu-Léger's approach would caution against the rejection of material such as Joshua from the Christian tradition, Assmann's approach highlights the presence of 'noninstrumentalisable, heretical, subversive and disowned' material. In other words, whilst it may be important not to 'reject' the book of Joshua from Christian 'cultural memory', this does not imply that it has, of necessity, to be 'used'; rather, it is a call to *respect and recognize* its presence in the tradition *as* part of the tradition that forms Christian identity. Such a conclusion is, perhaps, not particularly novel in the Christian tradition.[18] For example, Gregory of Nyssa in his first homily on Ecclesiastes writes,

> In all the other scriptures [i.e., other than Ecclesiastes], whether histories or prophecies, the aim of the book also includes other things not wholly of service to the Church. Why should the Church be concerned to learn precisely the circumstances of battles, or who became the rulers of nations and founders of cities, which settlers originated where, or what kingdoms will appear in time to come, and all the marriages and births which were diligently recorded, and all the details of this kind which can be learned from each book of scripture? Why should it help the Church so much in its struggle towards its goal of godliness?[19]

In other words, there is precedent within the tradition for an approach to the Old Testament that cherishes it as Scripture but does not require its 'utilization' or 'application' in any straightforward way.

---

[18] Throughout this introduction I will draw upon figures in the Christian tradition in order to indicate the way in which the approach that I am developing is properly Christian and properly theological even though I shall also make extensive use of contemporary anthropology. My use of anthropology should be construed as being conducted within a wider theological frame of reference, something that I hope will be clear.

[19] Homily 1, trans. S.G. Hall and R. Moriarty in S.G. Hall (ed), *Gregory of Nyssa: Homilies on Ecclesiastes: An English Version with Supporting Studies* (Berlin: Walter de Gruyter, 1993), 33-4.

Thus given the apparent impasse reached with regard to Joshua when its significance is discussed in hermeneutical terms, on empirical sociological grounds, consideration of cultural memory would suggest that 'abandoning' Joshua is unwise. Cultural memory provides one with a frame of reference that resists the rejection of Joshua whilst not forcing its 'application'.

The Old Testament in the Christian Tradition

The second avenue of inquiry is the way in which the Old Testament has in fact been used within the Christian tradition. The simple sketch above, whilst indicating (all too crudely and briefly) the erosion of trust and confidence in Scripture, and Joshua in particular, only reflects the development of the understanding of the nature of Scripture in the modern and post-modern era. Might attention to the pre-modern era make the debate look rather different?

I begin by considering some of Origen's comments on biblical interpretation in his *On First Principles*. He comments,

> But if in every detail of this outer covering, that is, the actual history, the sequence of the law had been preserved and its order maintained, we should have understood the scriptures in an unbroken course and should certainly not have believed that there was anything else buried within them beyond what was indicated at a first glance. Consequently the divine wisdom has arranged for certain stumbling-blocks and interruptions of the historical sense to be found therein, by inserting in the midst a number of impossibilities and incongruities, in order that the very interruption of the narrative might as it were present a barrier to the reader and lead him to refuse to proceed along the pathway of the ordinary meaning: and so, by shutting us out and debarring us from that, might recall us to the beginning of another way, and might thereby bring us, through the entrance of a narrow footpath, to a higher and loftier road and lay open the immense breadth of the divine wisdom.

> And we must also know this, that because the aim of the Holy Spirit was chiefly to preserve the connexion of the spiritual meaning, both in the things that are yet to be done and in those which have already been accomplished, whenever he found that things which had been done in history could be harmonised with the spiritual meaning, he composed in a single narrative a texture comprising both kinds of meaning, always, however, concealing the secret sense more deeply. *But wherever the record of deeds that had been done could not be made to correspond with the sequence of the spiritual truths, he inserted occasionally some deeds of a less probable character or which could not have happened at all, and occasionally some which might have happened but in fact did not.* Sometimes he does this by a few words, which in their bodily sense do not appear capable of containing truth, and at other times by inserting a large number. ...

> All this, as we have said, the Holy Spirit supervised, in order that in cases where that which appeared at the first glance could neither be true nor useful we should be led on to search for a truth deeper down and needing more careful examination, and should try to discover in the scriptures which we believe to be inspired by God a meaning worthy of God. ...
>
> *And so it happens that even in them the Spirit has mingled not a few things by which the historical order of the narrative is interrupted and broken, with the object of turning and calling the attention of the reader, by the impossibility of the literal sense, to an examination of the inner meaning.*[20]

Thus Origen was well aware and not at all bothered that there were 'historical difficulties' in Scripture, an observation that was not uncommon in the early patristic writers. But such 'historical difficulties' or 'contradictions' gradually became seen to be something problematic and were treated as apparent rather than real, and thus obscured in the tradition.[21] But rather than dismissing texts with historical difficulties as 'untrue', or seeking to offer a plausible reconstruction of the history behind the text, or a harmonization of texts, Origen saw these difficulties as a hermeneutical cue to seek the text's significance somewhere other than in the 'literal' or 'historical' sense.[22]

---

[20] *On First Principles*, Latin Text, IV.ii.9, in G.W. Butterworth (trans.), *Origen: On First Principles* (Gloucester: Peter Smith, 1973), 285-7, emphasis added.

[21] See e.g. R.W. Southern's discussion of the rise of work on harmonization of the biblical materials in Scholastic thought (R.W. Southern, 'The Sovereign Textbook of the Schools: the Bible' in *Scholastic Humanism and the Unification of Europe* (Oxford: Blackwell, 1995), 1.102-33). See also G.R. Evans, *The Language and Logic of the Bible: The Road to Reformation* (Cambridge: CUP, 1985) 114-20 on the development of reading strategies to avoid contradictions in the Bible.

[22] See B. Smalley, *The Study of the Bible in the Middle Ages* (Oxford: Basil Blackwell, 3rd ed. 1983) for general discussion of trends in biblical interpretation, esp. 281-308 on the decline of 'spiritual reading' and rise of concern with the 'letter'. (See also G.R. Evans, *The Language and Logic of the Bible: The Earlier Middle Ages* (Cambridge: CUP, 1984), 67-71 for the shift in perception of *historia* and the development of the sense of 'the letter'.)

Defining what is meant by the 'literal sense' is surprisingly difficult even if it seems intuitively clear. The problem is highlighted in David Dawson's comments on Hans Frei's work: 'Frei's concept of the Bible's literal sense, never simple, changed over the course of his career. His usual claim, developed in a number of early writings, was that the Bible's literal sense is constituted by the way its realistic, true-to-life stories aptly depict the way things are regarded as customarily happening in the world. Late in his career, Frei characterized the literal sense more as a consensus decision by the Christian community about how to read certain texts than as an inherent feature of certain kinds of literary narratives.' (J.D. Dawson, *Christian Figural Reading and the Fashioning of Identity* (Berkeley: University of California Press, 2002), 143).

But a similar move occurs in relation to ethical difficulties. In Augustine's discussion of literal interpretation in *On Christian Doctrine* he discusses criteria for determining where Scripture is to be read figuratively,[23] suggesting that, 'Whatever there is in the word of God that cannot, when taken literally, be referred either to purity of life or soundness of doctrine, you may set down as figurative. Purity of life has reference to the love of God and one's neighbour; soundness of doctrine to the knowledge of God and one's neighbour.'[24] In other words, an 'ethical difficulty' with a scriptural text—a text that does not have reference to love of neighbour for example—is a hermeneutical cue to promote its significance somewhere other than in the 'literal' sense. Whilst one might think that Augustine would then understand Joshua's significance figuratively, he does not. For example, in *Questions on Joshua,* commenting on Josh 11:14 Augustine states, 'One should not at all think it a horrible cruelty that Joshua did not leave anyone alive in those cities that fell to him, for God himself had ordered this.'[25] Thus although Augustine does not reject the 'literal sense' of Joshua, his ethical-theological hermeneutic paves the way within the tradition for one to do so.

However, returning to Origen, in his *Homilies on Joshua* ethical difficulties in the scriptural text function for him rather like historical difficulties—such difficulties are a hermeneutical cue to seek the significance of the text somewhere other than in the literal sense. In his homily on Josh 10:20-26 he remarks,

> But Marcion and Valentinus and Basilides and the other heretics with them, since they refuse to understand these things in a manner worthy of the Holy Spirit, "deviated from the faith and became devoted to many impieties," bringing forth another God of the Law, both creator and judge of the world, who teaches a certain cruelty through these things that are written. For example, they are ordered to trample upon the necks of their enemies and to suspend from wood the kings of that land that they violently invade.
>
> And yet, if only my Lord Jesus the Son of God would grant that to me and order me to crush the spirit of fornication with my feet and trample upon the necks of the spirit of wrath and rage, to trample on the demon of avarice, to trample down boasting, to crush the spirit of arrogance with my feet, and, when I have done all these things, not to hang the most exalted of these exploits upon myself but upon his cross. Thereby I imitate Paul, who says, "the world is crucified to me," and, that which we have already related above, "Not I, but the grace of God that is in me."
>
> But if I deserve to act thus, I shall be blessed and what Jesus said to the ancients will also be said to me, "Go courageously and be strengthened; do not be

---

[23] *On Christian Doctrine*, 3.5-11 (*NPNF* I.2, 1168-74).
[24] *On Christian Doctrine*, 3.10.14 (*NPNF* I.2, 1172).
[25] Augustine, *Questions on Joshua* 16 (*ACCS*, 67. Cf. also *Questions on Joshua* 10-11 in *ACCS*, 46).

afraid nor be awed by their appearance, because the Lord God has delivered all your enemies into your hands." If we understand these things spiritually and manage wars of this type spiritually and if we drive out all those spiritual iniquities from heaven, then we shall be able at last to receive from Jesus as a share of the inheritance even those places and kingdoms that are the kingdoms of heaven, bestowed by our Lord and Savior Jesus Christ, "to whom is the glory and the dominion forever and ever. Amen!"[26]

What is interesting is that this ethical-theological hermeneutic operated precisely *in contrast to* the hermeneutic of the Gnostic 'heretics' who asserted that the hermeneutically significant level of the Old Testament was found in the 'literal sense' of the text.

Thus the Old Testament functioned as Scripture in the emerging 'orthodox' Christian church precisely through 'spiritual reading' where historical and ethical problems were understood to exist in the text as cues to such a mode of reading. Indeed, this kind of spiritual or allegorical interpretation typified much of the early church.[27] Whilst allegorical interpretation is often regarded as

---

[26] *Hom. Josh.* 12.3, 123-4.

[27] See F.M. Young, *Biblical Exegesis and the Formation of Christian Culture* (Cambridge: CUP, 1997) for discussion of the nature of such interpretation, and differences between the Alexandrian and Antiochene traditions. Origen is typical here, at least in the Alexandrian tradition, of these kinds of hermeneutical moves. For example, in *The Life of Moses* Gregory of Nyssa suggests, 'Do not be surprised at all if both things—the death of the firstborn and the pouring out of the blood—did not happen to the Israelites and on that account reject the contemplation which we have proposed concerning the destruction of evil as if it were a fabrication without any truth. For now in the difference of the names, Israelite and Egyptian, we perceive the difference between virtue and evil.' (II.100, p.77). It is interesting that whilst interpreters within the Antiochene tradition are keen to 'uphold' the literal or historical sense of Scripture, in interpreters who seek any contemporary 'application' it is effectively a 'spiritual' sense that is used, although it is described in terms of typology or *theoria* rather than *allegoria* (see e.g. Theodoret of Cyrus, *Quest. Josh*, preface (p.261); 2.2 (pp.267-9); 12 (pp.285-7)).

However, by the time that we get to Calvin we find a very different response to the historical and ethical difficulties. For example, he comments on Josh 10:18, 'The enemy having been completely routed, Joshua is now free, and, as it were, at leisure, to inflict punishment on the kings. In considering this, the divine command must always be kept in view. But for this it would argue boundless arrogance and barbarous atrocity to trample on the necks of kings, and hang up their dead bodies on gibbets. It is certain that they had lately been raised by divine agency to a sacred dignity, and placed on a royal throne. It would therefore have been contrary to the feelings of humanity to exult in their ignominy, had not God so ordered it. But as such was his pleasure, it behoves us to acquiesce in his decision, without presuming to inquire why he was so severe.' (J. Calvin, *Commentaries on the Book of Joshua*, (Grand Rapids: W.B. Eerdmans, ET:1949), 157-8). Ironically Calvin is in a sense closer to the Gnostic heretics here than to interpreters such as Origen and Gregory of Nyssa, even though his exegesis is also in some senses simply a devel-

lacking hermeneutical control, it is interesting to note how 'stable' and consistent the allegorical readings of Joshua were—for example with regard to Rahab and to Jericho. This suggests that Joshua was read within a tradition that in fact offered a hermeneutical control and guide to its ongoing significance. Joshua was not read in isolation from the remainder of what emerged as Christian Scripture, and its reading was guided by the developing Christian tradition. Indeed, the importance of tradition, and the *regula fidei* as guiding interpretation was developed by Irenaeus, again in opposition to the Gnostics.[28] Thus we find an awareness of the importance of the reception of a text and the context in which it is used within the early Christian tradition—scriptural texts are not 'freely floating' objects to be interpreted in isolation from each other and the tradition of which they are a part. Irenaeus' response to conflicting interpretations was not to seek to determine what a given text 'really meant' through appeal to a 'presuppositionless' or 'scientific' exegesis, but rather to demonstrate that the significance of a text, as a *Christian* text, was bound up with its position and reception within the particular tradition—or one might say within the 'interpretative community'.

In summary then, we see an awareness of historical and ethical difficulties in Old Testament narratives, and that often this was not seen as a problem but as a hermeneutical cue to seek a 'spiritual meaning'. Moreover, just as the development of hermeneutical theory in the twentieth century highlighted the importance of the reader and their context for the interpretation of a text, so we have seen an awareness of the importance of the interpretative tradition associated with the reception of a scriptural text, and how such a tradition guides the 'good' interpretation of a given scriptural text *as Christian Scripture,* as a text that constructs Christian identity. This is not to say that a univocal 'correct' meaning was imposed on any given text for a plurality of interpretations is evidenced, even if they cluster around a 'stable core'. The tradition sought to foster good interpretation of biblical texts *used as Christian Scripture.*[29]

---

opment of Augustine's (cf. e.g. *Questions on Joshua* 16), in which he stresses the 'literal sense' of the text understood at 'face value'.

An interesting example of the tension between the kinds of reading exemplified by Origen and Augustine in relation to 'Christian warfare' is found in Gratian's *Decretum* C.23 q.1-5. (See my 'Joshua and the Crusades' (forthcoming) for further discussion of Gratian.) I think that the essential difference between the two forms of reading the text (Origen and Augustine/Calvin) is located in the way in which basic human ideas of morality inform the hermeneutical and theological frames of reference for reading scriptural texts, even as both approaches seek to uphold the enduring value of the difficult texts, unlike the heretics whom Origen refers to, for whom the moral difficulty was a cue to reject the text.

[28] Cf. e.g. *Adv. Haer.* 1.8.1.
[29] Cf. W.S. Green's comments on Jewish midrash ('Romancing the Tome: Rabbinic Hermeneutics and the Theory of Literature', in *Semeia* 40 (1987): 147-68) in which he

Thus there is a rich theological resource within the Christian tradition that is fully cognizant of the historical and ethical difficulties with Joshua, but uses them as a cue for a certain kind of interpretation that offers guidance for what it means to read Joshua as Christian Scripture *well*. Thus the contemporary interpreter of Joshua as Christian Scripture may, and perhaps ought to, refuse some of the interpretative moves encouraged by certain forms of modernity and post-modernity, even if the interpreter may also benefit greatly from both modern and post-modern biblical scholarship in order to understand Joshua better, as we shall see.

The Nature of Scripture and How we Learn to Speak of God

In the light of historical criticism one cannot simply return to patristic interpretation of the Old Testament and re-assert it. On the one hand, it may need some correction for in places it seems implausible, particularly in the details, even if it points towards a good 'frame of reference' for reading difficult texts. On the other hand, we have become more aware of the human dimensions of Scripture; one can no longer assert that it is 'divine revelation' in any straight-forward sense, and thus automatically trustworthy and true.[30] Thus we need to consider the nature of the material that we have in front of us in Scripture—in Joshua.

Indeed, Rowan Williams suggests that '[t]heology ... is perennially liable to be seduced by the prospect of bypassing the question of how it *learns* its own language'.[31] He suggests that revelation is associated with 'the dialectical process of its historical reflection and appropriation'[32] and that '"revelation" includes, necessarily, "learning about learning"'.[33] In other words, it can be all too easy to simply appeal to Scripture as 'divine revelation' in order to trump the demanding questions that occur in relation to it. Since it is no longer possible to

---

argues that although different interpretations are given in any midrash-compilation, they do, however, operate within a 'narrow thematic range'. The various explanations are thus *mutually reinforcing* rather than conflicting, and alleged multiple meanings are multiple variations on a single meaning. By providing multiple warrants for what is essentially the same message, it *restricts* interpretative options (162-3); 'The rabbinic interpretation of scripture, therefore, was anything but indeterminate or equivocal. Rather, it was an exercise—and a remarkably successful one—in the dictation, limitation, and closure of what became a commanding Judaic discourse.' (165).

[30] In other words, if one is to listen seriously to contemporary scholarship one must take seriously the possibility that Marcion was correct, or find a way to reconstrue the debates in such a way as to make the issues look rather different. This book is an attempt to explore the latter possibility.

[31] R. Williams, 'Trinity and Revelation' in *On Christian Theology* (Oxford: Blackwell, 2000), 131-47, here, 131.

[32] Ibid., 132.

[33] Ibid., 135.

simply assert the divine nature of Scripture,[34] one must engage with this process of 'learning about learning'. If we return to where we began, cultural memory, situated in a theological context, may be a helpful place to situate a discussion of how we 'learn about learning' with reference to that which we might wish to call 'revelation'. How is the church's cultural memory formed, and how is the life of the community shaped via scriptural texts; how can we 'learn about our learning'? I suggest that whilst it needs to be stripped of its negative connotations, 'myth' is a helpful category for reflecting upon this learning process when situated in a theological context, and in the context of cultural memory.

---

[34] Whilst one cannot simply *assert* it, one need not *deny* it either. A pointer to a way forward to the 'recovery' of the divine nature of Scripture might be found in Thomas Aquinas in his development of the somewhat neglected notion of *concursus* with regard to causality (see e.g. *Summa Contra Gentiles* III.2, and cf. 1 Thess 2:13). This is not the place to develop this idea in detail in relation to Scripture, save to say that the notion of *concursus* allows one to speak, simultaneously, of the human and divine nature of the material that is in front of us.

2. LEARNING TO SPEAK OF GOD THROUGH MYTH— APPROACHING JOSHUA AS MYTH

An Introduction to Myth

It is generally through 'important narratives' that people, both individually and as communities, gain a sense of identity and learn to speak about themselves and of what is of 'ultimate importance'. It is largely through such narratives that cultural memory is negotiated and constructed,[1] and by studying the nature of what have been called histories, stories and myths that we can 'learn about our learning'. Whilst in modern Western thought there has been a tendency to distinguish between the genres of history, story and myth in terms of content, value and function, I propose to reconsider these distinctions. For want of a better term, and it is a very inadequate term given its history of use, our learning and shaping of identity may nevertheless be considered using the category of 'myth', when suitably construed, for it will include history, story and other symbolic resources. In other words, one might say that cultural memory, and identity, is constructed through myth. Indeed, Jan Assmann suggests that the 'stories of the Exodus, Sinai, the wilderness, and conquest, or the stories about the patriarchs [understood as myth] ... are without any doubt foundational stories determining the memory and identity of Israel as a religious and ethnic community, taking place not "in illo tempore" but in historical time (however fictional this placement may be).'[2] He goes on to generalize this concept of *historia sacra* as he terms it to

---

[1] Cf. J. Assmann, 'Myth as *historia divina* and *historia sacra*', in D.A. Green and L.S. Lieber (eds.), *Scriptural Exegesis: The Shapes of Culture and the Religious Imagination: Essays in Honour of Michael Fishbane* (Oxford: OUP, 2009), 13-24. Previously Jan Assmann coined the term 'mnemohistory', i.e., history as it is remembered, as the 'proper way of dealing with the working of cultural memory' (*Moses the Egyptian: The Memory of Egypt in Western Monotheism* (Cambridge MA: Harvard University Press, 1997), 15). Also see A. Kirk, 'Social and Cultural Memory', in A. Kirk and T. Thatcher (eds.), *Memory, Tradition, and Text: Uses of the Past in Early Christianity* (Semeia Studies 52; Atlanta: SBL, 2005), 1-24 who discusses cultural memory in these terms. However, the approach that I shall develop indicates that the way in which texts shape identity occurs slightly differently from the way in which Kirk suggests.

[2] Assmann, 'Myth', 21.

understand the foundational myths of other peoples as their *historiae sacrae*. They are then to be defined as representations of their specific normative past based on (a) a concept of connective justice or morality; (b) a notion of sacrality, be it the will of God or an emphatic notion of community, nation, and empire; and (c) an idea of promise, project or program involving goals to achieve, ideals to realize, and values to enforce.[3]

This 'shaping of identity' through 'myth' needs careful elucidation. 'Myth' is a category that anthropologists have used to describe the means by which people learn to shape their identities and lives and relate to the community of which they are a part. Perhaps one might say then that it is by the cumulative accretion, juxtaposition and reception of 'myths' that 'cultural memory' is formed, developed and realized. So the study of myth is crucial to the understanding of cultural memory, and hence to self-understanding and to 'learning about learning', and thus, in the Christian context, to our understanding of Scripture, its relationship to Christian identity, and to how we learn to talk about God. Thus I shall focus on addressing the use of the category 'myth' in relation to Joshua.

A full treatment and analysis of the development and use of the category 'myth' is beyond the scope of this thesis. I offer here, however, an indicative account of how the idea of 'myth' is understood and used in contemporary anthropology and what its significance might be in general terms before looking at certain approaches in detail that appear to have heuristic value for the interpretation of Joshua.

The nineteenth and twentieth centuries witnessed the growth of a plethora of approaches to myth,[4] and so the term 'myth' has a problematic history of use, and current usage of the term by anthropologists is varied. Often, and particularly in biblical studies, it is used pejoratively, especially when used in a non-technical fashion, being associated with either primitive science or false consciousness—essentially that which is naively 'untrue'. But recent anthropological studies of myth highlight the importance of 'myth' as an ineluctable pan-cultural phenomenon that helps people and societies to make sense of the world and orientate themselves within it, with 'myth' having many functions and meanings in this regard.[5] Theorists of myth in the nineteenth and twentieth centuries sought to reify 'myth', providing accounts of the essence of myth according to differing understandings of human nature, seeking to address the

---

[3] Ibid., 22.
[4] See A. von Hendy, *The Modern Construction of Myth* (Bloomington: Indiana UP, 2002) for analysis of major approaches to myth in the nineteenth and twentieth centuries.
[5] R.A. Segal (*Myth: A Very Short Introduction* (Oxford: OUP, 2004), 56-7) notes that Mircea Eliade argued this, even if myth is 'camouflaged' today. Segal goes on to consider how the stories of John F. Kennedy Jr. and George Washington might be said to reflect contemporary myth.

origin, content or function of myth as they understood it. Recognizing the problems of approaching what has been termed 'myth' in these ways, towards the end of the twentieth century there has been a tendency either to abandon the search for an 'essentialist' definition of myth, or to combine varied approaches to provide a 'thick description' of myth, with the assumption being that most previous approaches to myth have identified *an* aspect of something called 'myth'. Thus the definition of 'myth' has been and remains problematic.

One contemporary theorist seeking a thick description of myth is William Doty. He defines myth via the following statement:

> A mythological corpus consists of (1) a usually complex network of myths that are (2) culturally important (3) imaginal (4) stories, conveying by means of (5) metaphoric and symbolic diction, (6) graphic imagery, and (7) emotional conviction and participation, (8) the primal, foundational accounts (9) of aspects of the real, experienced world and (10) humankind's roles and relative statuses within it.
>
> Mythologies may (11) convey the political and moral values of a culture and (12) provide systems of interpreting (13) individual experience within a universal perspective, which may include (14) the intervention of suprahuman entities as well as (15) aspects of the natural and cultural orders. Myths may be enacted or reflected in (16) rituals, ceremonies, and dramas, and (17) they may provide materials for secondary elaboration, the constituent mythemes (mythic units) having become merely images or reference points for a subsequent story, such as a folktale, historical legend, novella, or prophecy.[6]

Despite its attractiveness, the difficulty with Doty's approach is that it reflects a juxtaposition and conflation of various approaches that, in places, reflect essentially different understandings of human nature and of myth that may be mutually incompatible.[7] Whilst more work is therefore required for this ambitious project, this definition as it stands has heuristic value since it is suggestive of the kind of 'objects' that we are talking about in connection with myth. It indicates the complex and rich variety of ways in which one's worldview, identity and existence are shaped. Therefore, if Joshua can be shown to have sufficient resonance or 'family resemblance' with the kind of materials identified by

---

[6] W.G. Doty, *Mythography: The Study of Myths and Rituals* (Tuscaloosa: University of Alabama Press, 2nd ed. 2000), 33-4. In general his work appears to be well received in reviews and summaries of the field, although there are some important criticisms, discussed below. See R.A. Segal, review of *Mythography: The Study of Myths and Rituals* (Tuscaloosa: University of Alabama Press, 1986), by W.G. Doty, in *JAAR* 56 (1988): 149-52 (review of 1st ed.); L. Coupe, review of *Mythography: The Study of Myths and Rituals* (Tuscaloosa: University of Alabama Press, 2nd ed. 2000), by W.G. Doty, in *Religion* 32.2 (2002): 166-8; L.A. Northup, 'Myth-placed Priorities: Religion and the Study of Myth' in *Religious Studies Review* 32.1 (2006): 5-10.

[7] See e.g. Robert Segal's critique in his review of *Mythography*.

Doty's definition, then it is suggestive of the value of seeking to understand Joshua, and crucially, its significance and use, in terms of what the various theories of myth behind Doty's definition suggest that myth is, and how the significance of myths are manifested.

I will sketch very briefly how Joshua does indeed resonate with this description in order to suggest that a 'mythical approach' is a reasonable approach to pursue.[8] First, Joshua is clearly culturally important and part of a network of myths that are culturally important by virtue of their inclusion in Scripture. Secondly Joshua is a story (I will leave the 'imaginal' aspect of it to one side for the moment) that involves symbol, such as the symbolic nature of crossing the Jordan (Josh 3-4),[9] of Jericho (Josh 6),[10] and of the characters of Rahab (Josh 2) and Achan (Josh 7),[11] that invites emotional conviction and participation (e.g. Josh 23-24). Thirdly, Joshua is a foundational account for Israel that establishes statuses, values and norms for society, such as through the stories of Rahab and Achan, the law (e.g. Josh 8:30-35) and the distribution of the land (Josh 13-21). Fourthly, Joshua narrates suprahuman intervention, such as in the parting of the waters of the Jordan (Josh 3-4) and in the battle narrated in Josh 10. Finally, it provides material for further elaboration, such as one finds in the Psalms (e.g. Ps 114), the New Testament (e.g. Acts 7, Jas 2:20-26) and the Christian tradition (e.g. Origen's homilies). This very brief sketch indicates that Joshua appears to have significant resonances with material that is termed mythical, and hence that analyzing Joshua from the perspective of myth may be fruitful. Thus Joshua's significance is likely to be illuminated by the ways in which these theories of myth suggest that myths find their significance.[12]

There may well be difficulties with Doty's definition as it stands. But what is attractive about his approach is that it seeks to work from a 'family resemblance' between objects that might be called 'myth', rather than from pre-understandings of the nature of humanity that are specific to certain disciplines, and in which one's theory of myth is tailored to fit. He recognizes that different theorists of myth have produced *partial* accounts of how people and communities shape their existence and orientate themselves in the world from the per-

---

[8] The details of this will be filled out in chapter 8.
[9] Cf. L.D. Hawk, *Joshua* (Berit Olam; Collegeville: The Liturgical Press, 2000), 59-61.
[10] Cf. R.D. Nelson, *Joshua* (OTL; Louisville: Westminster John Knox Press, 1997), 91.
[11] Cf. F.A. Spina, *The Faith of the Outsider: Exclusion and Inclusion in the Biblical Story* (Grand Rapids: W.B. Eerdmans, 2005), 52-71.
[12] There has been surprisingly little work done on Joshua 'as myth'. One study is N.A Soggie (*Myth, God, and War: The Mythopoetic Inspiration of Joshua* (Lanham: University Press of America, 2007)). Soggie considers the development of the text of Joshua using a psychological approach to myth. His work has rather different concerns in view than mine.

spective of different disciplines in the humanities, and that some synthesis is required to establish a complete picture. As Richard Walsh puts it,

> Mythographers are ruthless tailors fitting their subjects to their Procrustean beds. That the academy's various methods and subject areas are themselves such *a priori* patterns is most obvious to those outside the methods and areas in question. ... [W]e will surely object to myth's reduction to mere psychology, sociology, economics, or so forth unless one of those areas is our own comfortable bed.[13]

It is too ambitious a project to seek to develop an adequate definition of myth here, and not necessary for my thesis.[14] But if one is to heed Doty and Walsh's comments on the one hand, and Doty's critics on the other, perhaps one may start by considering whether various approaches to myth that appear 'fitting' within a theological anthropology might, when used on their own terms, indicate ways of understanding Joshua that illuminate some aspects of Joshua and its reception and use that it would be difficult to discern otherwise. This avoids the very real difficulty of defining myth adequately, or of forcing our understanding of Joshua or myth into a Procrustean bed.[15] It is a less ambitious approach that makes no general (and unnecessary) claims concerning the nature of myth. It is an approach that might help one to understand Joshua better, and thus how to read and use it well. Thus there may be some theories of myth that are not appropriate to use to analyze Joshua either because they address different kinds of material, or because they may reflect a (theologically or anthropologically) poor interpretation of human nature. In other words, my project here is to

---

[13] R.G. Walsh, *Mapping Myths of Biblical Interpretation* (Playing the Texts 4; Sheffield: Sheffield Academic Press, 2001), 54. Cf. Ernst Cassirer's comments, 'Every scholar still found in myth those objects with which he was most familiar. At bottom the different schools saw in the magic mirror of myth only their own faces. The linguist found in it a world of words and names—the philosopher found a primitive philosophy—the psychiatrist a highly complicated and interesting neurotic phenomenon.' (*The Myth of the State* (New Haven: Yale UP, 1946), 6.

[14] Moreover, perhaps it is an *impossible* task to define myth, if, for example, one may seek an analogy with the Neo-Wittgensteinian refusal to define 'art' essentially. Rather, one might only be able to seek to identify and to discuss 'family resemblances' in the consideration of myth, which is the approach taken here. For discussion of the question of the definition of art see N. Carroll, 'Art, Definition and Identification', in *Philosophy of Art: A Contemporary Introduction* (Routledge Contemporary Introductions to Philosophy; London: Routledge, 1999), 206-67.

[15] Cf. John Rogerson's concluding comments in what is still, probably, the major work on myth and the Old Testament: '[M]yth has been used in so many senses in Old Testament interpretation that it would be impossible and undesirable to try to find a single definition for the term, and to force all relevant material or evidence into the mould that resulted.' (J.W. Rogerson, *Myth in Old Testament Interpretation* (BZAW 134; New York: Walter de Gruyter, 1974), 174).

consider whether Joshua has sufficient resonances with what particular theorists of myth have studied and categorized as myth (in their terms) to use their theories of myth to help one to understand Joshua. Thus my selection of and appeal to various theories of myth is essentially heuristic—I shall demonstrate that certain theories of myth provide tools or perspectives that help one to understand Joshua.[16]

Different theories of myth often identify rather different classes of objects as myth, or seek to address rather different questions relating to their origin, function or use. But it is appropriate to analyze Joshua using a variety of approaches to myth, with each perspective being potentially illuminative, provided that Joshua 'intersects' sufficiently with the concerns of the particular approach in question. This might lead to the criticism that one is using theories simply because they work—but the point of a good theory is precisely that it does work, that it provides a compelling explanation of empirical data. So, for example, whereas some theories stress myth as consciously shaping the human or the society, whilst others regard it as shaping identity at a subconscious level, there is no necessary inconsistency in applying both theories simultaneously provided that one grants that people can be shaped both consciously and subconsciously by the same material. The task is, then, to discern when a particular approach is appropriate and leads to good interpretation of the material, even if a particular approach only offers a partial account of the material.

Given my aim of reading Joshua as Christian Scripture, I shall locate this work on myth in a theological frame of reference; in other words, I shall grant descriptive and explanatory power to the anthropological approaches whilst not granting them autonomy. Anthropological theory does not provide the ultimate level of explanation, even as theology does not bypass anthropology. Thus I do not wish to develop a solely phenomenological approach, but a theological approach that is informed by and in dialogue with anthropology.

However, placing anthropological approaches to myth in a theological context can be as illuminative and 'empowering' as it is restricting, since, for example, theological accounts of human nature traditionally identify the importance of both 'rational' and 'emotive' aspects to human nature, and the need for their development and transformation. So it is likely that 'Christian myths' will seek to shape both aspects of the person, and thus one would expect such 'myths' to have both intellectual and emotional aspects. Thus one would expect that a text such as Joshua ought to be analyzed through approaches to myth that stress its intellectual aspects—such as those identified by Claude Lévi-Strauss in structuralism, for example, *in combination with* approaches that stress emotive aspects, such as those identified by Victor Turner, for example. In this way we may give a sufficiently full account of a work such as Joshua, *even if* Lévi-

---

[16] I am indebted to Prof Robert Segal for suggesting this approach to me in preference to an approach that starts by seeking to define myth.

Strauss would deny the importance of emotive aspects to myth as *he* views myth. Moreover, inasmuch as a theological anthropology identifies humans as being societal in nature, sociological and political approaches to myths are likely to be appropriate tools to use also. Thus a theological anthropology invites a broadening, an 'opening up' of possibilities for interpretation, as much as it might be said to represent a narrowing and constricting influence.

We will now explore these kinds of approach to myth further since they appear to be potentially fruitful for interpreting Joshua. This is not to suggest that *only these* approaches to myth might contribute to interpreting Joshua, but that together, they are, nonetheless, likely to provide a good account of Joshua. I shall not develop psychological approaches to myth directly in any depth, although such approaches have influenced other approaches that I wish to consider in detail. In this way psychological approaches do have an indirect impact on the approaches to Joshua that I wish to develop. I shall, however, make some brief comments on psychological approaches below and indicate how they may helpfully contribute to our understanding of the importance of the desire for 'rest' in Joshua for example.

Ideological, Sociological and Political Approaches to Myth

Joshua is certainly ideological literature (I do not use the term in any pejorative sense here), being originally concerned with shaping the identity of the nation of Israel. Joshua thus has political significance.[17] Moreover, Joshua continues to be used and discussed in political and colonial / postcolonial debate, and its significance is sometimes construed in these terms today, leading Michael Prior, for example, to engage in a moral critique of the Bible.[18] But ideological approaches

---

[17] See L.L. Rowlett, *Joshua and the Rhetoric of Violence: A New Historicist Analysis* (JSOTSup 226; Sheffield: Sheffield Academic Press, 1996) and R.B. Coote, 'The Book of Joshua', in *The New Interpreter's Bible* (Nashville: Abingdon, 1998), 2.555-719 for two readings of Joshua that major upon its political dimensions. My analysis will, however, run in a rather different direction from Rowlett and Coote's. Their readings are rather strongly dependent upon a particular historical reconstruction of the origins of the book and, in Coote's case, upon a particular understanding of the significance of such origins for the later usage of the text. See chapter 9 for further discussion.

[18] M. Prior, *The Bible and Colonialism: A Moral Critique* (The Biblical Seminar 48; Sheffield: Sheffield Academic Press, 1997). See also D. Mbuwayesango, 'Joshua' in D. Patte (ed.), *Global Bible Commentary* (Nashville: Abingdon Press, 2004), 64-73 for a reading of Joshua with postcolonial concerns in view. Furthermore, for the political implications of Joshua in regard to the modern state of Israel see N.S. Ateek, *Justice and only Justice: A Palestinian Theology of Liberation* (Maryknoll: Orbis Books, 1989), esp. 75ff (discussed below in chapter 3) and G.R. Tamarin, *The Israeli Dilemma: Essays on a Warfare State* (Rotterdam: Rotterdam University Press, 1973), esp. 183-90. Tamarin's closing comment, written in an epilogue following in the wake of the political difficulties

to myth are by no means uniform—one finds very different understandings of the relationship between myth and ideology in the works of Karl Marx, George Sorel and Bronislaw Malinowski for example.[19]

Engels describes ideology as 'a process accomplished by the so-called thinker consciously, it is true, but with a false consciousness. The real motive forces impelling him remain unknown to him ... As all action is mediated by thought, it appears to him to be ultimately based upon thought',[20] representing the kind of view that has led to many pejorative construals of ideology expressed as myth. Theologically speaking, such a 'hermeneutic of suspicion' highlights the need for discernment in appropriating what is presented in 'scriptural myths'; theologically speaking, humanity is understood to be distorted by sin, and this distortion may be reflected in some of the motives that led to the production of the texts that we now have as Scripture. However, these texts have persisted in use, indeed becoming Scripture at some remove from their original context, suggesting that God has, nonetheless, been discerned as in some sense speaking through these texts.[21] Broadly speaking I suggest that a 'hermeneutic of trust' towards scriptural texts is, theologically speaking, to take precedence over a 'hermeneutic of suspicion', even if the discernment of their proper use that is not based upon a false consciousness is an ongoing process.

Moreover, in relation to Sorel, who views myth as ideology that serves to topple society, Robert Segal suggests that how much his theory 'actually illuminates any myth beyond labelling it as such ... is not easy to see.'[22] In other words, having labelled something as 'ideology', which may or may not be understood pejoratively, some approaches might not take the interpreter any further. Granted, Joshua is ideological—but then what follows from this?

However, some theories of myth more aimed at the use of myth in society may supply further understanding of Joshua. Malinowski, for example, notes the importance of myth as a charter for society, and that it is a 'reality lived' and a 'hard-working, extremely important cultural force', or 'active force',[23] and that '*myth* comes into play when rite, ceremony, or a social or moral rule demands

---

that the publication of his research caused are suggestive; 'I never dreamt that I would become the last victim of Joshua's conquest of Jericho...' (190).

[19] See e.g. von Hendy, *Myth*, 278-303 for a summary of ideological treatments of myth (in which he includes structuralism).

[20] Cited in von Hendy, *Myth*, 280.

[21] Thus there are two issues here—the expression of an ideology that motivated the production of a text and the ideology associated with its ongoing use. The ideology associated with its production may or may not reflect the ideology of later use. But arguably of course, the ongoing use of a text may be understood as reflecting a distorted or false consciousness.

[22] Segal, *Myth*, 128-9.

[23] B. Malinowski, 'Myth in Primitive Psychology' in *Magic, Science and Religion and other Essays* (Westport: Greenwood Press, 1984), 93-148, here 97-101.

justification, warrant of antiquity, reality, and sanctity'[24] being an 'ever-present, live actuality'.[25] In other words, myths locate various aspects of society and life in society as rooted in an ancient past in order to grant their legitimacy. Furthermore, Abizadeh suggests that in relation to the way that national myths function to fashion the identity of a national group, the correspondence between the narrated myth and 'actual events' is often ambiguous,[26] but again, by setting the myth in a foundational time it grants it legitimacy, being something that the society can construct itself upon.

I shall return to the ambiguous relation of myth to history later, but for now I simply wish to observe the tendency to set narratives that shape or reinforce the existence of societies in a prototypical time in order to grant their legitimacy and form the basis of a secure cultural memory. This might raise the possibility that Joshua may not be particularly concerned with a prototypical conquest *per se,* but may take this as its *setting* and reflect some aspects of the memory of Israel's early existence.

Psychological Approaches to Myth

I will begin my brief consideration of psychological approaches to myth[27] with René Girard's work, an apparently 'obvious' starting point for reading Joshua as it is concerned with 'sacred violence'. Girard understands the anthropological characteristic that is most fundamental to human behaviour to be *mimesis*. Mimesis occurs in the imitation of the desire within two people for the same

---

[24] Ibid., 107.

[25] Ibid., 126.

[26] A. Abizadeh, 'Historical Truth, National Myths and Liberal Democracy: On the Coherence of Liberal Nationalism' in *The Journal of Political Philosophy,* 12:3 (2004): 291-313. Cf. D. Miller, *On Nationality* (Oxford: OUP, 1995), esp. 35-9, who also notes that such myths are rarely 'complete falsehoods' (38).

[27] Many other psychological approaches could be considered here, but space prevents this. For example, from a Jungian perspective Edward Edinger summarizes Joshua thus: 'Psychologically the Promised Land can be seen as an area of the unconscious which the imperative of individuation requires to be assimilated by the ego. This area is specifically assigned to the ego by the Self but still must be conquered by the efforts of the ego. The land is not vacant but occupied. It is studded with fortified cities; that is, it contains defended unconscious complexes which must be resolved before it can be assimilated. Joshua's conquest of Canaan is a symbolic picture of how to deal with the unconscious and its hostile complexes under certain circumstances.' (*The Bible and the Psyche: Individuation Symbolism in the Old Testament* (Toronto: Inner City Books, 1986), 65). There are some interesting resonances here with Origen's spiritual reading of Joshua, but an analysis of these will have to wait for another occasion. Another psychological approach that relates to the development of the text is that of Soggie's (*Myth, God, and War*).

'object', a desire that escalates into a rivalry, which becomes a conflict for the sake of conflict with the importance of the object of desire dissolving in the process. The two rivals become mirror images of each other, 'mimetic doubles'. When played out at the societal level others gradually join the conflict, conflict that can reach epidemic proportions and threaten the existence of a society. But when this 'contagion' of mimetic rivalry reaches a boiling point, peace mysteriously emerges: The 'mimetic contagion' is 'scapegoated' onto a victim, who is then deemed responsible for all the social chaos. The victim is killed by 'mob violence', and peace emerges. But for this peace to emerge requires that the lynching of the victim is not seen for what it is.[28] Jeffrey Carter elaborates on Girard's theory:

> Societies ... have discovered a means to end the cycle of violence caused by mimetic desire. They have discovered the "mechanism of the surrogate-victim," the practice of transferring the interior violence of the group (social chaos, sense of sin, evil, impurity) to a surrogate, a scapegoat, who can be expelled from (i.e., killed by) the community. This scapegoat, Girard notes, must be unable to retaliate and thereby extend the cycle of violence; it must be somewhat marginalized from the group, not fully a member but not completely foreign either. Domesticated animals, non-human community members, are ideal victims. Active in this mechanism is a "mob mentality," one that blames some innocent figure for social evil and that believes salvation (the return of stability and order) will come from eliminating that figure. By virtue of an unconscious process, "bad violence" threatening the very order of society is removed with an act of "good violence." Curiously, Girard continues, when the mechanism of the surrogate victim works, and the community is essentially saved from itself, members may look back and understand the victim as a savior. Whoever was at first worthy of blame is later remembered as beneficent, as the being who helped (perhaps even voluntarily—choosing to die) the community overcome a dangerous crisis. Being the locus of both good and bad violence, the victim acquires an air of mystery, of awesome power, potentially dangerous but generous, transcendent but nearby—all characteristics, in short, of the sacred. Girard concludes, the surrogate victim becomes, for the community, a divine being, a power to be worshipped, a founding ancestor who continues to protect and provide, bless and punish.[29]

Thus if the scapegoating is successful, it leads to a paradoxical and ambiguous representation of the scapegoat in subsequent myths via a process that Girard terms 'double transference'.[30]

---

[28] A. Marr, 'Violence and the Kingdom of God: Introducing the Anthropology of René Girard', in *ATR* 80.4 (1998): 590-603, here 590-91.

[29] J. Carter, 'René Girard' in *Understanding Religious Sacrifice: A Reader* (London: Continuum, 2003), 239-75, here 240.

[30] C. Fleming, *René Girard: Violence and Mimesis* (Cambridge: Polity Press, 2004), 62.

But this is not the case in Joshua. Indeed, Girard notes that sometimes 'the myth fails'; the violence does not become sacralised and 'double transference' fails to occur.[31] In this case, he suggests that such texts describing the events be termed 'texts of persecution', rather than myths, being texts that have undergone a process of demythologization, texts that sit between 'archaic mythical representations and radical demystifications of collective violence'. They are texts that are provided by the persecutors that distort, in characteristic ways, the character of those persecuted.[32] Is Joshua a 'text of persecution' then? Whilst Girard has written on a number of biblical texts, I am not aware of any discussion of Joshua in his work,[33] although others have sought to apply his work to Joshua.[34]

Gordon Matties also considers the applicability of Girard's theory to reading Joshua.[35] He notes,

> According to Girard, these foreigners [the Canaanites, etc.] are presented "in terms of a 'fictive' foreign threat." In this case, therefore, the insider-outsider dynamic in the plot of Joshua is not at all about shaping the identity of a community in front of the text; rather, it obscures a conflict behind the text in a generative act of violence. Reading Joshua with Girard's interests in mind would not simply describe how the narrative functions to shape corporate identity in the present, but would uncover how the hidden violence inherent in the community is linked, through the narrative, to original violence against the outsider.[36]

He goes on to note that a reading of Joshua from a Girardian perspective is unable to account for the cultic framing of the narrative, the 'exceptional outsiders' (such as Rahab), the problems of geographical boundary definition,[37] and the story of Achan. Indeed, Rahab and Achan's stories occupy much narrative

---

[31] Cf. Segal's comments on Girard's approach to myth: 'For him, literature is the legacy of myth, which recounts, albeit in distorted form, the ritualistic sacrifice of an innocent victim, who can range from the most helpless member of society to the king. ... Instead of functioning to explain the killing, as other myth-ritualists would assume, myth for Girard functions to hide it—and thereby to preserve the stability of society.' (R.A. Segal, *Theorizing about Myth* (Amherst: University of Massachusetts Press, 1999), 45).

[32] Fleming, *Girard*, 102-103.

[33] Likewise, Gordon Matties notes that with regard to Girard's work, 'Joshua has been one of those texts that has been avoided' ('Can Girard help us to read Joshua?', in W.M. Swartley, *Violence Renounced: René Girard, Biblical Studies, and peacemaking* (Telford: Pandora Press, 2000), 85-102, here 85).

[34] E.g. Coote, 'Joshua', esp. 617-8. Whilst Coote uses Girard's categories, I am not convinced that his is a Girardian reading as such. Rather, it seems that Girard's *categories* suit Coote's interpretation of Joshua.

[35] Matties, 'Girard'.

[36] Ibid., 91.

[37] Ibid., 95.

space in Joshua, indicating that they are a major concern—but Girard's theory does not account for this. Thus Matties concludes,

> Girard's approach seems unable to do two things: first, it does not pay enough attention to all details of a text; second, in its focus on the world hidden behind the text, it does not clearly address reception of the text by later readers in front of the text. With respect to both concerns, Girard's hermeneutic seems to offer a limited understanding of the formative and transformative function of the narrative. What it does well, however, is to offer critical tools by which to offer a critique of the violent mechanisms so often justified by texts like Joshua.[38]

Thus, leaving aside questions of the validity of Girard's theory generally, it appears that it does not help one to read Joshua.

However, Girard's work helpfully draws attention to the broader psychological issues of *projection* and *desire* in Joshua. Regarding projection, one might be able to understand the portrayal of the Canaanites as a 'symbolic' group onto whom those characteristics that are deemed irreconcilable with Israelite group identity are projected.[39] Whilst Joshua says little about the characteristics of the Canaanites, etc., in its cultural (and canonical) context such a projection, and its content, is clear (e.g. Lev 18:24; Deut 9:5; Zech 14:21).[40] But then if this is indeed an important way in which the identity of Israel was constructed, i.e., by indicating what her identity was not by projecting those characteristics that are incompatible with her identity onto another 'symbolic' group, it is then interesting to consider the *nature* of the projected undesirable characteristics, those that define the 'outsider', something that structuralist analysis, that I will discuss below, often does not consider.[41]

---

[38] Ibid., 95.

[39] Cf. Doty, *Mythography*, 63 (cited above) on myth as projecting identity, and also Hawk, *Joshua*, xxviii for a similar suggestion. Also P.D. Stern (*The Biblical ḥerem: A Window on Israel's Religious Experience* (Brown Judaic Studies 211; Atlanta: Scholar's Press, 1991)) notes that a practice like חרם 'reflects a certain mythicization of the enemy as the monster of chaos' (224).

[40] In Zech 14:21 כְּנַעֲנִי probably functions as an idiom for 'merchant'. But Izak Cornelius suggests that the term retains a negative image when used in this sense (see 'כְּנַעַן', in *NIDOTTE*, 2.669).Thus if the term does function as an idiom and carries a negative sense, it probably serves to strengthen the idea that 'Canaanite' functions as a symbol or 'root metaphor' in a pejorative fashion, as it shows how the metaphorical sense of 'Canaanite' is developed in a particular (negative) direction in connection with traders—i.e., bad traders are 'like' Canaanites. See the discussion on symbol below.

[41] Cf. Paul Ricoeur's comments: 'Structuralism, to my mind, is a dead end the very moment when it treats any "message" as the mere "quotation" of its underlying "code." This claim alone makes structural method structuralist prejudice. Structuralism as ideology starts with the reversal in the relation between code and message which makes the code essential and the message unessential. And it is because this step is taken that the text is killed as message and that no existential interpretation seems appropriate for a

Turning to desire, writing on Joshua, Daniel Hawk suggests that

> Within the context of the story, Israel's desire is clearly for the land. Canaan is "a land flowing with milk and honey" (Num. 14:8; Deut. 11:9), offering rest, security, and abundance. Life in the land represents "the goal and desire of the people of God" ... Yet more than a destination, it promises a profound fulfillment—Israel in the land is Israel identified, coherent, and completed.
>
> Life in the land is also life with Yahweh, who gives the land (Josh. 1:2-5; 13:6 and confirms the promise by removing those who stand as obstacles to Israel's fulfillment (Josh. 8:18; 10:11; 11:6; 23:5,9-10).[42]

Indeed, the desire for √נוח (rest) in Joshua (e.g. 1:13, 15; 21:44; 22:4; 23:1), a special quality of life which represents the goal of and consummation of Joshua's campaign,[43] seems particularly important. Joshua can be said to be expressive of a desire for a particular quality of life, a desire that Butler notes is eschatologized in the prophetic materials (Isa 11:2; 14:3,7; 28:12; 32:18, cf. Dan 12:13).[44] In other words, one might say that, psychologically speaking, Joshua is not so concerned with conquest *per se,* but rather with the desire for living peacefully at *rest* in the land as YHWH's people, a desire that has clear eschatological dimensions, even if it is rest that is achieved through struggle and conflict perhaps.[45] Thus 'spiritual' or 'typological' readings of Joshua that have taken the possession of the Promised Land to be a 'type' of Christian 'heavenly inheritance'[46] do in fact reflect that which Joshua is expressive of, but using the symbolism of a new context. In other words, some of the instincts of traditional Christian readings may have been correct, reflecting what is expressed in the text, even if they may have been poorly articulated.

---

message which has been reduced to a pure epiphenomenon of the "codes." ... I call dead end not all structural analysis, but only the one which makes it irrelevant, or useless, or even impossible to return from the deep-structures to the surface-structures.' (P. Ricoeur, 'Biblical Hermeneutics', in *Semeia* 4 (1975): 29-148, here 65).

[42] L.D. Hawk, *Every Promise Fulfilled: Contesting Plots in Joshua* (Louisville: Westminster John Knox Press, 1991), 141.

[43] Nelson, *Joshua,* 31. It is interesting that the root is also used in Josh 3:13; 4:3,8 and 6:23 which might point to the importance of נוח as a *Leitwort* in Joshua.

[44] T.C. Butler, *Joshua* (WBC 7; Waco: Word Books, 1983), 21.

[45] Of course it may be objected that belligerent groups often desire peace through violence on their own terms.

[46] E.g. in Calvin: 'But in Scripture sometimes God, in conferring all these earthly benefits on them, determined to lead them by his own hand to the hope of heavenly things. ... [I]n the earthly possession [the Israelites] enjoyed, they looked, as in a mirror, upon the future inheritance they believed to have been prepared for them in heaven' (*Inst.* II.11.1, 450-51).

Existential and Symbolic Approaches to Myth

Robert Segal suggests that '[b]ecause myth concerns the human experience of the world, not to say the deepest anxieties experienced in the world, it would seemingly have existential import'.[47] Moreover, Doty suggests that myths provide us with projective models of roles and of aspirations toward becoming 'something other than what we are, of ways of imagining new possibilities as to who we are', whilst providing a sense of a person's role in the universe.[48] This is reminiscent of Rudolf Bultmann's classic existential approach to myth in which he stated that, 'The real purpose of myth is not to present an objective picture of the world as it is, but to express man's understanding of himself in the world in which he lives. Myth should be interpreted not cosmologically, but anthropologically, or better still, existentially.'[49] Myths are important for shaping and developing life.

I would now like to base my discussion of symbolic and existential aspects of myth on the work of two figures, figures who have been, in rather different ways, very influential in the study of myth from these perspectives, Paul Ricoeur and Victor Turner.

Paul Ricoeur

Paul Ricoeur's work on symbol, myth and narrative, work which spanned several decades and reflected, as he put it, a journey from existentialism to the philosophy of language,[50] provides a basis for a discussion of symbols and of existential approaches to myth. However, 'symbol' is a concept that is as problematic as 'myth', perhaps because discussions of symbol and myth often occur together.[51] Indeed, Louis Dupré suggests that there is a 'dialectical relation between myth and symbol', where symbols 'need the verbal interpretation of the myth' and 'the symbol is the exegesis of the myth'.[52] Thus the concept of symbol will require careful development here in relation to myth.

Whilst there were developments in his thinking, Ricoeur retained a 'rich' understanding of symbols and myth throughout his career; for Ricoeur symbols discover rather than invent, reflecting the 'capacity of the cosmos to signify'; whilst symbols and myths require hermeneutics and interpretation, this is

---

[47] Segal, *Myth*, 118.
[48] Doty, *Mythography*, 72-3.
[49] R. Bultmann, 'New Testament and Mythology', in H-W. Bartsch (ed.), *Kerygma and Myth* (London: SPCK, ET 1953), 1.10.
[50] Cf. von Hendy, *Myth*, 306-307.
[51] See J.W. Heisig, 'Symbolism' in M. Eliade (ed.), *The Encyclopedia of Religion* (New York: Simon & Schuster Macmillan), 13.198-208 for a summary of approaches to symbol.
[52] L. Dupré, *Symbols of the Sacred* (Grand Rapids: Eerdmans, 2000), 91-2.

grounded in the 'sacredness of nature'.[53] Andrew von Hendy suggests that Riceour's approach 'is our finest theory of myth that confronts the century's linguistic turn and yet maintains its roots in the sacred.'[54] Ricoeur's account may be theologically attractive, for one can construe his position as expressive of a doctrine of creation in which the world is a place that is 'graced', is 'meaning-full' and able to symbolize the divine.

In his early work Ricoeur suggests that

> the symbol conceals in its aim a double intentionality. Take the "defiled," the "impure." This significant expression presents a first or literal intentionality that, like every significant expression, supposes the triumph of the conventional sign over the natural sign. Thus, the literal meaning of "defilement" is "stain," but this literal meaning is already a conventional sign; the words "stain," "unclean," etc., do not resemble the thing signified. But upon this first intentionality there is erected a second intentionality which, through the physically "unclean," points to a certain situation of man in the sacred which is precisely that of being defiled, impure. The literal and manifest sense, then, points beyond itself to something that is *like* a stain or spot. Thus, contrary to perfectly transparent technical signs, which say only what they want to say in positing that which they signify, symbolic signs are opaque, because the first, literal, obvious meaning itself points analogically to a second meaning which is not given otherwise than in it ... This opacity constitutes the depth of the symbol, which, it will be said, is inexhaustible. ...
>
> I cannot objectify the analogical relation that connects the second meaning with the first. It is by living in the first meaning that I am led beyond it itself.'[55]

Moreover, regarding the relationship between myth and symbol Ricoeur goes on to remark that, 'I shall regard myths as a species of symbols, as symbols developed in the form of narrations and articulated in a time and a space that cannot be co-ordinated with the time and space of history and geography according to the critical method.'[56] However, this, it seems, is perhaps an unnecessarily restrictive view of myth, something that I shall return to below. But Ricoeur's account of symbol needs careful nuancing, as it is open to misconstrual. Jacques Waardenburg observes that

> Anthropologists have shown the tremendous importance of the cultural tradition and context in which symbols occur. In order to understand a symbol, these should be thoroughly known since they influence heavily the choice, concrete

---

[53] P. Ricoeur, *Interpretation Theory: Discourse and the Surplus of Meaning* (Fort Worth: The Texan Christian UP, 1976), 62-3; cf. von Hendy, *Myth*, 309.
[54] von Hendy, *Myth*, 313.
[55] P. Ricoeur, *The Symbolism of Evil* (Boston: Beacon Press, ET: 1969), 15. Cf. also Sandra Schneider's helpful discussion on symbol (S.M. Schneiders, *The Revelatory Text* (Collegeville: The Liturgical Press, 2nd ed. 1999), 33-40).
[56] Ricoeur, *Symbolism*, 18.

form, and meaning of symbols and since they throw light on the need for symbolic expression at all in the given circumstances.

> Sociologists have stressed that symbols must be generally accepted by a group, community, or society in order to persist and that there must be a certain consensus on their meaning for them to be effective.[57]

Whilst one might think that this account differs significantly from Ricoeur's 'rich' account, in fact it does not, for Ricoeur states elsewhere that 'I demonstrated the non-existence of the naturally symbolic, that a symbolism only functions within an economy of thought, within a structure'.[58] In other words symbols have a societal or contextual aspect and require interpretation.

For Ricoeur symbols (and hence myths) contain a surplus of signification and meaning,[59] and he suggests that 'a symbol cannot be exhaustively treated by conceptual language' with symbols thus giving rise to endless exegesis.[60] Von Hendy suggests that for Ricoeur symbols are always mediated by language, where symbol is fused with myth, and hence that 'symbol is always mediated by narrative'.[61] Thus in Ricoeur's later work there is a shift to discourse analysis, and he develops the idea that 'discourse produces a "surplus of meaning," in the disclosure of "a world that constitutes the reference of the text"'.[62] Despite a shift from symbol and myth to metaphor and narrative, von Hendy observes, correctly I think, that narrative and myth 'may express something much nearer to identity than Ricoeur's historical separation of them has allowed him to face up to',[63] reflecting my observation above that Ricoeur's approach to myth *per se* is not only unnecessarily restrictive, but too restrictive. Thus it is appropriate to read a text such as Joshua from the perspective of Ricoeur's work on both narrative and myth—and allow both perspectives to illuminate each other—without worrying unduly about questions of classification.

As *narrative* Joshua discloses a world—the 'world of the text'—that is the reference of the text, whose 'referential claim is nothing other than the claim to *redescribe* reality'.[64] In other words, viewed from this perspective, the narrative of Joshua pictures a world that redescribes reality. As an act of discourse one

---

[57] J. Waardenburg, 'Symbolic Aspects of Myth' in A.M. Olson (ed.), *Myth, Symbol and Reality* (Notre Dame: University of Notre Dame Press, 1980), 41-68, here 45-6.

[58] P. Ricoeur in 'Claude Lévi-Strauss: A Confrontation', in *New Left Review* I/62 (Jul-Aug 1970): 57-74, here 63. Indeed, if Rahab can be understood to be a symbolic character, just what it is that she might be construed to symbolize varies from context to context even to the extent of an inversion of meaning—see chapter 3 for discussion.

[59] Ricoeur, *Interpretation*, 55.

[60] Ibid., 57.

[61] von Hendy, *Myth*, 309-10.

[62] Ibid., 308-309, cf. Ricoeur, *Interpretation*, 92.

[63] von Hendy, *Myth*, 312.

[64] P. Ricoeur, 'The Narrative Function', in *Semeia* 13 (1978): 177-202, here 194-5.

may understand Joshua to be an invitation existentially to enter this 'strange new world' and allow it to transform and affect one's own everyday world—it is a narrative concerned with conversion and transformation. But this world requires *interpretation* for its appropriation, and given the problematic nature of the material in Joshua at the 'literal level' this is no easy task. But there is a 'surplus of meaning' in discourse such as Joshua, manifested where the 'world of the text' is appropriated within the 'world of the reader'. This is a 'revelatory' process:

> why call it revelatory? ... Here truth no longer means verification, but manifestation, i.e. letting what shows itself to be. What shows itself in each instance a proposed world, a world I may inhabit and wherein I can project my ownmost possibilities. ... And the intended implicit reference of each text opens onto a world, the biblical world ... The proposed world that in biblical language is called a new creation, a new Covenant, the Kingdom of God, is the "issue" of the biblical text unfolded in front of this text.[65]

This idea of 'manifestation' is important for Ricoeur, and has some affinities with Barth's and Wittgenstein's attempts to move beyond modernist concerns and metaphysical dilemmas regarding verification and certainty.[66] I shall return to these questions in chapter 3, where I shall develop notions of 'manifestation' and 'testimony'. But *as narrative* Joshua shows a 'proposed world' that one can chose to enact (or not) in 'the real world', in an existential sense, by a process of 'conversion' through the imagination. But how does one *discern* the way in which one *ought* to allow oneself to be 'converted' by a text like Joshua? In what way does it present a 'world of the text' that is to be entered?[67] Or, to use Ricoeur's language, in what sense might one say—and indeed can one say—that the world that Joshua depicts is a picture of the world of the Kingdom of God, even if it is imperfect? And where do its imperfections lie? Granted that it is part of the *Old* Testament, it is likely that the picture will need 'perfecting'.

However, before tackling these questions there is one common difficulty that I wish to deal with now concerning the relationships between fiction, history, myth and truth. In 'The Narrative Function' Ricoeur discusses at length

---

[65] P. Ricoeur, 'Toward a Hermeneutic of the Idea of Revelation', in P. Ricoeur (ed. L.S. Mudge), *Essays on Biblical Interpretation* (London: SPCK, 1981), 73-118, here 102-103.

[66] Cf. M.I. Wallace, *The Second Naiveté: Barth, Ricoeur, and the New Yale Theology* (Studies in American Biblical Hermeneutics 6; Georgia: Mercer UP, 1990); N.B. MacDonald, *Karl Barth and the Strange New World within the Bible: Barth, Wittgenstein, and the Metadilemmas of the Enlightenment* (Paternoster Biblical and Theological Monographs) (Carlisle: Paternoster, 2000).

[67] Indeed, Robin Parry suggests that for Ricoeur '[e]xactly how the "worlds" interact seems to be less than fully clear' (*Old Testament Story and Christian Ethics: The Rape of Dinah as a Case Study* (Paternoster Biblical Monographs) (Bletchley: Paternoster, 2004), 17). I shall try to develop this, in particular using the work of Victor Turner, below.

the nature of 'historiographical' and 'fictional' narratives, problematizing the distinction between them, arguing on the one hand that 'history' requires 'emplotment' and interpretation through a narrative framework, and, on the other hand, that fictional narratives are grounded in historical existence. Crucially he argues that

> both history and fiction refer to human action, although they do so on the basis of two different referential claims. Only history may articulate its referential claim in compliance with rules of evidence common to the whole body of science. In the conventional sense attached to the term "truth" by the acquaintance with this body of science, only historical knowledge may enunciate its referential claim as a "truth"-claim. But the very meaning of this truth-claim is itself measured by the limiting network which rules conventional descriptions of the world. This is why fictional narratives may assert a referential claim of another kind, appropriate to the split reference of poetic discourse. This referential claim is nothing other than the claim to *redescribe* reality according to the symbolic structures of the fiction. And the question, then, is to wonder whether in another sense of the words "true" and "truth," history and fiction may be said to be equally "true," although in ways as different as their referential claims.[68]

Thus describing a narrative as 'fiction' is not to say that it is 'untrue'.

Likewise theorists of myths have, from various perspectives, shown the ambivalent relationships between 'history', 'myth' and 'truth'.[69] For example, Seth Kunin remarks, 'The [biblical] narratives are given an historical framework; nonetheless they seem to work in the same way as mythological material.'[70] Conversely, accounts of 'history' can also be symbolic, with historical events construed symbolically with existential importance.[71] The issue at stake with regard to the biblical narratives is thus not that of historical veracity, but of whether, and how,[72] they paint a *good, fitting* or *faithful* (even if imperfect) portrait of 'the Kingdom of God'. So with Barth one may say that

> the idea that the Bible declares the Word of God only when it speaks historically is one which must be abandoned, especially in the Christian Church. One consequence of this misunderstanding was the great uncertainty of faith which resulted from an inability wholly to escape the impression that many elements

---

[68] Ricoeur, 'Narrative Function', 194-5.
[69] See e.g. above on national myths, and also e.g. S.D. Kunin, *We Think What We Eat: Neo-structuralist Analysis of Israelite Food Rules and Other Cultural and Textual Practices* (JSOTSup 412; London: T&T Clark, 2004), 20-22. I shall return to the significance of 'history' in Western modernity below.
[70] Ibid., 20.
[71] Schneiders, *Revelatory Text*, 36-7.
[72] I.e., the tendency has been to assume that the world of the text paints its picture at the 'literal level', whereas I wish to suggest that the portrait is painted at the 'symbolic' or 'spiritual level', to use the traditional Christian term.

in the Bible have the nature of saga, and an ignorance of where and how to draw the line which marks off what is finally historical and therefore the true Word of God. But in other cases it led to a rigid affirmation that in the Bible, as the Word of God, we have only "historical" accounts and no saga at all—an affirmation which can be sustained only it we either close our eyes or violently reinterpret what we see. In other cases again it resulted in an attempt to penetrate to a "historical" kernel which is supposed to give us the true, i.e., "historical" word of God—the only trouble being that in the process it was unfortunately found that with the discarding of saga we do lose not only a subsidiary theme but the main point at issue, i.e., the biblical witness. We have to realise that in all three cases the presumed equation of the Word of God with a "historical" record is an inadmissible postulate which does not itself originate in the Bible at all but in the unfortunate habit of Western thought which assumes that the reality of a history stands or falls by whether it is "history."[73]

Returning now to symbol, Daniel Hawk's comments on the Jordan crossing demonstrate how attention to symbol is illuminative for Joshua:

> The crossing itself is an event highly symbolic of Israel's transformation from a disordered to an ordered people. The narration of the event has a mythic quality, and its etiological elements in particular sanction and reinforce the symbolic network which constitutes Israel's perception of reality. By crossing the Jordan, Israel moves from wilderness—the place of chaos—to the promised land—the place of order.
>
>> In and through the myth, "land" becomes a cipher for a total social order. The move into the land is nothing short of that creative change from chaos to ordered cosmos. ...[74]
>
> By crossing the Jordan, Israel enters a bounded place and leaves the vast expanse of the wilderness. The transformation is made possible by Yahweh, "frame-maker, boundary-keeper and master of transformations" ... who, represented by the Ark, stands between chaos and ordered existence. The narrative thus accentuates the liturgical elements of the episode in order to focus the reader's attention on the symbolic significance of the boundary being traversed. The priests, who oversee Israel's maintenance and traversing of boundaries, stand, appropriately, in the middle of the border-region to mediate journey of the entire people from wilderness to promised land. Extensive preparations are undertaken to ensure that the crossing is made in an orderly and integrated manner (3:1-13), and this is precisely what is done. Throughout the episode, the ostensive plot depicts the Jordan crossing in terms of wholes and boundaries.

---

[73] *CD* III/I, 82. For the move away from history and the importance of Barth see MacDonald, *Karl Barth*. MacDonald suggests that during the Enlightenment there was a shift away from the classic Christian paradigm of 'faith seeking understanding' to one of 'faith requiring justification'.

[74] Quoting L.L. Thompson, 'The Jordan Crossing: $ṣidqot\ Yahweh$ and World building', in *JBL* 100.3 (1981): 343-58.

Thus Israel as a people has crossed over into a new, ordered existence with Yahweh (who confirms the transformation with a miraculous stoppage of the water).[75]

But symbols, metaphors, and myths, whilst initially having great creative power and the ability to give rise to endless exegesis, can, and often do, become 'tired' or 'dead',[76] or, as Doty puts it, they 'become locked into single-meaning codes, where each term "stands for" only one meaning'.[77] Indeed Waardenburg suggests that when symbols are used in sacred myths 'the symbolization used in a myth can become so strong that not only is the referent of the myth and symbol absolutized but the symbolic instrument itself becomes sacralized and consequently absolutized.'[78] This process can be described as the 'tiring', 'rationalizing' or 'objectification' of myths.[79] Crucially then, 'myths', such as Joshua,[80] that are expressed as 'history-like' narratives will tend to lose their proper existential significance through a process in which there is a shift in the perception of the location of their significance. They are read in a different way, where a rather different 'world of the text' is construed, a world that has become 'historicized' and its significance sought in such terms—the myth 'dies' as Claude Lévi-Strauss puts it. The importance of the myth's existential character may be obscured.[81] Lévi-Strauss notes that

> Historicized myths are well-known throughout the world; a particularly striking example is the mythology of the Zuni indians of the South Western USA, which has been 'historicized' (on the basis of material which is not so historicized) by native theologians in a way comparable to that of other theologians on the basis of the ancestral myths of Israel.[82]

---

[75] Hawk, *Every Promise*, 95.

[76] Cf. S. McFague, *Metaphorical Theology: Models of God in Religious Language* (Philadelphia: Fortress Press, 1982), 41.

[77] Doty, *Mythography*, 52.

[78] Waardenburg, 'Symbolic Aspects', 57. Cf. his comments a little later, where he notes that making an implicit myth explicit is a kind of objectification of the myth, and a degree of rationalization (59).

[79] Ibid., 56; Doty, *Mythography*, 138-40.

[80] For convenience of expression I shall refer to Joshua and to other biblical and post-biblical material as 'myth' even though I have noted the difficulties of reifying the concept of 'myth' and thus of finally identifying any object as such.

[81] See C. Lévi-Strauss, 'How Myths Die', in *Structural Anthropology 2* (Chicago: Chicago UP, 1976), 256-68 and discussion in Kunin, *We Think What We Eat*, 204. Lévi-Strauss does not speak in existentialist categories but rather in terms of the 'destructuring' of a myth. However, through neo-structuralism (see below) I will develop the idea that structure *as given content in a particular myth* has existential significance.

[82] C. Lévi-Strauss in 'Claude Lévi-Strauss: A Confrontation', in *New Left Review* I.62 (Jul-Aug 1970): 57-74, here 63. Cf. also Jean-Pierre Faye's comments (ibid.), 67.

Waardenburg suggests that one way of 'liberating' a 'tired myth' is to assimilate the myth in question to a new myth that has wider claims and possibilities with regard to the interpretation of reality.[83] But this process, of the assimilation of a myth into other myths, is in fact something that is inherent to myth when considered as part of a network of myths that shapes the life of a community. For example, Lévi-Strauss comments that

> A mythic system can only be grasped in *a process of becoming*; not as something inert and stable but in a process of *perpetual transformation*. This would mean that there are always several kinds of myths simultaneously present in the system, some of them primary (in respect of the moment at which the observation is made) and some of them derivative.[84]

These observations regarding 'objectification' or 'historicization' coupled with the notions of 'surplus of meaning' or 'endless exegesis' have important implications for understanding the significance, reception and use of Joshua. In the Christian tradition one can track the 'transformation' or 'assimilation' of Joshua as it was read in the light of the New Testament materials in, say, Origen's *Homilies on Joshua*. Combining Joshua with, for example, Eph 6 gave rise to a powerful, existential development of the symbolic nature of the world of Joshua's text into what the patristic writers termed the 'spiritual sense' of the text, something that I would call the second-order, symbolic sense when developed in a new context. For example, in a homily on Joshua Origen suggests

> [D]oubtless the wars that are waged through Jesus [Joshua], and the slaughter of kings and enemies must also be said to be "a shadow and type of heavenly things," namely, of those wars that our Lord Jesus with his army and officers— that is, the throngs of believers and their leaders—fights against the Devil and his angels. For it is he himself who strives with Paul and with the Ephesians "against sovereigns and authorities and the rulers of darkness, against spiritual forces of wickedness in heavenly places." ... The kingdoms of earth are not promised to you by the Gospels, but kingdoms of heaven. These kingdoms, however, are neither deserted nor abandoned; they have their own inhabitants, sinners and vile spirits, fugitive angels. Paul, sounding the apostolic trumpet, exhorts you to the battle against those who dwell there. Just as Jesus said then that your war would be against the Amorites and Perizzites and Hivites and Jebusites, likewise Paul also declares to you here, saying, "Your fight will not be against flesh and blood," that is, we shall not fight in the same manner as the ancients fought. Nor are the battles in our land to be conducted against humans "but against sovereigns, against authorities, against the rulers of darkness of

---

[83] Waardenburg, 'Symbolic Aspects', 56.
[84] C. Lévi-Strauss, *From Honey to Ashes* (New York: Harper and Row, ET: 1973), 354.

this world." Certainly you understand now where you must undertake struggles of this kind.[85]

The early church fathers, especially in the Alexandrian tradition, were sensitive to Joshua's symbolic and existential nature, often showing little concern for the significance of 'history' in Joshua whilst indicating ways in which it may be enacted in a new context. But over time this symbolic power was lost as Joshua's significance was located increasingly in historicizing terms.[86] The tradition moves from Origen's spiritual reading, through Augustine's slightly more literal approach (as may be seen with regard to some of his interpretation of Joshua[87]) to Calvin's 'literal' reading in his commentary on Joshua into the problems that we now encounter through historical and ethical critical concerns.[88] Joshua has become 'tired', with its significance assumed to lie in historicizing terms. Moreover, there has been the particular trend in modern Western thought to privilege 'history', and an epistemology associated with it, over attentive, imaginative, or 'prophetic' discernment, a privileging which is, interestingly, itself a 'mythic perception of reality', as W.T. Stevenson has outlined.[89] This, coupled with the 'tiring' of myth, has been a 'double whammy' for texts such as Joshua, for we have become quite unable to 'hear' the text—Canaanites, and their genocide, have been historicized, leading in turn to ethical objections to the text read 'as history'. The possible existential nature of the text

---

[85] *Hom. Josh.* 12.1. See also Gregory of Nyssa, 'The Lord's Prayer', Sermon 1, in *St. Gregory of Nyssa: The Lord's Prayer, The Beatitudes* (Trans. H.C. Graef) (ACW 18; New York: Paulist Press, 1954) 30-31, for a similar move.

[86] One may track a trajectory throughout the history of the church as regards biblical interpretation in this way. For example, whilst Origen did not attempt to harmonize the gospels Augustine did, and by the middle ages complex and ingenious attempts to harmonize them were well developed, reflecting a growing concern with 'history'. See R.W. Southern, 'The Sovereign Textbook of the Schools: the Bible' in *Scholastic Humanism and the Unification of Europe* (Oxford: Blackwell, 1995) 1.102-33, and the discussion in chapter 1 above.

[87] E.g. *Questions on Joshua* 16.

[88] Whilst, as we saw above, Calvin offers a typological interpretation of the Promised Land in the *Institutes*, there is no sign of this kind of interpretation in his commentary on Joshua, suggesting something of a tension in his approach to Scripture and theology and their relationship.

[89] W.T. Stevenson, 'History as Myth: Some Implications for History and Theology', in *Cross Currents* 20.1 (1970): 15-28: 'My thesis is that what is commonly termed "history" is a mythic perception of reality. When one stands within this myth, all reality is seen as being historical in nature. ... No more damning criticism can be made of anyone than that of having falsified history, i.e. of having tampered with the "true" and the "sacred". ... Consequently, I believe that what is often called "historical consciousness" conforms essentially to what Eliade calls "myth," and hence I believe that we are justified in asserting that history is a mythic way of viewing reality.' (17-19).

has been obscured or lost. But how then are mythical texts such as Joshua to be appropriated existentially?

Victor Turner

Victor Turner has developed an 'existential' approach to myth in relation to the idea of 'enactment'. For Turner myth is associated with performance, performance that has often been understood in terms of ritual and transition. But Turner has developed and extended conceptions of 'ritual', 'transition' and 'performance' to encompass the 'enaction' of *social actions* in daily life as shaped through myth. He concludes *From Ritual to Theatre*:

> When we act in everyday life we do not merely re-act to indicative stimuli, we act in frames we have wrested from the genres of cultural performance. And when we act on the stage, whatever our stage may be, we must now in this reflexive age of psychoanalysis and semiotics as never before, bring into the symbolic or fictitious world the urgent problems of our reality. We have to go into the subjunctive world of monsters, demons, and clowns, of cruelty and poetry, in order to make sense of our daily lives, earning our daily bread. And when we enter whatever theatre our lives allow us, we have already learned how strange and many-layered everyday life is, how extraordinary the ordinary. We then no longer need in Auden's terms the "endless safety" of ideologies but prize the "needless risk" of acting and interacting.[90]

So for Turner myths are enacted and 'performed' in daily life, with myths providing the symbolic, existential contours that evoke certain kinds of action and interaction.[91]

In his earlier work Turner suggested that myths 'treat of origins, but derive from transitions ... Myths are *liminal* phenomena: they are frequently told at a time or in a site that is "betwixt and between".'[92] Here, he develops the notion of myths as 'liminal phenomena' from Arnold van Gennep's work on rites of passage, but suggests that myths have a liminal character even where they are not bound to rites. Importantly he remarks that myths

> involve a restructuring of social relationships—with the possibility of conflict and disorder. The well-known amorality of myths is intimately connected with their existential bearing. The myth does not describe what ought to be done ... Liminal symbolism, both in its ritual and mythic expressions, abounds in direct

---

[90] V. Turner, *From Ritual to Theatre: The Human Seriousness of Play* (New York: PAJ, 1982), 122.
[91] Cf. also his comments in his introduction (ibid., 7-19).
[92] V. Turner, 'Myth and Symbol', in D.L. Sills (ed.), *International Encyclopedia of the Social Sciences* (Macmillan & The Free Press, 1968), 10.576-81, here 576. Note that here Turner develops a notion of myth that is (I think unnecessarily) rather more narrow than the one that I am developing—I would not limit myths to treatments of origins.

or figurative transgressions of the moral codes that hold good in secular life, such as human sacrifice, human flesh eating, and incestuous unions of brother-sister or mother-son deities or their human representatives. Thus the theory that myths are paradigmatic (Eliade 1957) or that myths afford precedents and sanctions for social status and moral rules (Malinowski 1925) requires some sort of qualification. Myths and liminal rites are not to be treated as models for secular behavior. Nor, on the other hand, are they to be regarded as cautionary tales, as negative models which should not be followed. ... Liminality is pure potency, where anything can happen, where immoderacy is normal, even normative, and where the elements of culture and society are released from their customary configurations and recombined in bizarre and terrifying imagery. Yet this boundlessness is restricted—although never without a sense of hazard—by the knowledge that this is a unique situation and by a definition of the situation which states that the rites and myths must be told in a prescribed order and in a symbolic rather than a literal form. The very symbol that expresses at the same time restrains; through mimesis there is an acting out—rather than the acting— of an impulse that is biologically motivated but socially and morally reprehended.[93]

In other words, myths for Turner have symbolic and existential characteristics and are, in some sense, to be 'enacted'. But crucially they are not to be enacted in any *straightforward* way, simply by modelling behaviour to follow for example. This provides an important perspective on the idea of the 'world of the text' of the myth, and on the way that mythical texts might invite us to 're-imagine' our world. The 'world of the text' is not simply that which is presented to us at 'face value'. These are crucial observations, for there are clear resonances with what Turner describes as the characteristics of myth and the contents of Joshua, such as the חרם, and the restructuring of social relationships.

In terms of discerning Joshua's significance, coupling Turner's remarks on both the role of myth and its amoral nature with traditional interpretation of the Old Testament, and with our consideration of the 'historicization' of myths and symbols, we see that Joshua's significance is located neither in a 'literal sense' nor 'historical sense', nor indeed in a 'moral sense', but rather in something approaching what the Christian tradition has termed the 'spiritual sense', a sense that might be termed the 'second-order symbolic sense' today. Then, re-appropriating Barth one might say that:

The idea that the Bible declares the Word of God only when it speaks *ethically or historically* is one which must be abandoned, especially in the Christian Church. One consequence of this misunderstanding was the great uncertainty of faith which resulted from an inability wholly to escape the im-

---

[93] Ibid., 577. It is important to emphasize here that this is myth according to Turner's conception of it, and so given the broader perspective that I am developing here, this analysis should be understood to refer to *one kind* of myth—i.e. there may be other narratives that one might label 'myth' that do not share these characteristics.

pression that many elements in the Bible have the nature of *myth*, and an ignorance of where and how to draw the line which marks off what is finally *ethical or historical* and therefore the true Word of God. But in other cases it led to a rigid affirmation that in the Bible, as the Word of God, we have only "ethical" accounts and no *myth* at all—an affirmation which can be sustained only if we either close our eyes or violently reinterpret what we see. In other cases again it resulted in an attempt to penetrate to an *"ethical" or "historical"* kernel which is supposed to give us the true, i.e., *"ethical" or "historical"* word of God—the only trouble being that in the process it was unfortunately found that with the discarding of *myth* we do lose not only a subsidiary theme but the main point at issue, i.e., the biblical witness. We have to realise that in all three cases the presumed equation of the Word of God with an *"ethical" or "historical"* record is an inadmissible postulate which does not itself originate in the Bible at all but in the unfortunate habit of *contemporary* thought which assumes that the *validity and enduring significance of a narrative* stands or falls by whether it is *"ethical" or "historical"*.[94]

Indeed, we may discover ways in which Joshua is to be 'enacted and performed' in the Christian context through its juxtaposition with new myths such as Eph 6 in Origen's *Homilies on Joshua,* as we saw above. Thus the Christian interpreter of the Old Testament is not *necessarily* forced to have to simply 'shape up' to and accept narratives that portray an 'immoral' God at face value, and provide an apologetic for such material such as one finds in Calvin's comments on Josh 10:18 for instance:

> Joshua is now free ... to inflict punishment on the kings. In considering this, the divine command must always be kept in view. ... But as such was [God's] pleasure, it behoves us to acquiesce in his decision, without presuming to inquire why he was so severe.[95]

But neither is one forced to reject such immoral material as the word of God as the Marcionites wished to. Rather, in the light of Turner's observations, the contemporary Christian interpreter is freed to re-appropriate the kind of approach found in Origen or Gregory of Nyssa. Ethical difficulties in a narrative indicate that one should seek its significance somewhere other than in its 'literal sense', or what it appears to say 'at face value'. This is a reflection of the nature of the material that we have.

So Joshua, and its use, resonates with the kind of approach to myth that Victor Turner develops. One should not be surprised that Joshua contains amoral and unethical material, being something that it shares with other 'myths'. Joshua provides a symbolic existential resource that is to be enacted or performed in

---

[94] Cf. *CD* III/I, 82, cited above.
[95] Calvin, *Joshua,* 157-8.

some sense, although this is something that will require careful elucidation and development when we come to consider the text in detail in chapter 8.

Structuralist Approaches to Myth

An important approach to the study of myth is the structuralist approach of Claude Lévi-Strauss. In an introduction to his approach he outlines two aspects of this approach that have been foundational to it, and to developments of it. First, he suggests that myths are viewed as having a dynamic significance:

> our method eliminates a problem which has been so far one of the main obstacles to the progress of mythological studies, namely the quest for the *true* version, or the *earlier* one. On the contrary, we define myth as consisting of all its versions ... a myth remains the same as long as it is felt as such.[96]

Secondly, he notes that 'mythical thought always works from the awareness of oppositions towards their progressive mediation'.[97] Robert Segal summarizes the importance of this aspect of Lévi-Strauss's approach thus:

> Lévi-Strauss ... treats myth as a coldly intellectual phenomenon: the oppositions expressed in myth constitute logical puzzles rather than existential predicaments. Myth involves thinking, not feeling. At the same time myth involves more the process than the content of thinking. Here Lévi-Strauss anticipates the focus of contemporary cognitive psychologists. ...
>
> Lévi-Strauss alone dispenses with the plot, or 'diachronic dimension', of myth and locates the meaning of myth in the structure, or 'synchronic dimension'. Where the plot of a myth is that event A leads to event B, which leads to event C, which leads to event D, the structure, which is identical with the expression and resolution of contradictions, is either that events A and B constitute an opposition mediated by event C, or that events A and B, which constitute the same opposition, are to each other as events C and D, an analogous opposition, are to each other.[98]

In practice structuralist readings often highlight questions of identity construction. And Joshua can be read as being concerned with the construction of identity and the tempering of 'contradictions', such as in the stories of Rahab and Achan, which suggests that a structuralist approach is an appropriate tool for studying Joshua.[99] Moreover, given that Joshua is interpreted and developed,

---

[96] C. Lévi-Strauss, 'The Structural Study of Myth' in *The Journal of American Folklore* 68.270 (Oct.-Dec. 1955): 428-44, here 435. Note the similarities between this comment and the ones above on the development of myth.
[97] Ibid., 440.
[98] Segal, *Myth,* 118-9.
[99] I.e., these characters, and their fates, represent 'contradictions' to the accepted norms of Israelite society, with Rahab being the Canaanite prostitute who behaves like an Israelite

often homiletically, at some length in the Christian context, for example by Origen, this indicates again the appropriateness of a structuralist analysis, since structuralism is concerned with the development of myths into 'new myths' in new contexts. Indeed, structuralist analysis provides an interesting way of understanding and viewing Christian allegorical reading of the Old Testament.[100]

However, structuralist approaches have been widely criticized, perhaps most notably by Ricoeur, who said of Lévi-Strauss,

> as far as you are concerned there is no 'message' ... you despair of meaning; but you console yourself with the thought that, if men have nothing to say, at least they say it so well that their discourse is amenable to structuralism. You retain meaning, but it is the meaning of non-meaning, the admirable syntactical arrangement of a discourse which has nothing to say.[101]

In light of this sort of criticism, Seth Kunin has developed the structuralist work of Lévi-Strauss in new directions into what he terms 'neo-structuralism'.[102] It is his approach that I will discuss now, being an important development and improvement of classical structuralism that makes it more attractive and amenable to synthesis with other approaches to myth, especially in a theological context.

Kunin suggests that the basis of structuralist theory is that

> all cultural objects will have as their foundation an unconscious underlying structure. Cultural objects from the same context will largely share the same underlying structural equation. ... [S]tructure at its deepest level organizes patterns of categories that are abstract and contentless—it is the pattern that is significant rather than the meanings articulated by that pattern. The pattern, however, should also be seen as the basis for creating meaningful cultural objects. Structure provides the underlying logic that allows things to be said and to be understood. It creates the logical possibilities that determine how and what can be meaningfully communicated.[103]

---

and is spared, whilst Achan is an Israelite who behaves like an idolater and is executed. More trivially perhaps, Joshua reflects the juxtaposition of portraits of complete and partial conquest (Josh 10:28; 11:12-23; 12:7-24; 21:43-45; 23:9-10; 24:11-13 cf. Josh 9:14-27; 11:22; 15:63; 16:10; 17:11-12; 19:47). Such 'contradiction' draws attention to the mythical nature of the material, and suggests that Joshua *uses* the tempering of such contradictions to serve its very function.

[100] See R.B. Williams, 'Origen's Interpretation of the Old Testament and Lévi-Strauss' Interpretation of Myth', in A.L. Merrill and T.W. Overholt (eds.), *Scripture in History & Theology: Essays in Honor of J. Coert Rylaarsdam* (*PTMS* 17; Pittsburgh: The Pickwick Press, 1977), 279-99 for a structuralist analysis of Origen's use of the Old Testament.

[101] Ricoeur, 'Confrontation', 74. See also P. Ricoeur, 'Biblical Hermeneutics', 65.

[102] Kunin, *We Think What We Eat*.

[103] Ibid., 7.

Learning to Speak of God through Myth 41

In developing neo-structuralism he introduces distinctions into levels of structure and narrative.[104] But he is less ambitious than Lévi-Strauss and other structuralists who seek to impose a 'particular content or meaning on a biological or universal level', for neo-structuralism is interested in 'culture specific aspects of structure rather than the biological'.[105] Crucially he notes that 'many readings of structuralism viewed it as denying human agency both in the creation of cultural artefacts and in practice', and thus neo-structuralism seeks to account for such agency:

> Agency comes into play in the process of emphasizing or de-emphasizing aspects of structure, particularly in cases of cultural overlap. This process leads to possible transformation in structure, and thus removes the static view of culture that is often associated with structuralism. ... Agency provides one of the motors for structural transformation. Agency, which is largely conscious, does not directly change underlying structure, rather it privileges different aspects of the structural equation, and by so doing leads to a slow process by which models of categorization and thinking can change.[106]

He introduces three structural levels and a narrative level for analysis which he denotes S^1, S^2, S^3 and N. S^1 is the most basic and abstract level, related to the biological structure of the human brain as capable of structuring; S^2 is the next structural level, which has no informational content, and is 'understood to be unconsciously shaped by a culture', providing the basis for the nature of categorization and the relationships between categories in order to create culturally meaningful patterns;[107] the S^3 level is culture and context specific, containing available mythological elements (*mythemes* or symbols) that find meaning in relation to other mythemes or symbols in that cultural context. Finally, it is at the N level that these symbols or mythemes are combined into a narrative that is the myth that one analyzes.[108] So, for example, in a given culture the S^2 level reflects the existence of abstract categories, say A and B, and the relationships between them, such as where A and B are mutually exclusive categories with mediation or transformation between them being impossible, as Kunin identifies is the case in Ancient Israel. This structure then finds expression in concrete terms at the S^3 level, for example in the categorization of animals as 'clean' or 'unclean' in Ancient Israel, or in the categorization 'priests' and 'non-priests' for example. The point is that the basic underlying structure at the S^2 level is 'recapitulated' in various ways throughout the culture.[109] These 'concrete' categories,

---

[104] Ibid., 5.
[105] Ibid., 6. '[T]he holy grail of classical structuralism was the discovery of the underlying structures of the brain that were shared by all human beings.' (7).
[106] Ibid., 6.
[107] Ibid., 11.
[108] Ibid., 7-14.
[109] Ibid., 25-7.

understood as symbols or mythemes, are then woven into material at the N level, forming actual myths that explore the significance of these categories and their relationships in practice.

Kunin introduces a

> definition of myth [that] works on two levels both of which arise from structuralist theory. The underlying structure of the definition is 'highly structured narrative (or related) material'. This definition ... sees myth as that body of material in which the structures are most strongly articulated. The definition at this level is open-ended; it makes no determination either to content or function. The next level of definition narrows this range to narrative or related material (for example genealogies) that is used by a particular community to structure its understanding of self and the world.[110]

Thus a narrative that is 'mythical' in this sense requires analysis at both structural and narrative levels, and these analyses will inform one another, suggesting that the approaches of Kunin and Ricoeur may inform each other.[111] So whilst for Lévi-Strauss myths are 'coldly intellectual', for neo-structuralism, when viewed at the narrative level, space is created for more existential and emotional

---

[110] Ibid., 20.

[111] Kunin tends to concentrate on structural concerns. Whilst Ricoeur was at odds with classical structuralism, as we have noted, it appears that neo-structuralism, as Kunin sets it up, is more amenable to use alongside Ricoeur's approach. However, one potential difficulty in using the approaches together relates to the question of symbols, for in many ways Kunin remains close to Lévi-Strauss' account of symbols as conventional with their meaning determined by their structural role and their placement within a set of structural relations (ibid., 13-14, 35), whilst Ricoeur is understood to offer a somewhat more 'transcendental' account of symbols. For example, Lévi-Strauss stated that 'here I am perhaps in disagreement with Paul Ricoeur—symbols, to use a term he is particularly fond of, never have any intrinsic significance. Their meanings can only be "positional" meanings, and it follows that they cannot be available to us in the myths themselves, but only be reference to the ethnographic context, i.e. to what we know about the way of life, the techniques, the ritual and the social organization of the societies whose myths we wish to analyse.' ('Confrontation', 60). But in response Ricoeur suggested that, 'I demonstrated the non-existence of the naturally symbolic, that a symbolism only functions within an economy of thought, within a structure; that is why hermeneutics will never be possible without structuralism' (ibid., 63). This would suggest that the two approaches to symbol are not in fact incompatible. Indeed, Kunin grants that symbols work simultaneously on several levels and are multivocal (*We Think What We Eat*, 35-6), so, although differently developed, these accounts of symbol are closer than they may have been assumed to be. It seems that there is space for a nuanced account of symbol, in which different symbols may be understood as functioning in different ways depending on both their nature and their context of use. As symbols are polyvalent different aspects may be significant or insignificant in different contexts, but arguably they find significance owing to their 'nature'.

aspects to be significant; symbols may take on a richer sense in this domain. Indeed, I noted earlier that from the perspective of a theological anthropology that it is likely that Christian myths will involve both intellectual and emotive dimensions. In other words, 'structural' and 'existential' concerns may be interrelated and function together, so a myth that has 'tired' (or 'died') at the structural level is likely to tire or die at the existential level, with its significance seen only in 'historicizing' terms as suggested above.

Neo-structuralist analysis suggests that *transformation* of myths, and structure, occurs at several levels as they are received and used. It occurs at the N level, where transformations of the narrative, or developments of it, tend to *crystallize* and articulate the issues present in the myth if these elements are not culturally problematic, or to *cloud* the issues if they are culturally problematic. Through such development *mythemes* can be given different emphases or prominence. Kunin denotes the process of transformation at the S^3 level as *bricolage,* reflecting changes in the elements out of which myths are constructed, as the cultural context changes. 'It is through bricolage that new elements are unconsciously categorized and assembled to create new cultural constructs.'[112] But neither of these processes transform the underlying structure.

However, in an important departure from classical structuralism Kunin introduces the idea of *agency*. Whilst it relates to processes of transformation at all levels, it is important to highlight the role of agency with regard to the most significant forms of transformation, transformations at the S^2 level, the underlying structure. It 'comes into play through the individual's conscious and unconscious emphasis or privileging of aspects of the underlying structural equation.' Differing emphases 'will shape [a group's] own conscious and unconscious use of the underlying structure, and can, through pushing at the edges of the system, shift it as it transforms through time. This process is facilitated in cultural situations in which different cultural equations come into contact'.[113] Kunin describes the 'conscious articulation of this form of agency' as *jonglerie,* or 'identity juggling'. It

> encapsulates the process by which individuals privilege different elements of their cultural repertoire at different points in time depending on context and individual choice. *Jonglerie* is not a random process, it allows the individual to highlight or select different aspects of their identity and thereby to shape and reshape different levels of their use and experience of structure. The theoretical concept of *jonglerie* highlights the constant process of conscious and unconscious negotiation of identity and the fact that all identities are in some sense contested.[114]

---

[112] Kunin, *We Think What We Eat,* 18.
[113] Ibid., 22.
[114] Ibid., 23.

So we see here how concerns relating to ideology come into play, and of how the development of the significance of a narrative relates to issues of structure, and vice versa, and how this is played out at conscious and subconscious levels. Crucially, the construction of identity developed from the narrative or N level may differ from the underlying construction of identity reflected at the structural levels. This difference may occur when the narrative is composed so as to 'push' the underlying structure of the context against which it is composed, or when the narrative is used in new contexts in which the underlying structure against which it is appropriated differs from that against which the narrative was composed. The consideration of both levels of significance is thus important for understanding the text and its use.

Thus for a biblical text that contains 'structured material' such as Joshua, viewing it as myth in this perspective will highlight the structural categories that the text reflects and their relations, and in particular, the ways in which 'tensions' in categorization are tempered with regard to the construction of identity. When read canonically, such an approach may indicate the presence of a 'pushing' of the ideology of the categorization and structural relationships in Joshua, since different structural relationships may be discerned in Joshua from those in Deuteronomy for example. Indeed, Joshua is concerned with the structure of insider:outsider definitions and relationships as demonstrated in the stories of Rahab and Achan for example, stories which, as well as subconsciously *reflecting* an underlying structure, represent an ideological 'pushing' of the structure. Rahab, the 'outsider', appears to gain the status of an 'insider', something that arguably the underlying structure does not normally permit, for Israelite identity was essentially genealogically (or at least ethnically) constructed, and does not allow transformation between categories, or their mediation.[115] But it is the narrative level discourse that gives content to how identity is constructed with reference to these categories and their relationships.

Moreover, this neo-structuralist approach indicates that texts such as Joshua will find their significance developed through juxtaposition with other myths, and will be subject to development at both structural and narrative levels. Indeed, an interesting shift takes place with the juxtaposition of these Old Testament texts with those of the New, for a shift in underlying structure occurs in the New Covenant. At the S^2 level an important transformation takes place, for in the Christian context mediation between categories, and transformation between categories is now possible and indeed inherent to the underlying structure of Christian identity.[116] Non-Christians can convert to become Christians, demonstrating transformation, whereas non-Israelites could not, on the whole, convert

---

[115] Ibid., e.g. 168-92, esp. 181-4; 238-46. See chapters 8 and 9 for development of these ideas, and consideration of the slightly more ambiguous status of Rahab in the narrative than traditional readings have tended to assume.

[116] Ibid., 238-46.

to become Israelites, for Israelite identity was essentially genealogically or ethnically determined.[117] Mediation is possible, and indeed necessary, in the Christian context too, such as in Jesus who shares human and divine natures, or in the Christian who is simultaneously a 'sinner' and a 'saint'. Moreover in the Christian context, at the S^3 level certain distinctions found in the Old Testament, such as those between clean and unclean animals lose significance as they are inherently associated with the underlying old structure of thought, and so there is a change at the S^3 level. Certain myths and mythemes thus cease to have significance, becoming simply 'records of the past'—important records, as cultural memory would indicate, but records that no longer have direct existential significance, such as perhaps Antiochene exegesis of the Old Testament as exemplified in Theodore of Mopsuestia. The distinction between clean and unclean animals for example is something inherently bound up with the nature of the Old Covenant and its underlying structure (in the neo-structuralist sense of the term), and is thus a concern that does not find a trajectory into the New Covenant (cf. Acts 10-11). Thus texts that are concerned with the distinction no longer find Christian significance, and their significance as Scripture may be accounted for in terms of certain forms of cultural memory, with such texts no longer having existential significance. Finally, with changes in cultural context there is development at the N level, and so for example when Old Testament images of actual violence and warfare become problematic in the Christian era there is a tendency to develop or 'cloud' these difficulties at the N level by developments of the material into new myths via allegorical and spiritual reading, such as in Origen's *Homilies on Joshua*. Warfare becomes spiritual warfare. Thus different contexts imply different construals of what marks acceptable or good symbolism.

Hence a neo-structuralist approach draws attention to major transformations of *all* Old Testament materials, and not just legal materials for example, when they are taken into the church, a point that is often obscured, but one that neo-structuralism highlights.[118] One might say that two different 'cultural memories' emerge with the Old Testament (or Hebrew Bible) as their shared core. So when an Old Testament text is read in a Christian context important transformation of its significance necessarily takes place at various levels for *theological* reasons that can be described in *structural* terms. Difference in the underlying structures is one way of expressing the 'oldness' of the Old Testament, and is something

---

[117] The exceptions, such as Rahab, Ruth and Naaman are just that, reflecting the pushing of the structure, but are well known stories to Christians precisely because they reflect an attempt to move to a structure that includes conversion. Kunin demonstrates that some of the more difficult texts in Genesis (e.g. Gen 34) are a more accurate reflection of the underlying Israelite structure.

[118] See my 'Towards a Christian Hermeneutic of Old Testament Narrative: Why Genesis 34 fails to find Christian Significance' (forthcoming in *CBQ*) for development of this point.

that is significant theologically and hermeneutically. But Joshua is almost unique here, for perhaps more than any other Old Testament text it reflects a pushing of the underlying structure towards that of the New Covenant, reflected in the possibility of transformation between categories, i.e. of 'conversion'. One might say that it is a preparation for the Gospel, and hence the widespread typological use of Rahab, where her 'faith' is transposed into a new key, with Christ now taken as the object of faith, is understandable.[119] So in this sense, perhaps Joshua more than most other Old Testament narratives *is* amenable to use in a Christian context. But for this to occur developments must take place at the narrative level to suit the new cultural context, a new cultural context that arises from the Incarnation. The necessary transformation of reading strategy often occurred through allegorical interpretation and spiritual reading—a transformation of mythemes in a new cultural context. Hence Rahab is universally a 'type' for the faithful Christian convert, with her house a type of the church.[120] Whilst often seen as fanciful and arbitrary,[121] allegorical and typological interpretations of the Old Testament were in fact fairly stable as I remarked in chapter 1. Rahab is a 'type' for the Christian convert exercising faith in some way, and so 'spiritual' readings do in fact provide a culturally stable 'traditional' resource and 'new myth' into which Joshua is assimilated and used, contributing to the formation of Christian 'cultural memory'. Moreover, whilst allegorical interpretations have been criticized for disregarding the narrative movement, often being 'atomistic' readings of the text, from a structuralist perspective this diachronic narrative movement may be insignificant; it is the synchronic relations that count, and so *from this perspective* it would seem that one can produce a good reading of the text that neglects its narrative flow and plot development, even if it may be necessary to read the text 'holistically' and not 'atomistically' in order to properly appropriate the text as discourse.

In summary then, the importance of a neo-structuralist approach for reading Joshua is clear, for it has great potential to illuminate a number of aspects of the text and its subsequent reception, use and development.

Reading Joshua with Mythical Perspectives

A text that is mythical in the sort of ways identified above finds its meaning and significance expressed and developed in a number of different ways. Sensitivity

---

[119] See chapters 8 and 9 for development of this.

[120] E.g. Heb 11:31; Jas 2:25; 1 Clem 12; Origen, *Hom. Josh.* 3.5; Cyprian, *Letter* 69.4; Chrysostom *Homilies on Repentance and Almsgiving* 7.5.16; Cyril of Jerusalem *Catechetical Lectures* 2.9 (in *ACCS Josh*, 12-15). Moreover, Rahab is understood typologically in some Antiochene exegesis, such as in Theodoret of Cyrus (*Quest. Josh.* 2.2, pp.267-8).

[121] I think that it can be as regards many details.

to the mythical character of a text indicates that its significance is not only or necessarily located in its 'literal', 'historical' or 'first-order' sense; rather its significance lies 'beyond' this, which is something that traditional spiritual reading of the Old Testament has sought to capture, even if inadequately. Thus as 'myth' an Old Testament narrative may be understood as a particular cultural expression that testifies in an existentially engaging fashion to an imaginative world that seeks to shape the way in which the community and the individual lives, thinks and feels, especially as these relate to response to God. Such concerns can often be analyzed and (partially) understood in terms of structural level concerns. The significance of such a narrative is located in terms of this shaping of identity, shaping that may or may not relate straightforwardly to the 'literal sense' of the narrative, and may or may not endure beyond a rather limited context of use, even if its 'historical effects' endure from the perspective of cultural memory. Where its significance does endure a 'mythical' Old Testament narrative is likely to need careful re-expression as symbols come to be construed and used differently.

Reading Joshua in this way, the focus is taken off construing Joshua's significance in terms of a bloody genocide and xenophobia. Rather, the book of Joshua is a narrative set in a foundational, prototypical time—a setting that grants the narrative legitimacy—and a narrative that expresses a desire for rest. 'Typological' readings that develop the story eschatologically can be seen as developing what is already there, and not as readings that impose an alien and unjustifiable sense on the text. A neo-structuralist approach indicates that Joshua may be understood as tackling difficult and searching questions of identity construction, relations to others, and to the land in ways that are ideologically disturbing for some construals of Israelite identity. The story of Rahab challenges the perception of the 'otherness' of the outsider; the story of Achan confronts the comfortable insider, and the story of the altar building (Josh 22) qualifies the status of the land.[122] In other words, approaching Joshua 'as myth' appears to offer insights into what the book of Joshua sought to achieve as discourse as well as indicting how the book's significance develops in new contexts to form Christian cultural memory, in the Christian context.

Finally, to draw together the work of Ricoeur, Turner and Kunin, I will explore one specific and important way in which the meaning of myths is located 'below the surface'. Myths sometimes narrate immoral behaviour. Whilst the neo-structuralist and existential approaches to myth develop the significance of symbols in rather different ways, there are some similarities in the way in which, according to both accounts, symbols may of necessity be morally problematic through a property that I will term a 'limit-situation'. Doty remarks that

---

[122] See chapters 8 and 9.

48   *Reading Joshua as Christian Scripture*

> Myths belong to poetic attempts to express this there-ness [of the world and being] in all its aspects, whether subsequently named sacred or profane, beneficent or maleficent. They express limit-situations, boundaries, not through explanation but as ennarrations, storied presentations of powerful experiences transcending the expressivity of ordinary language.[123]

'Limit-situation' is a helpful way of expressing the nature of some of the material that we find in myth.[124] The idea functions in several related yet distinct ways. First, in the most straightforward way, it acts as an exemplar. In Gen 22 Abraham's obedience in being prepared to sacrifice Isaac demonstrates 'in the limit' what obedience looks like. It provides an existential 'paradigm' that is to be enacted in less extreme ways in ordinary life. The story demonstrates in an existentially demanding fashion what obedience to God entails in its most demanding form. Secondly, again with reference to Abraham, Kunin has indicated the logic behind Abraham's incestuous relationship with Sarah. Here, the 'limit-situation' is genealogical closeness. From a structuralist perspective an incestuous relationship is *logically required* in the case of the patriarchs in order to preserve genealogical identity, even though this relationship is prohibited in the levitical legislation on incest (Lev 18:9-18). Thus *structural* and *narrative* needs are in opposition, and here structural rather than narrative concerns dominate.[125] Here we have a 'limit-situation' necessitated by Abraham, and his wife, being 'the limit' of Israel as its origin. In this sense, this 'limit-situation' is not something to aspire to in the same way as Abraham's obedience, but it engenders the need to marry within the community of Israel to preserve identity. It evokes the enaction of marrying within ethnic Israel. But in both cases the expression of a 'limit-situation' necessitates the portrayal of immoral behaviour, behaviour that is not to be emulated but enacted at another existential level. I shall argue in chapters 6, 8 and 9 that חרם reflects a limit-situation too, although perhaps in a slightly different way again in Joshua.

In summary, reading Joshua 'as myth' illuminates its real significance, and draws attention to ways in which its significance endures through its reception and use. However, whilst this sort of approach indicates how one might *account* for Joshua and the hermeneutics of its reception and use, it does not reveal how, and whether, it *ought* to be received and used, and thus how one assesses the sense in which it might be 'normative', 'revelatory' or 'true'. I shall now turn to these concerns.

---

[123] Doty, *Mythography*, 103.
[124] 'Limit-situation' is discussed from a slightly different angle in Paul Ricoeur's essay 'Biblical Hermeneutics'.
[125] Cf. Kunin, *We Think what we Eat*, 119.

3. THE HERMENEUTICS OF READING JOSHUA AS CHRISTIAN SCRIPTURE

In chapter 2 I considered how we may 'learn about our learning' in essentially 'phenomenological' terms through a *descriptive* account of how, in general, communities learn and shape their identity and existence through 'myth', considered in the context of 'cultural memory', and I also provided some initial reflections upon the significance of this for how Joshua might shape Christian identity. I developed an account of how symbols and stories *do* function and develop. But it is neither an account of how they *ought* to function and develop, nor of whether they are in any sense 'normative' or 'true'. But the Christian interpreter will wish to ascertain whether the Old Testament narratives can be said to be 'true'. Moreover, whilst in different ways Paul Ricoeur, Victor Turner and Seth Kunin's analyses provide the basis for the development of descriptive accounts of the reception and interpretation of Joshua in Origen's *Homilies,* for example, can such *interpretation* be said to be 'true'? And what then ought the interpreter of Joshua to seek to interpret—the text itself or the text together with the tradition of its reception and development into new myths?

Whilst it is tempting to frame the question in this way, relating to 'truth', this predicate may be unhelpful or misleading, as we saw in Ricoeur's analysis of history and fiction in 'The Narrative Function', owing to the difficulty of knowing where to locate (and so how to assess) a text's referentiality, and thus to the difficulty of defining 'truth'. Moreover, it is difficult to see how a development of a myth in, say, neo-structuralist perspective, if construed as an 'interpretation', can be said to be 'true' or not *qua* interpretation. Rather, I wish to suggest that it will be more profitable for the Christian interpreter of the Old Testament to ask whether, and if so then in what sense, a text such as Joshua can be said to offer an iconic *faithful and fitting* 'redescription' of the world that invites the reader, and the community that values the text, into new ways of understanding and relating to God and to the world, and of new ways of 'being in the world' that lead to fuller and more faithful participation in their humanity as created in the image of God and perfected in Christ.[1] We may then speak of

---

[1] I take this as a basic assumption for this discussion for reading Joshua *as Christian Scripture,* even if it is not entirely unproblematic.

the text as being *revelatory* if it can be understood in this way in a particular context.[2]

However, a text (here, Joshua), a myth as a story, can be appropriated in different ways by different readers, or at least by different 'interpretative communities', giving rise to 'new' myths, as we saw from a neo-structuralist perspective. Does one therefore need to speak of both a text *and* a particular tradition of reception *together* as being 'faithful and fitting', and hence (in the Christian context) 'revelatory' (or not), and not just a text? As we saw in chapter 1, Irenaeus argued that one *does* need to interpret a scriptural text as embedded within the Christian tradition, and not in isolation from it *if it is to be interpreted as Christian Scripture*, just as recent accounts of postmodern hermeneutical theory would suggest more generally regarding the role of reading communities. But there are two issues here; first, the fittingness of the history of reception of a text with respect to the text, and secondly, the fittingness of text together with its interpretation with respect to the bigger questions of appropriate human response to God. I would now like to turn once again to Paul Ricoeur to consider these issues.

The Hermeneutics of Texts

Ricoeur suggests that 'literary texts involve potential horizons of meaning, which may be actualized in different ways',[3] but also that not all interpretations are equal, with there being means of arbitrating between interpretations.[4] Mark Wallace helpfully interprets Ricoeur here through Beardsley's guidelines of *plenitude* and *fittingness*; interpretations should be 'fitting' even though a text gives rise to a plenitude of interpretations.[5] Thus in terms of plenitude, if a literary text portrays a world—the world of the text—then this world is amena-

---

[2] I.e. I wish to allow for the possibility that certain Old Testament texts were 'revelatory' in their original context in a way that they are not for Christians today. The contemporary value of texts such as these may be upheld owing to their value as Scripture through the concept of cultural memory; the community lives in the light of the history of their effects in the sense that, for example, a text may be said to be a preparation for the gospel. I think that such a position is reflected in the Antiochene tradition of reading the Old Testament, especially in Theodore of Mopsuestia (see R.A. Greer, *Theodore of Mopsuestia: Exegete and Theologian* (London: The Faith Press, 1961), 86-111).

[3] P. Ricoeur, *Interpretation Theory: Discourse and the Surplus of Meaning* (Fort Worth: The Texan Christian UP, 1976), 78.

[4] Ibid., 79.

[5] M.I. Wallace, *The Second Naiveté: Barth, Ricoeur, and the New Yale Theology* (Studies in American Biblical Hermeneutics 6; Georgia: Mercer UP, 1990), 65. Cf. also S.M. Schneiders, *The Revelatory Text* (Collegeville: The Liturgical Press, 2nd ed. 1999), xxx, who uses the category of 'ideal' meaning instead of the categories of plenitude and fittingness, being based on Ricoeur's work.

ble to various interpretations and 'actualizations' as it meets the 'world of the reader', perhaps just as our experienced world is. Different 'traditions of reception' may then accentuate and develop different aspects of the world portrayed by a text, whilst allowing other different aspects to recede, in rather different ways. These developments may relate to the world of the text as it appears 'at face value', or to what it is that is symbolically reflected by the world of the text. So, in the case of Joshua there is a tradition of reception that, crudely speaking, develops 'spiritual' concerns, another that develops historical concerns, and others that develop colonial/postcolonial concerns. Without a wider frame of reference than the text of Joshua all these construals *might* be possible fitting construals of the text, as text. 'Plenitude' refers to the possibility of there being a variety of possible interpretations of the text owing to its inherent surplus of meaning. But then the tradition of which Joshua is a part, and the juxtaposition of other texts with Joshua in the canon of Scripture restricts (or highlights) the interpretations that one might wish to call constraints of 'fittingness' that guide the use of the text in a particular context. The question is then that of what a good context of use is, and how the text is read well within that context.[6]

In his work on discourse Ricoeur suggests that 'the object of hermeneutics is not the "text" but the *text as discourse* or *discourse as the text*'[7] where, 'Discourse consists of the fact that someone says something to someone *about something*. "About something" is the inalienable referential function of discourse. Writing does not abolish it, but rather transforms it.'[8] However, elsewhere he develops the idea of a revelatory function of what he terms *poetic discourse*[9] through the concepts first of writing; '[writing] produces a form of discourse that is immediately autonomous with regard to the author's intention. ... [I]n this autonomy, is already contained ... the *issue* of the text which is removed from the finite intentional horizon of the author';[10] secondly of 'work':

> By [work] I mean the shaping of discourse through the operation of literary genres such as narration, fiction, the essay, etc. By producing discourse as such and such a work taking up such and such a genre, the composition codes assign

---

[6] Thus I shall draw upon examples of Joshua's interpretation to consider how the plenitude of the text has been explored, and whether such explorations are in fact fitting with respect to the text.
[7] P. Ricoeur, 'Biblical Hermeneutics', in *Semeia* 4 (1975): 29-148, here 67.
[8] P. Ricoeur, 'Naming God', in *Figuring the Sacred* (Minneapolis: Fortress Press, 1995), 217-35, here 220.
[9] For Ricoeur, 'poetics' does not designate a literary genre, 'but rather the totality of these genres inasmuch as they exercise a referential function that differs from the descriptive referential function of ordinary language and above all of scientific discourse.' (P. Ricoeur, 'Toward a Hermeneutic of the Idea of Revelation', in P. Ricoeur (ed. L.S. Mudge), *Essays on Biblical Interpretation* (London: SPCK, 1981), 73-118, here, 100).
[10] Ibid., 99.

to works of discourse that unique configuration we call a style. This shaping of the work concurs with the phenomenon of writing in externalizing and objectifying the text into what one literary critic has called a "verbal icon";[11]

and thirdly of 'world of the text':

> By this I mean that what is finally to be understood in a text is not the author or his presumed intention, nor is it the immanent structure or structures of the text, but rather the sort of world intended beyond the text as its reference. In this regard, the alternative "either the intention or the structure" is vain. For the reference of the text is what I call the issue of the text or the world of the text. The world of the text designates the reference of the work of discourse, not what is said, but about what it is said. Hence the issue of the text is the object of hermeneutics. And the issue of the text is the world the text unfolds before itself.[12]

Moreover, elsewhere he remarks on the phenomenon of 'traditionality' that

> [a] trait that a narrative theology may retain ... concerns the *role of tradition* not only in the transmission but also in the reception and the interpretation of received stories. This phenomenon of traditionality is very complex because it relies on the flexible dialectics between innovation and sedimentation. It is sedimentation that we ascribe to paradigms that help a typology of emplotment to emerge and to get stabilized. But the opposite phenomenon of innovation is no less prominent. Why? Because paradigms generated by a previous innovation provide guidelines for further experimentation in the narrative field. In this dialectic between innovation and sedimentation a whole range of solutions is deployed between the two poles of servile repetition and calculated deviance, passively through all the degrees of *déformation réglée*.[13]

This is another perspective for considering, or for talking about, the development of the use of texts such as Joshua in addition to the perspectives introduced in the discussion of myth in chapter 2. Crucially, we may take the embedding of a text such as Joshua within the canon of Scripture as a vital stage in this process of reception, affecting its ongoing significance. Such a text is now part of a *new* act of discourse, one that has community assent, an act of discourse that transforms and perhaps directs the way in which Joshua might be construed.[14] Ricoeur suggests that,

---

[11] Ibid., 99-100.
[12] Ibid., 100.
[13] P. Ricoeur, 'Toward a Narrative Theology: Its Necessity, Its Resources, Its Difficulties', in *Figuring the Sacred*, 236-48, here 240.
[14] Here it is not necessary to appeal to an 'intentionality' in this transformation and direction of reading when considered from the perspective of the cultural factors leading to the production of the canon. At the theological level this process might be described in terms of the action of the Holy Spirit as 'primary cause' working through the 'secondary causes' of the human processes involved in the compilation of Scripture.

this interweaving brings into play a reading of the biblical writings laid out as one vast "intertext." This reading must of course take into account the historical-critical method, but it cannot be reduced to it. Where the historical-critical method focuses on the differences between the diverse literary layers brought together in the final redaction, in order to re-establish the *Sitz-im-Leben* of this or that narrative or this or that institution, the reading I am proposing begins from the fact that the meaning of the recounted events and the proclaimed institutions has become detached from its original *Sitz-im-Leben* by becoming part of Scripture, and this Scripture has so to speak substituted what we may call a *Sitz-im-Wort* for the original *Sitz-im-Leben*. My reading shall begin from here, from the *Sitz-im-Wort* of events, actions, and institutions that have lost their initial roots and that, as a consequence, now have a textual existence. It is this textual status of the narratives, laws, prophecies, wisdom sayings, and hymns that makes these texts contemporary with one another in the act of reading. This synchronic reading is called for to complete the diachronic approach of the historical-critical method. This synchronic reading is at the same time an intertextual reading, in the sense that, once they are apprehended as a whole, these texts of different origins and intentions work on one another, displacing their respective intentions and points, and they mutually borrow their dynamism from one another. So read, the Bible becomes a great living intertext, which is the place, the space for a labor of the text on itself. My reading, in short, seeks to grasp this labor of the text upon itself through an act of reconstructive imagination.[15]

Several implications may be drawn from Ricoeur. First, the 'fittingness' of an interpretation of a text is not straightforwardly related to the author's intention, to the text as artefact, or to the tradition that the text is embedded in; rather, it sits in tension with all three. On the one hand, a tradition cannot impose *any* reading on the text, for the text 'as work' needs to be respected—it is 'about something'. However, on the other hand, the text in some sense 'belongs to' the tradition that values and uses it. So certain post-colonial readings of Joshua, for example those that read Joshua from a Canaanite perspective with Rahab becoming identified as a 'traitor' or 'collaborator with imperialism' rather than as a model of faith,[16] may not provide genuinely *Christian* interpretations of the text precisely because they are readings from an antagonistic perspective that is not fitting for the use of text, both with respect to the text as an act of discourse *and* with respect to its use in the Christian tradition.[17] Joshua is concerned with shaping those inside the community that values the text and is not concerned

---

[15] P. Ricoeur, 'Biblical Time', in *Figuring The Sacred*, 167-80, 171.

[16] See D. Mbuwayesango, 'Joshua' in D. Patte (ed.), *Global Bible Commentary* (Nashville: Abingdon Press, 2004), 64-73, here 66 and M.W. Dube, 'Rahab says Hello to Judith: A Decolonizing Feminist Reading', in R.S. Sugirtharajah (ed.), *The Postcolonial Biblical Reader* (Oxford: Blackwell, 2006), 142-58, here 156.

[17] Of course any interpreter may be free to read any text from whatever perspective they desire; the question is what is *claimed* for the interpretation.

with providing an 'outsider' perspective, a perspective that will naturally look rather different. However, this is not to say that all fitting readings must be traditional, for as Ricoeur noted, traditionality is complex, involving sedimentation and *innovation*. So some postcolonial readings might provide innovations that are in a sense 'revelatory' and lead the use of Joshua within the Christian tradition forward. Thus interpretation is a matter of dialectics; the tradition in dialectic with itself via the contemporary context (i.e., contemporary 'innovation' in dialogue with the 'sedimentation' of the existing deposits within the tradition that are in some sense authoritative), and the tradition of reception itself in dialogue with the original act of discourse reflected in the text.

Secondly, since the interpreter is concerned with the kind of world 'intended beyond the text', which is not quite the 'author's intention' or 'the text itself', this world needs to be 'accessed' through 'critical' tools that relate to genre, literary techniques of composition, lexicography, etc., But this does not necessarily imply that understanding the *precise* historical circumstances that led to the production of the text is required. Rather, what is required is *sufficient* knowledge of the historical context of a text so as to make it intelligible—but this might be rather little. The difficulty is ascertaining what counts as sufficient knowledge. It seems impossible to generalize, and care is required here in not seeking to claim that too much is required, not least since it is so difficult to establish with any confidence the historical context of Joshua's composition. Scholars continue to debate Josianic, exilic and other contexts for the 'most significant' stage of Joshua's composition. But even when the context *is* 'known',[18] one can only speculate on the intention that lies behind the work. Those who assume a Josianic context for Joshua tend to read Joshua as reflecting royal propaganda, sometimes pejoratively,[19] whilst those who assume an exilic context read Joshua in terms of the hopes for return from exile of a beleaguered community.[20] But what is the significance of the 'identification' of such for understanding Joshua's theological significance? It is not clear that as much

---

[18] R.D. Nelson ('Josiah in the Book of Joshua', in *JBL* 100.4 (1981): 531-40) develops a case for a Josianic context. But the matter is not straightforward. For example it is difficult to know which direction dependency might run (i.e., whether the account of Josiah is based upon a story of Joshua, or whether Joshua is 'invented' by Josiah or for his own benefit), if indeed there is any dependency. Moreover, if Josiah's account does reflect a rather tendentious narrative of the Deuteronomist, perhaps rather little may be said as regards historical reconstruction and in particular the relationships between vaguely similar texts, as *both* accounts might be later inventions to suit a later context.

[19] E.g. R.B. Coote, 'The Book of Joshua', in *The New Interpreter's Bible* (Nashville: Abingdon, 1998), 2.555-719, e.g. 584-5, who takes it as supplying justification to the House of David's claim to land.

[20] E.g. J.F.D. Creach, *Joshua* (Interpretation) (Louisville: John Knox Press, 2003), 30; W.A. Brueggemann, *Theology of The Old Testament: Testimony, Dispute, Advocacy* (Minneapolis: Fortress Press, 1997), 209-11.

follows as Coote or Creach, for example, would like, for we still do not know what the act of discourse of Joshua sought to achieve, *other than through the text itself*. For instance if Joshua did arise in a Josianic context then it might not have been used coercively originally. Moreover, the study of myth indicates that questions of 'persistence' are at least as important as those of origin, and, as we shall see below, it is through the *persistence* of particular ways of construing a text, i.e., the 'world of the text', that its 'revelatory significance' is 'testified' to. In summary, an Old Testament text such as Joshua is part of a tradition, or of traditions (taking tradition(s) here to mean the tradition(s) that Joshua arose *from*), and an awareness of such tradition(s), their language and concerns, is likely to assist in making the text intelligible as a public act of discourse.[21]

Thirdly, if one traces the development of the tradition of which Joshua was *already* a part then the notion that Joshua reflects an act of 'discourse' becomes rather complex. Let us suppose that Joshua *was* composed from a number of disparate sources. These sources are themselves already acts of discourse that the author(s) of Joshua edited into a *new* act of discourse, to create a particular 'world of the text'. But then the placement of Joshua into the canon of Scripture is *another* act of discourse, yielding *another* 'world of the text' through juxtapositions of texts to create meanings that might or might not have been intentional.[22] Indeed, the concept of canon does not rely upon intentionality, rather it relies upon the juxtaposition of a collection of texts that the community has discerned to be of particular importance and significance that are generative of the community's identity,[23] an identity created and worked out through both the discords and the harmonies of the texts as they are read together. The canonical context thus provides a 'filter' that is of particular hermeneutical significance for considering how the plenitude and fittingness of Joshua's interpretation might play out. This 'world of the text', its interpretation and appropriation is then developed in the subsequent tradition of its reception which occurs in the dialogue between the contemporary context of the interpreter and of the tradition leading to it, and *the canon in particular*. So this criterion of 'fittingness' is complex, and one might regard the whole *process* of the composition *and reception* of Joshua as (at least potentially) 'revelatory', even if there are spurious and wrong twists and turns within the process as well as healthy develop-

---

[21] See chapter 4.

[22] Moreover, this process might reflect several acts of discourse given the gradual emergence of the canon through intermediate stages.

[23] Cf. J.W. Rogerson, 'Towards a Communicative Theology of the Old Testament', in J.G. McConville and K. Möller (eds.), *Reading the Law: Studies in Honour of Gordon J. Wenham* (London: T&T Clark, 2007), 283-96, who is cautious of notions of 'intentionality' in relation to the canon. Here he develops notions of canon in terms of cultural memory.

ments, again implying the need for a dialectical aspect to interpretation.[24] But it is important to note that a story that is used in another story can have its meaning transformed by the process; a seemingly minor redactional gloss can transform the meaning of a text, either clarifying or obscuring the 'world of the text'.[25] In summary then, interpretation and revelation are caught up in this whole *process* of tradition and discourse, and not primarily in a punctilinear moment within it,[26] even if there are such punctilinear moments within the tradition, especially as 'actions in history' perhaps, that do have a special revelatory character that is foundational,[27] such as the crucifixion and resurrection.[28] Theologically speaking, the 'revelatory' character of Joshua might be said to be manifested in the processes of sedimentation and innovation in its reception and use in the tradition. So the notion of plenitude expresses the possibility that the tradition can 'open up' possibilities for interpretation of the text that are genuine developments that may be termed 'revelatory' in themselves, such as reading Joshua in terms of the spiritual life, whilst the notion of fittingness restricts possibilities for interpretation, for example by suggesting that the 'colonial' use of Joshua is a poor way of construing the text, because it does not sit well with canonical texts that stress the love of neighbour and God's desire for the salvation of all for instance. The criterion of 'fittingness' thus forms the basis for arbitrating between differing interpretations, even though a plurality of 'good' interpretations may exist.[29]

However, whilst this starts to tackle the question of what 'faithful and fitting' means from the perspective of the Christian tradition, it says rather little about whether Joshua and the tradition that it is embedded in are 'faithful and fitting' in the sense that I introduced earlier, where I sought to associate this description with the idea of 'revelation' and of good re-description of the world that leads humanity to its proper *telos*. But as Kevin Vanhoozer asks with refer-

---

[24] Theologically speaking, this idea of the revelatory process would seem to be a reflection of the dynamic activity of the Holy Spirit as leading into truth.

[25] I shall discuss Josh 6:19 and 24 from this perspective in chapter 8.

[26] As, it seems, was the basic assumption of much modernist biblical interpretation, such as the 'original event'.

[27] See below.

[28] I.e., *some* texts will have the fittingness of their interpretation constrained by historical concerns—'what happened' if you like, but even here such events are subject to interpretation and development within a tradition—they are not 'naked facts'; cf. W. Pannenberg, 'Dogmatic Theses on the Concept of Revelation', in W. Pannenberg (ed.), *Revelation as History* (London: Sheed & Ward, 1969), 123-58, esp. 137, 152-3. For example, the gospels draw upon the traditional material (the cultural memory) formed by what Christians term the Old Testament to interpret the life of Jesus.

[29] As noted earlier, Schneiders helpfully introduces the notion of 'ideal' meaning (even if the term is a little awkward) in the sense that good readings will share a certain 'family resemblance'.

ence to Ricoeur's work, 'What is the difference between an imaginative way of being-in-the-world that is a genuine individual or social possibility and a utopian dream derived from the pathology of hope?'[30] Whilst Vanhoozer wishes to appeal to aspects of historical veracity to provide an epistemological warrant, as is common in modernity, this will not do, owing to the nature of much 'revelatory' material as 'poetic discourse'.[31] Appealing to history in *this* way reflects a mythical perception of reality rampant in modernity,[32] but it is an epistemology that is simply not available. How might one proceed? Perhaps it is better to speak in terms of *manifestation* rather than of *verification*. To this I shall now turn, considered through the notion of 'testimony'.

The Significance of Testimony

Developing Ricoeur's work, Rowan Williams asks,

> How ... do we speak of revelation? The point of introducing the notion at all seems to be to give some ground for the sense in our religious and theological language that the initiative does not ultimately lie with us; before we speak, we are addressed or called. Paul Ricoeur, in an important essay on the hermeneutics of the idea of revelation, has attempted to link the concept with a project for a 'poetics', which will spell out the way in which a poetic text, by offering a frame of linguistic reference other than the normal descriptive/referential function of language, 'restores to us that participation-in or belonging-to an order of things which precedes our capacity to oppose ourselves to things taken as objects opposed to a subject'. The truth with which the poetic text is concerned is not verification, but manifestation. That is to say that the text displays or even embodies the reality with which it is concerned simply by witness or 'testimony'. ... It displays a 'possible world', a reality in which my human reality can also find itself: and in inviting me into its world, the text breaks open and extends my own possibilities. All this, Ricoeur suggests, points to poetry [sc. poetic discourse] as exercising a *revelatory* function—or, to rephrase this in the

---

[30] K. Vanhoozer, *Biblical Narrative in the Philosophy of Paul Ricoeur* (Cambridge: CUP, 1990), 240. He suggests, 'Lacking in Ricoeur's otherwise brilliant philosophical rehabilitation of metaphor is any indication of how one may judge the difference between good and bad metaphors. ... The question is simply this: if metaphors are our only access to a redescription of the real, how can we know whether or not to believe the metaphor? If what the metaphor affirms cannot be checked by non-metaphorical means, how can we tell the difference between a helpful and a misleading metaphor?' (66).

[31] See P. Ricoeur, 'The Narrative Function', in *Semeia* 13 (1978): 177-202. Here, I use the term 'revelatory' in a somewhat broader sense than it has often been construed in the Christian tradition, although perhaps Ricoeur allows the term to slip a little too far.

[32] See W.T. Stevenson, 'History as Myth: Some Implications for History and Theology' in *Cross Currents* 20.1 (1970): 15-28.

terms proposed at the beginning of this paragraph, it manifests an initiative that is not ours in inviting us to a world we did not make. ...

Revelation, on such an account, is essentially to do with what is *generative* in our experience—events or transactions in our language that break existing frames of reference and initiate new possibilities of life. ... And to recognize a text, a tradition or an event as revelatory is to witness to its generative power. It is to speak from the standpoint of a new form of life and understanding whose roots can be traced to the initiating phenomenon. ...

Thus 'revelation' is a concept which emerges from a questioning attention to our present life in the light of a particular past—a past seen as 'generative'. In terms of the scriptural history of Israel, the events of the Exodus were revelatory insofar as they were generative of the community of Israel itself and Torah was revelatory because it was what specified the form of life of that community.[33]

Ricoeur proceeds to develop this notion of testimony,[34] suggesting that

To be a witness is to have participated in what one has seen and to be able to testify to it.

On the other hand, testimony may break away from the things seen to such a degree that it is concentrated on the quality of an act, a work, or a life, which is in itself a sign of the absolute. In this second sense, which is complementary to the first sense, to be a witness is no longer to testify that . . . , but to testify to. . . This latter expression allows us to understand that a witness may so implicate himself in his testimony that it becomes the best proof of his conviction.[35]

And elsewhere that

Testimony should be a philosophical problem and not limited to legal or historical contexts where it refers to the account of a witness who reports what he has seen. The term testimony should be applied to words, works, actions, and to lives which attest to an intention, an inspiration, an idea at the heart of experience and history which nonetheless transcend experience and history. The philosophical problem of testimony is the problem of the testimony of the absolute or, better, of absolute testimony of the absolute.[36]

He goes on to relate the idea of testimony to symbol in a way reminiscent of the discussion above on 'fittingness':

---

[33] R. Williams, 'Trinity and Revelation', in *On Christian Theology* (Oxford: Blackwell, 2000), 131-47, here 133-4.
[34] A notion also developed by Walter Brueggemann in his *Theology of The Old Testament*.
[35] Ricoeur, 'Toward a Hermeneutic', 113.
[36] P. Ricoeur, 'The Hermeneutics of Testimony', in *Essays on Biblical Interpretation*, 119-54, here 119-20.

> The symbol is not obliterated ... its double meaning, its opacity, renders it inexhaustible and causes it never to cease giving rise to thought. But it lacks—or can lack—historic density; its meaning matters more than its historicity. As such it constitutes instead a category of the productive imagination. Absolute testimony, on the contrary, in concrete singularity gives a caution to the truth without which its authority remains in suspense. Testimony, each time singular, confers the sanction of reality on ideas, ideals, and modes of being that the symbol depicts and discovers for us only as our most personal possibilities.[37]

Finally Ricoeur considers the importance of testimony in Scripture:

> A theology of testimony which is not just another name for the theology of the confession of faith is only possible if a certain narrative kernel is preserved in strict union with the confession of faith. The case par excellence is the faith of Israel which, at first, confessed Yahweh by relating the facts of deliverance which punctuate the history of its liberation. Every "theology of the traditions," following von Rad, is built on this basic postulation that the *Credo* of Israel is a narrative confession on the model of the nuclear *Credo* of Deuteronomy 26:5-9. Where a "history" of liberation can be related, a prophetic "meaning" can be not only confessed but attested. It is not possible to testify *for* a meaning without testifying *that* something has happened which signifies this meaning. The conjunction of the prophetic moment, "I am the Lord," and the historical moment, "It is I, the Lord your God, who has led you out of the land of Egypt and out of the house of bondage" (Exodus 20:2)—is as fundamental as the conjunction of the prophetic moment and the juridical moment. A tension is thus created between confession of faith and narration of things seen, at the heart of which is renewed the ever present tension between the judgment of the judge, who decides without having seen, and the narration of the witness who has seen. There is therefore no witness of the absolute who is not a witness of historic signs, no confessor of absolute meaning who is not a narrator of the acts of deliverance.[38]

So in a sense, the importance of 'history' is not abandoned in this account. But here we encounter a difficulty, perhaps one that Williams repeats,[39] with regard to the nature of the Old Testament materials. Whilst the Old Testament materials are certainly *generative,* perhaps they do not 'testify' in quite the sense that Ricoeur envisages, being of a more 'poetic' nature (to use his term) than he grants. Gerhard von Rad's *Credo* has not been well received in Old Testament scholarship, and a good number of scholars, partly on the basis of the current state of archaeological research, suggest or assume that there was never an Israelite exodus from Egypt, something which might find support from a

---

[37] Ibid., 121-2.
[38] Ibid., 133-4.
[39] This is not quite clear, for he goes on to cite N.K Gottwald, *The Tribes of Yahweh: A Sociology of the Religion of Liberated Israel, 1250-1050 BCE* (The Biblical Seminar 66; Sheffield: Sheffield Academic Press, 1999).

'mythical' reading of the book of Exodus.[40] Now, Exodus, for example, is generative of the identity of a community in the way that Williams suggests, and it is testified to in this fashion in history in the sense that Exodus *has* generated a community with certain characteristics. The identity thus generated might well be said to lead to the 'enhancement' of the life of the community that values the work. But, in all likelihood, it does not provide the kind of testimony that Ricoeur wishes. It is, however, at the very least a symbolic story testifying *to the experience of Israel*, and so even if there was not a 'historical exodus' from Egypt, the story may still be understood to testify to an actual 'exodus experience' for Israel in the more 'historical' form that Ricoeur seeks, but *told in symbolic form whilst having a 'historical' basis nonetheless*. The book of Exodus would then represent a symbolic way of telling of such foundational, generative experience using available cultural resources to interpret an 'exodus experience' that invites existential participation—i.e. to continue to experience 'exodus'.[41] But in fact we find the resource in Ricoeur's essay itself to overcome the difficulty in his proposal, for he suggests that, 'Applying this relation to testimony and to the relation of confession to narration points up that the manifestation of the absolute in persons and acts is indefinitely mediated by means of available meanings borrowed from previous scripture.'[42] In other words, the book of Exodus may not represent a straightforward testimony to actual historical events as narrated at 'face value', but it is testimony to a *manifestation* of God to Israel using available meanings, perhaps such as Egypt as symbolizing oppression and bondage.

Returning to Joshua, one may suggest that Joshua represents the manifestation of the divine summons in some sense, but in a sense yet to be clarified. It is testimony to a manifestation of the divine in some way, but not in a straightforward sense that construes the book of Joshua as testimony to historical events as narrated.[43] The sense in which Joshua is testimony is interpreted, clarified,

---

[40] I.e., a number of the major motifs in Exodus reflect ANE mythology set in a 'history like' narrative (see e.g. J.D. Levenson, *Creation and the Persistence of Evil* (Princeton: Princeton UP, 1988), 75-6). The textual evidence need not suggest, however, that there was not an exodus from Egypt, and the archaeological evidence remains open to revision.

[41] In relation to this question, and that of the conquest, Neil Soggie develops the notion of an 'inspiration event' that lies behind the narrative—whilst the narrative is not 'history' in the modern sense, a 'historical event' lies behind it that inspires it. (N.A Soggie (*Myth, God, and War: The Mythopoetic Inspiration of Joshua* (Lanham: University Press of America, 2007), e.g. 7, 17, 29-30 and 110-11).

[42] Ricoeur, 'Hermeneutics of Testimony', 145.

[43] Examples of indicators within the text itself that it is not a 'historical record' are the nature of the 'spy' mission (Josh 2), the location of Rahab's house (which needs to be in the city wall to suit the dynamics of Josh 2, but a location that is problematic for Josh 6—something that the narrative passes over in silence, but a problem that has been discussed in Jewish exegesis (see R. Drucker, *The Book of Joshua: A New Translation with a*

developed, refined and, perhaps, corrected through further manifestation of the divine and testimony to the divine in the tradition,[44] a process that is revelatory and generative of a community transformed into ways of being and action that reflect God's *telos* for humanity. For the Christian the central locus of the manifestation of the divine and testimony to the divine is in Jesus and the narratives of the gospels.

Thus one may say that Joshua is revelatory today as Christian Scripture if it is generative of contemporary Christian life and experience by providing a faithful and fitting witness to God by developing the existential significance of foundational 'inspiration events' into the present. The interpreter's task is to consider whether, and if so how, it is, which is something of a dialectical process as outlined above concerned with exploring the plenitude—or surplus of meaning—and fittingness of the text with respect to its tradition of reception when viewed from the interpreter's contemporary context. Whilst one might like to 'stand outside' the tradition to seek to discern an objective view of its truth, in doing so one cuts oneself off from the very manifestations which make such discernment possible. But one must thus recognize the provisionality of the tradition itself that is oriented towards an eschatological *telos*. In Brueggemann's terms the tradition, including the biblical tradition perhaps, contains both 'testimony' and 'counter-testimony' to the manifestation of the divine.[45] Manifestation, testimony and discernment are intimately related.

But what does the interpretative task involve in more practical terms? Returning to the questions raised at the end of chapter 2, is the task for the contemporary Christian interpreter of Joshua primarily to take the narrative, *as*

Commentary anthologized from Talmudic, Midrashic and Rabbinic Sources (New York: Mesorah Publications, 1982), 178-9), and the tension between narratives of complete and partial conquest (Josh 10:28; 11:12-23; 12:7-24; 21:43-45; 23:9-10; 24:11-13 cf. Josh 9:14-27; 11:22; 15:63; 16:10; 17:11-12; 19:47). Moreover, in canonical perspective there is tension between the ways in which it was envisaged that Israel possessed the land—in Exod 23:20-33 it is envisaged that the locals will simply vanish (כחד, 23:23), whereas they are to be destroyed (חרם) according to Deut 7:1-5, whilst Lev 18:25 envisages the land 'vomiting out' (קיא) the locals. Whilst it is possible to harmonize the accounts of Rahab's house—for example by suggesting that most but not all of the wall of Jericho collapsed, this reading strategy seems to undermine the thrust of the narrative—that through YHWH's power the wall was completely removed.

[44] In other words, some sort of notion of 'election' is needed in this account—that God manifests himself to particular people and communities at particular times. I do not wish to claim that such manifestation can be 'known' as being such 'from nowhere' on formal grounds; rather it requires an act of acceptance that forms the grounds for the kind of analysis here, even if such manifestation also provides testimony in itself to encourage the acceptance of it as such. In traditional Christian categories such acceptance is accounted for in terms of grace and faith.

[45] See his *Theology of the Old Testament*.

narrative, in the 'literal sense' of its locutions and in all its particularity as being the place in which one, in some sense, expects to locate its 'normative' or 'authoritative' significance, with an existential response being called forth from this level of significance? *Or,* following the lead of Nicholas Lash, as read through the existential account of myth developed in chapter 2, once one understands 'what was once achieved, intended or "shown"' by the book of Joshua, as would be reflected in terms of concrete expressions or enactments of actual human practice and behaviour, expressions and enactments that are appropriations of the *symbolic sense* of *the world of the text,* is the interpretative task then to consider how what the narrative witnesses to *in this sense* might be faithfully and appropriately expressed and enacted today?[46] With regard to Joshua it would appear that it is mostly the latter,[47] as I shall now seek to clarify.

The question is made more complex not just because of differences in cultural context, where differences in interpretation may arise simply from different forms of concrete practices, but also as regards the normativity of what is witnessed to, particularly for a text that relates to the Old Covenant—such a text might have an intrinsic theological 'oldness' that restricts its significance (and revelatory character) to the context of the Old Covenant (without denying that it is an 'inspired' text). From the perspective of cultural memory the text would still be important, as it narrates the roots and identity of the Christian community, even if it might not have continued revelatory significance beyond this. But cultural memory is not static, and so these questions must, first of all, be considered in the light of further manifestation of the divine. *Discernment,* often of a theological nature, is thus required in interpretation; to what extent does not just the narrative, but what the narrative witnesses to in its symbolic sense, resonate with the testimony and witness of the Christian tradition, and in particular, to the witness of God in Christ, even if Joshua might 'push' such a later witness in challenging and demanding ways?[48] So what is required, if 'enduring normative significance' (in some existential or theological sense perhaps) is to be found, is that in this engagement of 'testimony with testimony' sympathetic 'resonances' exist between Joshua, later aspects of the tradition (the

---

[46] N. Lash, 'What might Martyrdom mean?', in *Theology on the Way to Emmaus* (London: SCM, 1986), 75-92, here 89-91. It would remain important not to dispense with the narrative since it is *this narrative* that forms Christian cultural memory. However, the corresponding forms of practice and behaviour that might be encouraged today might look rather different from those envisaged or achieved in its ancient Israelite context.

[47] In other biblical texts, such as the gospels, the *balance* may look rather different, with a greater emphasis on the 'literal sense' of the narrative. I wish to leave this as an open question requiring further exploration.

[48] I.e., Joshua needs to be given space to say something 'in its own right'. A criterion for discernment of the appropriation and enactment of Joshua is not just that of whether what it says may be gleaned from elsewhere, in the New Testament for example.

canon in particular), and the contemporary context as one seeks to probe the 'world of the text' and its appropriation and enactment in all its fullness.

But when the narrative 'world of the text' of Joshua confronts the world of the reader situated in a different cultural context, what the narrative *witnesses to*, i.e., 'what was once achieved, intended or "shown"' by the book of Joshua in terms of concrete enacted expressions of human practice and behaviour that arise from the appropriation of the world of the text *reflected* in the narrative might need to be re-expressed faithfully today in concrete expressions of human practice and behaviour that are very different. If, as I shall argue, Joshua is primarily concerned with questions of the identity and character of Israel, then its contemporary interpretation may not then be concerned *necessarily* with questions like, 'What does it mean to practice חרם today?', or perhaps even, 'What does it mean to put away idols today?'—questions that focus on interpretation at the *narrative* level. Instead, perhaps the focus will be on questions like, 'What does it mean to respond faithfully to God today in a multi-cultural society?' and, 'What is it that constitutes the identity of God's people today amid a seemingly fragmented church, and how should those who consider themselves to be inside the Christian community live and relate to those seemingly outside this community?', for these are the kinds of questions that reflect what Joshua sought to address in the concrete aspects of ancient Israelite life.[49] To tackle these questions today with respect to our communities *is* to interpret Joshua today.

As I noted earlier, perhaps, to use the traditional Christian grammar, this is akin to the 'spiritual' or 'figural' sense of Joshua, the need for which was recognized in part through a close reading of the literal sense of the text—and a realization that this was problematic. 'Spiritual reading' of Joshua attempted to re-express in concrete ways in the Christian context what it was that Joshua witnessed to, recognizing that the text needed to be re-expressed using new symbols and to be enacted existentially if it was to be used faithfully.[50] Attention

---

[49] Cf. Lash: 'What might "witness" or "martyrdom" mean, today? The form of the question, derived from models of interpretation the inadequacy of which I have tried to indicate, is unsatisfactory. It should rather be: What form might contemporary fidelity to "the testimony of Jesus" appropriately take? And this is a practical and not merely a theoretical question. It is a question that will continue, often in darkness, strenuously to engage all those resources of integrity and discernment without which patterns of human action are not responsibly undertaken or pursued. And it will also continue to engage all those resources of textual, historical and literary criticism without which the New Testament scholar cannot competently perform his indispensable function. That function, I have suggested, is an aspect, but only an aspect, of the broader task of Christian interpretative practice, of the attempt to bear witness faithfully and effectively to God's transformative purpose and meaning for mankind.' (*Martyrdom*, 91-2).

[50] Spiritual reading strategies also took their cue from the observation that 'Joshua' and 'Jesus' are identical names in Greek ('Ιησοῦς). It was, therefore, natural to recontextualize Joshua in Christian terms, possibly (indirectly) influenced by Stoic etymology (cf. D.

to such reading strategies force one to consider what the text is really 'about'.[51] This is where neo-structuralist analysis, relating to the construction of identity, or psychological analysis, reflecting desire, for example, come in, drawing attention to what is, in some sense, 'below the surface'—or manifested in the symbol. However, the possibility remains that a given Old Testament text is rendered otiose in a sense in the Christian context, finding its significance in the limited yet important sense indicated by cultural memory—that it forms part of the historical foundations on which Christian identity, and the Christian community, is formed.[52]

The Life of Symbols

The most basic, and possibly the most important single aspect of this process of appropriation and enactment concerns the use and interpretation of symbols (being, arguably, the 'building blocks' of myth). It is one of the biggest difficulties that the interpreter will encounter. This is for a number of reasons: symbols are contextual, and it is only by 'living with' the 'concrete' aspect of the symbol that one is led beyond its 'first-order' sense and into an understanding of what it expresses; but symbols are polyvalent by nature, and also affective, suggesting that their meaning cannot be exhausted noetically; they are prone to ossification with corresponding loss of meaning; indeed their meaning can be inverted in new contexts,[53] and they are important in the construction of cultural memory.

Dawson, *Allegorical Readers and Cultural Revision in Ancient Alexandria* (Berkeley: University of California Press, 1992)). I shall argue that there were significant inadequacies in such readings whilst they pointed in the right direction and had the right instincts, unlike much modernist interpretation.

[51] For example, the film *Titanic* (Twentieth Century Fox and Paramount Pictures, 1997, dir. James Cameron) is really 'about' a tragic love story rather than the maiden voyage of the Titanic, even though it is set in this context. I am grateful to my colleagues at the Biblical Hermeneutics seminar at Spurgeon's College in 2003-2004 for this observation. Similarly whilst Joshua is set in the context of conquest, it may not really be *about* conquest as such.

[52] I argue elsewhere ('Towards a Christian Hermeneutic of Old Testament Narrative: Why Genesis 34 fails to find Christian Significance' (forthcoming in *CBQ*)) that this is the case with Gen 34 since the text is problematic at narrative *and* structural levels in the Christian context. This is not to deny the inspiration of such a text *per se*, but rather to suggest that the 'revelatory significance' (in the sense that such a text is to evoke a response of enactment) is confined to a particular context.

[53] E.g. the 'symbol' of the dispossession of the Canaanites in Joshua has very different meanings depending on whether one reads it with Israelite or Canaanite eyes.

In the context of symbols used of God, the problem is tackled by Sallie McFague, who is concerned that 'models of God' (to use her term) become idolatrous or irrelevant.[54] She suggests,

> We are concerned, in part, not only to avoid idolatry—any identification of our words or traditions with being-itself—but also to show the relevance of the Christian tradition to those whose experience the tradition has rejected or distorted. Therefore, Ricoeur's correction of Gadamer is critical to us. For ... if the Bible is understood as a poetic classic or classic model, its metaphorical characteristics mean that tension, dialectic, openness, change, growth, and relativity must be intrinsic to a proper understanding of its authority. Thus, reform and revolution, perhaps one or both, are features integral to biblical authority. To question linguistic distortions within Scripture and the tradition would not be alien or wrong, but precisely what is called for, given the particular kind of text the Bible is and its authority. To see false consciousness, to unearth deceptions and prejudices due to cultural biases, to substitute revised metaphors and models for distorted ones—all of this would be not only permissible but what a theology based on Scripture as poetic classic must do. Metaphorical theology, most basically, insists on the dialectic of the positive and the negative, on the "is and is not," and that tension permeates every aspect of it.[55]

But the difficulty of using symbols to speak of God is raised much earlier, for example in the treatment of Exod 15:3, 'The Lord is a man of war; the Lord is his name' in *Shirata IV* of the *Mekhilta according to Rabbi Ishmael*,[56] which I propose to consider carefully in regard to its sensitive use of symbol.[57] Here, a number of scriptural texts that offer different metaphorical or symbolic descriptions of YHWH as a warrior are reviewed (none of which, interestingly, include Joshua[58]) whilst considering various parallels at a human level for understanding what a 'man of war' is like. But the repeated refrain, 'But the One who spoke and brought the world into being is not that way' demonstrates a profound sensitivity to the nature of metaphor and religious language here—God is *not like* human pictures of a 'man of war', although in another sense 'he is'. This is how symbol and metaphor may be understood—as something that 'is' and 'is not', opening up the possibilities of new ways of thinking and feeling about

---

[54] S. McFague, *Metaphorical Theology: Models of God in Religious Language* (Philadelphia: Fortress Press, 1982), 2 and 145.
[55] Ibid., 64-5. I think that she overstates the case, but her general point is valid.
[56] See e.g. J. Neusner, *Mekhilta according to Rabbi Ishmael: An Analytic Translation* (Brown Judaica Studies 148, Atalanta: Scholars Press, 1988), vol. 1. The translations here are Neusner's.
[57] The midrash is, however, exceptionally complex, and is beyond the scope of the present work.
[58] This seems significant granted the parallel of the Jordan crossing with the sea crossing in Exodus, and the numerous places in Joshua that one might expect the rabbis to explore in this context.

something difficult to apprehend. Moreover, the conclusion in the midrash, 'If the Israelites *are in need*, the Omnipresent makes war for them' is most important. The perception of YHWH as fighting on one's behalf is limited to the context of the 'needy' (and here, specifically, needy *Israel*). It is not used in relation to stances of power or aggression; YHWH does not fight as the aggressor on campaigns of conquest, which might explain the lack of reference to Joshua here. Moreover, YHWH's fighting is also motivated by love; 'How then can Scripture say, "The Lord is a man of war"? "On account of the love that I bear for you [Israel], and on account of the sanctification that you bear, I shall sanctify my name through you." (IV.5.C-D).[59] This section of the *Shirata* moves to a conclusion by combining the two parts of the lemma, 'The Lord is his name: *With his name he makes war*, and he hardly needs any of those measures'. This is the conclusion of a discussion of the means by which YHWH fights, reinterpreting the various scriptural metaphors. Moreover, in closing (IV.6.C), the role of Israel in such warfare is indicated with three scriptural citations indicating that Israel's role is to call upon the name of YHWH (1 Sam 17:45; Ps 20:8; 2 Chr 14:10). Thus the mode by which YHWH is understood to fight, and how Israel is to participate in this, is reconfigured, and this seems to be the point of this part of the *Shirata*. As Jacob Neusner comments,

> This stunning and moving composition holds together, beginning to end, in a sequence of elegant and powerful constructions. ... We start with a specification that the Lord is master of all media of war, we end with the conclusion that the Lord needs none of those media. We identify the Lord as a man of war, but then show that the Lord is in no way comparable to a man of war, making war in a supernatural way, specifically by retaining, even while making war, the attributes of mercy and humanity. So God exhibits all manner of attributes, No. 1, but needs none of them. And however multifarious the attributes, it is always one and the same God, so. No. 2. the sustained and exquisite exercises, Nos. 3, 4, with their recurrent patterns, then undertake that comparison and contrast that shows God to be like the man of war, yet wholly other. It seems to me that the compilers of these materials ... have formed a composition of enormous strength and cogency and made a fundamental point and fully articulated it in detail.[60]

Thus we discover a profound appreciation of the nature and value of religious language, and an indication of how difficult symbols may be dealt with in imaginative ways that are faithful to the tradition that leads to further affectual and existential meditation on the symbol, and on the nature of God—an exploration of the plenitude of the symbol in ways fitting with the tradition.

It is interesting to compare this treatment in the *Shirata* with Origen's treatment of Josh 10:40-43:

---

[59] Ibid., 195.
[60] Ibid., 195-6.

The Hermeneutics of Reading Joshua as Christian Scripture 67

> I myself think it is better that the Israelite wars be understood in this way, and it is better that Jesus [Joshua] is thought to fight in this way [that the names of the cities carry a spiritual significance] and to destroy cities and overthrow kingdoms. For in this manner what is said will also appear more devout and more merciful, when he is said to have so subverted and devastated individual cities that "nothing that breathed was left in them, neither any who might be saved nor any who might escape."
>
> Would that the Lord might thus cast out and extinguish all former evils from the souls who believe in him—even those he claims for his kingdom—and from my own soul, its own evils; so that nothing of a malicious inclination may continue to breathe in me, nothing of wrath; so that no disposition of desire for any evil may be preserved in me, and no wicked word "may remain to escape" from my mouth. For thus, purged from all former evils and under the leadership of Jesus, I can be included among the cities of the sons of Israel, concerning which it is written, "The cities of Judah will be raised up and they will dwell in them."[61]

In both Origen's homily and the *Shirata*, an ethical concern leads to an imaginative, yet traditionally stable, construal of the texts within a wider (scriptural) frame of reference that is generative of new ways of saying something further about God and his relationship with humanity, and is thus, arguably, 'revelatory'. In the *Shirata,* there is a 'corporate' concern; that YHWH fights for *Israel* when in need, whereas in Origen, it is a more individual concern that is spiritualized with YHWH fighting for 'my soul', against the evils within. But what is interesting is that during this phase of the traditions both Jewish and Christian readings reflect an ethical sensitivity that leads interpreters to understand the significance of certain scriptural texts to be other than that which a 'straightforward' reading of the text would suggest, even if such interpretation remains rooted in the symbol. This is a rather different approach from Calvin's, and perhaps Augustine's for example,[62] and from interpreters in the modern period, an approach (or approaches) that reflect the ossification of the symbol and the myth; a form of idolatry perhaps, in McFague's terms.

Symbols need imaginative, careful treatment. Naim Stifan Ateek, a Palestinian Christian, highlights the problematic nature of the symbolism of the Old Testament when used in new contexts, especially in a Palestinian context today. He notes that

> if some parts of [the Bible] are applied literally to our situation [as Palestinians] today the Bible appears to offer to the Palestinians slavery rather than freedom,

---

[61] *Hom. Josh. 13.3*, p.127.
[62] Calvin gives priority to a different theological frame of reference in his hermeneutics—that of Rom 9:20-21, which allows God to do what he wants, and suggests that we should not complain (*Commentaries on the Book of Joshua*, (Grand Rapids: W.B. Eerdmans, ET: 1949), 164). Cf. the discussion in chapter 1.

injustice rather than justice, and death to their national and political life. Many good-hearted Christians have been confused or misled by certain biblical words and images that are normally used in public worship; words that have acquired new connotations since the establishment of the state of Israel. For example, when Christians recite the *Benedictus,* with its opening lines "Blessed be the Lord God of Israel, for he has visited and redeemed his people," what does it mean for them today? Which Israel are they thinking of? What redemption?[63]

Here, he cites Arnold Toynbee to illustrate the problem of the symbol *Israel:*

> This traditional spiritual connotation of the name "Israel" has been supplanted today by a political and military connotation. Today, if I go to church and try to join in the singing of the Psalms, I am pulled up short, with a jar, when the name "Israel" comes on to my lips. The name conjures up today a picture of a small, middle-Europe type state, with bickering political parties like all such states, with a rigid—and unsuccessful—foreign policy with respect to its neighbours and with constant appeal to the Jews of the world either to send them money or to come themselves. This picture has now effaced that one in our minds. It has effaced it, whoever we are: Jews or Christians, diaspora Jews or Israelis, believers or agnostics. The present-day political Israel has, for all of us, obliterated or, at least, adumbrated, the spiritual Israel of the Judeo-Christian tradition. This is surely a tragedy.[64]

Ateek continues that since the establishment of the State of Israel 'many previously hidden problems [in the Bible] suddenly surfaced. The God of the Bible, hitherto the God who saves and liberates, has come to be viewed by Palestinians as partial and discriminating. ... [Allegorization and spiritualization] do not meet the challenge of the political abuse of the Bible.'[65]

Ateek raises some real, searching difficulties here regarding the appropriation of the symbol of *Israel,* let alone the Canaanites and their genocide. However, there are difficulties with Toynbee and Ateek's comments, for it seems that the 'traditional spiritual connotation of the name "Israel"' as formed in the liturgy is in fact precisely a *spiritualized* interpretation of the 'Israel' portrayed in the Old Testament; from what we know of the history of ancient Israel it is hard to avoid the conclusion that ancient Israel was not altogether unlike 'a small, middle-Europe type state, with bickering political parties like all such states, with a rigid—and unsuccessful—foreign policy with respect to its neighbours'. In other words, the reality of such symbolism when it is not, in

---

[63] N.S. Ateek, *Justice and only Justice: A Palestinian Theology of Liberation* (Maryknoll: Orbis Books, 1989), 75-6.
[64] From Elmer Berger, *Prophecy, Zionism and the State of Israel*, introduction by Arnold J. Toynbee, cited in Ateek, *Justice,* 76.
[65] Ibid., 77-8.

some sense, construed in a 'second-order' or indeed 'spiritual' sense is probably always rather messier, and perhaps more idolatrous, than one might like.[66]

But regarding the symbolism of the inhabitants of the land, Ateek notes that 'some contemporary Jewish militants have debated the use of "genocide" to deal with the Arab problem', such as Rabbi Moshe Segal who compared the Palestinian residents of the West Bank and Gaza to the Amalekites.[67] Ateek notes that by labelling the Palestinians as "Amalek" 'they do not fall under the category of "all creatures" and therefore "mercy" does not apply to them.' Rabbi Segal is not alone, Ateek notes, since Rabbi Israel Hess published an article 'The Genocide Ruling of the Torah' in which he also compared the Arabs to Amalek and stated that their extermination has been mandated by the Torah.[68] This is comparable with some instances of the 'Christian' use of these texts, such as by the Puritan emigrants to America.[69]

The *Shirata,* Origen, Rabbi Segal, Rabbi Hess and the Puritan emigrants all exhibit a desire to explore imaginatively the plenitude of various symbols to suit the use and needs of a particular context. What sets them apart, however, is the 'fittingness' of their exploration of the symbolism with regard to its status as discourse, and with respect to the wider canon of Scripture and the tradition of its reception and use. This is why some readings should be rejected, even as readings such as these demonstrate the potential and problems of symbols.

Summary

I have sought to develop the question of how we 'learn about our learning' in the Christian context beyond the largely descriptive and phenomenological aspects studied in chapter 2 to consider the sense in which our learning can be said to be 'revelatory' and not the result of a false consciousness. I developed first the notions of plenitude and fittingness as categories by which the significance of a 'mythical' scriptural text is explored, before turning to consider how ideas of manifestation and testimony can help to foster a well-founded attitude of trustworthiness towards such a text *together with* the tradition associated with its use,

---

[66] I do not wish to denigrate the very real problems that Ateek raises, but rather to show that the problems can look rather different.

[67] R.I. Friedman, "No Land, No Peace for Palestinians" in *The Nation* (April 23, 1988), 563), in Ateek, *Justice,* 84.

[68] Ateek, *Justice,* 85, again citing Friedman.

[69] Cf. R.A. Warrior, 'Canaanites, Cowboys and Indians: Deliverance, Conquest, and Liberation Theology Today' in D. Jobling, *et al.,* (eds.), *The Postmodern Bible Reader* (Oxford: Blackwell, 2001), 188-94.

whilst also indicating where this might be problematic and need correction.[70] It is in the *use* of a text, and its juxtaposition with other 'myths' that what is of enduring significance in the world of the text is manifested and crystallized, and its 'revelatory significance' shown and developed. But this is not to argue for an 'evolutionary positivism', for as we have seen, it is possible to read and use texts badly, and myths can 'tire' through 'historicization', which is why criteria of testimony and 'fittingness' are required.

Indeed, we have seen that 'traditionality' is a complex notion, involving a dialectic between innovation and sedimentation, which works to assist in the formation of a constructive appropriation of a text such as Joshua through a field of tension between the text, Joshua, as an act of discourse, and its juxtaposition with other texts and their use in the later tradition, in which the canonical context is one of particular hermeneutical and theological significance, and with the contemporary horizons and concerns of the interpreter. The good interpretation of different texts will involve the relative privileging of these different 'poles' in this process, requiring a questioning, attentive stance on the part of the interpreter. Working in this way the text may be appropriated in innovative yet faithful and fitting ways that are generative of human transformation towards the human *telos* in God. In this process the 'poles' of the 'final form' of the text as discourse and of the 'canonical form' are privileged, but not determinative.

Moreover, we saw that it is neither possible nor necessary to know and understand fully the precise historical circumstances that resulted in the production of a text in order to understand it as an act of discourse; rather, it is an awareness of the traditions, and 'public codes of production', in which the text is situated that provide the basis for understanding the text as discourse—as an icon—and making it intelligible so as to be able to read and appropriate it well.

We also considered different ways in which a mythical text might find significance, such as at the narrative level or at some level 'beneath' the narrative and how this might be reflected in different contexts. This raised the possibility that for the Christian interpreter certain texts, such as Gen 34, might be rendered otiose in the context of the New Covenant in any sense beyond that of their place in the cultural memory of the church, which is, nonetheless, an important role. Finally, we turned to the interpretation of symbols as a particularly important illustration, and building block, of this process of appropriation of scriptural myth.

---

[70] In other words, I suggest that the fundamental stance be one of trust rather than suspicion, with it being the revelation of God in Christ that forms the fundamental means of discernment in this process.

SECTION II

MAKING JOSHUA INTELLIGIBLE AS DISCOURSE: STARTING TO READ WELL

In chapter 2 I discussed questions of underlying Israelite 'structure' (in neo-structuralist perspective) as one important feature against which the composition of Joshua as discourse could be made intelligible and understood. I suggested in chapter 3 that in order to read and appropriate Joshua well, it is necessary to understand it as an act of discourse that is embedded in a tradition that reflects various public 'codes of production'. In this section I wish to develop the question of how Joshua is made intelligible further, considering three areas that are of particular importance; first, the general nature of the tradition(s) that Joshua is embedded in (chapter 4); secondly, the slightly more specific question of Joshua's genre and its relation to 'conquest accounts' (chapter 5), and thirdly the specific question of the significance of חרם (chapter 6), being a major theme of the book of Joshua.

4. JOSHUA AS PART OF TRADITION(S)

What counts as *sufficient* knowledge of Joshua's historical context to make it intelligible? I suggested that it may be beneficial to situate the book of Joshua within the tradition(s) that generated and received it so as to understand the kinds of issues that are at work in the text. Such attention establishes an understanding of the text that will provide a sense of 'fittingness' by which the 'plenitude' of imaginative readings of the text in other contexts may be judged—it reveals the nature of the 'world of the text' and indicates the kinds of boundary that one might expect its interpretation to have when it is appropriated in new contexts.

In this chapter I will consider features in the text of Joshua which, when situated within the context of the Old Testament, might indicate the nature of the tradition(s) that Joshua reflects with a view to establishing what it means to read the text well as discourse. This is a task that is related to (although different from) that of identifying Joshua's compositional history through source, redaction or composition criticism, for example. Indeed, the task of reconstructing the compositional history of an Old Testament text has always been a difficult one, demonstrated in the continual revision of established paradigms as well as the coexistence of competing models of, for example, the nature of the Deuteronomistic History. Therefore arguments for what it means to read an Old Testament text well that are strongly dependent on particular reconstructions of the text's history may be seen as problematic. For this reason I wish to avoid such dependency as far as possible, preferring to speak of only what is necessary for good interpretation of a text as discourse.

As we shall see, from a historical-critical perspective, these difficulties seem all the more acute in the light of recent trends in pentateuchal criticism where recourse to putative Yahwist and Elohist sources is often no longer made to account for the composition of the Pentateuch / Hexateuch. The composition of the Pentateuch is accounted for via 'Priestly' and 'non-Priestly' materials, often by expanding the scope of what is taken to be Deuteronom(ist)ic (or related) material to account for the 'non-Priestly' material. Moreover, the compositional relationship between these materials and the final form of the Pentateuch and indeed the Hexateuch is debated. There is yet to emerge an overall consensus, and many of the results that are claimed have been contested.[1] Space prevents discussion and analysis of these trends in recent scholarship, for such

---

[1] See E. Blum, *Studien zur Komposition des Pentateuch* (BZAW 189; Berlin: Walter de Gruyter, 1990); T.B. Dozeman and K. Schmid (eds.), *A Farewell to the Yahwist? The Composition of the Pentateuch in Recent European Interpretation* (SBL Symposium 34; Atlanta: SBL, 2006); J.C. Gertz, *Tradition und Redaktion in der Exoduserzählung: Untersuchungen zur Endredaktion des Pentateuch* (FRLANT 186; Göttingen: Vandenhoeck & Ruprecht, 2000); J.C. Gertz, K. Schmid and M. Witte (eds.), *Abschied vom Jahwisten: Die Komposition des Hexateuch in der jüngsten Diskussion* (BZAW 315; Berlin; Walter de Gruyter, 2002).

The discussions centre around the question of the relationship between the patriarchal and exodus (and conquest) traditions, and in particular the origins and extent of their literary combination. Increasingly, this literary combination is being seen as a Priestly work, P^g, the *Priestergrundschrift,* although the nature and extent of P^g is debated. See e.g. K. Schmid, 'The So-called Yahwist and the Literary Gap between Genesis and Exodus', in *A Farewell to the Yahwist?* 29-50, and for discussion of the extent of P^g see T. Pola, *Die ursprüngliche Priesterschrift: Beobachtungen zur Literarkritik und Traditionsgeschichte von P^g* (WMANT 70; Neukirchen-Vluyn: Neukirchener, 1995); E. Otto, 'Forschungen zur Priesterschrift', in *Th R* 62 (1997): 1-50.

The various proposals differ significantly. So, for example, Erhard Blum (*Studien zur Komposition des Pentateuch*) accounted for the composition of the Pentateuch in terms of a post-Deuteronom(ist)ic (i.e., post-DtrG and post Dtn) D-Komposition (KD) which was incorporated (along with Dtn) into a so-called P-Komposition (KP). The P-Komposition is seen by Blum as a 'composition' in its own right rather than being a 'redaction' or a 'source', although he allows for KD and KP as using earlier separate materials. He confines KP to the Pentateuch, and thus argues that the 'Priestly' material in Josh 18-19 (see below) is in fact part of a 'Priestly-like' supplement (224-8). His position developed in a 2002 essay ('Die literarische Verbindung von Erzvätern und Exodus. Ein Gespräch mit neureren Endredaktionshypothesen', in *Abschied vom Jahwisten,* 119-56) in which he identifies a non-Priestly patriarchal narrative that is independent of KD, as well as a significant 'Hexateuch redaction' that presupposes the 'P-layer' and has its goal in Josh 24.

William Johnstone speaks of a "D-version" and "P-edition" to describe the composition of the Pentateuch in which the "P-edition" is a greatly expanded edition of the "D-version" which reflects a 'continuous pre-P presentation [which] should be associated with Deuteronomy and the Deuteronomistic literature' ('The Use of the Reminiscences in Deuteronomy in Recovering the Two Main Literary Phases in the Production of the Pentateuch' in *Abschied vom Jahwisten,* 247-73, here 247-8).

Jan Christian Gertz' model for the composition of the Pentateuch identifies a Priestly narrative (being the narrative that originally unified earlier diverse narratives in the Pentateuch) together with a 'non-Priestly' narrative that are combined at a late stage in what he terms the *Endredaktion* which seeks to reconcile Priestly themes with Deuteronom(ist)ic ones.

However, not everyone is willing to say 'farewell to the Yahwist', such as David Carr, Christoph Levin, and John Van Seters, although their understanding of the Yahwist

discussion is somewhat peripheral to the nature of the argument that I wish to develop. What I take as generally agreed is that there is material that may be labeled 'Priestly' and material that may be labeled 'Deuteronom(ist)ic' in terms of style, concerns and language, and that there is some continuity in the nature of the material categorized as such in contemporary scholarship with the older uses of these categories (categories which are, after all, scholarly constructs aimed to have heuristic value in terms of explaining the texts and modeling the histories behind them).[2]

I suggest that in Joshua there is a substantial section of material that may be thought of as essentially shaped by 'Deuteronomistic' concerns (Josh 1-12 and 23) and a substantial section that may be thought of as shaped by essentially 'Priestly' concerns (Josh 13-22). I do not wish to make claims of a historical

---

differs significantly from how the Yahwist has been understood traditionally. Indeed, in addition to the essays in *Farewell to the Yahwist* for discussion and critique of these trends see for example C. Levin, 'The Yahwist: The Earliest Editor in the Pentateuch', in *JBL* 126.2 (2007): 209-230; M. Vervenne, 'The Question of "Deuteronomic" Elements in Genesis to Numbers', in F. García Martínez, *et al.*, (eds.) *Studies in Deuteronomy in Honour of C.J. Labuschagne on the Occasion of his 65th Birthday* (VTSup 53; Leiden: E.J. Brill, 1994), 243-68; J. Blenkinsopp, review of E. Blum, *Studien zur Komposition des Pentateuch* in *CBQ* 54.2 (1992): 312-3; G.I. Davies, review of J.C. Gertz, K. Schmid and M. Witte (eds.), *Abschied vom Jahwisten*, in *Bib Or* 62.3-4 (2005): 315-6; G.I. Davies, review of J.C. Gertz, *Tradition und Redaktion in der Exoduserzählung* in *JTS* 53.2 (2002): 571-5 and J. Van Seters, review of E. Blum, *Studien zur Komposition des Pentateuch* in *JBL* 111.1 (1992): 122-4.

[2] For my purposes I shall simply refer to 'Priestly' material, being material that has clear resonances with 'classical' Priestly material, and to 'Deuteronomistic' material, being that which is classically taken to be Deuteronomic or Deuteronomistic, such as in the treatments by Weinfeld or Driver (see below). So, for example, if Blum is correct that Josh 18-19 represents a post-Priestly supplement rather than being 'Priestly' *per se*, or if the view that P understood as P^g does not extend into Joshua is correct, it makes little difference to my thesis—the point is that such texts may be construed with 'Priestly' concerns in view, even if the texts in fact reflect a dialogue with such concerns. See Pola, *Die ursprüngliche Priesterschrift*, 107-8 for discussion of Joshua in relation to P^g, and for analysis of the problematic usage of the term 'Priestly' or the siglum 'P' see R. Rendtorff, 'Two Kinds of P? Some Reflections on the Occasion of the Publishing of Jacob Milgrom's Commentary on Leviticus 1-16', in *JSOT* 60 (1993): 75-81. As Rendtorff indicates, perhaps the problem may be traced to a division of P into narrative and legal/cultic materials by Wellhausen, a distinction that some scholars develop and some elide.

Indeed, the terminology used in recent debate and its significance is often complex and difficult to follow, especially in recent discussion, with the significance of the proliferation of descriptive categories being unclear. For example, what is the significance, or heuristic value, of employing the category 'Deuteronomic' in the appellation 'proto-Deuteronomic'? (Cf. Vervenne, '"Deuteronomic" Elements', 251-4). I shall use a rather simplified 'classical' terminology in what follows.

nature regarding the nature of the redaction of Joshua, but rather to observe that there are 'decisive' levels of composition in Joshua that imply that some parts of Joshua are read well with what have traditionally been labeled Deuteronomistic concerns in view and other parts with what are traditionally labeled Priestly concerns in view.[3]

If it should turn out that what might be labeled 'Deuteronomistic' in outlook is far more extensive than previously thought, or involves more dialogue within the tradition than previously thought, then it would seem that what has traditionally been thought of as 'Deuteronomistic' in fact represents a particular sub-tradition of this broader tradition that exhibits certain marked features. It is still valuable (minimally at a heuristic level) to regard this traditional Deuteronomistic material as having its own particular concerns, and to interpret texts within this material relative to these concerns. In other words, identification of material relative to the older paradigm has real heuristic value as regards understanding what it means to read certain texts well.

Moreover, whilst vocabulary has often been taken to be an indicator of sources or traditions, scholars are becoming increasingly cautious of using vocabulary as such an indicator. Whilst I think that it is correct to be cautious,

---

[3] I think that there may be a number of places where Priestly or post-Priestly influences on Josh 1-12 are in evidence. Sometimes these can be identified as additions, such as in 6:19 and 6:24, and my argument is that such additions can distort or at least obscure the real concerns of a substantially complete story that is better understood with reference to different (i.e. Deuteronomistic) concerns (see chapter 6). From a compositional perspective, the question is then one of whether one wishes to speak of prior influence, 'light touches', or a major stage of redaction or composition. I think that this is a very difficult question to address. From my perspective the question is that of what counts as a 'decisive' stage of composition that establishes what frame of reference might be employed to read a text well, and thus whether additions such as 6:19 and 6:24 enhance or distort the interpretation of the text.

However, the absence of any (traditionally identified) 'Deuteronomistic' language or concerns in the 'Priestly' section of Joshua (apart perhaps from 21:43-45 and 22:1-9) would tell against treating this part of the work as essentially the work of a post-Priestly redactor who sought to harmonize Deuteronomistic and Priestly traditions. That said, Gertz argues that Josh 20 reflects the mixture of the 'linguistic style' of a dtn/dtr tradition and the conceptions of a late-Priestly tradition from Num 35:25ff (*Die Gerichtsorganisation Israels*, 151-7, esp. 155 and 157). Moreover, Axel Knauf argues that Josh 21:43-45 is a reflection of 'P-Theologie in D-Sprache' (*Josua* (Zürcher Bibelkommentare AT 6; Theologischer Verlag Zürich, 2008), 21). Gertz does not discuss other texts in Josh 13-22, but on the basis of my discussion below, I think that it is difficult to detect any significant Deuteronomistic influence in this section of Joshua overall, as classically construed. But the observation that the final form of Joshua integrates Priestly and Deuteronomistic sections points toward a 'post-Priestly redactor' of the work. Overall, there has been relatively little discussion of Joshua in this body of scholarship, with Josh 24 being the notable exception, a text that I do not wish to focus upon.

especially where small sections of text are concerned, nonetheless the use of vocabulary, or at least vocabulary when used in certain ways, can be a useful (if not determinative) pointer that identifies accessible features within a particular set of texts that distinguish these texts from other texts. It indicates something that a set of texts share 'as works', a feature that calls for explanation, being an indicator that texts with a shared vocabulary might reasonably be read with similar concerns and conceptualities in view, even if care is required so as to allow for the possibility of development and subsequent adoption of particular vocabulary in new contexts and traditions.[4]

So what I suggest is that features in certain texts that have traditionally led to such texts being categorized as 'Priestly' or 'Deuteronomistic' do provide a means for talking about real 'family resemblances' in texts that, on the one hand, call for explanation, and, on the other hand, provide features of the collection of such texts 'as works' that are suggestive of what it means to read such texts well. In other words, in many cases traditional analyses of texts in terms of the scholarly constructs 'Priestly' and 'Deuteronomistic' retain heuristic value as tools for reading such texts well, however these constructs may (or may not) end up being recontextualized in the long run with advances in scholarship. In what follows the discussion will be framed in terms of traditional paradigms, for it is within this framework that most discussion on Joshua has been conducted.

Turning more specifically to work on Joshua now, I begin by considering the composition of Joshua as a means of considering the tradition(s) of which it is a part, and thus the concerns that are likely to be reflected in the text. Volkmar Fritz considers Joshua to be the product of a basic DtrG/H account subsequently redacted through what he terms a later Deuteronomistic RedD stage, a RedP (Priestly) stage and through 'redactions of a different kind' (*Redaktionelle Zusätze verschiedener Art*). He provides a detailed analysis of and commentary on the book based upon these assumed layers.[5] Michaël van der Meer offers a more detailed analysis of certain sections of Joshua, introducing a pre-Deuteronomistic level of composition, and traces pre-Dtr, DtrH, DtrN, RedP and Proto-MT layers.[6] Indeed, attempts to trace increasingly refined compositional 'layers' abound. For example, with regard to Josh 6, Schwienhorst claims to

---

[4] Cf. e.g. Vervenne, '"Deuteronomic" Elements', 253-4, and also John Van Seters' comments on the approach of Vervenne and H. Ausloos (*A Law Book for the Diaspora: Revision in the Study of the Covenant Code* (Oxford: OUP, 2003), 70-71).

[5] V. Fritz, *Das Buch Josua* (HAT I/7; Tübingen: J.C.B. Mohr (Paul Siebeck), 1994). Whilst identifying these redactional layers, unlike other commentators he appears to leave the question of their dating open. A weakness identified in Fritz' approach is his lack of concern with the LXX (A.G. Auld, *Joshua Retold: Synoptic Perspectives* (Old Testament Studies; Edinburgh: T&T Clark, 1998), 145).

[6] M.N. van der Meer, *Formation and Reformulation: The Redaction of the Book of Joshua in the Light of the Oldest Textual Witnesses* (Leiden: Brill, 2004).

detect a basic ancient account, a Yahwist redaction, subsequent DtrH, DtrP and DtrN redactions, followed by various post-Deuteronomistic glosses and additions.[7] But as Römer and de Pury observe with regard to the reconstruction of multiple levels of the Deuteronomistic material, 'The attribution of texts to one of these multiple levels risks therefore being done according to more and more arbitrary criteria and leads to allocations that are less and less verifiable.'[8]

Likewise Richard Nelson comments,

> Some have proposed dividing DH in Joshua into more than one deuteronomist. However, unlike the situation in Judges or Kings, evidence is lacking in Joshua for a second deuteronomist with a theological viewpoint different from DH or using a distinct vocabulary. The only possible exception might be the addition of chapter 24.[9]

Nelson does, however, recognize the presence of pre-Deuteronomistic material in Joshua, but suggests that the Deuteronomistic material 'represents more than just a series of isolated expansions or incidents of retouching, but is a comprehensive redaction or act of authorship'.[10] This would suggest that the Deuteronomistic level(s) of redaction provide a decisive stage of composition—an act of discourse that transforms and shapes whatever earlier materials are used, which would imply that seeking to 'peer behind' the Deuteronomistic level(s) of composition is unnecessary, and possibly likely to mislead.[11] However, granted the difficulty in identifying possible levels of Deuteronomistic composition, they nonetheless have sufficient 'family resemblance' to be labeled 'Deuteronomistic', and this knowledge may be sufficient to make the text intelligible—i.e., simply knowing that the text is read well with broadly Deuteronomistic concerns in view. However, Nelson notes that the 'deuteronomistic redactional presence is ... noticeably absent from the description of land distribution (chaps. 13:1-

---

[7] L. Schwienhorst, *Die Eroberung Jerichos: Exegetische Untersuchung zu Josua 6* (Stuttgart: Katholisches Bibelwerk, 1986).

[8] T. Römer and A. de Pury, 'Deuteronomistic Historiography: History of Research and related Issues', in A. de Pury, *et al.*, (eds.), *Israel Constructs its History: Deuteronomistic Historiography in Recent Research* (JSOTSup 306; Sheffield: Sheffield Academic Press, 2000), 24-141, here 72. For a summary of the history of research into the Deuteronomistic History see this, or for a fuller treatment T.C. Römer, *The So-Called Deuteronomistic History: A Sociological, Historical and Literary Introduction* (London: T&T Clark, 2005). For another perspective, and a theory that seeks to replace that of Martin Noth's, see K.L. Noll, 'Deuteronomistic History or Deuteronomic Debate? (A thought experiment)', in *JSOT* 31.3 (2007): 311-45.

[9] R.D. Nelson, *Joshua* (OTL; Louisville: Westminster John Knox Press, 1997), 6.

[10] Ibid., 6.

[11] Unless of course Joshua's significance is to be construed in terms of a 'historical record' that might have been distorted by later editors, but as the overall thrust of this work shows, this is not the case.

21:42 apart from 14:6-15),'[12] where he detects Priestly language and outlook. Moreover, he detects a number of 'P-like touches' elsewhere (e.g. 3:4; 4:19; 9:15b and 18-21) which 'definitely indicate that Priestly redactional interests played a role in the creation of the final form of Joshua.'[13]

Most recently however, Axel Knauf summarizes his view of the compositional history of Joshua in his commentary on Joshua, a work that accounts for some of the recent developments in pentateuchal criticism outlined above. Knauf suggests that Josh 6* and 10* represent the earliest material, material associated with Exod 14* as an early version of an exodus-conquest story. He argues that it would be inconceivable to have an exodus account without an account of conquest. He then traces a 'D-redaction' that encompasses Exod 2* to Josh 11*, reflecting a theological and political movement that generally became accepted during the fifth century. However, D provoked a 'counter-project', namely P. Along with H, P is now represented in Joshua in 4:19a; 5:10-12; 18:1 and 24:29b according to Knauf. He suggests that whereas D was exclusive, P is inclusive, and argues that it makes sense to regard Josh 18:1 as the natural original conclusion of P. Knauf then detects a 'Hextateuch redaction' that represents a dialogue between D and P, reflected in the addition of Josh 3-4, the ark material to Josh 6, the basic material of Josh 14-17*, and Josh 21:43-45. Next, he identifies a prophetic or 'book' redaction in the addition of Josh 1 and 24 in order to shape Joshua as a prophetic book in its own right before a 'Joshua-Judges redaction', represented in Josh 18:2-19:48 and Josh 23, a redaction that links Joshua with Judges. Finally, he postulates a 'Shechem redaction', in which, for example, Shilo is replaced with Shechem in Josh 24:1.[14]

It is interesting that Knauf does not discuss Josh 2, 7-8 or 9 in his treatment of Joshua's composition. Elsewhere in his commentary he suggests that Josh 2 interrupts Josh 1 and 3, being one of the latest additions to the book. It has traces of post-classical Hebrew and reflects an anti-war tradition.[15] Likewise Josh 9 is discussed as an addition in similar fashion to Josh 2, with its shaping taking place in the last quarter of the fifth century after the Hextateuch redaction.[16]

However, I will argue in chapters 6 and 8 that Josh 2 and 7-8 are intimately bound up with Josh 6, and that Josh 9 is similarly related to Josh 10-11. Taken together, these stories reflect a 'decisive level' of composition into a single discourse with a clear literary and theological function based around the use of the Deuteronomistic (rather than Priestly) conception of חרם. Whether Knauf, for example, is correct in his diachronic reconstruction of the text, the point is that it is Deuteronomistic concerns that drive the text of Josh 1-12 and not

---

[12] Ibid., 6.
[13] Ibid., 9.
[14] Knauf, *Josua*, 17-22.
[15] Ibid., 46.
[16] Ibid., 90-91.

necessarily the concerns of possible antecedent versions. Thus the issue for us is that of the discernment of *decisive* levels of composition coupled with the development of conceptual categories to aid reading the text that we now have well. If Knauf is correct, and if I am correct in my analysis of חרם, then Josh 6 in the form that we know have functions in a very different way from that in which its antecedent version functioned. But to attempt to recover and read Josh 6 in an earlier form is not to read the book of Joshua—it is to read an earlier composition. Of course, if the aim of Joshua is to provide a historical witness then this is a problem that needs resolution—but I am arguing that Joshua is 'poetic discourse', to use Ricoeur's term.[17] Furthermore, I will argue that Josh 22, for example, is read well within the context of Joshua with Priestly concerns in view, even though this narrative is not attributed to P construed as P^g.

In summary, there is no consensus regarding the compositional history of Joshua. A variety of different recent proposals exist, with there being no agreement even on the question of whether or not the Priestly narrative extends into Joshua. However, I have argued at length that for my purposes of reading Joshua as Christian Scripture this need not matter. My concern is to find interpretative lenses that will help one to read the narrative well. I will consider how the categories 'Deuteronomistic' and 'Priestly', as more classically understood, provide interpretative lenses that have heuristic value toward this end.

With all this in mind, I shall develop, in general terms, the nature and significance of the Deuteronomistic and Priestly traditions associated with Joshua,[18] using the studies of Moshe Weinfeld and Joseph Blenkinsopp as starting points. I do not intend to provide another account of Joshua's compositional history, or a comprehensive and exhaustive breakdown of which verses are read with specifically Deuteronomistic or Priestly concerns in view. Rather, I will briefly paint an indicative picture that highlights in broad terms some of the Deuteronomistic and Priestly resonances (as they have classically been labeled) in the major sections of Joshua with a view to considering how to read the text that we now have well as discourse.

---

[17] Indeed, if my analysis in chapters 6 and 8 is correct, then it is quite possible that there never were antecedent versions of Josh 6 and 10 in the way that Knauf proposes. The assumption in critical scholarship often appears to be that Joshua provides a witness to earlier traditions, such as in Josh 6, but perhaps Joshua has somewhat greater unity in composition than critics often grant. For example, there is no tradition of the destruction of Jericho outside the book of Joshua (although there is the rebuilding of Jericho in 1 Kgs 16:34) which might be taken to suggest that the account was written for the book as it now stands in the ways that I suggest later on. In this case the terminus of a 'pre-Joshua' exodus-conquest story might be quite different from a 'Jericho tradition'.

[18] Generally speaking, I shall not seek to differentiate between layers in the Priestly and Deuteronomistic materials as I think that this is rather too ambitious a project, and, as the study unfolds it will be seen that this is unnecessary on the whole. I shall draw attention to the few places where it might be important as they arise.

Deuteronom(ist)ic Affinities in Joshua

In *Deuteronomy and the Deuteronmic School* Weinfeld identified the following verses in Table 4.1 below as being indicative of distinctive Deuteronomistic language in Joshua:[19]

Chapter	Verses
1	5, 6, 7, 8, 9, 11, 13, 15, 18
2	11
3	
4	24
5	1
6	
7	5, 9, 11, 15
8	1, 22, 31, 32
9	24, 27
10	8, 25, 28, 30, 33, 37, 39, 40
11	8, 11, 14
12	6, 7
13	
14	8, 9, 14
15	
16	
17	
18	3
19	
20	
21	42, 43
22	3, 5
23	1, 3, 4, 5, 6, 7, 8, 9, 11, 12, 13, 14, 15, 16
24	2, 7, 14, 16, 17, 18, 31

Table 4.1: Instances of Distinctive Deuteronomistic Language in Joshua

Some discussion of and modifications to this list are needed. Whilst Weinfeld does not consider the use of חרם in Joshua to be distinctively Deuteronomistic, I shall argue in chapter 6 that חרם here is distinctively Deuteronomistic, apart from 6:19 and 24 which appear to be later additions influenced by Lev 27. Thus references to חרם in Joshua are instances of Deuteronomistic language. Furthermore, identifying מלא אחר יהוה ('to fill up after', i.e. 'to follow with loy-

---

[19] See M. Weinfeld, *Deuteronomy and the Deuteronmic School* (Oxford: Clarendon, 1972), 320-65.

alty/perfection' (Weinfeld)) which occurs in Josh 14:8, 9, 14 (cf. Deut 1:36; Num 14:24 and 32:11-12) as Deuteronomistic is questionable;[20] in context, Josh 14 seems to be referring to, and using, the language of Num 14, and thus the use of this phrase in Josh 14 cannot be said to be specifically Deuteronomistic in the fairly specific sense that I am advocating. This would suggest that there are in fact only two instances of distinctive Deuteronomistic language in Josh 13:1-21:42, namely Josh 14:8 and 18:3.

Most significantly, absent is any חרם vocabulary in Josh 13-22, a root that dominates the accounts of conquest in Josh 1-11, but is absent in places where one would expect it in 13-22.[21] But other Deuteronomistic terms are also absent from Josh 13:1-21:42. There is no language of סור; no references to 'not turning to the left or right' and no references to 'turning away from foreign gods', language used in 23:6 and 24:14, 23. In particular, it is interesting that 13:1-7 does not contain these Deuteronomistic features. Also lacking is אמץ (be strong) which occurs in Josh 1:6, 7, 9, 18 and 10:25 in relation to 'being strong and courageous'.[22] It is clearly important in Josh 1, and thus if Josh 13 in some sense parallels Josh 1, its absence here is striking. However, it is also lacking in Josh 23-24, but here חזק (be strong) is used in relation to obeying the law (23:6), as in Josh 1 (e.g. 1:6-7). Whilst חזק occurs in Josh 13:1-21:42 (14:11; 17:13 and 18) (and P), it only occurs here in connection with military/physical strength and not obeying torah.

So absent from Josh 13:1-21:42 is much of the Deuteronomistic language that one might expect if it was Deuteronomistic. There are only two instances of (possibly) Deuteronomistic features here in 14:8 and 18:3, which might reflect later glosses. Thus Josh 13:1-21:42 cannot be said to be 'Deuteronomistic'.

Finally, with the possible exception of Josh 24:31, according to Weinfeld, all the other uses of what he identifies as Deuteronomistic language in Josh 24 have, in fact, pre-Deuteronomistic use also.[23] Thus these cannot be said to be distinctly Deuteronomistic.

Thus Weinfeld's list needs some revision (see Table 4.2 below).

Priestly Affinities in Joshua

What then of the Priestly character of Joshua? Some time ago Joseph Blenkinsopp argued that 'the tendency to deny to P any significant contribution to

---

[20] Cf. Ibid., 337.
[21] E.g. Josh 17:13, where ירש (*hiphil*) with infinitive absolute is used, which reflects the language of Num 32-33 rather than Exod 23:20-33, suggesting dependency on the conquest tradition represented in Numbers rather than that of Exodus (or Deut 7:1-5).
[22] Cf. esp. Deut 31:6-7, 23 (also 2:30, 3:28 and 15:7).
[23] Weinfeld, *Deuteronomy*, 320, 332 and 357.

[Joshua] ... needs to be reversed',[24] and suggests the following as possible Priestly elements:

> Twelve stones set up in the Jordan (4:9)
> Date of the crossing of the Jordan (4:19)
> Celebration of Passover according to the P chronology (5:10-12)
> Covenant with the Gibeonites (9:15-21)
> Completion of the conquest (11:15,20)
> Introduction to the allotment of territory (14:1-5)
> Setting up of the sanctuary at Shiloh (18:1)
> Completion of the allotment of territory (19:51)
> Allotment of levitical cities (21:1-8)
> Decision about the altar of the Transjordanian tribes (22:10-34)
> Death of Phineas (24:33)[25]

Moreover, Weinfeld comments that

> Traces of the Priestly source are clearly evident in Josh. 14:1-21:40 not only in the terms and expressions employed (cf. 14:1-5; 18:1-10; 19:49-51 and chs. 20–1) but also in the disposition of the material. The material in these chapters has been arranged in the same manner as was the Priestly tradition in Num. 26-36. The partition of the land in the presence of Joshua and Eleazar coupled with the underlying geographical lists in Josh. 14-19 corresponds to the charge of dividing the land and the related genealogical and geographical lists in Num. 26-7, 32-4; the assignment of the cities of refuge and the Levitical towns in Josh. 20-1 is the implementation of the related commands recorded in Num. 35. Josh. 14:1-21:40 in general appear to have been edited by a Priestly redactor and subsequently incorporated *en bloc* by a deuteronomic editor.[26]

In terms of a brief initial sketch, the following might be identified as Priestly language in Joshua:

---

[24] J. Blenkinsopp, 'The Structure of P', in *CBQ* 38 (1976): 275-92, here 287.

[25] Ibid., 288-9. It is not clear that 11:15 and 20 are particularly Priestly however. The Priestly influence on the Jordan crossing narrative in Josh 3-4 has been developed by J. Wagenaar, 'Crossing the Sea of Reeds (Exod 13-14) and the Jordan (Josh 3-4): A Priestly Framework for the Wilderness Wandering', in M. Vervenne (ed), *Studies in the Book of Exodus: Redaction–Reception–Interpretation* (BETL 126; Leuven: Leuven UP, 1996), 461-470. He finds Priestly influences in Josh 3-4 in 3:1, 4, 8, 15; 4:15-24 (466).

[26] Weinfeld, *Deuteronomy*, 182. Weinfeld does not see P as presupposing cult centralization in Jerusalem (as opposed, he suggests, to D) (183). Moreover, he suggests that 'The redaction of the book of Joshua similarly points to P's preceding D. As it was the Deuteronomist who gave the book its frame (ch. 1 = introduction, ch. 23 = conclusion) we may infer that the Priestly material' was redacted by the Deuteronomic editor and consequently antedated D.' (182).

עדה

Hurvitz notes that עדה is a 'Priestly term',[27] which occurs in Joshua in Josh 9:15, 18 (twice), 19, 21, 27; 18:1; 20:6, 9; 22:12, 16, 17, 18, 20 and 30, but significantly not in Josh 7 which Josh 22 alludes to.

מקלט

The use of מקלט for 'city of refuge' only occurs in the Old Testament outside Joshua in Num 35:6, 11, 12, 13, 14, 15, 25, 26, 27, 28, 32; 1 Chr 6:42 and 52. It occurs in Joshua in Josh 20:2, 3; 21:13, 21, 27, 32 and 38, but, significantly, it does not occur in the Deuteronomistic account of the cities of refuge. Thus in this regard Josh 20-21 follows Numbers not Deuteronomy.[28] Moreover, the use of גר in Josh 20:9 reflects Num 15:15-16,[29] and not the parallel text in Deuteronomy (Deut 19:1-8 and 4:41-43). Thus Josh 20-21 reflects the Priestly text of Numbers, rather than the parallel text in Deuteronomy.

גורל

'Allotment' (גורל) occurs twenty-six times in Josh 13-21 (14:2; 15:1; 16:1; 17:1, 14, 17; 18:6, 8, 10, 11; 19:1, 10, 17, 24, 32, 40, 51; 21:4, 5, 6, 8, 10, 20 and 40). It occurs five times in Leviticus, seven times in Numbers. It does not occur in Deuteronomy, Kings or Josh 1-12 and so may be said to be Priestly.

כבש and כלה

כבש (subdue) occurs in the summary statement in Josh 18:1. Although it only occurs once in the book of Joshua, its presence in this summary statement indicates that it is important. Elsewhere it is used in Gen 1:28, which is significant as it relates to the role of humanity in creation, and in Num 32:22 and 29, which is again significant as Josh 18:1 represents the fulfilment of Num 32. It occurs a further nine times in the Old Testament, but not in Deuteronomy or Kings.[30] Similarly, Brueggemann has compared the 'finishing' (כלה) of Gen 2:1-

---

[27] A. Hurvitz, *A Linguistic Study of the Relationship between the Priestly Source and the Book of Ezekiel: A New Approach to an Old Problem* (Cahiers de la Revue biblique 20; Paris: J. Gabalda, 1982), 66.

[28] cf. Nelson, *Joshua*, 229: the 'unrevised text' (OG) of Josh 20:1-9 'has its closest relationship to Num 35:9-15. He notes that Noth argued that Num 33:50-35:29 is dependent upon Josh 14-21.

[29] 'a Priestly concern': Nelson, *Joshua*, 229-30.

[30] Josh 10:40-41 uses נכה for subduing or smiting the land, which is common throughout D and P (e.g. Num 32:4 uses נכה).

2 with the completion of the tabernacle (Exod 39:32 and 40:33) and with the 'finishing' of Josh 19:49-51 as a Priestly theme.³¹

אהל מועד

אהל מועד (Tent of Meeting) occurs in Josh 18:1 and 19:51. It occurs many times in Exodus, Leviticus and Numbers, but only once in Deuteronomy (31:14), which Driver, for example, suggests is 'in a passage belonging not to D, but to JE'.³²

נשׂיא

נשׂיא (leader) occurs in Joshua in 9:15, 18, 19, 21; 13:21; 17:4; 22:14, 30 and 32. It is a Priestly term, occurring sixty-two times in Numbers, four times in Exodus, once in Leviticus, being absent in Deuteronomy, and occurring only twice in Samuel-Kings.³³

אחזה

אחזה (possession) occurs in Joshua in 21:12, 41; 22:4, 9 and 19. It occurs only once in Deuteronomy, in 32:49, but is common in Leviticus and Numbers.

Eleazar the priest
Eleazar the priest, prominent in Numbers but not Deuteronomy, has an important role in Joshua: in 14:1, in allotting inheritance; in 17:4 in the appeal to him by Zelophehad's daughters; in 19:51, in the division of inheritance at Shiloh, and in 21:1 the heads of Levites come to him. He has similar, if not quite equal (cf. 13:1) stature to Joshua in Josh. 13-21.

Thus there are indeed a number of Priestly affinities that can be identified in Joshua.

---

³¹ W.A. Brueggemann, *Theology of The Old Testament: Testimony, Dispute, Advocacy* (Minneapolis: Fortress Press, 1997), 533. Auld argues that כבש in Gen 1:28 is a late addition based upon Josh 18:1 (*Joshua Retold*, 66).
³² S.R. Driver, *A Critical and Exegetical Commentary on Deuteronomy* (The International Critical Commentary; Edinburgh: T&T Clark, 3rd ed. 1902), xiii. In light of recent trends in pentateuchal criticism it may be unwise to seek an ascription to JE—the point is that this phrase is not Deuteronomistic as traditionally understood.
³³ As with עדה it is interesting that נשׂיא occurs several times in Josh 9, suggesting that it has a Priestly flavour. However in Josh 9 we find ברית and כרת (Josh 9:6, 7, 11, 15 and 16), which are not in Leviticus or Numbers, but thirteen times in Deuteronomy (significantly 7:2) and six times in Exodus, seven times in Genesis. So the 'body' of Josh 9 appears to be Deuteronomistic as well.

A Summary of the Deuteronomistic and Priestly Affinities in Joshua

In summary then, I suggest that the following are instances of characteristic Deuteronomistic and Priestly language in Joshua, summarized in Table 4.2. I do not claim that this is a comprehensive list, but it is an indicative sketch of the distribution of what are the most readily identifiable instances of Deuteronomistic or Priestly language or concerns. Such a sketch is, I hope, sufficient to establish the point that I wish to make regarding the composition of Joshua.

Chapter	Deuteronomistic elements	Priestly elements
1	5, 6, 7, 8, 9, 11, 13, 15, 18	
2	10, 11	
3		1, 4, 8, 15
4	24	9, 15-24
5	1	10-12
6	17, 18, 21	
7	1, 5, 9, 11, 12, 13, 15	
8	1, 22, 26, 31, 32	
9	6, 7, 11, 15, 16, 24, 27	15-21, 27
10	1, 8, 25, 28, 30, 33, 35, 37, 39, 40	
11	8, 11, 12, 14, 20, 21	15, 20
12	6, 7	
13		21
14	8	1-5
15		1
16		1
17		1, 4, 14, 17
18	3	1, 6, 8, 10, 11
19		1, 10, 17, 24, 32, 40, 51
20		2, 3, 6, 9
21	42, 43	1-8, 10, 12, 13, 20, 21, 27, 32, 38, 40, 41
22	3, 5, 20	10-34
23	1, 3, 4, 5, 6, 7, 8, 9, 11, 12, 13, 13, 14, 15, 16	
24	31	33

Table 4.2: Provisional Summary of Deuteronomistic and Priestly Language in Joshua

The affinities of 13:1-21:41 with Numbers, rather than with Deuteronomy or Exodus are interesting: the language of entrance to the land reflects Num 32-33 rather than Exod 23:20-33; the account of the cities of refuge in Josh 20-21 reflects Num 35 rather than Deut 4 and 19; the use of כבש in Josh 18:1 reflects the fulfilment of Num 32; Caleb's story reflects Num 13:1-33 (Caleb is only mentioned briefly in Deuteronomy in 1:36); the story of Zelophehad's daughters (Josh 17:3-4) reflects Num 27:1-11 and 36:1ff; the reference to Balaam (Josh 13:22) reflects Num 22-24; the prominence of Eleazar the priest (Josh 14:1; 17:4; 19:51 and 21:1) reflects Num 26:1, 27:2, etc. (he is only mentioned in Deuteronomy in 10:6 in passing); Phinehas, the son of Eleazar (Josh 21:1; 22:13, 31, 32 and 24:33) again reflects Numbers (Num 25:7, 11; 21:16) and not Deuteronomy; the status of the Transjordan tribes (Josh 13:8ff and 22) reflects Num 32; the Levitical cities (Josh 21) reflects Num 35, and the division of the land in Josh 13-21, and the concern with driving the locals out and taking possession, reflects the fulfilment of Num 33:50-56, with the boundaries of Josh 13:1-7 reflecting Num 34—as Nelson notes, 'The description of the "land that remains" in [13:]2-6 is coterminous with neither the following tribal allotments nor the Deuteronomistic conception of idealized borders. It reflects instead a tradition of expansive borders over much of Syria-Palestine also found in Num 34:1-12 and Judg. 3:3.'[34] Finally, it is interesting to consider the importance of Gilgal and Shiloh in the two 'sections' of Joshua: Gilgal is referred to ten times in Josh 1-12, and twice in 13-21, whilst Shiloh is never referred to Josh 1-12, but seven times in 13-21, again suggesting something of a partition of the materials.[35]

The Significance of the Deuteronom(ist)ic and Priestly Affinities in Joshua

Joshua appears to be comprised of sections that are read well with what have traditionally been termed as Deuteronomistic concerns in view, namely Josh 1-12 and 23, and sections that are read well with what have traditionally been

---

[34] Nelson, *Joshua*, 164. Auld argues that Josh 13-21 and the end of Numbers were drafted and re-drafted alongside each other, and so emerged together (A.G. Auld, *Joshua, Moses and the Land* (Edinburgh: T&T Clark, 1980)).

[35] But cf. chapter 7 for the possibility of some references to Gilgal as being late additions. Moreover, in light of the tendency to account for progressively more of the material in Numbers to various forms of 'D' influence, appealing to Numbers here in relation to differentiating the material in Joshua might be problematic. Whilst I am yet to be convinced of the pervasiveness of such 'D' influence in Numbers, even if one grants such influence then one is still left with two 'sets of material' in Joshua that use different vocabularies and relate to different sets of texts with different concerns in view. In this case, whilst the appellations I use might benefit from revision, their heuristic value would, I think, remain as a useful way of talking about the differences of the sections of Joshua, suggesting a basis for understanding what it means to read the texts well.

termed Priestly concerns in view, i.e. Josh 13-22 The Deuteronomistic sections reflect the concerns of Deuteronomy, and Deut 7 especially, whilst the Priestly sections reflect Priestly concerns, and Numbers in particular. However, Josh 1-12 also shows a number of allusions to or resonances with Numbers, as we shall see in chapter 8. There is also evidence of Priestly influence on this material in Josh 1-12, 'light touches' as Nelson describes it, influences that may go beyond some of those noted above. These influences might indeed be regarded as being more extensive and significant than 'light touches'.[36] Furthermore, as we shall also see in chapter 8, Josh 22:10-34 appears to allude to the stories of Rahab and Achan, suggesting some interdependency of various sections of Joshua. All this suggests that the compositional history of Joshua is complex.

I will not probe Joshua's compositional history further. All I wish to observe is that Joshua reflects the conflation of what one might term a substantially Deuteronomistic account of entrance to the land and a substantially Priestly account of the settlement of the land. Each section of the book may be made intelligible and read well against the concerns of these backgrounds.

What I wish to draw from this brief and rather provisional sketch of Joshua relates to the idea of testimony on the one hand, and appreciating how to read a text well on the other. Regarding reading the text well, knowing that Josh 1-12 and 23 reflect Deuteronomistic concerns at a decisive stage of composition suggests that these texts may be read well with Deuteronomistic concerns in view. Thus one would expect to read the text in terms of obedience to the law and the avoidance of idolatry for example. Similarly, knowing that Josh 13-22 reflect Priestly concerns suggests that one might expect to read these texts well in terms of Priestly conceptions of purity of the land for example. Moreover, one is invited to read Josh 18:1 and 19:49-51 in terms of the Priestly creation narrative in which the settlement of the land is viewed as, in some sense, reflecting the completion of creation and the fulfillment of the divine command to subdue the land; Joshua interprets and is interpreted by Genesis. Thus the text of Joshua represents the testimony of two traditions to the manifestation (in some sense) of the divine in Israel, and what constitutes an adequate response to such manifestation.

But the synthesis of these Deuteronomistic and Priestly traditions in Joshua is significant, however this came about historically, for it is testimony to the *compatibility* of these two traditions that offer two perspectives on the early life of Israel in the land. Joshua has in its favour the weight of the assent of two major strands of Israelite tradition, testifying to the discernment of the manifestation of the divine in Israel. The two testimonies thus mutually reinforce and complement each other, providing testimony to the revelatory character of the material in Joshua, for here we have two traditions that are usually discussed in

---

[36] See e.g. Wagenaar, 'Crossing the Sea of Reeds' for discussion on the nature of the Priestly influence on Josh 3-4 as we now have it.

isolation but are synthesized in Joshua. But as well as being mutually reinforcing, the fusion of these two traditions in Joshua reflects a new act of discourse that invites one to read the whole of Joshua from a broader perspective; it invites the Priestly material to be read from a Deuteronomistic perspective and vice versa. This 'testimony' is testimony to the opening up of new interpretative possibilities as these two testimonies to the same divine reality (viewed from different perspectives) coalesce, and invite an exploration of the 'plenitude' of the texts of each tradition in new ways, an innovation in the tradition. So, for example, one could construe the settlement of the land as the fulfillment of the creation mandate to 'subdue' the land in terms of the eradication of idolatry and obedience to God.

However, as indicated in chapter 3, it is important to consider the text from the perspective of the traditions with respect to which it arose first, reflecting important levels of composition, in order to read it well. Then one may consider how the text might be appropriated and read well at a later point in the tradition when the traditions have merged, reflecting the 'field of tension' that the interpreter must work in. This will become clear in chapter 6 when we consider חרם. But first, we shall consider questions relating to Joshua's genre in regard to the category of 'conquest account'.

5. THE GENRE OF JOSHUA — CODES OF PRODUCTION AND USE OF LITERARY CONVENTIONS

Considering Joshua 'as myth' has done much to elucidate the genre of Joshua, and thus to indicate how to read it well. But might one say more regarding particular 'composition codes' associated with Joshua, a consideration of which might contribute to the understanding of its meaning?[1] One approach to the question of 'composition codes', or perhaps one might say genre, in relation to Joshua has been the study of ANE 'conquest accounts'. Indeed, K. Lawson Younger Jr. compares Josh 9-12 with ANE 'conquest accounts'.[2]

Similarities Between Joshua and ANE Conquest Accounts

Younger cites a number of examples of ANE texts that have significant resonances with Josh 9-12. For example, there are some similarities between Josh 10 and Assyrian Royal Inscriptions, such as in the *Annals of Tiglath-Pileser I*:

> With my valorous onslaught I went a second time to the land of Kadmuhu.
> I conquered all their cities.
> I carried off without number their booty, possessions, and property.
> I burned, razed (and) destroyed their cities.
> Now the remainder of their troops, which had taken fright at my fierce weapons and had been cowed by my strong and belligerent attack, in order to save their lives took to secure heights in rough mountainous terrain.
> I climbed up after them to the peaks of high mountains and perilous mountain ledges where a man could not walk. They waged war, combat, and battle with me; (and) I inflicted a decisive defeat on them.
> I piled up the corpses of their warriors on mountain ledges like the Inundator (i.e. Adad).
> I made their blood flow into the hollows and plains of the mountains.

---

[1] Cf. the discussion of Paul Ricoeur's work in chapter 3. 'Composition codes' reflect the existence of tacit public agreements relating to factors such as genre that influence how a work is understood.

[2] K. Lawson Younger Jr., *Ancient Conquest Accounts: A Study in Ancient Near Eastern and Biblical History Writing* (JSOTSup 98; Sheffield: JSOT Press, 1990) (hereafter *ACA*). I shall assume here that it is possible to identify 'conquest account' as a genre, following Younger.

I bro[ught do]wn their booty, possessions and property from the secure heights of the mountains.
(Thus) I ruled over the entire land of Kadmuhu; and I annexed (it) to the borders of my land.³

Furthermore the Hittite *Detailed Annals of Muršili II* provides an interesting comparison with the story of the Gibeonites:

> When the people of the city of Azzi saw that fighting (their) strong cities I subjugated them:
> —the people of Azzi, who have strong cities, rocky mountains, (and) high difficult terrain—
> they were afraid!
> And the elders of the land came before me,
> and they bowed themselves down at (my) feet.
> And they spoke:
> > "Our lord! Do not destroy us!
> > Lord, take us into servitude,
> > and we will begin to provide to (your) lordship troops
> > and charioteers.
> > The Hittite fugitives which (are) with us, we will provide these."
> Then I, my sun, did not destroy them.
> I took them into servitude;
> and I made them slaves.⁴

Likewise an Egyptian text of Ramesses III's account of his victory over the Libyans in the fifth year at Medinet Habu also has some resonances with the story of the Gibeonites:

> ... we were trapped, they drew us in like a net. The gods caused us to succeed, indeed, (merely) to offer us up, to overthrow us for Egypt! (So,) let us make a *brt* (a treaty) with [the Egyptians (?) before they de]stroy us
>
> ... your terror seizes them, cowed, miserable and straying. They all make a *brt* (a treaty), bringing their tribute [on their backs ..., and coming with prai]se to adore [him = the king].⁵

We see the motifs of terror and fear here, which are commonly reflected elsewhere too.⁶ Moreover, several motifs that occur in Josh 10 reflect Sargon's *Letter to God*:

> Metatti, (the ruler) of Zikirtu, together with the kings of his neighboring regions I felled their assembly (of troops). And I broke up their organized ranks. I brought about the defeat of the armies of Urartu, the wicked enemy, together

---

³ Aššur prism, III.7-31, in *ACA*, 83-4.
⁴ *KBo IV 4 Rs IV.28-37* in *ACA*, 159.
⁵ From *KRI* V, 58-66 in *ACA*, 204.
⁶ *ACA*, 221-2.

with its allies. In the midst of Mt. Uauš he came to a stop. I filled the mountain ravines and wadis with their horses. And they, like ants in straits, squeezed through narrow paths. In the heat of my mighty weapons I climbed up after him; and *I filled ascents and descents with the bodies of (their) fighters. Over 6 'double hours' of ground from Mt. Uauš to Mt. Zimur, the jasper mountain, I pursued them at the point of the javelin.* The rest of the people, who had fled to save their lives, whom he had abandoned that *the glorious might of Aššur my lord, might be magnified, Adad,* the violent, the son of Anu, the valiant, *uttered his loud cry against them; and with the flood cloud and hail-stones (lit. 'the stone of heaven' [NA₄ AN-e]), he totally annihilated* [qatu] *the remainder.* Rusa, their prince, who had transgressed against Samaš and Marduk, who had not kept sacred the oath of Aššur, the king of the gods, became afraid at the noise of my mighty weapons; and his heart palpitated like that of a partridge fleeing before the eagle. Like a man whose blood is pouring out from him, he left Turuspâ, his royal city. Like a roaming fugitive *he hid in the recesses of his mountain.* Like a woman in confinement he became bedridden. Food and water he refused in his mouth. And thus he brought a permanent illness upon himself. *I established the glorious might of Aššur my lord, for all time to come upon Urartu. I left behind a terror never to be forgotten in the future.*[7]

Here we find hailstones as a 'divine weapon', annihilation of the enemy (but not with the root חרם or equivalent[8]), fleeing and hiding in a mountain, and terror and fear, as per Josh 10. Thus, as Younger argues, a number of motifs in Joshua seem to reflect standard ways of telling certain types of story, and hence in particular, we have instances of 'mythical' (in the more traditional sense of the word) motifs in Joshua that reflect their usage elsewhere, an observation that lends support to the kind of reading of Joshua that I am proposing.

Moreover, if one looks further than Younger's study, Joshua has resonances with other ANE texts. Fleming compares the collapsing walls of Jericho with *ARM* 1 135:8-10, where Išme-Dagan announces that he made the wall of Qirhadat fall, although 'by breaches'.[9] He also notes that with regard to the ark, sacred personnel are essential to any movement of Yahweh's cultic presence, 'as they would be for the transportation of divine statues in the wider ancient Near East'.[10] In other words, Joshua contains a number of 'traditional motifs', and understanding them as such helps one to understand the nature and significance of the text of Joshua.

---

[7] From *MDOG* 115 (1983), 82-3, in *ACA*, 210.
[8] חרם occurs in the Mesha Inscription; see chapter 6.
[9] D.E. Fleming, 'The Seven-Day Siege of Jericho in Holy War' in R.Chazan, *et al.*, (eds.), *Ki Baruch Hu: Ancient Near Eastern, Biblical and Judaic Studies in honour of Baruch A. Levine* (Winona Lake: Eisenbrauns, 1999), 211-28, here 216-7. He notes that in Akkadian texts the 'collapse' of a city wall describes a victorious siege (see *CAD maqatu* 1a) (216).
[10] *Ibid.*, 217.

Differences Between Joshua and ANE Conquest Accounts

However, these similarities should not obscure the many differences. First, the account of the fall of Jericho in Josh 6 is not a siege account, and I am not aware of any extant ANE account that is quite like the fall of Jericho.[11] Secondly, the only undisputed references to חרם (or lexical equivalents) outside the Old Testament in a sufficiently ancient era to be of relevance for Joshua are found in the Mesha Inscription and in the Ugartic 'Incantation against Infertility' (*KTU* 1.13);[12] it is a very rare way of describing warfare or conquest in the ANE. Thirdly, the Assyrian sources especially, whilst similar in reporting mass destruction, differ from Joshua in that they are usually narrated in the first person (perhaps suggesting that they exist to bolster the reputation of the king) and contain far more graphic accounts of slaughter than Joshua does. It is interesting that they often use simile and metaphor to do this, something absent from Joshua. For example, in the *Gebal Barkal Stela of Thutmose III*; 'I slaughtered them (the enemy) like they had never existed, prostrating them in their blood, casting (them) down in heaps';[13] in the Annals of Tiglath-Pileser I, 'The corpses of their warriors I laid out like grain heaps on the open country',[14] and 'I piled up the corpses of their warriors on mountain ledges like the Inundator (i.e. Adad). I made their blood flow into the hollows and plains of the mountains',[15] and Sennacherib claims, 'I harvested their skulls like shrivelled grain and I piled (them) into heaps'.[16] Fourthly, the Hittite accounts, whilst not always narrated in the first person, tend to report the capture of people and not their destruction even though they regularly have reports of burning cities.[17] An interesting exception is in Muršilli II's account that commemorates the victory of his father Suppiluliuma;

> (So) my father went against him.
> And the gods ran before my father:
> the Sun Goddess of Arinna, the Storm god of Hatti, the Storm
> god of the Army, and the Lady of the Battlefield.

---

[11] One would expect accounts narrating the collapse of walls elsewhere, as this is simply a means of overthrowing a city.

[12] The other possible reference is in the Sabean text RES 3945—the question is how one dates this text. See L.A.S. Monroe, 'Israelite, Moabite and Sabaean War-ḥērem Traditions and the Forging of National Identity: Reconsidering the Sabean Text RES 3945 in Light of Biblical and Moabite Evidence', in *VT* 57.3 (2007): 318-341. Also chapter 6 for discussion of חרם.

[13] See *ACA*, 217.

[14] *ACA*, 223.

[15] *ACA*, 83-4.

[16] *ACA*, 224.

[17] e.g. *KBo* III 4 Vs II.1-6, in *ACA*, 156.

(Thus)he slew the aforementioned whole tribe,
and the enemy troops died in multitudes[18]

Finally, and perhaps most significantly, Joshua does not 'feel' like any of these 'conquest accounts'; in Joshua little space is given to describing conquest and warfare *per se,* the accounts of Rahab (Josh 2 and 6), and Achan (Josh 7) are unlike anything else one finds in 'conquest accounts', as is the altar building of the tribes of the Transjordan (Josh 22), and the framing of the book (Josh 1 and 23-24) arguably shows more interest in obedience to the law and serving God than in conquest *per se,* even if it has rhetorical dimensions. Likewise, the distribution of the land (Josh 13-21), and in particular the establishment of cities of refuge and cities for the Levites (Josh 20-21) seem to share little with 'conquest accounts'. In other words, at the level of 'genre', Joshua cannot be described as a 'conquest account', if indeed such a genre can be identified in the ANE.

Summary

Whilst Joshua shares a number of motifs from accounts that narrate conquest in the ANE that accentuate its 'mythical' character, there are too many important differences to conclude that Joshua's genre is accounted for in terms of being a 'conquest account' and that the nature of such accounts should shape one's understanding of Joshua.[19] But awareness of such accounts highlights the stylization of the material in Joshua, in particular of the difficult material in Josh 10-11, accounts that speak of mass destruction in terms of חרם. To חרם we must now turn.

---

[18] Frag. 15 F Col. iv-G Col. i.5-10. See H.G. Güterbock, 'The Deeds of Suppiluliuma as Told by His Son, Muršilli II', in *JCS* 10 (1956): 41-130; L.L Rowlett, *Joshua and the Rhetoric of Violence: A New Historicist Analysis* (JSOTSup 226; Sheffield: Sheffield Academic Press, 1996), 90-91.

[19] Moreover, granted the similarities and differences with a wide range of ANE 'conquest accounts', it seems perilous to use a supposed similarity with, for example, neo-Assyrian accounts to derive a historical context for Joshua.

6. UNDERSTANDING THE SIGNIFICANCE OF חרם

חרם is a major theme in Joshua and thus it is important to understand its significance if one is to make the act of discourse that Joshua represents intelligible. The significance of the use of the verb and noun √חרם (as homonym I rather than homonym II 'net') is difficult to determine, for the usage of the root intersects with various apparently contradictory categories.[1] The verb is usually understood to refer to destruction in a sacral sense, but as attempts to translate Josh 6:17 indicate, its sense is problematic.[2] The root occurs frequently in Deuteronomy and Joshua in relation to the conquest, in 1 Samuel with regard to Saul, and in the prophetic materials, but is very rare in the remainder of the Old Testament, apart from Lev 27, being absent from the Psalms. Moreover, accounts in Deuteronomy that use the verb חרם have parallels in Exodus and Numbers where the root is not used.[3]

---

[1] The most comprehensive recent study of חרם is Philip Stern's, perhaps replacing that of C.H.W. Brekelmans as the standard work. (P.D. Stern, *The Biblical Herem: A Window on Israel's Religious Experience* (Brown Judaic Studies 211; Atlanta: Scholars Press, 1991); C.H.W. Brekelmans, *De herem in het OT* (Nijmegen, 1959). Other treatments include: H.H. Cohn, 'ḥerem' in *EJ* 8, 344-56; Y. Hoffman, 'The Deuteronomistic Concept of the Herem', in *ZAW* 111.2 (1999): 196-210; N. Lohfink, '*ḥāram*' in *TDOT* V, 180-99; R.D. Nelson, '*Ḥerem* and the Deuteronomic Social Conscience', in J. Lust and M. Vervenne (eds.), *Deuteronomy and Deuteronomic Literature: Festschrift C.H.W. Brekelmans* (Peeters, 1997), 39-54; C. Schäfer-Lichtenberger, 'Bedeutung und Funktion von Ḥerem in biblisch-hebräischen Texten', in *BZ* 38 (1994): 270-75. Moreover, there are important discussions in חרם in M. Fishbane, *Biblical Interpretation in Ancient Israel* (Oxford: Clarendon, 1985), 200-209; J. Milgrom, *Leviticus 23-27* (AB 3B; New York: Doubleday, 2000), 2417-21 and G.M.H. Ratheiser, *Mitzvoth Ethics and the Jewish Bible: The End of Old Testament Theology* (London: T&T Clark, 2007), 307-15.

Stern distinguishes a 'war-חרם' from a 'priestly-חרם' (represented in Lev 27), which he argues is a later re-interpretation of חרם in a peaceful cultic setting, but still involving separation, inviolability, holiness and destruction. (Stern, *ḥerem*, 125-6), a distinction that I shall develop. He argues that the earlier war-חרם is deeply rooted in mythic conceptions, with the execution of חרם interpreted as a participation with YHWH in fighting the forces of chaos to secure order (220-21).

[2] E.g. 'devoted for destruction' (NRSV); 'devoted' (NIV); 'under the ban' (NAS); 'set apart' (NET); 'devoted under the curse of destruction' (NJB); 'doomed to destruction' (NKJ); 'completely destroyed as an offering' (NLT).

[3] E.g. Deut 2:24-3:11 reflects Num 21:21-35 using חרם.

Whilst one might hope to gather extra-biblical evidence from other ANE texts that would illuminate the use of חרם in the Old Testament, the evidence, discussed in detail in Stern's study, is surprisingly sparse. The root occurs in the Mesha Inscription (MI), and in the Ugaritic text, 'An Incantation Against Infertility' (*KTU* 1.13), in verbal form in both cases. These are the only two undisputed extant uses of the root *ḥrm*, or its semantic equivalent, in ANE texts outside the Old Testament that are likely to have been composed in the same era as, or earlier than, Joshua in which a sense of annihilation is implied.[4] Thus Joshua does not simply reflect a common cultural context or a common depiction of something like 'holy war', in the same way as it does not reflect ANE 'conquest accounts' as we saw in chapter 5. However, the verb *ḥarāmu* (II) meaning 'to separate' occurs in Akkadian texts, and is possibly associated with women who are 'socially set apart'.[5] This usage has not been seen as particularly important for understanding the biblical חרם,[6] although I shall return to this notion of separation later. Other parallels have been sought, such as the *assaku* in the Mari letters, yet this appears to be a rather partial parallel, and as likely to mislead as to help.[7] But in the MI and *KTU* 1.13 the verb *ḥrm* is associated with destruction. Indeed, in *KTU* 1.13 *ḥrm* is used in parallel with *hrg*, although the text is fragmentary and difficult to interpret.[8] The MI is more promising, and here חרם is used (line 17) in a way apparently similar to that in Deuteronomy and Joshua, relating to the mass destruction of a group of people (here in the MI, the Israelites) in battle by divine sanction. But one may render the verb in a number of ways in the MI, and so perhaps it does not advance one's understanding of biblical חרם. However, Stern notes that in the biblical narratives and in the MI חרם is associated with גרש, הרג, ירש and אחז which, he suggests, 'form a small glossary which could be used to describe the struggle for control of land'.[9]

חרם occurs in essentially three different contexts in the Old Testament. First, in the Deuteronomistic materials the verb is associated with annihilation, with the noun being used to denote that which is to be annihilated. In Deuteronomy

---

[4] The root occurs in the Sabean text RES 3945. A date in the fifth century for this text has generally been accepted, although L.A.S. Monroe has recently argued for a date in the seventh or eighth century ('Israelite, Moabite and Sabaean War-*ḥērem* Traditions and the Forging of National Identity: Reconsidering the Sabean Text RES 3945 in Light of Biblical and Moabite Evidence', in *VT* 57.3 (2007): 318-41). As both the dating of this text and its interpretation are problematic, as Monroe's study indicates, I shall not consider it further here.

[5] '*ḥarāmu*' in *CAD* vol.6 'ḫ', 89-90.

[6] Stern, *ḥerem*, 8.

[7] See Stern, *ḥerem*, 5-87 for a full discussion of the parallels that have been proposed. It will become clear that trying to read חרם in terms of *assaku* (and vice versa) is indeed misleading, at least for understanding חרם in Deuteronomy and Joshua.

[8] See ibid., 5-6 for a discussion of the text.

[9] Ibid., 225.

חרם is used in relation to the command to annihilate the inhabitants of Canaan during the conquest, but also in relation to Israelite settlements where other gods are worshipped (Deut 13:13-19 (Heb.)). Secondly, in the prophetic literature the verb is used in an eschatological/apocalyptic sense to describe the fate of the nations, and Babylon in particular (Jer 51:1-3), but again, it is also used in relation to Israelites (Isa 43:28). Thirdly, the root occurs in the Priestly materials, usually in the sense of something or someone that is 'irrevocably dedicated' to YHWH (Lev 27:21, 28-29).

Whilst there has been a tendency to read חרם in these contexts together as expressing an essentially similar concept, there are problems. In Deuteronomy what is declared חרם is to be detested and abhorred (תעב, שקץ, Deut 7:25-26), yet in Leviticus, and in other Priestly material, that which is חרם is associated with that which is holy (קדש) to YHWH, where the noun חרם is associated with land and objects irrevocably handed over to the priests (Lev 27:21, 28-29; Num 18:14; Ezek 44:29; Ezra 10:8, and perhaps Josh 6:19). So comparison of Lev 27 with Deut 7, texts which seem to offer paradigmatic accounts of חרם in the Priestly and Deuteronomistic materials, indicates that there may be a confusion of categories, with the usage of the root being different in each case. However, in Deuteronomy and Joshua, what is חרם is 'חרם ל 'to' (?) 'יהוה' (e.g. Josh 6:17), resembling the vocabulary associated with offerings. This might be said to connect with the Priestly use of the term after all. Moreover, initial readings of Deut 7, 13 and Josh 7 give the impression that חרם objects may be viewed as a 'contagion', which has clear resonances with Priestly categories and conceptualities, although the objects that are declared חרם varies in the Deuteronomistic literature (Josh 6 cf. Josh 8).

So, leaving aside the prophetic literature, three questions arise from reading Deut 7, 13, Josh 6-7 and Lev 27 in their literary contexts. First, comparing Josh 6:19 and 24 with Deut 7:25-26, how can that which is categorized as קדש here in Josh 6:19 and 24 also be categorized as תעב and שקץ in Deut 7:25-26? Secondly, does the grammar of חרם as ליהוה חרם in Josh 6:17 support a 'sacrificial' understanding of חרם in the Deuteronomistic materials? Thirdly, do Deut 7, 13 and Josh 6-7 imply that חרם objects are viewed as a contagion?

Re-examining the 'Priestly-like' Approaches to חרם in the Non-Priestly Literature

חרם *and the categories of* קדש, תעב *and* שקץ

In Josh 6:17 Joshua orders that Jericho and everything in it 'are to be חרם'. The execution of this command is reported in 6:21 and 24 where it appears that total destruction is envisaged. However, 6:19 and 24 report that precious metallic objects are קדש to YHWH and are to go into the treasury. This report can be understood in three different ways. First, perhaps the metallic objects were implicitly understood as not being חרם. Secondly, perhaps the conception of חרם found in the Priestly materials exists here, and is in fact associated with the Deuteronomistic conception. Thirdly, whilst the Priestly conception is in view here, such a conception may be distinct from the Deuteronomistic conception, with these verses representing a Priestly (or Priestly influenced) gloss.

In the context of Josh 7 it seems that the metals *were* categorised as חרם (7:1, 21), as Deut 7:25-26 would suggest, where the language of coveting in both accounts invites them to be read together. But Deut 7 implies that all objects designated as חרם, including the metals from which they were made, should have been destroyed, as would Josh 7:12. Indeed, Josh 7 does not suggest that the required corrective action arising from Achan's crime is to return the items that he took to the treasury, but to destroy them. Moreover, objects that are חרם are to be detested and abhorred (תעב, שקץ, Deut 7:25-26) as we have seen. This sits uneasily with categorization of the חרם metals as קדש in Josh 6:19 and 24; would one place that which is to be detested and abhorred into YHWH's treasury and call it 'holy'?[10]

So, coupled with the observation that the clauses relating to the metals in Josh 6:19 and 24 can be removed from the story without loss to its flow, good grounds exist to suppose that Josh 6:19 and 24 are later Priestly (or Priestly influenced) additions.[11] Indeed, this trajectory of reading a Priestly conception of חרם into the account is further developed in 4Q379 3 II, 5-6, which is a reworking of Josh 6-7, where allusion to Lev 27:28-29 is explicit.[12]

Thus it is preferable to differentiate distinct uses of חרם, senses that we might call a Deuteronomistic sense, associated with תעב and שקץ, and a Priestly sense associated with קדש, even if both senses involve the idea of 'separation' in some way.[13] But are there grounds for construing חרם, in its Deuteronomistic sense, as being an 'offering' (Deut 13:16-17 (Heb); Josh 6:17), a question to which we now turn.

---

[10] Cf. Schäfer-Lichtenberger, 'Bedeutung und Funktion'; '*Qdš* und *ḥrm* symbolisieren hier zwei verschiedene Sphären, die strikt voneinander geschieden sind. Ḥerem ist die Gegensphäre zum Heiligen.' (274).

[11] Cf. J.S. Kaminsky ('Joshua 7: A Reassessment of the Israelite Conceptions of Corporate Punishment', in S.W. Holloway and L.K. Handy (eds.), *The Pitcher is Broken: Memorial Essays for Gösta W. Ahlström* (JSOTSup 190; Sheffield: Sheffield Academic Press, 1995), 315-346, here 329-30).

[12] H.D. Park, *Finding Ḥerem? A Study of Luke-Acts in the Light of Ḥerem* (Library of New Testament Studies 357; London: T&T Clark, 2007), 84.

[13] I shall go on to argue that there is a distinction to be made between what might be termed a *Deuteronomic* חרם and a *Deuteronomistic* qualification and use of the Deuteronomic idea. For now, it will suffice to consider both under the heading of 'Deuteronomistic' for convenience as the conception is sufficiently similar even if the use differs.

חרם *and the language of 'offering' to YHWH*

The grammar of חרם as being ליהוה is found only in Josh 6:17 in the Deuteronomistic materials, and only Micah 4:13 and Lev 27 elsewhere, although the language of Deut 13:16-17 (Heb) is taken to reinforce this conception of חרם as 'sacrificial offering'. When compared with the usage of זבח it is suggestive of interpreting חרם using the category of 'offering'. Indeed, Joel Kaminsky suggests that

> when one treats something as חרם, it means that the object is consecrated or dedicated in an almost sacrificial manner. Support for such an understanding of the חרם can be found in several biblical passages. Notice the way in which Deut. 13:17 uses terminology that is strongly reminiscent of the language surrounding the idea of sacrifice ... Sacrificial terminology can also be found in Josh. 6:17a ... and in Lev. 27:28b.[14]

In Josh 6:17 Jericho is to be חרם ליהוה, and in Micah 4:13 it is the unjust gains of the nations that החרמתי ליהוה. But what does ליהוה mean in these contexts? Deut 13:16-17 (Heb) is an important text. It commands the חרם of an Israelite town where people have been led astray to worship other gods, stating that everything in the town is to be gathered in the square and burnt כליל ליהוה. Here, כליל is usually taken to mean 'whole burnt offering' (cf. Deut 33:10), which would obviously associate חרם with the idea of 'offering', clarifying the sense ליהוה. But it is equally possible to read כליל adverbially, for emphasis, i.e., reading 'the city and all its plunder *in its entirety*', which would reflect the more common usage of כליל.[15] Significantly, when used in Leviticus כליל is only used in the sense of completeness, suggesting that it is not part of the vocabulary of offerings. Moreover, dis-associating חרם from the category of offering is supported by the use of the categories relating to 'detesting' (תעב, שקץ) in relation to חרם (Deut 7:25-26)[16] - would one offer something detestable to YHWH?

How then does the *lamed* function in ליהוה? Does it connote 'to YHWH', and if so then what does this mean? Or 'for YHWH', or 'on behalf of YHWH', maybe to emphasise agency; i.e. that חרם is conducted on YHWH's behalf as the

---

[14] Kaminsky, 'Joshua', 331.

[15] It occurs in Exod 28:31; 39:22; Lev 6:15, 16; Num 4:6; Judg 20:40; Isa 2:18; Lam 2:15; Ezek 16:14; 27:3; 28:12 in the sense of completeness, and Deut 33:10; 1 Sam 7:9 and Ps 51:21; in the sense of offering. Cf. Lohfink, '*ḥāram*', 184 who questions whether כליל 'was perceived as a sacrificial term' here.

[16] See also Nelson, '*Ḥerem*', who argues that חרם is not to be understood in sacrificial terms (47). But later I shall argue that it is not a property of חרם-ness *per se* that makes an object detestable; rather it is its association with idolatry. But here my argument is simply that it is unlikely that a detestable object would be considered an acceptable offering.

Understanding the Significance of חרם   99

result of a divine command?¹⁷ Whatever the precise sense, ליהוה need not connote an idea of offering or sacrifice; its usage is far wider.¹⁸ However, evidence from the Mesha Inscription might support the 'sacrificial' understanding. In the MI it is possible that חרם (line 17) may be associated, via parallelism, with what is described earlier as a רית (satiation?) to the god Kemosh (line 12) which might suggest that חרם in its ANE context is associated with the idea of offerings.¹⁹ However רית is used in conjunction with הרג (line 11) and not חרם, and if רית derives from רוה it may have a less 'technical' and more metaphorical sense. Indeed רוה is associated with חרם in Isa 34:5, and has a metaphorical sense.²⁰ Moreover, הרג occurs 172 times in the Old Testament but never in conjunction with ליהוה, suggesting that the usage of the roots in the MI do not map directly onto those in the Old Testament.

Hence the association of חרם with the category of 'offering' in the Deuteronomistic materials is problematic, although the grammar of its usage might account for the emergence of the Priestly conception of חרם, maybe through texts like Micah 4:13, perhaps together with other ANE conceptions of חרם such as is expressed in the MI. But the root חרם may have suited the purpose of the Deuteronomist because it was a rare term associated with separation and annihilation on the one hand, and the divine sphere on the other. Thus it is a 'difficult' and exceptional category; understanding חרם as being ליהוה grants the term a narrower and more precise sense than terms such as שמד and הרג which are never used in conjunction with ליהוה, which thus suggests that חרם has a mythical association relating in a rather ambiguous way to the divine sphere in a way that other terms relating to destruction do not—it has a liminal nature.²¹ Perhaps 'for YHWH' is the best rendering of ליהוה.

---

[17] See B.K. Waltke and M. O'Connor, *An Introduction to Biblical Hebrew Syntax* (Winona Lake: Eisenbrauns, 1990), 205-212 for discussion of the wide range of uses of the preposition.

[18] Cf. e.g. Gen 24:26; Deut 1:41; 16:1; 1 Sam 1:3; 2:8; 3:20; 2 Sam 21:6; 1 Kgs 6:1-2; 19:10 and 2 Kgs 6:33 for a variety of senses for ליהוה.

[19] רית (line 12) is usually rendered 'satiation' from רוה, although it is, as Stern notes, something of an interpretative crux (*ḥerem*, 32). Cf. also K.A.D. Smelik, 'Moabite Inscriptions' in *CoS* II, 137-8

[20] See also Nelson, 'Ḥerem', 47-8. Nelson suggests that 'Isa 34,5-7 uses sacrifice as a poetic metaphor. The most natural reading is to construe *ḥerem* and sacrifice as two successive images illustrating the frenzied attack of Yahweh's sword.' (47).

[21] Cf. Stern, *ḥerem*, 220-24.

חרם, *contagiousness and impurity*

It has become popular to regard חרם objects as a 'contagion'.[22] This appears to stem from Josh 6:18; 7:10-15; Deut 7:25-26 and perhaps Deut 13:13-19 (Heb). For example, Kaminsky suggests that 'The sacral character of חרם also extends to the effect it has on those who misuse it. It is clear from Deut 7:25-26 ... and from Josh 6:18 ... that when one misappropriates חרם, one runs the risk of having the tabooed status of the חרם transferred to oneself.'[23] He elaborates on this in a footnote,

> this is wholly analogous to the contagiousness of the state of impurity, and a provision of the law of impurity is really the best commentary on the story of Achan's crime ... (Num. 19:14)' ... [I]t is important to recognize that ~rx can spread and thus can be described as something that is contagious.[24]

and develops it further in his reading of Josh. 7:

> חרם is sacral in nature and has the ability to transmit its taboo status to those who misappropriate it. That this factor is operational in this narrative is stated rather explicitly in Josh. 7:12 ... This verse appears to indicate that all Israel has, at least temporarily, become חרם. Verse 15, in which God orders that Achan and everything he owns be burned, suggests that the tabooed status of misappropriated objects spreads to Achan's family and possessions.[25]

However, I shall argue that it is a mistake to regard חרם objects as a contagion, and hence argue that it should not be interpreted via this or similar Priestly-like categories. I shall demonstrate that, first, חרם is not associated with the use of the vocabulary of Priestly categories relating to contagion or impurity; secondly, חרם is not associated with any conceptually equivalent Deuteronomistic categories, and thirdly, in the texts that might appear to support understanding חרם in terms of contagion, a rhetorical understanding of the texts offers a better construal of חרם, with the texts being read 'rhetorically' rather than 'ontologically'.

First, חרם is never associated with the vocabulary of 'spreading' as per other Levitical notions of impurity or uncleanness, or indeed of 'spreading' generally; חרם is never used in conjunction with פרש or פשה, which it might be if it were understood using the Priestly categories of 'contagion' or 'contamination' (cf. Lev 13-14). Furthermore, the language for 'unclean-ness' and 'clean-ness' or

---

[22] See e.g. L.D. Hawk, *Joshua* (Berit Olam; Collegeville: The Liturgical Press, 2000), 100; R.D. Nelson, *Joshua* (OTL; Louisville: Westminster John Knox Press, 1997), 101; J.F.D. Creach, *Joshua* (Interpretation; Louisville: John Knox Press, 2003), 72-4; Kaminsky, 'Joshua', 331ff; Lohfink, '*ḥāram*', 194.
[23] Kaminsky, 'Joshua', 331.
[24] Ibid., 331-2.
[25] Ibid., 336-7.

Understanding the Significance of חרם   101

purity does not fit; neither טמא nor טהר are ever used in conjunction with חרם. Moreover, the language of 'transmission' for טמא uses the verb נגע (touch), a verb not used in conjunction with חרם. What is more, such unclean-ness is temporary and can be removed by appropriate procedures, which is not, it seems, the case with חרם.[26] Finally, the lack of Priestly terminology, especially in Josh 7, is striking considering the use of מעל, a Priestly term, here. Taken together, these observations suggest that it is a category mistake to interpret חרם via categories such as purity/impurity and/or contagion, for חרם is not 'talked about' in this grammar.[27]

Secondly, the phrase ידבק בידך 'cling to the hand' used in relation to חרם in Deut 13:18 (Heb) might be said to express an idea of 'contagion' in a different idiom; in Deut 13:13-19 an Israelite town is to be subject to חרם if people have been led to worship other gods, with an additional note in 13:18 stating that חרם objects must not to 'cling to the hand' (ולא־ידבק בידך מאומה מן־החרם). דבק occurs seven times elsewhere in Deuteronomy, five times to describe 'holding fast' to YHWH (Deut 4:4; 10:20; 11:22; 13:5 and 30:20) and twice with references to diseases 'clinging' to one (Deut 28:21, 60). It occurs three times in Joshua, twice with reference to clinging to YHWH (Josh 22:5; 23:8) and once with reference to clinging to the survivors in the land, as a warning against doing so (Josh 23:12). Thus it seems that more than simply coming into contact is implied by the idiom; rather, it implies an 'attachment' to the object(s) in question, suggesting that 'contagion' may be an inappropriate description. However, the language of 'bringing into the house' of objects associated with idols in Deut 7:25-26 might be said to resonate with that of the unclean-ness that results from discases in the house which cause all who enter the house to be unclean (Lev 14:46-47). But, as with Deut 13:13-19, in the context of 7:25, it seems that more than literally 'entering the house' is envisaged for the idea of coveting is introduced in Deut 7:25, being similar to that of 'attachment' in Deut 13:18.

Thirdly, the 'threats' relating to חרם—that *you* may end up as subject to חרם if *you* 'involve yourself' with חרם objects inappropriately - have a *rhetorical* force, relating to the avoidance of idols, and to not coveting, rather than an *ontological* force; these texts do not describe the process by which חרם is 'transmitted'. Indeed, in Deut 7, 13 and 20, what is to be detested is not חרם objects *per se* as if they have some ontological property of 'חרם -ness', rather it is idols, the *practices* of idolatry and the worship of other gods that are to be

---

[26] Cf. Lev 11:24-28 in relation to touching the carcasses of unclean animals, and Lev 12:4 where uncleanness, cleanness (טהרה) and touching (נגע) holy things (קדש) are established in a matrix, a matrix from which חרם is absent, except in Lev 27 where חרם is associated only with קדש, which I suggest represents a development of חרם in a different context.

[27] Moreover, the term 'contagion' was made popular in relation to the purity laws of Leviticus by Mary Douglas (*Purity and Danger* (London: Routledge & Kegan Paul, 1966)), but I am not aware of her ever using 'contagion' in relation to חרם.

detested. Deut 20:17-18 indicates that the concern for 'spreading' is not for the spreading of חרם, but of the teaching that encourages the worship of other gods. Thus these texts reflect warnings against idolatry and covetousness, rather than explanations of a transmission process of a supposed 'חרם property'. To use the language developed in chapter 2, these texts represent 'limit-situations' as myths that function to shape what it is that is to characterize the identity of Israel, rather than actual 'legal' practice. The continual struggle against idolatry and the worship of other gods in the 'biblical history' of Israel suggests that if Deut 13:13-19 (Heb) had been practised to the letter, little would have remained of Israel! Indeed, the Temple Scroll (11Q19, LV, 6-12) which re-writes Deut 13:16-18 to require the whole city to have fallen into idolatry, indicates that a problem was perceived with the literal application of Deut 13,[28] and thus 11Q19 reflects a tradition associated with the text that clarifies its use, indicating that חרם does function symbolically here as a 'limit-situation' to evoke radical separation from idols and idolatry. These injunctions seek to inculcate an attitude of careful avoidance of idols and other gods. Indeed, Deuteronomy itself may be construed as a mythical narrative that shapes the life and identity of Israel in some of the ways outlined in chapter 2; it is not a 'legal code' in the modern sense.[29]

Finally, Josh 7 is best construed via the 'rhetoric of חרם', for another difficulty that Kaminsky's analysis raises is that if, as he suggests, Israel has become 'temporarily' חרם in Josh 7:12,[30] then this sits uncomfortably with the assumption that declaring something חרם is an irrevocable declaration relating to the ontological state of an object, an assumption probably made via the influence of Priestly conceptions of חרם.[31] The solution is to read Josh 7:12-13 'rhetorically' rather than 'ontologically'. Josh 7:12-13, together with Josh 6:18 form warnings embedded in rhetorical contexts. Whilst one might claim that the 'interpretative keys' of 7:1 and 11 suggest that חרם objects are a contagion, Josh 7:11, reporting YHWH's response to Joshua, can be understood in two ways. It could be understood to imply that the problem here is the contagiousness of the חרם *per se*, or that the issue is really that violation of the חרם represents disobedience, and in fact symbolises covenant violation. The importance of the latter concern is indicated in 7:11 and in 7:21 where Achan confesses, for here the use of גנב (steal) in 7:11 reflects the Decalogue's language (Deut 5:19), as does חמד

---

[28] Cf. Park, *Ḥerem*, 68-71.
[29] This assertion does, of course, need further development, but cf. N.M. Sarna, *Exploring Exodus: The Origins of Biblical Israel* (New York: Schocken Books, 1996), 168-70 on the way that law codes functioned in the ANE.
[30] Kaminsky, *Joshua*, 336-7.
[31] Cf. Nelson, '*Ḥerem*', 44-5; Hawk, *Joshua*, 100-101. What is often evident in the discussions is a conflation of the concept of חרם in Lev 27 with that in Deuteronomy, Joshua, and other ANE texts.

(covet) in 7:21.³² Indeed, if one reads on into Josh 8 (8:2), what is declared חרם varies (cf. 6:17-18 and Deut 7:25-26), which again suggests that an ontological conception of חרם or 'contamination' is not the primary issue.

Thus covenant violation is really the issue,³³ which the חרם violation symbolises. The presence of חרם objects is not a problem because they contaminate the Israelite camp with a property of 'חרם-ness', but because their presence is symbolic of covenant violation. Covenant violation cannot exist in Israel, since obedience to the covenant is what constitutes Israel's identity as a community in response to YHWH. Israel's identity—and very existence—can only be restored when obedience is restored through the destruction of the חרם objects, as per YHWH's original injunction.³⁴ Moreover, Achan, as the one symbolizing covenant violation cannot 'exist' in the community either. Thus it is not so much חרם objects that have a 'sacral character', but the covenant, that is here *symbolized* through חרם.³⁵ The concern of the story is that of identity construction with respect to the covenant. The covenant, and obedience to it, is central to the characterization of Israel's identity. To use the language developed in chapter 2, and to anticipate the more detailed analysis of Josh 7 in chapter 8, Josh 7 presents, as myth, a story as a 'limit-situation' that indicates that disobedience to the covenant makes one an 'outsider', symbolized by the death of the offender and their family.

Summary

There has been a tendency to read conceptions of the priestly-חרם into the Deuteronomistic accounts of חרם which has led to a skewed and incorrect understanding of the narratives dealing with it. But we have seen how the grammar associated with חרם is suggestive of its development in the preistly

---

³² Moreover, the use of כחש (deceive) in 7:11 may amplify the issue at stake. However, כחש and the context of stealing seems to reflect Lev 5:21ff (Heb), a resonance strengthened via the use of מעל here and in Josh 7:1. The use of מעל is all the more significant in Josh 7:1 as it is so rare in the Deuteronomistic literature (only Deut 32:51; Josh 7:1; 22:16, 20 and 31), but common in, e.g. P and Chr. However, the resolution of the offence is very different in Leviticus from that in Joshua.
³³ Cf. R.S. Hess, *Joshua* (TOTC; Leicester: IVP, 1996), 149-50.
³⁴ The observation that the silver and gold are to be destroyed here, rather than put into the treasury is a further indicator that Josh 6:19 and 24 are later glosses.
³⁵ However, we see here an exploration of the polyvalency of the symbol of חרם in a particular (narrative) context. Perhaps it is the association of חרם with the 'sacred sphere' in some sense that is suggestive for its use in relation to the covenant since it resonates with the sacredness of the covenant. This symbolic (or metaphoric) mode of association thus invites new ways of thinking about each concept (חרם and the covenant) in the light of each other.

sense.[36] Historically speaking such a development is plausible granted that in Leviticus for example the priestly-חרם only occurs in Lev 27, which is perhaps the paradigmatic text dealing with the priestly-חרם, a text that is widely acknowledged to be a late addition to Leviticus. Thus it is plausible that the Deuteronomistic conception of חרם reflects an early appropriation of this rare Western Semitic term, whilst its Priestly conception reflects an exilic (or later) development of the Deuteronomistic conception, however one wishes to date the core of the Priestly and Deuteronomistic materials.[37]

---

[36] See Lohfink's discussion of Brekelmans' study in *TDOT*, esp. 185ff for an account that would suggest an alternative reconstruction of the development of the term, treating the more 'Priestly' conception as primary, a view that seems to have been followed often. My analysis, rather like Stern's, seems to point in the opposite direction.

[37] Lev 27:21, 28-29 is the main text dealing with the 'priestly-חרם. Gerstenberger suggests that Lev 26 was probably the original conclusion of Leviticus, as it was common for ANE legal collections, etc. to conclude with such imprecatory formulae as we find here (E.S. Gerstenberger, *Leviticus* (Louisville: WJKP, ET: 1996), 399). Moreover, he claims that Lev 27 differs in 'form and content' from the rest of the book, forming a 'kind of price list for redeeming persons and objects promised to God through a vow' (ibid., 436; Cf. M. Noth, *Leviticus* (OTL; London: SCM, Rev. ET: 1977), 203). Importantly, there is general agreement that Lev 27 is an 'appendix' added at a relatively late stage to Leviticus. Indeed, Jacob Milgrom who argues for a rather earlier date for P (and H) than most argues that the logical closure of H (the later material, parts of which are 'demonstrably exilic', he claims) is Lev 26 (Milgrom, *Leviticus 23-27*, 2407-2409. (See also his 'Priestly ("P") Source' in *ABD*, 5.454-61). However, he notes that the valuation of fifty shekels for an adult male (27:3) suggests a pre-exilic date for some of the materials of Lev 27 (ibid., 2409), and thus it is difficult to know where to situate the חרם materials of Lev 27, even if they were only incorporated into the book at a late stage. They are probably late, but could be seventh or eighth century (cf. 27:3). What does a wider analysis of the Priestly materials suggest?

Apart from Lev 27 there are no references to the root חרם at all in Leviticus, except a homonym in Lev 21:18. But if the חרם concept in Lev 27 were early, it is surprising that it is not referred to in the 'earlier redaction' of Leviticus. This adds weight to the suggestion that the חרם in Lev 27 is a relatively late development in P and/or H. Moreover, the only references in the Old Testament to the root חרם in the sort of way that it is used in Lev 27:21-29, i.e. its association with the priests, the treasury and the category קדש are Num 18:14; Ezra 10:8; Ezek 44:29 (cf. Num 18:14) and possibly Josh 6:19 and 24. Clearly Ezra 10:8 is late. Ezek 44:29 is exilic or later, and Num 18:14 is very similar to Ezek 44:29, and Budd suggests that in Num. 18:14 the author uses '*ḥērem* as an alternative to the *terumah* contribution' (P.J. Budd, *Numbers* (WBC 5; Dallas: Word, 1984), 206), and that Num 18:14 is *dependent* upon Ezek 44:29, placing it in a late fifth century context where it was necessary to reform the 'clerical office' (202, 206-207). Such a historical reconstruction, although plausible, is difficult to substantiate. But, if Num 18:14 were early, it would be exceptional, with Lev 27 being the only other candidate for an early usage of a priestly-חרם. Thus it seems most likely that the priestly-חרם is indeed a late concept, with Josh 6:19 and 24 reflecting it as later glosses to a stable text.

A Mythical Approach to the Deuteronomistic חרם

Having argued what חרם is not, we must now consider what it is. An initial reading of the Deuteronomistic materials gives the impression that חרם as a verb is a term used as a divine command that connotes annihilation, either of people or of objects. I shall argue that a mythical reading of the texts is appropriate and indicates that חרם functions symbolically. As a symbol חרם takes the image of annihilation as its first-order, literal or concrete sense, a sense that is 'literal' within the portrayal of the text, but a sense that points to its real significance in a 'second-order' or 'opaque' sense that may be described in neo-structuralist terms. This sense, as evoked through the literal sense of the symbol, forms the basis for the existential appropriation and enactment of חרם, as I shall now develop. First, I shall consider temporal perspectives on חרם to assist in establishing its symbolic and mythical character, before considering, secondly, what its significance is by studying the way in which its second-order sense was construed and developed within Israel according to the witness of various biblical texts, i.e., according to how it was *used*. But crucially, we shall see that חרם in Joshua (and 1 Samuel) functions symbolically in a way that is different from its symbolic use in Deuteronomy, even though its use in these texts builds upon its sense in Deuteronomy.

Temporal perspectives and the mythical nature of חרם

Outside Deuteronomy and Joshua, references to 'deuteronomistic-חרם' are rare. In Judges, Samuel-Kings and Chronicles it occurs in relation to activities that trace back to the conquest in some sense (Judg 1:17; 1 Kgs 9:21 and 1 Chr 4:41). It also describes the actions of others (2 Kgs 19:11 (and parallels, 2 Chr 32:14 and Isa 37:11)), where the verb is attributed to Sennacherib, an interesting observation given that the root חרם, or equivalent, does not appear in any Akkadian texts. Likewise in 2 Chr 20:23 חרם is used in relation to the action of the Ammonites and Moabites against the men of Mount Seir. In 1 Kgs 20:42 it is used in relation to a man (Ben Hadad) whom a prophet said should die, but whom Ahab allowed to live. 1 Kgs 20:42 is an unusual text, and Stern regards it as an attempt to develop a parallel with Saul, noting, moreover, a possible association, or wordplay with חרם II 'net'.[38] The usage of חרם in Judg 21:11 is unusual, and difficult to explain; Stern merely suggests that it is 'isolated'.[39] Finally, it occurs in 1 Sam 15, a text that I wish to leave to one side for the moment, but will return to in chapter 9, as its significance here is best explained after considering the role of חרם in Joshua. Thus the virtual absence of חרם from Judges, Samuel-Kings and Chronicles is striking, suggesting that it is not part of

---

[38] Stern, *ḥerem*, 178-83.
[39] Ibid., 160-63.

Israel's vocabulary of warfare, or indeed of any concept like 'Holy War' *per se*.[40] Similarly, the absence of חרם from the Psalms is surely significant, particularly in contexts where it might have been expected, such as Ps 135, 136 and 137. If the Psalms reflect Israel's regular grammar of response to YHWH, then it is striking that חרם is absent. So, leaving Deuteronomy and Joshua aside for a moment, taken together, these observations suggest that deuteronomistic-חרם is not a category that Israel uses to describe her existence or narrate her actions in the present, suggesting that חרם is 'displaced' from the present.

However, חרם *is* developed and used in an other-worldly eschatological direction in the prophetic materials.[41] Its use here is varied, but when associated

---

[40] For this reason, and, since as will become clear, I do not think that Joshua is really about warfare, I shall not discuss 'holy war' and the debates surrounding it (See G. von Rad, *Holy War in Ancient Israel* (Grand Rapids: W.B. Eerdmans, ET:1991); S. Niditch, *War in the Hebrew Bible* (Oxford: OUP, 1993)). It will be clear that I do not follow von Rad or Niditch. Peter Craigie's comments on von Rad are apt; 'While war was religious by association, it was no more a cultic and holy act than was sheep shearing.' (*The Problem of War in the Old Testament* (Grand Rapids: W.B. Eerdmans, 1978), 49). See Ratheiser, *Mitzvoth Ethics*, 307-10 for a recent summary of research on the concept of 'holy war'. One of the main difficulties has been, I think, a tendency to conflate the Priestly and Deuteronomistic conceptions of חרם. However, whilst 'holy war' might be an unhelpful category, it is clear that Israel (and Judah) fought wars like everybody else (and emerged as a nation through warfare), and that from other texts from the ANE that it was common to presume that deities were involved in human warfare. I do not think that Joshua tells us much about, or is really concerned with warfare in Israel, however, as will become clear.

[41] In the prophets the verb חרם is used in an eschatological or future sense in Isa 34:2, 5; 43:28; Jer 25:9; 50:21, 26; 51:3; Dan 11:44; Micah 4:13 and Zech 14:11, where it is used as part of the language of poetic prophetic oracles that are replete with metaphor. (It also occurs in the MT of Isa 11:15, but this appears to be a textual corruption—see Stern, *ḥerem*, 192.) It also appears in Isa 37:11 in a non-Priestly, non-futuristic sense. Now:

1. In Isa 37:11 (and parallel, 2Kgs 19:11) חרם is the verb that Sennacherib is reported to use in relation to what he has done to other nations. It is clearly referring to destruction, and Hezekiah's prayer in response suggests an association with the destruction of gods and idols (37:18-19);
2. In Isa 34:2, 5; Jer 50:21, 26; 51:3 חרם is used as a verb in an eschatological/apocalyptic context to describe what YHWH will do to the nations (Isaiah) or Babylon (Jeremiah). Jeremiah makes more explicit the association between sins and חרם, but again, חרם clearly refers to destruction;
3. In Isa 43:28; Jer 25:9; Zech 14:11 it is Jacob, Judah or Jerusalem that is the object of the verb חרם. In Isaiah and Jeremiah it is used in the context of a vision of the imminent future where it is understood as YHWH's punishment and functions as a warning. In Zechariah it is in an eschatological context, where Jerusalem will suffer חרם no more;

with YHWH and/or Israel, חרם is either a judgment that will fall upon Israel/Judah in the near future, or it is an expression of YHWH's (eschatological) wrath against the nations. But it is a concept of the future, which, mythologically speaking, provides the contours for an existential response of Israel in the 'here and now'; do not go after the nations and their ways, and do not worry about them, for they are doomed, as will *you* be if *you* keep following their gods. But whilst Israel was prophetically threatened with חרם unless she changed her ways (Isa 43:28; Jer 25:9 and Zech 14:11), when punishment is said to have occurred it was not interpreted using the category of חרם. So here, חרם is pushed into the future as a 'rhetorical' anticipatory category, again displacing it from the present even if it has significance in the present in an existential sense.

Apart from Joshua and Deuteronomy, there are no other instances of 'deuteronomistic-חרם' in the Old Testament, other than in 1 Sam 15, which I shall return to in chapter 9, where I shall suggest that חרם functions in a similar way here to that in Joshua. Now, Joshua places the portrayal of a 'literal חרם' in the prototypical past. This sense of the prototypical past is reinforced through references to the Anakim and Rephaim, mythical giants and ghosts from the distant past that dwelt in the world of Joshua's חרם, a world that is very different from the Israelites' everyday experienced world. Indeed, the conclusion of the conquest in Josh 11 is described in terms of the destruction of these 'mythical beings',[42] with the result that Israel settles in the land and enjoys rest from warfare (Josh 11:21-23), encouraging the reader to associate the world of a practice of 'literal חרם' with an other-worldly prototypical past.

Moreover, it is generally uncontroversial to suggest that Deuteronomy and Joshua represent retrospective re-tellings or interpretations of the conquest tradition, and thus it is very unlikely that any such conquest was interpreted using the category of חרם at the time. Indeed, חרם seems to reflect one of three different interpretations or 'portraits' of Israel's entrance to the land.[43] Exod

---

4. In Dan 11:44 חרם appears in an apocalyptic context, but it is one of the kings in Daniel's vision that is the subject of the verb, and it is simply 'many people' that is the object, and is a result of this king's great rage;
5. In Micah 4:13 חרם appears in an apocalyptic/eschatological vision, but it is the 'unjust gains' of the nations that are the object of the verb חרם, and are said to be חרם 'to YHWH'. The usage here is thus slightly ambiguous, occupying a position that resonates both with the 'war-חרם' and the 'priestly-חרם'.

[42] Num 13:1-33; Deut 2:11; 3:11; 9:1-3; Josh 11:21-23. I use 'mythical' here in the more traditional sense of the word. See e.g., B.A. Levine, *Numbers 1-20* (AB 4A; New York: Doubleday, 1993), 378-9 and the discussion on Josh 11-12 in chapter 8.

[43] Moreover, if the patriarchal and exodus traditions are to be understood as *competing* myths of Israel's emergence in the land, then a fourth portrait of Israel's 'entrance' in the land exists—one of peaceful emergence in the land. See K. Schmid, 'The So-called Yahwist and the Literary Gap between Genesis and Exodus', in T.B. Dozeman and K.

23:20-33 envisages the locals 'disappearing' or 'vanishing' (23:23, כחד (hiphil)) rather than being subject to חרם, and Lev 20:22-26 envisages the land 'vomiting' (קיא) people out who defile it, be that Israelites or others (Lev 18:25, 28 and 20:22).[44] In other words, here חרם has 'literary' rather than 'literal' existence, being only one of three portraits of how Israel took possession of the land, and a retrojection into the past in the textual world. The commands of Deut 7:1-26 (cf. 20:16-18) are a later retrojection that is 'fulfilled' in Joshua, but in the prototypical past. Indeed, Josh 23-24, which draw, in some sense, the ongoing charge to Israel into the world of the reader do not mention חרם or the destruction of the property of others—only of one's own idols, although separation from 'the

---

Schmid (eds.), *A Farewell to the Yahwist? The Composition of the Pentateuch in Recent European Interpretation* (SBL Symposium 34; Atlanta: SBL, 2006) 29-50, esp. 49.

[44] I suspect that the Deuteronom(ist)ic tradition re-tells other traditions by using חרם as a retrospective interpretative category (Deut 2-3, cf. Num 21:21ff; Deut 7, cf. Exod 23:20-33; 34:10-14 and Num 33:50-56; see e.g. Fishbane, *Biblical Interpretation,* 200-203 for the dependency of Deut 7 on Exod 23:20-33). However, whilst Driver, for example, had ascribed 23:20-33 to E / R[JE] (*Exodus,* xxvi-xxvii) it has become increasingly common to ascribe Exod 23:20-33 to 'D' (e.g. J.P. Hyatt, *Exodus* (NCB; London: Marshall, Morgan & Scott, 1971), 250, taking Exod 23:20-33 as an RD revision of E), or, more recently to treat it as post-D material that might be dependent upon 'D' (e.g. E. Blum, *Studien zur Komposition des Pentateuch* (BZAW 189; Berlin: Walter de Gruyter, 1990), 377, taking Exod 23:20-33 as presupposing DtrG and K_D) rather than material upon which Deut 7 drew. John Van Seters offers a summary of the debate on the history of Exod 23:20-33 and its relationship to Deut 7 in the process of formulating his own proposal that Exod 23:20-33 is dependent on Deut 7 and is to be ascribed to J, whom Van Seters dates late (*A Law Book for the Diaspora: Revision in the Study of the Covenant Code* (Oxford: OUP, 2003), 67-81). See also H. Ausloos, 'Deuteronom(ist)ic Elements in Exod 23,20-33? Some Methodological Remarks', in M. Vervenne (ed), *Studies in the Book of Exodus: Redaction—Reception—Interpretation* (BETL 126; Leuven: Leuven UP, 1996), 481-500; H. Ausloos, 'Exod 23,20-33 and the "War of YHWH"', in *Biblica* 80.4 (1999): 555-63, and H. Ausloos, 'The "Angel of YHWH" in Exod. xxiii 20-33 and Judg. ii 1-5. A Clue to the "Deuteronom(ist)ic" Puzzle?', in *VT* 58.1 (2008): 1-12. Ausloos draws attention to some of the difficulties in too readily attributing Deuteronom(ist)ic influence to Exod 23:20-33 ('Deuteronom(ist)ic Elements') and concludes in another essay, 'The comparison of Exod 23 with the (Deuteronomistic) scheme of YHWH-war ... is not truly indicative of the dependence of Exod 23 on Deuteronomistic literature. On the contrary, the language that seems to be connected with the "war of YHWH" rather suggests that the author(s) of Exod 23 has/have made use of a terminology that was peculiar to a tradition about YHWH as warrior, which probably has been used by the author(s) of the (Deuteronomistic) scheme as well.' ('Exod 23,20-33 and the "War of YHWH"', 563). Whilst my suspicion is that Deut 7 *is* dependent on Exod 23:20-33, as this is not a claim that I need to make (although it might make my argument look more attractive), then owing to the complexities of the debate as it currently stands I shall refrain from arguing for any particular position here.

locals' is commanded. The only remaining text in Deuteronomy that mentions חרם not in the context of the prototypical time of the conquest is Deut 13:13-19 (Heb), a text that we have already considered as a 'limit-situation' that rhetorically exhorts the avoidance of idolatry, and is a text in which חרם is self-directed against Israel.

In summary, literal חרם only exists in the textual world; it is 'never now', even if the symbol has a second-order sense that relates to life 'here and now' in a sense that I shall now develop, relating to the avoidance of idolatry and the worship of other gods, at least in Deuteronomy. Crucially though, I shall argue later in chapter 9 that it has a rather different significance in Joshua, even though it builds upon this sense in Deuteronomy.

The significance of חרם — *its symbolic sense in Deuteronomy*

The 'literal' practice of חרם only exists in the textual world, and then in the distant past or in the distant future, and 'never now'. Indeed, even in Deut 7:1-5, the injunctions not to intermarry or to make covenants with the local inhabitants (7:2b-3) suggests that the חרם injunction of 7:2a was not understood as a command to actually practice total annihilation. It would seem then that for Deut 7:1-5 the enactment of the text that was envisaged related more to radical separation rather than annihilation, with 7:2b-3 giving content to how חרם was to be enacted. Is this borne out elsewhere?

Turning to Josh 23-24, these chapters construe Israel's ongoing task in terms of being careful to obey the law (23:6); not to associate with the nations who remain in the land (23:7); not to serve other gods (23:7); to love YHWH (23:11), and not to intermarry (23:12). If Israel obeys this charge, then YHWH will continue to drive the other nations out (23:13). What is noteworthy is that there is no call for Israel to engage in fighting of any kind, nor indeed to destroy the idols and altars of the surviving nations. There is only a call for Israel to throw away *her own* idols (24:14 and 23). The only remaining injunction from Deut 7:1-5 with regard to the surviving nations is the command not to intermarry. Thus it would appear that the way in which the חרם injunctions in Deuteronomy are to find existential significance and be enacted according to Josh 23-24, and thus for the task of Deut 7:1-5 to be completed,[45] is via separation, negatively, and obedience to the law, positively. Josh 23-24 thus provides us with an interpretation of or 'homily' on Deut 7:1-5.

So Josh 23-24, however it relates diachronically in compositional terms to the remainder of Joshua, can be regarded as a theological commentary on Joshua and the 'deuteronomistic-חרם' of Deut 7:1-5. But is it a *faithful* commentary and testimony to חרם? It is not the only material that provides clues to the significance of the 'deuteronomistic-חרם'. Indeed, I would like to consider the use of

---

[45] Since Josh 23-24 imply that the task is incomplete.

the terms בדל (separation) and קיא (vomit) in the Priestly materials. בדל is used in the sense of the setting apart of Israel from the nations, and for distinguishing clean from unclean in Lev 20:22-26,[46] where קיא (vomiting) is the term used for the expulsion of people from the land who defile it, be that Israelites or others (Lev 18:25, 28 and 20:22) who are 'sent out' by YHWH (שׁלח, Lev 20:23) in order to allow Israel to posses (ירשׁ, 20:24) the land. This is summarised in Lev 20:26—'You shall be holy to me; for I the LORD am holy, and I have separated (בדל) you from the other peoples to be mine.' (NRSV)

Comparing Lev 20 with Deut 7, where the possession of the land is achieved via חרם, it appears that the Deuteronomist and the Priestly writer draw upon different symbols to portray the 'clearing of space' in the land for Israel, and her 'separation' from others and their evil practices.[47] The Priestly writer uses the symbol of vomiting to portray a somewhat inexplicable disappearance of 'outsiders', whilst the Deuteronomist uses a symbol relating to annihilation that perhaps offers a more 'realistic' account of the disappearance of outsiders. Moreover, the Deuteronomist uses the single symbol of חרם whilst the Priestly writer uses the symbol קיא along with the category בדל. Both symbols (חרם and קיא) interpret Israel's possession of land, but each symbol evokes a different affectual aspect—a feeling of sickness toward the detestable practices of the locals and their effects for the Priestly writer, and a sense of conflict, annihilation, and a call to action for the Deuteronomist. In other words the Priestly writer affectually describes the effect of evil and those who practice it (picture vomit), whereas the Deuteronomist affectually describes how the removal of evil is to be effected (picture radical annihilation). So, for P the affectual concern is to make you feel sick about idolatry, whilst for D it is to make you want to wipe it out, with it being a struggle to do so, with this struggle being construed using concepts relating to annihilation. Moreover, the use of קיא in relation to both Israelite and outsider who practice evil in Leviticus is mirrored by the use of חרם in relation to the annihilation of idolatry both in outsiders (Deut 7) and in Israelites (Deut 13). In other words then, there is a sense in which symbolically קיא maps on to חרם.

However, the second-order sense of both symbols (חרם and קיא) is בדל (separation), as demonstrated in Ezra; it seems that both symbols had become problematic or 'tired', and thus the second-order sense of the symbols (בדל) is made explicit here, where Ezra draws upon the ideas of Lev 20 and Deut 7. In Ezra 6:21 בדל refers to Israel separating herself from the unclean practices of the gentiles; in 9:1 it refers to a failure to separate from the detestable practices of the stereotypical 'anti-elect' nations, and similarly in 10:11 where a note

---

[46] It is also a refrain in Gen 1 (1:4, 6, 7, 14, 18), the Priestly creation account, indicating its importance as a Priestly concept.

[47] Likewise, as noted above, Exod 23:20-33 offers another perspective—the locals will simply כחד (hiphil)—vanish?

about foreign wives is added. Ezra 9:1 and 10:11 are particularly interesting, for 9:1ff appears to have Deut 7:1ff in mind, where חרם is now interpreted as בדל. Thus the association of separation with חרם is clear, reflecting the neglected Akkadian root *ḫarāmu*, with the idea of separation developing the 'second-order' sense of חרם, the sense that is of existential significance regarding its use in Deuteronomy. It is בדל that expresses the significance of the Deuteronomic conception of חרם in the Priestly (and Priestly influenced) materials.[48]

Summary

חרם in Deuteronomy shapes attitudes toward idols - avoid idols and separate yourself from anything that is likely to lead to idolatry, with the symbol perhaps evoking a sense of conflict in the struggle to do so. Josh 23-24 do, therefore, provide a fitting and faithful portrait of how חרם is to be enacted, making explicit what it means to obey Deut 7. But in neo-structuralist perspective deuteronomistic-חרם, in the 'world of the text' of Deuteronomy, can be viewed as constructing Israel's identity by denying the possibility of mediation between Israel and the local peoples. Any attempt to 'mediate' between categories results in annihilation or death, symbolizing expulsion from the community. Josh 23-24 indicates then how this 'non-mediation' is to be enacted in practice, i.e. through separation, especially in the avoidance of intermarriage, and the avoidance of idolatry (as per Deut 7:2b-3). Or, to view it from another perspective, there is no mediation possible between the covenantal relationship with YHWH and attachment to idols.

But does Josh 1-12 simply portray the fulfilment of Deut 7, and of the wider Pentateuchal promises of the land, when, for example, so much narrative space is devoted to the sparing of Rahab, a Canaanite prostitute, and to the execution of Achan, an Israelite from the tribe of Judah? We must now turn to the text of Joshua to consider this question. I shall argue that whilst in one sense Joshua *does* portray the fulfilment of Deut 7, and of the promise of the land to the Patriarchs, its literary use of חרם is in fact far more subtle and searching, being used symbolically to pose probing questions concerning Israel's identity and self understanding, *qualifying* some of the assumptions of Deuteronomy—in particular, how the boundaries of the community are to be defined, and thus the practice of separation.

---

[48] Moreover, it is interesting that Origen construes the חרם of Jericho (or rather ἀνάθεμα as he would have read it in the Greek) in terms of separation—the church should be separate from the ἀνάθεμα of worldly ways—they should not be introduced into the church (*Hom. Josh.* 7.4, pp.78-9).

Conclusion

In conclusion, I have sought to 'clear the ground' of misconceptions of חרם, and the kind of material that we are dealing with so that we may 'hear' Joshua in a sense that is fitting to the text as an act of discourse, from which a plenitude of interpretations may arise that will use the text well.

I have argued that there are different conceptions of חרם in the Old Testament. First, it may be divided into Priestly and non-Priestly usage. In its non-Priestly sense it only has 'literal' existence in the textual world in a prototypical past or eschatological future. It is 'never now', even if it evokes an enactment of its symbolic (or rhetorical) sense in the 'here and now'. Thus the non-Priestly conception of חרם may be divided into uses in Deuteronomistic and prophetic senses. In its Deuteronomistic sense the symbol is used to evoke separation of Israel from idolatrous non-Israel. However, I shall go on to show that even its Deuteronomistic usage and significance may be divided into what might be termed a properly *Deuteronomic* sense (as expressed in Deut 7:1-5) and a strictly *Deuteronomistic* sense as expressed in Josh 1-12 (and 1 Sam 15), a sense which utilizes the Deuteronomic conception of חרם so as to qualify it, in the book of Joshua at least.[49]

---

[49] In a sense the conception is the same, but the *use* of the concept in literary and symbolic terms is significantly different.

SECTION III

READING JOSHUA

Having laid the groundwork for the Christian appropriation of Joshua, we may finally turn to such appropriation. In chapter 7 I consider the fundamental yet difficult question of the actual text of Joshua to be used. In chapter 8 I develop a reading of Joshua as discourse, within the horizons of its context in the Old Testament, in order to consider what it might mean to appropriate it in a 'fitting' way. I also give consideration here to the way in which Joshua *has* been interpreted in the Christian tradition, before in chapter 9 developing a constructive account of how Joshua might be read as Christian Scripture today.

7. THE TEXT OF JOSHUA

Clearly it is important to address the question of which textual witness to the book of Joshua is to be preferred for its use as Christian Scripture. When Joshua is read from the perspective of myth, this question is more complex than seeking to discover the earliest witness to the text, a notion that is problematic in itself in any case, because the use of the category of myth introduces the importance of the idea of the development and use of a text—a later version of a text might be a preferable version to use in the shaping of the identity of a community.

Differences in the Textual Witnesses to Joshua

The difficulties associated with the text of Joshua are vast. Space permits only a brief sketch of the issues, although, as I have indicated, the issues posed for a 'mythical' reading are rather different from those normally posed by textual criticism. There are many differences between the extant textual witnesses to Joshua, most notably between the LXX versions and the MT, but also between these and the fragmentary texts of Joshua discovered at Qumran (4QJosh^a (4Q47),[1] 4QJosh^b (4Q48)[2] and XJoshua[3]), which are the most ancient textual witnesses to Joshua.[4] There are a number of studies on the text,[5] and commentators often discuss the differences between the versions with a view to seeking the 'earliest recoverable text'. Only the more recent commentaries have the

---

[1] Preserving Josh 8:34-35, 5:2-7; 6:5-10; 7:12-17; 8:13-14, 18(?); 10:2-5, 8-11; See E. Ulrich, '4QJosh^a', in E. Ulrich, *et al.*, (eds.), *Qumran Cave 4.IX. Deuteronomy, Joshua, Judges, Kings* (*DJD* 14) (Oxford: Clarendon, 1995), 143-52.

[2] Preserving Josh 2:11-12; 3:15-4:3; 17:1-5, 11-15; See E. Tov, '4QJosh^b', in *DJD* 14, 153-60.

[3] Preserving fragments of Josh 1:9-12 and 2:4-15; See J. Charlesworth, 'XJoshua', in J. Charlesworth, *et al.*, (eds.), *Miscellaneous Texts from the Judean Desert* (*DJD* 38; Oxford: Clarendon, 2000), 231-9.

[4] See M.N. Van der Meer, *Formation and Reformulation: The Redaction of the Book of Joshua in the Light of the Oldest Textual Witnesses* (Leiden: Brill, 2004), 93-114.

[5] Most notably those of M.L. Margolis, (*The Book of Joshua in Greek According to the Critically Restored Text with an Apparatus Containing the Variants of the Principal Recensions and of the Individual Witnesses* (Paris: Librairie Orientaliste Paul Geuthner, 1931-1938), Part 5 (Philadelphia: Annenberg Research Institute, 1992)), A.G. Auld, (*Joshua Retold: Synoptic Perspectives* (Edinburgh: T&T Clark, 1998)), K. De Troyer, (*Rewriting the Sacred Text: What the Old Greek Texts tell us about the Literary Growth of the Bible* (Atlanta: SBL, 2003), esp. 29-58), and Van der Meer, *Formation*.

benefit of access to the Qumran witnesses, published in 1992 and 2000 (XJoshua).⁶ Whilst there are numerous minor differences amongst the witnesses, there are several major differences, with the LXX generally witnessing to a considerably shorter text than the MT. I shall now consider some of the more significant differences.

The OG of Josh 2:14 reads, 'The men said to her, "Our life in exchange for yours [pl]!" She said, "When Yahweh gives you the city, deal loyally and faithfully with me." whilst the MT reads, 'The men said to her, "Our life in exchange for yours [pl]! If you [pl] do not tell this business of ours, when Yahweh gives us the land we will deal loyally and faithfully with you [sg]."'⁷ Here, Nelson suggests that the differences reflect a concern for secrecy in the MT relative to the OG, with the OG demonstrating a misreading of an earlier text that changes the speaker to Rahab for the second statement. If Nelson is correct, as well as a possible misreading of an earlier text in the OG, the differences are explained by a differing emphasis in the OG, with it being a deliberate 'retelling' of the story.

Josh 5 is perhaps one of the most notable differences between the three sets of witnesses. There are significant differences in 5:2-6 between the OG and the MT. The OG mentions two groups with reference to the circumcision that takes place; those born in the wilderness and those who left Egypt uncircumcised. The emphasis is on those 'born on the way' and thus Nelson detects a concern with 'new beginnings' reflected in the text of the OG, contrasting the two generations. But he argues that the MT modifies v.2-9 from an earlier text, witnessed to in the OG, to improve its 'logic and orthodoxy', carefully specifying that all men of war had perished in the wilderness, and insisting that all Israel had been circumcised at the exodus. Moreover, linking Passover with eating the harvest does not occur in the OG, with the link made only in the MT. The MT additions in v.10-12 seek to enhance the Passover's orthodoxy. Careful distinction of the days is made, with unleavened bread being eaten on the day after Passover, reflecting Lev 23:5-6 'and other P texts'. He suggests that eating unleavened bread originally had nothing to do with the ritual eating of unleavened bread, with it being co-ordinated through textual expansion in the MT. Rather than being cultic, eating the unleavened bread here originally marked the transition in to the new land.⁸ However, Van der Meer offers a different analysis, arguing that the MT preserves an earlier text with the OG reflecting a heavily interpretative translation of a Hebrew text similar to the MT to transform the story into a more plausible account of the events whilst exhibiting 'a concern for the individual responsibility for the disobedient behaviour of [the] older generation, and thus for the innocence of the Israelites of the younger generation'.⁹ Whichever

---

⁶ The most helpful commentary in this regard is that of R.D. Nelson, *Joshua* (OTL; Louisville: WJKP, 1997) (even though he does not have access to XJoshua) in which a translation of the MT is provided alongside a translation of the 'earliest recoverable text' based on the OG.
⁷ Nelson, *Joshua*, 39.
⁸ Ibid., 75-80.
⁹ Van der Meer, *Formation*, 408-15.

reconstruction is correct, one may see that the text was used and developed according to particular concerns—either to improve the orthodoxy of the text or to emphasize the innocence of the new generation.

Also notable is the difference in Josh 5 between 4QJosh^a, the OG and the MT, for the account of the altar building (8:30-35 in the MT) occurs, with minor differences, after 9:2 in the OG, and before 5:2 in 4QJosh^a. Nelson suggests that the OG would connect the 'kings' reaction immediately to the story of Ai', whereas 4QJosh^a emphasizes the fulfillment of Deut 27, with the command to construct the altar being fulfilled *as soon as* Israel had crossed the Jordan. He concludes that 'this unit is manifestly disconnected from its context whichever of the three possible locations one chooses.'[10] Perhaps the MT emphasizes 'all systems go' after the ambiguities and difficulties in relation to Rahab, Achan, Jericho and Ai. The placement of the pericopae in 4QJosh^a, whilst emphasizing the fulfillment of Deut 27, also draws torah together with circumcision and Passover here, being three 'pillars' of Israelite identity, into this momentous occasion of crossing into the land, emphasizing the nature of Israel's identity, marked, moreover, by the construction of an altar.[11] Thus from a 'mythical perspective', one sees how different emphases are given to different aspects of the story in different ways of telling and using it.

There are many places where the OG is shorter, but where, although details are omitted, the gist of the text remains the same, even if different emphases may emerge. Nelson, for example, suggests that much of 6:3b-6, as well as some of 6:7-15 (MT) reflect additions to an earlier text represented by the OG. The processional aspects are less explicit in the earlier text. Thus the MT appears to reflect an emphasizing of ritual procession over the OG.[12] Likewise, the MT of 8:9-17 is longer than the OG and 4QJosh^a, and although the narrative may be 'rough and confused' as Nelson suggests, the overall gist of the story is similar in each account (that Joshua leads a successful ambush attack on Ai), although Joshua's role is more prominent in the MT.[13] Nelson prefers the thesis that the OG reflects an earlier text than the MT, with the MT an expansion of the OG, whilst Van der Meer views the OG as a condensed and simplified version of the story as found in the MT.[14]

Another sort of difference between the textual witnesses is demonstrated in Josh 10. Josh 10:15, 'Then Joshua returned and all Israel with him, to camp at Gilgal' (and similarly 10:43) appear to reflect MT additions. De Troyer comments, 'The Old Greek is a witness to a pre-Masoretic text of Joshua, in which

---

[10] Nelson, *Joshua*, 117.

[11] See chapter 8.

[12] Ibid., 83-5.

[13] Ibid., 110.

[14] Van der Meer, *Formation*, 476-8. He suggests that tensions arise in the MT owing to DtrH additions to a pre-DtrH account, tensions that the OG seeks to resolve. See also E. Tov, 'Midrash-type Exegesis in the LXX of Joshua', in *Revue Biblique* 85 (1978): 50-61 for discussion of ways of understanding the significance of the differences between the MT and LXX.

Gilgal did not play an important role. The place Gilgal, however, became crucial during the second century B.C.E., so it was imported into the Hebrew story of Joshua.'[15] Again, these additions are a further reflection of the 'mythical character' of Joshua, in that Joshua developed to meet the needs and circumstances of the community that used it so as to be a relevant, imaginative cultural resource to help the community shape and interpret its present life; it is a living rather than inert text. Such use witnesses to Joshua's ongoing significance in shaping the life of Israel.

However, in the account of the settlement of the land by the Danites, in 19:47-48 the OG offers a longer text in which Judah captures Leshem (LXX^A, or Lachish (LXX^B)) following the failure of the Danites to expel the Amorites. Nelson prefers the MT as a witness to an earlier text.[16] Likewise, the account of Joshua's death in 24:29-33 (MT) is longer in the OG, although again Nelson favours the MT as reflecting an earlier text, arguing that the OG seeks to coordinate the story with the continuation of the national story in Judges.[17] Moreover, the OG locates Joshua's farewell speech at Shiloh rather than Shechem (24:1) 'in order to harmonize with 18:1 and with the presence of the tabernacle at Shiloh (22:12, 29) to which a Greek plus in v.25 alludes'.[18] However, he suggests 'harmonization' occurs in a different direction in the account of the cities of refuge (20:3-6), in which the MT considerably expands the OG in order to coordinate the text with Num 35:25 and Deut 19:1-13.[19]

This brief sketch of some of the main differences between the different textual witnesses indicates the major difficulties associated with the text of Joshua. Whilst Nelson *tends* to prefer to view the OG as a witness to an earlier text than the MT in favour of the hypothesis that the OG shortened texts to give them greater coherence,[20] one sees, through Van der Meer's analysis that, as Auld notes, cautions remain in assuming that the LXX is a 'crown witness for an originally shorter Hebrew text'.[21] Indeed, it is not clear that the OG witnesses to a different, earlier text than the MT (or vice versa), since differences may be the result of deliberate changes to the text that reflect different emphases concerning the *use* of the text. In mythical terms, such development can be viewed as the crystallization of what the community sees as being (perhaps latently) implied in an earlier text, or an attempt to improve and clarify it. Alternatively, some developments in the text might reflect 'confusions' that distort the text, such as the likely additions of Josh 6:19 and 24 that reflect a Priestly conception of חרם that skews the text, but nonetheless reflects the use of the text in a new context.

---

[15] De Troyer, *Rewriting*, 30. She expands on this, arguing that Modein, the 'headquarters' of the Maccabean revolt became a 'quasi-Gilgal', signifying a new beginning for Israel (57-8).
[16] Nelson, *Joshua*, 225-6.
[17] Ibid., 280-3.
[18] Ibid., 264.
[19] Ibid., 227.
[20] Ibid., 110.
[21] Auld, *Joshua*, 145.

Or, some changes can be more 'imposed' on the text to 'force' its relevance in a particular context, again demonstrating the importance of 'use'. In other words, the whole process of Joshua's transmission is associated with redaction and use as much as with copying and preservation, and so, especially from a mythical perspective, the quest for an 'earliest recoverable text' appears misguided, since it fails to account for the text's use and development—and with texts composed from various sources, where does one locate the 'original' in any case? So perhaps the problem is that of determining the 'best' version of the text to use; additions to a text might 'improve' it by clarifying and developing it, or they might skew or distort it. The problem is one of deciding which reasonably 'stable' or 'mature' version of the text ought to be preferred.[22] But perhaps the notion of a 'best' version is also problematic. If different versions arose in different contexts to suit different needs, then perhaps the interpreter ought to seek not a 'best' version, but to consider what constitutes various 'fitting' versions of the text and how they might each be illuminative.

The Significance of the Choice of Text for Christian Reading

Should one prefer essentially the Hebrew or the Greek text as Christian Scripture, given that the Old Testament was often read and quoted in the New Testament and in the early church in the Greek? If, as argued in chapters 2-3 reception and use are important and contribute to the 'normativity' of the use of a text in shaping a community, then arguably the Christian interpreter could, or even should, read the Old Testament in the Greek versions, as the Orthodox church does. However, this introduces a difficulty beyond that of 'text', for it raises the question of transformation of meaning in translation. Of particular importance here is the translation of חרם, for it is rendered as ἀνάθεμα in the Greek of Josh 6:17, which is a crucial interpretative move that sets up all sorts of resonances and allusions that are not present in the Hebrew.[23] For example, one might expect the use of ἀνάθεμα in Gal 3:13 (citing Deut 21:23, applied to the crucifixion) to set up a resonance with its use in Joshua in the Greek, which (returning to Hebrew) might serve as the basis for a typology in which חרם could be said to be 'fulfilled' in Jesus on the cross, in that he takes the 'חרם of the world' onto himself,[24] perhaps reflecting a 'substitutionary' understanding of the crucifixion. But it is interesting that there is no evidence of that sort of move being made in the early Christian tradition, despite the common imaginative use made of similar typology. This observation might suggest that there was little interest in

---

[22] This idea is similar but not identical to that of the 'final form'.

[23] A similar problem occurs with translating חרם into English. Rendering it as 'destroy' shifts the meaning of the term, for Hebrew has other words for destroy (e.g. שמד) distinct from חרם.

[24] Cf. R.S. Hess: 'Christ takes upon himself the sin of the world and becomes the victim of the holy war that God wages against sin (2 Cor 5:21).' (*Joshua* (TOTC; Leicester: IVP, 1996), 46).

interpreting the crucifixion using the category of 'substitutionary atonement' within the early church.[25]

However, whilst the Greek versions of the Old Testament shaped the early church, the MT has generally been favoured by Christian scholars over the last few centuries, and thus has been the privileged version for translations of the Bible into the vernacular, and thus the version of the text that has most shaped the contemporary church. So in terms of reception and use both the OG and MT versions have certain claims to normativity. But as noted in chapter 3 the job of interpretation is worked out in the dialectic between the significance of the text as 'original' act of discourse and later significance and usage of the text, and thus if the original pole is to be favoured, then the earliest recoverable text would be favoured.

Summary

The difficulties with the text of Joshua, and the choice of text for use, are, at one level, immense. Even though space prevents detailed discussion of the variations in the versions, it is not clear which version ought to be favoured in any case—an earlier 'original' form or a later 'improvement'. I shall take the pragmatic decision to favour the MT, largely on the basis of its general privileging today. But, at another level, as we have seen, whilst there are numerous differences between the textual witnesses, in most cases they represent changes in emphasis rather than gist, and so in most cases the concern is an academic historical one, and not a concern for the Christian who wishes to 'use' the text as Scripture.

---

[25] Indeed, there appears to be little interest in the concept of 'justification' in this period, an exception being Origen's commentary on Romans in which he understands justification to occur through what might be termed the 'willed afflictions' of the Christian as they participate in Christ's suffering which 'occurs by dying to sin, and, if necessary, dying as a witness of Christ'. (K.D. Hall, 'Afflicted for Love: Willed Affliction and Salvation in Origen's Commentary on Romans', paper given at the Durham Patristics Seminar, 7th February 2008).

8. READING JOSHUA

In this chapter I shall read the book of Joshua 'chapter by chapter' providing something of a commentary (although not a full one) on the text and provide some examples of how it has been interpreted in the tradition, in a somewhat descriptive fashion. Then in chapter 9, I shall develop the question of what it might mean to read Joshua as Christian Scripture today in a more constructive sense, drawing all the threads of the discussion together.

Joshua 1

Josh 1 provides a summary, and perhaps theological interpretation, of Joshua as a whole, comprising four speeches (vv.2-9, 10-11, 12-15 and 16-18) that centre on crossing, conquest, allocation of land, and obedience to law. It reflects a number of quotations from or allusions to Deuteronomy (e.g. Deut 7:24; 11:24-25 and 17:18-19),[1] suggesting that Joshua interprets and is to be interpreted by Deuteronomy. Moreover, Brevard Childs suggests that Josh 1, 12 and 23 reflect the shaping of Joshua's final form and provide a framework that offers an 'elaborate and highly reflective theological interpretation of the conquest of the land'.[2] Josh 1 also provides continuity with Israel's story thus far as narrated in the Pentateuch, and so read canonically Joshua becomes a part of the narrated history of Israel. It also 'legitimates' the book, being set in an important prototypical time with the voices of YHWH, Moses and Joshua appearing to coalesce.[3]

---

[1] R.D. Nelson, *Joshua* (OTL; Louisville: Westminster John Knox Press, 1997), 28-9.

[2] B.S. Childs, *Introduction to the Old Testament as Scripture* (Philadelphia: Fortress Press, 1979), 244. More recently see E.A. Knauf, *Josua* (Zürcher Bibelkommentare AT 6; Theologischer Verlag Zürich, 2008), 16-22 for discussion of the redactional history of the book. Knauf suggests that Josh 1 and 23 form parts of two distinct late redactions. But as I indicated in chapter 4, I am not concerned with seeking to trace 'redactional layers'; rather, I am concerned with how (or whether or not) material such as Josh 1 provides a good or fitting interpretation and 'commentary' of the book, and with how it might guide interpretation of the material, whether it is a later addition or not.

[3] Cf. L.D. Hawk, *Joshua* (Berit Olam; Collegeville: The Liturgical Press, 2000), 6; R. Polzin, *Moses and the Deuteronomist: A Literary Study of the Deuteronomistic History* (New York: Seabury Press, 1980), 75.

However, there are themes that one might expect to find here, but do not. Particularly significant is the *absence* of חרם and of any other term such as שמד that might imply that genocide or destruction is central to the book. If Josh 1 does provide a theological summary of the book, then the absence of חרם here is striking, which might suggest that Joshua is not really 'about' conquest at all. Moreover, another significant absence, both here and elsewhere in Joshua, is any reference to the sinfulness of the nations that are to be driven out. The Canaanites, etc. are not mentioned here. Nowhere does Joshua seek to explain or justify the extermination of the Canaanites because of their sinfulness, *unlike* Deuteronomy (e.g. Deut 9:4-5).[4] Whilst their sinfulness may be implied from the cultural context, the absence of reference to it here is significant, again suggesting that Joshua is not trying to justify conquest. But does Josh 1 reflect a faithful and fitting 'commentary' on the book, whether it is a later addition or not? I shall argue that it does.

The unexpected absences of these themes in Josh 1 are complemented by what might seem to be unexpected transformations of military exhortation language. Michael Fishbane suggests that encased in the military exhortation formula (1:5-9) is a piece of 'aggadic theologizing' where Joshua is said to be strong and courageous *in obeying torah*, reflecting the transformation of physical prowess into spiritual fortitude, generating a new emphasis on the ideology of torah. Victory becomes conditional upon obedience to torah, and conquest is transformed from something inevitable and assured, based on ancient promises, into an event dependent upon faithfulness to covenant, reflecting the Deuteronomist's theology of history.[5] So one might say that we find here in the composition of the book itself a 'spiritualizing' move already which might be suggestive of the sort of frame of reference within which the book ought to be read if it is to be read well.

Moreover, the rhetoric of promise is synthesized with that of obedience, setting up a fruitful dialectic that enables human and divine faithfulness to be explored. The struggles and pain associated with warfare become metaphors for obeying the law, providing affectual, existential contours that evoke the challenges of torah obedience. But these struggles and concerns with obedience are held in tension with promise. Indeed, as well as an emphasis on obedience, a major theme here is the *gift* of the land, with √נתן occurring eight times in Josh 1. This gift represents fundamental confessional language throughout the book (2:9, 14, 24; 5:6; 8:1; 9:24; 18:3; 22:4; 23:13, 15-16; 24:13),[6] being important

---

[4] Apart, perhaps from Josh 11:19. Cf. E.F. Davis, 'Critical Traditioning: Seeking an Inner Biblical Hermeneutic', in *ATR* 82.4 (2000): 733-51.
[5] M. Fishbane, *Biblical Interpretation in Ancient Israel* (Oxford: Clarendon, corrected ed. 1986), 384-8.
[6] Nelson, *Joshua*, 31.

for understanding Israel's perception of her relationship to the land and of her relationship with YHWH.

But the special quality of life in the land given by YHWH is נוח, 'rest', (1:13 and 15), which represents the consummation of Joshua's career (Josh 21:44, 22:4; 23:1).[7] Butler suggests that

> נוח, "rest," is the new word of promise in this section. The term has a variety of contexts within the OT. The cult speaks of "divine deliverance" to the individual as bringing rest (Ps. 116:7; 23:2; Jer. 45:3; Job 3:13, 26; cf. Exod. 33:14). It also speaks of the cult as the place of divine resting (Ps. 132:8, 14; 1 Chr. 28:2; cf. the earlier ark tradition of Num. 10:33, 36; contrast the later prophecy Isa. 66:1). The early Sabbath commandments spoke of human rest (Exod. 23:12; cf. Deut. 5:14), which the priests reinterpreted to speak of divine rest (Exod. 20:11; cf. Gen. 2:2-4, שבת) The term appears also to have roots in early legal language (2 Sam. 14:17).
>
> Isaiah used the term to apply to the life God desired for his people, who rejected it (28:12). Prophecy then eschatologized the term (Isa. 14:3, 7; 11:20; 32:18; cf. Dan. 12:13). Prophetic schools also used the term to speak of the gift of the divine spirit (Num. 11:25-26; 2 Kgs. 2:15), a usage that also became eschatologized (Isa. 11:2; 63:14; Zech. 6:8).
>
> The Deuteronomistic school took up the term so widely used to speak of peace and rest from the problems of life and gave it a specific theological meaning: rest from war and enemies (Deut. 3:20; 12:9-10; 25:19). Our passage takes precisely this line from Deut. 3:20 and points it a step forward to its eventual realization (Josh. 21:44; 22:4; 23:1).
>
> ... Rest, not war, is the ultimate goal of Israel for the Deuteronomist. But he sees the dialectic that rest could be won only through war.[8]

These are important comments, reflecting the *desire* that Joshua expresses, when Joshua is read from the kind of psychological perspective discussed in chapter 2. In other words, they might be said to reflect a latent eschatological character to the book, which again helps to set the sort of frame of reference that is appropriate for reading the book—ultimately Joshua is not concerned with conquest, but with finding rest in peaceful covenantal life with YHWH.

Another *Leitwort* in Josh 1 which resounds throughout the book is עבר, used here in the sense of crossing the Jordan.[9] But boundaries, and their crossing, will be important throughout Joshua, with the Jordan crossing being the parade symbolic example. Indeed, Israel begins her journey by crossing the Jordan. But the 'Jordan valley not only constitutes a boundary but also a defining symbol and a point of reference. Traversing it signifies Israel's entry into the measure of

---

[7] Ibid., 31.
[8] T.C. Butler, *Joshua* (WBC 7; Waco: Word Books, 1983), 21-2.
[9] עבר occurs here in 1:2, 11 (twice), 14 (twice) and 15, and eighty-one times in Joshua.

life YHWH gives.'[10] We will see how this theme of crossing into (or out of) life with YHWH is recapitulated throughout Joshua. But for now, we may observe the symbolic character of the land, where the land symbolizes Israel's life with YHWH, and that crossing into the land (Israel) *symbolizes* crossing into this life in its fullness (as the fulfilment of promise). This symbolism is reinforced by the attention given to the Transjordan tribes (1:12-18). Here, they affirm Joshua's authority and respond in the most positive way possible (something that the other tribes are not reported as doing), indicating that they are indeed 'crossing into' the fullness of life with YHWH, even if not the land.[11]

Finally, the repeated use of כל (all/every)[12] is indicative of this fullness and completeness in all its aspects; of complete obedience to torah, of complete possession of the land, and of the unity of all Israel.

Attention to these themes is suggestive of the kind of existential significance of Joshua developed in section I. Butler's comments indicate that the idea of rest already has an eschatological trajectory, and is thus, perhaps, capable of construal in traditional Christian categories, finding continued significance in a Christian context. From the kind of 'mythical perspective' developed in section I, the idea of finding rest in 'life in the land' may find continuing significance, construed as symbolic of life in the eschaton, or of life in the 'kingdom of God' to use a New Testament idiom. If, as we shall see, Joshua may be understood in terms of what it means to possess the land and live in the land in the fullness of life that YHWH gives so as to move toward 'rest', then it suggests that in the Christian context Joshua *might* be understood to relate to what it means to live so as to move to possess or inherit the 'kingdom of God', an idea that will need further exploration.

Such attention to the symbolism makes Calvin's comments on the Promised Land intelligible,[13] as it does Origen's homily on the text, which illustrates the existential development of some of the themes identified above in the new Christian context:

> [W]e understand the promise to us from our Lord Jesus that "every place we set the soles of our feet" will be ours. But let us not imagine that we may be able to enter into this inheritance yawning and drowsy, through ease and negligence. The wrath of his own race possesses the angel [Lucifer]. Unless you vanquish this [wrath] in yourself and cut off all violent impulses of anger and rage, you

---

[10] Hawk, *Joshua*, 15.

[11] Cf. ibid., 15.

[12] Occurring fourteen times in Josh 1.

[13] *Inst.* II.11.1, pp.450-51, cf. chapter 2. It is interesting that Calvin develops this typology of the land in his *Institutes,* but not in his commentary on Joshua. Perhaps this indicates a tension between Calvin's appropriation of the tradition of interpretation which he has received and his own exegetical preferences, possibly reflecting a division that will become problematic for the theological interpretation of Scripture in the modern era.

will not be able to claim as an inheritance the place that angel once had. For you will not expel him from the land of promise by your slothfulness. In like manner, some angels incite pride, jealousy, greed and lust and instigate these evil things. Unless you gain the mastery over their vices in yourself and exterminate them from your land—which now through the grace of baptism has been sanctified—you will not receive the fullness of the promised inheritance.[14]

Origen's homily may be construed not as an exegesis of the text as such, even though it *is* a development of themes found in the text, but as an imaginative exploration of the significance of the symbolism in a new context as a *development* of the original act of discourse. Origen uses the idea of conquest as 'struggle' to affectually intimate something of the nature of the Christian life, and how this relates to Christians taking possession of their inheritance, perhaps reflecting a 'new myth' that might be revelatory in its own right. Whilst reading the text in a rather different way,[15] Calvin's comments on the text are not too far removed from Origen's:

> From this passage ... let us learn that we can never be fit for executing difficult and arduous matters unless we exert our utmost endeavours, both because our abilities are weak, and Satan rudely assails us, and there is nothing we are more inclined to than to relax our efforts. But, as many exert their strength to no purpose in making erroneous or desultory attempts, it is added as a true source of fortitude that Joshua shall make it his constant study to observe the Law. By this we are taught that the only way in which we can become truly invincible is by striving to yield a faithful obedience to God. Otherwise it were better to lie indolent and effeminate than to be hurried on by headlong audacity.[16]

In a sense then, traditional readings manifest what it is in the original act of discourse that can be developed, in an imaginative existential manner, to find enduring significance in a Christian context.

Joshua 2

Josh 2 is cast as a spy story, reflecting a common biblical motif relating to preparation for conquest (Num 13:1-33; Deut 1:22ff; Josh 7:2ff; Judg 1:23ff; 18:2ff). But is it really a spy story? The spies do no reconnaissance, and they do

---

[14] *Hom. Josh.* 1.6, p.34.

[15] I.e., I think that Origen reads the text within a 'spiritualizing' (or perhaps 'allegorizing') frame of reference whilst Calvin appears to wish to develop the 'literal sense' of the text in what seems to be more of a 'moralizing' direction, showing concern with 'the Law' for example, even if he also introduces Satan. But it is interesting that the two forms of interpretation appear to converge in terms of the practical implications drawn from the text.

[16] J. Calvin, *Commentaries on the Book of Joshua* (Grand Rapids: Eerdmans, ET: 1949), 30-31.

not return with any strategically useful information, and they are not criticised for this. Something else is going on. In addition to recalling the 'failed' mission of Num 13, via the note that spies are sent from Shittim and go immediately to a prostitute's house, Num 25 is evoked (in which Israelites staying at Shittim engaged in sexual activity with the Moabite women, who then led the Israelites into worshipping other gods, resulting in disaster). This would seem to lead the reader to expect disaster following the upbeat start of Josh 1. Indeed, the spies went and entered the house of a prostitute named Rahab and slept or lay there (Josh 2:1).[17] Recent commentators detect sexual innuendo here with the use of the verb שכב,[18] and allusions to Numbers are reinforced through the prostitute's name, Rahab, since the spies in Num 13:21 went as far as Rehob. The possibility of innuendo is further strengthened through the name Rahab, since *rhb* is used in Ugaritic epic to refer to female genitals.[19]

Having set the reader up to expect disaster, the story takes a new twist, losing interest in questions of sex, but with a further expectation of disaster introduced by the king sending messengers to Rahab. But then the story unfolds rather unexpectedly. Rahab hides the spies, lies to the king's messengers, and lowers the spies to safety outside the city whilst instructing them how to avoid capture. But crucially, in doing so, Rahab recounts significant events in Israel's story and makes the spies swear an oath to spare her.

Two major theological difficulties identified by commentators are the questions of how Rahab's deception is to be viewed, and of how the agreement she makes with the spies is understood in relation to the חרם injunction of Deut

---

[17] וילכו ויבאו בית־אשה זונה ושמה רחב וישכבו־שמה

[18] E.g. Hawk, *Joshua*, 40; J.F.D. Creach, *Joshua* (Interpretation; Louisville: John Knox Press, 2003), 32; Nelson, *Joshua*, 43.

[19] Creach, *Joshua*, 32. Moreover F.A. Spina suggests that the scarlet cord evokes erotic and sexual imagery, being a sign of prostitution (*The Faith of the Outsider: Exclusion and Inclusion in the Biblical Story* (Grand Rapids: Eerdmans, 2005), 62). However Hawk thinks the 'reddish colour at the window recalls the Israelite deliverance from death in Egypt (Ex. 12:1-32)' (*Joshua,* 49) whilst Creach finds the virtuous wife of Prov 31:10-31 (esp. 31:13, 21) evoked here (*Joshua*, 38-9). Let the reader decide! Moreover, in two 'crusade sermons' of the thirteenth century, one by James of Vitry and another by Gilbert of Tournai Josh 2 is interpreted through Ps 77:54 in the Vulgate. Ps 77:54 in the Vulgate reads: *et induxit eos in montem sanctificationis suae montem quem adquisivit dextera eius et eiecit a facie eorum gentes et sorte divisit eis terram in funiculo distributionis*. This reading derives from the LXX Ps 77:55 which reads ἐκληροδότησεν αὐτοὺς ἐν σχοινίῳ κληροδοσίας for the MT (Ps 78:55) ויפילם בחבל נחלה, taking חבל as cord or line rather than territory. In other words, it was through Rahab's cord that YHWH distributed the land to Israel, with Israel's hopes literally hanging by a thread here. I am not aware of this interesting and imaginative interpretative move having been made elsewhere. For the text of the sermons see C.T. Maier, *Crusade Propaganda and Ideology: Model Sermons for Preaching the Cross* (Cambridge: CUP, 2000), 103, 189.

7:1-5. Interestingly, the first difficulty seems to be more of an issue for earlier writers such as Augustine[20] and Calvin,[21] with the second being more an issue for more recent commentators. There is no explicit evaluation given on either point, through the narrator, or Joshua, or YHWH. Moreover, the resolution of the story is postponed until Josh 6 whilst one wonders what will happen; will Rahab be saved? Is the oath a violation of *torah* that will result in the premature end of the 'conquest'? The reader is left in suspense. However, even in Josh 6 no explicit evaluation of Rahab's status, or description of her future, is provided.

For now I would like to consider Rahab's characterization and character. Rahab is presented as the paradigmatic outsider—a Canaanite prostitute living in Jericho. The reader expects her to be trouble. But as the story unfolds one sees that appearances are deceptive. As Frank Spina observes, Rahab is certain that YHWH has given Israel the land, demonstrating trust in YHWH, and he observes that the phrase used by Rahab in 2:11,

כי יהוה אלהיכם הוא אלהים בשמים ממעל ועל־הארץ מתחת

is only used elsewhere by Moses (Deut 4:39) and Solomon (1 Kgs 8:23), placing her in the most esteemed company; her 'confession' is, arguably, better than Joshua's,[22] and she recites and interprets the major events of Israel's recent past. Moreover, the way she deals with the spies is interpreted using the fundamental covenant characteristic of חסד, and she appeals to the חסד that she has shown as the basis for her hope (2:12). Indeed

כי־עשׂיתי עמכם חסד

(lit. 'because I have 'done *ḥesed*' with you) evokes a number of texts,[23] and perhaps particularly significantly

ועשׂה חסד לאלפים לאהבי

(Deut 5:10; Exod 20:6) granted its context in the Decalogue. חסד is that which characterizes the way that YHWH deals with Israel, and occurs in the command relating to avoiding idolatry, something that is surely a concern in relation to Rahab. Likewise חסד characterizes YHWH in the foundational Exod 34:6-7, being the basis of Israel's hope, and חסד is also identified in Micah 6:8 as one of the three characteristics that are, taken together, what it essentially is that YHWH requires of the Israelite. Thus Rahab, despite appearing to be the paradigmatic outsider, actually manifests precisely that which characterizes the

---

[20] *Against Lying* 15.31-32, in *ACCS,* 10.
[21] *Joshua,* 46-8.
[22] Spina, *Faith,* 57-61.
[23] Interestingly it occurs in Genesis in ways that also indicate that 'outsiders' sometimes 'do better' than 'insiders'; e.g. in relation to Abraham and Abimelech (20:13, where Abraham seems to 'misuse' חסד, 21:23 whereas Abimelech grasps it).

centre of Israel's identity and existence. She displays the characteristics, both in terms of action and 'confession', of precisely that which is to characterize the 'insider', the 'model Israelite'. But it is interesting that her act of deception (also an act of courage perhaps), and her act of hiding the spies, are together interpreted as an act of חסד. This suggests that her action is to be construed positively, perhaps unlike in much Christian interpretation that has, through 'new myths', been preoccupied with other concerns (lying as violating an eternal moral law) that are in fact alien to the story, even if they are concerns that might naturally arise. So provisionally one might say that perhaps the 'tension' here that the interpreter works in draws the interpreter toward privileging the original act of discourse, rather than its later development, if the text is to be read well.

Moreover, חסד is a term that occurs in Deut 7:12 in the context of YHWH keeping his covenant according to what he שבע (swore) to the ancestors, another term important in Josh 2 (2:12, 17, 20). But it is Deut 7:1-5 that provides the חרם injunction, describing what Israel must do when they enter the land, and here in Josh 2 it is Rahab who uses the term for the first time in Joshua (2:10), which indeed is the only mention of the word until Joshua uses it in 6:17. In other words the reader is now disorientated and bewildered; all the locals were to be exterminated according to Deut 7 (or so it seems), but here is a local who, despite (very worrying) appearances, acts in every way like the best Israelite. Ironically, Rahab herself raises the question of Deut 7. Thus the story of Rahab may reflect a demanding test case of the interpretation of Deut 7.[24] Should the spies have sworn an oath to save her? What will happen to her? We must wait until Josh 6 to find out.

Joshua 3-4

The space devoted to the Jordan crossing, with its repetitive, slow narration imbues it with significance. Perhaps the mode of narration encourages the reader to imaginatively enter the experience and marvel at how YHWH brought Israel through the Jordan and into the land, and thus to reflect on what this signifies. Josh 3-4 narrates how YHWH powerfully brought a unified Israel from the 'liminal' wilderness across a boundary into the land. This miraculous crossing results in fear leading to discouragement for the Canaanites, etc., and fear leading to obedience (4:24), together with encouragement (3:10), for the Israelites. It also results in Joshua's exaltation (3:7; 4:14). The narrative 'looks back' to the exodus sea crossing to interpret the significance of the events (4:23), and 'looks ahead' to future generations of Israel with memorials (e.g. 4:20).

The ark is introduced for the first time in Joshua and it plays a prominent role here. Creach notes that

---

[24] Cf. Polzin, *Moses*, 87.

The portrait of the ark and its impact seems to include something from virtually every Old Testament voice. The ark is known by the familiar label "ark of the covenant" (3:6, 8, 14; 4:9), which is the favorite language of the Deuteronomic tradition; it is also called "ark of the testimony" (4:16), a title that derives from Priestly circles. The effect of the ark upon the waters of Jordan is similar to the portrayal in stories that understand the object as the invisible throne of God that scatters Israel's enemies (Num. 10:35-36) and accounts of the ark striking people dead with its supernatural energy (1 Sam. 6:19). The recognition of Levitical priests as bearers of the ark and the order for the people to remain at a distance from it (3:3-4) resemble the Chronicler's view that the Levites had exclusive responsibility for carrying the sacred chest (1 Chron. 15:2). Most significant is the fact that some of the traditions that give rise to these descriptions and portraits of the ark disagree as to the significance of the object. This point has been classically expressed as follows: some circles saw the ark as representative of the presence of God (2 Sam. 6:2), while the Deuteronomic tradition downplayed its importance and spoke of it as a container for the Ten Commandments (Deut. 10:1-5).[25]

Moreover, given the importance of 'rest' in Joshua (cf. Josh 1), the ark's role in Num 10:33 understood in terms of leading the people to a place of rest

וארון ברית־יהוה נסע לפניהם דרך שלשת ימים לתור להם מנוחה

is probably significant,[26] highlighting the importance of the theme for Joshua. Thus whilst this story probably has a complicated history in which both Priestly and Deuteronomistic elements are present in relation to the ark, the fusion of portraits reflects testimony to the fusion of the Priestly and Deuteronomistic traditions that we discussed in chapter 4. Thus one is encouraged to see the powerful presence of YHWH here reflected in the ark, being associated with the covenant and obedience to the Decalogue. It is, perhaps, the more Priestly images that dominate here, indicating the 'real presence' of YHWH among Israel, leading and guiding, present in the midst of the crossing of an insurmountable boundary.[27]

That the Jordan crossing represents the crossing of an important boundary is emphasized by the very dense use of עבר (twenty-two times in forty-one verses), marking the transition of a wandering people into a people with land, a land flowing with milk and honey, representing a change of status. As in Josh 1, national unity is stressed, demonstrated in the twelve-stone memorial (4:1-3, 8, 20) with the half-tribes explicitly included (4:12). But the significance of עבר is illustrated in Deut 29:11 and 30:18, and the reception and development of these texts in the Community Rule, 1QS, which uses עבר to describe 'crossing into'

---

[25] Creach, *Joshua*, 48.
[26] נוח occurs here in Josh 3:13; 4:3, 8, possibly indicating the use of a *Leitwort*.
[27] See also G.W. Coats, 'The Ark of the Covenant in Joshua: A probe into the history of a tradition', in *Hebrew Annual Review* 9 (1985): 137-57.

the covenant, identified with 'crossing' into the community. Indeed, 1QS i.16f reads, 'All who enter the order of the community shall cross (עבר) into the covenant in God's presence and do all that he commanded' and W.H. Brownlee notes that the community rule contains a 'liturgy' that enacts this crossing, a 'crossing ceremony' that is associated with lustration (1QS ii.25-iii.12),[28] and suggests that

> The fact that [Deuteronomy] 29:11 indicates the intention of "crossing into the sworn covenant" and 30:18 speaks of "crossing the Jordan" may have led the people of Qumrân to equate the two uses of the verb *'ābar*. Symbolically one was also passing over into the land which God had promised the patriarchs by covenant. This suits the military character of the procession as depicted in the Community Rule, making of the event an annual memorial of the Conquest.[29]

Moreover, he notes that the instructions for the order of the procession in the ceremony (1QS ii.19-25) evoke the instructions for the procession in Joshua. So the 'crossing' ceremony in the community is a form of 're-enactment' of the Jordan crossing in a new context, inspired by Joshua. In other words the community uses Joshua to (imaginatively) shape and interpret its existence, with Josh 3-4 symbolizing 'crossing into new life', something developed in Josh 5.

The crossing of the Jordan has a clear 'typological' link with the exodus sea crossing, understood as a mighty act of liberation testifying to YHWH's power (e.g. Exod 14:15-18; 15:1-21), and forms an interpretative lens through which to read the Jordan crossing (cf. Josh 4:23).[30] If the exodus crossing is to be interpreted as a redemptive act via creation themes, with YHWH 'creating' a people for himself in the deliverance at the sea,[31] then one may interpret the Jordan crossing as symbolizing another instance of YHWH's creative action. If life in the Promised Land represents life in all its fullness for Israel, where Israel may enter into rest with YHWH, then the crossing of the Jordan reflects the creation of and entrance into this new life. Indeed, it is significant that elsewhere the Jordan is not presented as a barrier to crossing into the land (cf. Gen 32:11; Josh 2:7; 22:19, 24-25; Judg 3:28; 8:4; 10:9; 12:5; 2 Sam 17:22),[32] which accentuates

---

[28] W.H. Brownlee, 'The Ceremony of Crossing the Jordan in the Annual Covenanting at Qumran', in W.C. Delsman, *et al.*, (eds.), *Von Kanaan bis Kerala: Festschrift für Prof. Mag. Dr. Dr. J.P.M. Van der Ploeg O.P. zur Vollendung des siebzigsten Lebensjahres am 4. Juli 1979* (Verlag Butzon & Bercker, 1982), 295-302, here 297-8.

[29] Ibid., 300.

[30] Cf. Fishbane, *Biblical Interpretation*, 350-63.

[31] See T.E. Fretheim, *Exodus* (Interpretation; Louisville: John Knox Press, 1991), 158ff; J.D. Levenson, *Creation and the Persistence of Evil* (Princeton: Princeton UP, 1988), 75-7.

[32] Cf. Nelson, *Joshua*, 59 and D. Jobling, "The Jordan as a Boundary': Transjordan in Israel's Ideological Geography', in *The Sense of Biblical Narrative: Structural Analyses in the Hebrew Bible II* (JSOTSup 39; Sheffield: JSOT Press, 1986), 88-134, here 125-6.

the symbolic nature of the mode of crossing here and its 'mythical' nature in both the traditional sense and the other senses developed in chapter 2. So Nelson suggests that the miraculous Jordan crossing is symbolic, ideological and confessional in significance (Josh 24:11; Ps 66:6; Micah 6:4-5).[33]

However, the narrative also interprets the symbol of crossing the Jordan as a witness to the power of YHWH to the peoples of the ארץ (earth/land)[34], and to Israel, so that they might 'fear' YHWH (4:24), which is probably to be construed in terms of obeying YHWH:[35]

למען דעת כל־עמי הארץ את־יד יהוה כי חזקה היא
למען יראתם את־יהוה אלהיכם כל־הימים

Furthermore, the crossing event is also interpreted in terms of encouragement for Israel, so that Israel would know that the 'living God' is amongst them, and that he will drive out the Canaanites, etc. (3:9-13). But Josh 3:7 (cf. 4:14) gives another interpretation of the water crossing; that Joshua would be exalted, and so that he, and Israel, would know that YHWH was with Joshua just as he was with Moses, thus legitmating Joshua. The narrative presents the events relating to the crossing as נפלאות (3:5), which, portraying the action of YHWH, by its very nature provides a rich, polyvalent symbol.[36]

Confessionally, when existentially appropriated the event provides a way of speaking of what YHWH has done 'for us/me'.[37] And this seems to be reflected in Ps 66 where YHWH's נורא עלילה 'awesome deed(s)' (v.5), such as the sea crossing (v.6)[38] are used as the grammar of discourse for the psalmist to interpret and reflect upon 'what God has done *for me*' (v.16). This symbol of sea / river crossing provides the means by which one may praise God for the way that he acts in *my* life. So from the perspective of cultural memory, such symbols provide a rich cultural resource that forms a grammar of discourse for the description of the experience of God, and for talk about God. Indeed, Walter Brueggemann begins his Old Testament theology at essentially this point, in a confessional mode—'*the beginning point for articulating an Old Testament*

---

[33] Nelson, *Joshua*, 9-60.

[34] ארץ might be taken either way. Possibly it referred to the Promised Land alone in its original context, but in light of the development of the idea that YHWH is lord of all the earth it reads naturally as a witness to all the earth in a later context.

[35] See R.W.L. Moberly, *The Bible, Theology and Faith* (Cambridge Studies in Christian Doctrine) (Cambridge: CUP, 2000), 80-97 for a discussion of the idiom of fearing YHWH.

[36] It is interesting that the narrative describes the 'event' of crossing in terms of the plural נפלאות.

[37] Whatever historical events do or do not lie behind the narrative; cf. the discussion of testimony in chapter 3.

[38] I think that Ps 66:6 refers to the exodus however.

theology is in the liturgical, public acknowledgement of a new reality wrought by Yahweh in the life of the speaker and in the community of the speaker.'[39]

Combining the imaginative use of symbols such as the Jordan Crossing to describe and confess what God has done 'for us/me', the observation that this crossing is related to entrance into life in its fullness, a life that brings rest, then given the presence of water it is not surprising that Christian interpreters have used this passage in relation to baptism. An interesting discussion of the traditional Christian interpretation of the Jordan crossing is found in Daniélou's discussion of Gregory of Nyssa's mystical writings:

> Gregory's doctrine on Baptism makes use of the various Biblical types, especially the crossing of the Red Sea. In another image which he uses we find the River Jordan considered as one of the rivers of Paradise, and this symbolism stresses the idea of rebirth—Baptism is thus represented as a return to the Garden of Eden. The entrance into the baptistery means that "the Garden of Paradise and, indeed, heaven itself is once again accessible to man" and that "the sword of flame no longer prevents his approach." ...
>
> Again, the Jordan is considered as a figure of Baptism in the traditional way, as for example, by reference to the cure of Naaman the leper, or to the entrance of the Jews into the Promised Land.
>
>> Cross the Jordan, [he says,] hasten towards the new life in Christ, to the land that bears fruit in happiness, flowing with milk and honey according to the promise. Overthrow Jericho, your former way of life! ... All these things are figures of the reality which is now made manifest. [*Against those who put off Baptism* (*PG* 46.421A)]
>
> But what is original with Gregory is the linking of the Jordan with the Garden of Eden. Taking up an idea which seems to have been first developed by the Gnostics, Gregory contrasts the rivers that flow down from Paradise with the Jordan, which flows back to heaven and has its source in Christ.
>
>> Hurry to my Jordan, not at the call of John, but at the command of Christ. For the river of grace does not rise in Palestine and flow into the nearby sea, but flows everywhere, circling the entire world, and empties into Paradise. For it flows in a different direction from those four streams which flow from Eden and bears a cargo much more precious than that which was borne out by them. ... For it brings back those who have been reborn by the Spirit. [*Against those who put off Baptism* (*PG* 46.420C)]
>
> The true Jordan that covers the entire world is the water of Baptism, consecrated by the Baptism of Christ, and it grows into an immense stream which carries men back to Paradise.[40]

---

[39] W.A. Brueggemann, *Theology of The Old Testament: Testimony, Dispute, Advocacy* (Minneapolis: Fortress Press, 1997), 126-8. Cf. also Fishbane's comments on the exodus-conquest 'typology' discussed earlier.

This kind of association is, perhaps, a development of what we find at Qumran. Indeed, Brownlee suggests that

> John's baptisms in the Jordan may also owe something to Qumrân. He was awaiting there the coming of a messiah, one mightier than he, who would judge as with fire all moral vipers and usher in the Kingdom of God. His insistence that the rite of baptism meant nothing except as people brought forth fruits worthy of repentance agrees precisely with the emphasis of 1QS iii,3-12, which declares that apart from an inner, spiritual cleansing, one remains a moral leper, to be called 'unclean, unclean". Like the Essenes, John was "preparing the way of the Lord in the wilderness". ... Crossing of the Jordan was also reminiscent of crossing the Red Sea (Josh. 4:23f.; Pss. 66:6; 114:3, 5). Hence baptism in the Jordan could suggest baptism in the Sea (I Cor. 10:2).[41]

Indeed, 'crossing the Jordan' symbolizes 'crossing' into the covenant or community or 'crossing into life',[42] as we saw above, and so the Christian development of the symbol is natural. Moreover, perhaps the interesting association that Gregory of Nyssa makes with Eden is reflective of an impulse to recognize the act of crossing the Jordan as being associated with ideas of creation in some sense, as we saw above.

Perhaps one reason why (Christian) allegorical or typological interpretation such as Gregory's has come to be seen as problematic is that it often seeks to present itself as being *the* 'real metaphysical meaning' of a text or event, being in some sense an 'exegesis' of it, which here might evacuate the original story of Joshua of significance in its own right.[43] However, a 'mythical approach' as outlined in chapter 2 does not make this move. Rather, used 'as myth' the Jordan crossing functions as a symbol whose significance in the story can be recaptured imaginatively in later contexts to interpret future instances of God's action in bringing into life. To evoke the image is to evoke all this power of God as wondrously acting. God's continual action of recreating people into communities that anticipates life in its fullness 'resting' with God continues to testify to the story of the Jordan crossing, with the Jordan crossing being an imaginatively rich, symbolic way of describing and imagining such action. This is simply the continuation of the interpretative process that Joshua represents, where Joshua

---

[40] J. Daniélou, *From Glory to Glory: Texts from Gregory of Nyssa's mystical writings* (London: John Murray, ET:1962), 19-21.

[41] Brownlee, 'Ceremony', 302.

[42] 'Crossing the Jordan' is an important motif in John's gospel (cf. John 1:28; 3:26 and 10:40), but I argue elsewhere ('"Bethany beyond the Jordan": The Significance of a Johannine Motif', in *NTS* 55.3 (2009): 279-94) that John in fact inverts the traditional symbol so that life in Christ is found by crossing *out of* the land.

[43] Cf. J.D. Dawson, *Christian Figural Reading and the Fashioning of Identity* (Berkeley: University of California Press, 2002) for a recent discussion of various modes of typological, allegorical and figural reading.

re-uses the exodus crossing in an imaginative way to say something similar but new about God's action amid his people in a new context, namely the entrance to the land in the world of the narrative. Perhaps the Jordan crossing might be described as a 'limit-situation' symbolically reflecting, toward the extreme, how one might construe divine action in the world and talk about it imaginatively.

However, the kind of Christian reading just outlined will need development so that the reader is drawn more fully into the world that the book portrays, i.e. to see what the fullness of life that is entered into looks like. Joshua is concerned with a number of aspects of this, as I shall go on to develop. Indeed, perhaps a weakness of traditional Christian readings of the Jordan crossing is that the crossing has been interpreted 'atomistically' and somewhat independently of its narrative context, a context that gives content to something of what is envisaged in the nature of the new life of the community being entered.

Finally however, a more recent example of this imaginative interpretation worked out in a 'performative' context is the final verse of William Williams Pantycelyn's 'Guide me, O thou great Redeemer':

When I tread the verge of Jordan,
Bid my anxious fears subside;
Death of Death, and hell's Destruction
Land me safe on Canaan's side:
Songs of praises I will ever give to thee.

Joshua 5:1-12

Josh 5 continues the story of Israel's journey into the land. There is further development in the locals' response as in Josh 2, where their hearts are said to melt in fear. The crossing of the Jordan is alluded to, reflecting the development of 4:24. Interestingly, there is, once again, no חרם here. This, coupled with the observation that Josh 5 is concerned with circumcision, Passover and eating from the land suggests that concerns of conquest are not really in view here. Josh 5 starts to indicate what 'new life' for Israel will look like and what is central to its construction, with the continued use of עבר inviting further reflection on this 'crossing' into new life, and the creation of a new people, or at least of a people with a new mode of life.[44]

Circumcision follows immediately from the crossing and symbolically confirms this transformation, reflecting the fulfilment of the ancestral promises, and emphasizes the centrality of circumcision in the construction of Israel's identity. YHWH is faithful in bringing the people into the land, and Israel is

---

[44] Placing the ceremony of 8:30-35 (MT) here in 4QJosh[a] (cf. chapter 7) makes good sense, for it draws the importance of torah into the construction of Israel's identity at this key prototypical moment.

faithful in an act that expresses the devotion of their ancestors. Moreover, the repetition of יצא (five times) to designate the previous generation contrasts with the current generation of those who have עבר (crossed) into the land.[45]

There are exegetical difficulties in Josh 5:1-12 that are related to the significant textual problems here. For example, commentators continue to discuss the question of what the 'disgrace of Egypt' refers to, the most likely candidates being a reference to slavery in Egypt or a failure to circumcise the exodus generation.[46] However, it does seem that the MT represents a redaction of an earlier text that is reflected in the OG, a redaction that was designed to improve the 'logic and orthodoxy' of the passage, both here and in relation to the Passover, as briefly discussed in chapter 7. But as I noted in chapter 7, the original version need not be the preferred version, and so there are numerous difficulties here that relate to the questions both of which version of the text is to be preferred for Christian use, and of the exegesis of the text. All I wish to claim is that the circumcision and Passover (and torah if we take 4QJosh[a]'s placement of 8:30-35 (MT) here) are significant 'pillars' upon which the new life of Israel in the land are to be founded. Continuity with Genesis-Exodus is demonstrated as well as the foundation of Israel's identity and existence in the new land, in a new phase of Israel's life, as a unified people seeking to 'rest' with YHWH. For this reason, I am inclined to think that 4QJosh[a]'s placement of 8:30-35 is the preferred location on the basis of a sensitivity to what Joshua is seeking to achieve here, whether or not this is the original location for the pericopae.[47]

However, Josh 5:1-12 is concerned specifically with the content of the new life of *Israel*, particularly as it is symbolized and expressed in its more ceremonial aspects, and thus one might not expect to find much Christian significance at the narrative level here, for Israel's identity is constructed here in elements expressive of the Old Covenant that are expressly modified and developed (Passover) or even abandoned, or at least very sharply reinterpreted (circumcision) in the New.[48]

---

[45] Hawk, *Joshua*, 77-80. There are a number of word-plays here, as elsewhere in Joshua. The root עבר is 'played with' in vv.10-12 where we find בערב, בערבות and מעבור ('in the evening', 'on the plains' and 'produce').

[46] See e.g. Nelson, *Joshua*, 76. How one understands this depends partly upon how one construes the history of the text.

[47] Cf. A. Rofé who notes that both 'the Mishna and Tosephta establish that the rites mentioned in Josh. 8:30-35 were performed immediately after the crossing of the Jordan [*M. Soṭah* 7.5; *t. Soṭah* 8.7].' ('The Editing of the Book of Joshua in the light of 4QJosh[a]', in G.J. Brooke (ed.), *New Qumran Texts and Studies: Proceedings of the first Meeting of the International Organization for Qumran Studies, Paris, 1992* (Leiden: E.J. Brill, 1994), 73-80, here 79).

[48] Indeed, the significance of the Passover is developed in a Christian context, but it is difficult to relate this directly to the *narrative* here, other than to say that the Last Supper is in a sense foundational to Christian identity in the way that Passover is to Israelite

One aspect of the story as it relates to the kind of fullness of life that is to be entered into here does find enduring significance for both Christian and Jewish communities—that of God's provision of food, and the way that one is invited to interpret it. The word אכל 'eat' is pivotal, used three times here, and Nelson suggests that here to eat the yield of Canaan is to claim the land; Israel does not have to wait for the completion of the conquest, for the gifts of the land are already available.[49] Brueggemann notes that

> The food does not need to appear surprisingly. It rises up from the land as gift. … The old land that Israel remembered so well, the land of slavery, even of banishment, was land by effort. And it was therefore precarious, requiring effort and attention. It was *demanding* land. The new land, the land given beyond the Jordan, the land of restoration, is land by graciousness.[50]

Thus Josh 5:10-12 makes the association explicit between YHWH's gracious, miraculous provision of manna, and his provision of food in the land. The only difference is the method by which he provides in each case, encouraging one to view food harvested from the land as a gift given through divine action, just like manna. Moreover, אכל is an important term in Lev 26 in the context of rewards for Israel for obedience and punishment for disobedience. Perhaps in Lev 26 the nature of Israel's eating symbolizes the nature of reward or punishment. Thus food, and eating, is symbolic in relation to the covenant. Thus the 'eating' of Josh 5 reflects a symbolic foundation of Israel's covenantal life, indicating blessed existence with YHWH in the land, as Israel 'rests' with YHWH through life in the covenant.[51]

Origen develops the issue of food in a slightly different direction. He suggests that

> Three kinds of food … are described. The first one we certainly enjoy when going out of the land of Egypt … Manna follows after this. But the third fruit we receive now from the holy land. … But, placed in the desert, that is, the condition of life in which we now are, we enjoy the manna only through what we learn by the instructions of the divine law.[52]

---

identity. This is the way that the story does find significance in the Christian tradition. But Origen does develop the narrative, noting that circumcision occurs before Passover, implying that nobody unclean may celebrate the Passover, which he then interprets in terms of receiving communion (*Hom. Josh.* 6.1, p.68).

[49] Nelson, *Joshua*, 78-80.

[50] W. Brueggemann, *The Land: Place as Gift, Promise and Challenge in Biblical Faith* (Overtures to Biblical Theology; Minneapolis: Fortress Press, 2nd ed. 2002), 47-48.

[51] For further reflection on the importance of food and land see E.F. Davis, *Scripture, Culture, and Agriculture: An Agrarian Reading of the Bible* (Cambridge: CUP, 2009).

[52] *Hom. Josh.* 6.1, p.69.

Thus Origen uses the exodus-wilderness-conquest cycle as a map for the Christian life, existentially interpreting the earthly Christian life as life in the wilderness, a life in which one is taught through divine instruction. What is interesting is that this sort of reading reflects a sensitivity to the idea of liminality that we briefly considered in chapter 2 through Victor Turner's work, and is something that I shall now develop. Together with the crossing of the Jordan as something of a recapitulation of the exodus crossing, the cessation of the manna upon the harvest from the land creates a certain symmetry of the 'conquest' with the exodus. Israel's life in the wilderness is now over as she enters the land, with a new status. Read canonically the exodus and 'conquest' reflect a transition, rather like a 'rite of passage', but of a whole community, Israel, from slavery to new life.[53]

The first major study of rites of passage was Arnold Van Gennep's (1909), whose work has been developed by Victor Turner. Van Gennep argued that beneath the diversity of human ritual there was a basic threefold scheme of phases of separation, segregation and incorporation (or pre-liminal, liminal and post-liminal phases). In the first phase (separation), people are separated from their former status and way of life in order to enter the second phase of seclusion during which time truths, values and new commitments are taught, before being incorporated into their new social status in the third phase.[54] Edmund Leach analyzes aspects of the exodus-conquest in terms of this model;[55] the Israelites journey to a land flowing with milk and honey from Egypt, a land of suffering, through the wilderness, a place of potential starvation and death, but a place where God is encountered in extraordinary ways, making it a liminal site. He suggests that

---

[53] See also J. Wagenaar, 'Crossing the Sea of Reeds (Exod 13-14) and the Jordan (Josh 3-4): A Priestly Framework for the Wilderness Wandering', in M. Vervenne (ed), *Studies in the Book of Exodus: Redaction—Reception—Interpretation* (BETL 126; Leuven: Leuven UP, 1996), 461-470 for reflections on these issues from the perspective of redaction history, although he inverts the traditional direction of the typology of the crossings (cf. Fishbane, *Biblical Interpretation*, 358-60). Wagenaar suggests, 'The Priestly writer, like the Yahwist before him, consciously parallels the Exodus from Egypt and the entrance into the promised land. In his perception, however, these events are not primarily a military operation, but part of a complex "rite de passage". Sea and Jordan represent the borders between the desert and the inhabitable land. The crossing of the Sea of Reeds as the counterpart of the crossing of the Jordan is an invention of the Priestly writer. In his view the crossing of the Sea of Reeds and the Jordan mark the beginning and the end of the wilderness wandering. The Priestly writer solemnly frames these events by the rituals of circumcision and Passover.' (470).
[54] D.J. Davies, *Anthropology and Theology* (Oxford: Berg, 2002), 123.
[55] E. Leach, 'Fishing for Men on the Edge of the Wilderness' in R. Alter and F. Kermode, *The Complete Literary Guide to the Bible* (Cambridge: Harvard UP, 1987), 579-99, esp. 584-9.

The prototype Wilderness is provided by the geographic environment of the wanderings in the Book of Exodus. If you are in Egypt, the Wilderness is where you get to if you cross the Red Sea; if you are in the land of Israel, the Wilderness is where you get to if you cross the Jordan. The Wilderness is the Other World. Entering or leaving the Wilderness symbolizes a metaphysical movement from the here and now to the timelessness of the Other or vice versa. ...

In this Other World everything happens in reverse. The heavenly bread falls from the sky like rain; the heavenly water does not fall like rain but emerges from a rock. Perhaps you think this polarity is a structuralist fantasy? On the contrary, the point is noted in the Talmud.

The end of the forty-year period of wandering in the Wilderness presents exactly the same set of motifs but in a different order: in Joshua 3-4 the Israelites cross the Jordan on dry land; in Joshua 5:2-9 there is a renewal of the rite of circumcision, which had been omitted during the wanderings in the Wilderness; at verse 10 the Israelites celebrate the Passover; at verse 12 the daily supply of manna ceases; in Joshua 6 the enemy (in this case the people of Jericho) are destroyed by divine intervention.

This symmetry cannot be accidental. The Wilderness is marked off as altogether Other. It is a world in which ordinary food is not available but in which God's chosen people are sustained with divine bread and divine water. It is a world in which the chosen prophets Moses and Joshua, and to a lesser extent Aaron and Miriam, converse directly with God. It is a world in which the rite of circumcision is not required (apart from the enigmatic exception of Gershom). It is a world with sharply defined water boundaries: the Red Sea on one side, the river Jordan on the other. In order to enter this sacred other world, ordinary people (other than chosen prophets such as Moses and Aaron) need divine intervention by which the water boundaries are made passable. It is a world which includes the mountain of God, Mount Sinai (Horeb), which is itself bounded, a world apart within a world apart (Exod. 19:12, 23-24).

Thus specified, the Wilderness, the Other World of things sacred, is in every respect the exact converse of the profane world that is familiar to ordinary people conducting their ordinary secular affairs.[56]

Thus it is possible to read the exodus-conquest as a 'rite of passage' for Israel, a rite of passage that is reinterpreted in terms of the Christian life in a Christian context, in which Israel (or the Christian) is 'separated' from her former state of slavery in Egypt (life under the power of sin) before being 'reincorporated' into the fullness of life in the land flowing with milk and honey (the goal of the Christian life as consummated divine union perhaps) after being 'segregated' for a period of divine instruction in which 'the law' is given (the Christian life now).

But is this only a Christian reading of the text? If the 'exodus-conquest' cycle portrayed in Exodus and Joshua may indeed be interpreted more existen-

---

[56] Ibid., 586-7.

tially as myth in the ways that I suggest, then perhaps, existentially speaking, the narrative of Exodus-Joshua may be reflective of the expression and desire of a 'rite of passage' for the life of Israel or the Israelite that finds continual appropriation and engagement at any and all times. The move towards rest and the fullness of life with YHWH begins, in the narrative sequence, with the initiatory stage of being freed from a life of slavery and oppression by YHWH's powerful deliverance that finds appropriate human response developed in the service of worship and obedience to YHWH through the covenant, something that one *learns as a process*. Indeed, Israel, and any Israelite, has to go through a process of *learning* the content of torah, and of learning how it is lived, something that is a lifelong, and thus one might say eschatologically orientated, process.[57] Existentially, and taking the narrative synchronically, life in the 'here and now' reflects the liminal phase, as one seeks continually to be freed from bondage and oppression (symbolized by life in Egypt) to progress into ultimate life and rest with YHWH (symbolized by life in the land). In other words, perhaps the Christian 'spiritual' reading such as we find in Origen is by no means an alien imposition of meaning on the Old Testament texts, but a development of what is actually expressed there.

Existentially then, the community, or the reader, is invited to interpret their life as a transition from a state of slavery and bondage into the fullness of life with God, via the wilderness, which is a liminal 'dangerous place', a place which has the quality of two different spheres of existence ('earthly'/'heavenly' perhaps) in which one is detached from one's former way of life and given divine instruction, being 'supernaturally' sustained. It is a place of possibility and transformation, and a powerful symbol for the Christian (and perhaps Jewish) life. In a sense the wilderness, as portrayed in the texts of the Old Testament, might be said to reflect a 'limit-situation', forming the contours for a detachment from the 'everyday' into a world in which the divine is most clearly manifested, and is thus not part of everyday experience as such. But maybe one is invited to interpret the reality of the 'ordinary' through the terms and symbolism of the wilderness, which is perhaps where the reader is to be located existentially. For example, daily provision of food 'in the ordinary' is likened to the provision of manna 'in the extraordinary', in the wilderness, through Josh 5. Life may be interpreted through the wilderness portrait, a portrait in which life is stripped to its barest essentials.

In summary, we see again that an anthropological perspective is able to make traditional Christian use of the text, such as Origen's, intelligible, indicat-

---

[57] Indeed, it is interesting to note that Van Gennep's theory was developed in relation to rites of passage for individuals rather than for societies. But here we may detect a Van Gennep sequence for the community of Israel. So there would appear to be an interesting interplay between the transition of the individual and the community as expressed in the narratives here.

ing that such reading does, in fact, demonstrate a sensitivity towards concerns that surround the text, even if such reading is not 'exegesis' *per se*.

Joshua 5:13-15

Josh 5:13-15 narrates Joshua's encounter with the commander of YHWH's army, a report that Nelson describes as a 'stunted, cryptic narrative [that] seems to break off before any real plot has a chance to develop and twists into a jarring ending that connects only ambiguously with the following story'.[58] Likewise Hawk suggests that it certainly 'halts the forward momentum' of the plot in Joshua, where one has an expectation of a better ending, especially when compared with Exod 3.[59] It is commonly supposed that the original ending of the story has been lost, with the real message of the commander now missing,[60] granted the jarring ending that the story now has. However, it is significant that despite this roughness no attempt has been made to smooth it through redaction, with no textual witness to a longer form. Moreover, even if the narrative had a 'satisfactory ending' that has been lost, the story would, probably, still be rather cryptic granted the nature of the figure appearing to Joshua and the response given to Joshua's question—it is an ambiguous response.

Indeed, there are various difficulties with the interpretation of this account. It is not clear whether to read ביריחו (5:13) as 'in Jericho' or 'near Jericho'.[61] Moreover, it is difficult to know what the significance of the drawn sword is. Other biblical examples would imply a message of judgement or warning (cf. Num 22:21-35; 1 Chr 21:14-16), whereas in the ANE context, in the *Annals of Assurbanipal* for example, Ishtar appears with a drawn sword to give a promise in a battle, and thus the drawn sword functions as a sign of encouragement.[62] This seems to point to an inherent ambiguity that is accentuated through the dialogue between Joshua and the mysterious commander. Joshua asks,

הלנו אתה אם־לצרינו

('Are you for us or for our adversaries?') to which the commander replies,

---

[58] Nelson, *Joshua*, 80.

[59] Hawk, *Joshua*, 83-5. Exod 3 is also assumed to read roughly owing to the history of the text; in particular the sign of 3:12 is difficult (see B.S. Childs, *Exodus* (OTL; London: SCM, 1974), 56-60. Perhaps then there is something that is often ambiguous and elusive about such narratives?

[60] E.g. P.D. Miller, *The Divine Warrior in early Israel* (Harvard Semitic Monographs 5; Cambridge MA: Harvard UP, 1973), 129.

[61] Nelson reads 'by Jericho' (*Joshua*, 73, 80-81) whilst Butler reads 'in Jericho' (*Joshua*, 54).

[62] *ANET*, 451. cf. J. Van Seters, 'Joshua's Campaign of Canaan and Near Eastern Historiography', in *SJOT* 4 (1990): 1-12.

לא כי אני שר־צבא־יהוה עתה באתי

('Neither. For I am the commander of the army of YHWH. Now I have come.')
The phrase שר־צבא־יהוה certainly locates the story in a context of warfare. But the response is unexpected; one would expect to find the commander on Israel's side, or at the very least on one side or the other. So, as Robert Polzin puts it, 'The situation is much more complex than the familiar answer of an authoritarian dogmatism would have it: "God is on our side; we have the promise made to our fathers, and the law given to Moses!" The commander's answer is not so clear cut.'[63] This suggests once again that Joshua is not, in any straightforward sense, simply a story of jingoistic conquest, even if it uses the discourse of conquest

Read in its current form, the encounter might be understood as anticipating the ambiguity of the question of whether 'God is on Israel's side' as a prologue to the stories of Jericho and Ai (and indeed the whole 'conquest'), reflecting the stories of Rahab and Achan. God is neither *straightforwardly* for Israel (i.e., for Israel on Israel's terms) nor *straightforwardly* against her enemies. Rather, as seen in the stories of Rahab and Achan, what matters is alignment with and obedience to YHWH; the right question is to ask whether one is 'for YHWH' or not, and not the other way around. The question that arises for the reader is *not* that of asking whether God is 'on my/our side', or a matter of trying to 'co-opt' God onto 'my/our side', but of asking whether I/we have 'aligned' myself/ourselves with God.

Josh 5:13-15 functions in its present form as an important interpretative key that introduces the material that follows, with the brief story encouraging reflection on three perspectives; one's own, one's adversaries, and God's. Josh 5:13-15 resists the collapsing of these three perspectives into two, which is what so often happens; there is 'us' and 'them', and God is (usually) on 'our' side. The text thus refuses to be co-opted to 'colonial' categories.

Joshua 6

Josh 6, which narrates the fall of Jericho, is an unusual story. There is no other account quite like it in the Old Testament, or in extant ANE texts. The story resolves Rahab's story and introduces Achan's. Indeed, Rahab and Achan are two important, contrasting, symbolic characters whose stories intersect at this symbolic city. Jericho, and its capture, symbolizes the 'conquest' and its nature perhaps. Jericho represents a terrifying, large fortified city (cf. Num 13:28; Deut 9:1ff), which would explain why it is singled out as a symbol. Coogan suggests that Jericho was well fortified from the Neolithic period onwards, with its fortifications being anomalous owing to their grand scale, which may have given

---

[63] Polzin, *Moses*, 112.

rise to a folk-tradition about the city.⁶⁴ In other words, Jericho had a cultural reputation that made it ripe for use as a symbol. Nelson suggests that

> Jericho is unique, however, because it serves as a paradigm for the entire conquest. Not only is Jericho Israel's first conquest, it is the gateway to Canaan, near a natural crossing point (4:19; 2 Sam. 10:5). The language of the Rahab story has already prepared the reader to equate Jericho with the land as a whole (2:1, 2, 9, 14, 18, 24). A second unusual feature is the secondary and unwarlike part played by Israel's fighters until trumpet and shout trigger the attack and slaughter. Israel engages in a symbolic, ritualistic siege of the city. Trumpets are detached from their battle situation (such as Judg. 7:15-22) and take on a liturgical flavor (as, e.g., Ps. 98:6). The war cry (Jer. 20:16) merges into a shout of cultic joy (1 Sam. 4:5-6). The seven-day timetable is of greater importance than maneuvers on the ground (contrast 8:3-22; 10:9-11; 11:7-8). For this reason the narrative problem is not really the size and extent of the enemy forces (as in 10:3-6; 11:1-5), but that Jericho is tightly closed up behind impregnable walls (v.1). Spectacular divine intervention resolves this problem when the wall collapses (literally "falls down in its place").⁶⁵

So whilst Jericho reflects the Israelites' fear that the land is impregnable (cf. Num 13), Josh 6 indicates that the 'conquest' will nonetheless occur, with divine aid, which will make it straightforward for the Israelites. Moreover, Jericho's fall is narrated in ritualistic terms, continuing the ritualistic nature of Josh 3-5 indicating the kind of sphere of significance that the narrative possesses. Indeed, the narrative commences with the cue that God has given (נתן) the city to the Israelites, re-iterated in Joshua's speech (6:16), reflecting Josh 1. The king of Jericho is un-named, enhancing the narrative's symbolic nature, which, coupled with the lack of explicit 'military' detail, and the small amount of narrative space given to reporting destruction and battle suggests that Josh 6 does not *function* as a military 'conquest account'. Indeed, eighty-six words are devoted to Rahab and 102 the destruction of Jericho, showing the importance of Rahab's rescue for this story.⁶⁶

What is the significance of the unusual procession? Fleming suggests that the siege of Jericho is transformed into a ritual procession by the ark and 'with a play on the common idea of siege as encirclement, where fixed encirclement becomes circumambulation (verbs סבב and נקף).'⁶⁷ He goes on to consider Josh

---

⁶⁴ M.D. Coogan, 'Archaeology and Biblical Studies: The Book of Joshua', in W.H. Propp, *et al.*, (eds.), *The Hebrew Bible and its Interpreters* (Winona Lake: Eisenbrauns, 1990), 19-32, here 22.
⁶⁵ Nelson, *Joshua*, 91.
⁶⁶ R.S. Hess, *Joshua* (TOTC; Leicester: IVP, 1996), 133-4.
⁶⁷ D.E. Fleming, 'The Seven-Day Siege of Jericho in Holy War' in R. Chazan, *et al.*, (eds.), *Ki Baruch Hu: Ancient Near Eastern, Biblical and Judaic Studies in honour of Baruch A. Levine* (Winona Lake: Eisenbrauns, 1999), 211-28, here 218.

6 in light of the *Keret Epic* (*KTU* 1.14). In the *Keret Epic* Keret is addressed in a dream by El to set out on a seven day march towards *Udm* (iii.2-10). Upon reaching *Udm*, rather than attacking, the army must remain silent (*dm*) for six days (iii.11-13) in contrast to normal siege procedure (iii.14-15). By the seventh day *Pbl* the king of *Udm* will be unable to sleep (iii.16-20)—a common expression of anxiety. Thus there are two seven-day periods 'to immerse Keret's mission in sacred time. By operating in seven-day intervals, Keret moves in synchronicity with El in heaven.' Fleming notes that although the number seven is widely used at Ugarit, the seven day period in Ugaritic texts 'applies more specifically to activity touching the divine sphere' (e.g. *KTU* 1.4.vi.24-33; 1.17.i.2-16, ii.30-40 and 1.22.i.21-26), and so he suggests that 'Repetition of the period in the Keret episode shows that the seven days ultimately belong not to siege as such but to intervals of activity under divine supervision and power.' Thus Fleming concludes that there is no need to see a hypothetical festival as the basis of the campaign, and hence that, 'In light of Keret, the seven days of the Jericho siege need not be attributed to a re-enacted festival drama but naturally belong to a narration about warfare by divine plan.'[68]

Hawk notes that יובל ('ram's horn', Josh 6:4, 5, 6, 8, 13) occurs elsewhere in the sense of 'ram's horn' only in Exod 19:13 in connection with Sinai, although it occurs elsewhere in the sense of 'Jubilee' (Lev 25; 27; Num 36:4). In Lev 25:8-55 the trumpet sound inaugurates the Jubilee after 'seven sabbaths of years, seven years, seven times' (25:8). But Hawk notes that there is a similar repetition of sevens in Josh 6; march for seven days, and seven times on the seventh day. From an intertextual perspective Josh 6 might then be read in terms of the transfer of property and possession of land as reflected in Lev 25. The Jubilee calls for the return of all land to its rightful owners and provides guidelines for the redemption and release of property (Lev 25:10, 25-34). Indeed, Hawk detects an allusion to the Jubilee here, with the fall of Jericho being like a Jubilee - the land is returned to its owner and Israel is given occupancy (cf. Gen 12:7; 15:18-21; 17:8; Exod 3:8, etc.). Moreover, he notes that YHWH has redeemed Israel from Egypt to become a people of his own possession (Deut. 4:20, cf. 7:8), and that a significant part of the Jubilee legislation concerns the redemption of slaves (Lev 25:39-55), a practice explicitly associated with YHWH bringing Israel out of Egypt and into Canaan.[69] Thus one might interpret the 'conquest' using the concept of Jubilee, and indeed given that Josh 6 follows almost immediately from the 'festal' material in Josh 5, with Josh 6 having its own ritualistic overtones, this has attractions.[70] In other words, the land is not

---

[68] Ibid., 221-3.
[69] Hawk, *Joshua*, 94-5.
[70] If one wishes to claim that this is more than an intertextual reading, then the difficult issue of showing the dependency of Josh 6 on Lev 25 is raised, or at least of the story in Josh 6 on the Jubilee concept in the sort of form that one finds it in Leviticus. But if much

interpreted as being 'stolen'; rather the divine owner of the land is giving occupancy to its rightful grantees.[71]

The חרם command here is extreme; *everything* is to be destroyed. But I suggest that the חרם functions here as a 'limit-situation' that is *required* to serve narrative and structural *requirements* of the story that relate, primarily, to the resolution of Rahab's story and to the introduction of Achan's story and what these stories seek to convey as understood in neo-structuralist terms. Without extreme חרם the stories of Rahab and Achan would not exist as Rahab might have survived the capture of Jericho anyway and Achan might not have committed an offence in taking some plunder. Rather, the extreme חרם enables the narrator to tell these stories, in stylized form that take their inspiration from other stories of conquest, so as to indicate that Israel's identity is, in fact, based upon doing חסד (Rahab), which symbolizes the heart of the covenant, and avoiding חמד (Achan), which symbolizes disobedience to the covenant, as we shall see. Interestingly, it seems that חרם relates only implicitly or secondarily to the annihilation of idolatry, and its sources, and only really when read in terms of Deut 7.

I argued in chapter 6 that Josh 6:19 and 24 were later glosses arising from the development of a more Priestly conception of חרם, glosses that have tended to skew the interpretation of Josh 6-7. Thus in one sense the earlier form of the story (without 6:19 and 24) might be said to have greater theological and 'revelatory' significance. But, in another sense, *once the basic story is understood*, these additions make חרם an increasingly paradoxical or mysterious category by drawing it into the domain of קדש, drawing it as a concept further into the divine sphere perhaps, which serves to distance חרם from the ordinary yet further, making it an increasingly difficult, liminal category.[72]

---

of 6:3-6 does reflect an 'MT revision' of an earlier text (cf. Nelson, *Joshua*, 83-4), then the importance of the sevens is stressed by this revision, perhaps drawing the story into closer proximity with the Jubilee concept in the reception, development and use of the text.

[71] The association with Lev 25 might be strengthened in the light of the association of the ideas in Josh 5 with Lev 26. Prof. E.F. Davis suggested to me that 'Leviticus 26 might be seen as depicting the un-Jubilee, when the connection between Israel's eating and the land is broken.' Indeed, perhaps the references to cities being laid waste here (e.g. 26:31, 33) has resonances with the destruction of Jericho in Josh 6. Taken together, intertextual resonances with Lev 25 and 26 invite a Priestly perspective for reading the story.

[72] So whilst a Priestly perspective for reading Josh 6 is invited through intertextual links with Lev 25 and 26, there are difficulties with reading Josh 6 using a Priestly conceptuality of חרם. This differentiated appeal to Priestly perspectives need not be a problem for the sort of reading that I am proposing for a tradition such as the Priestly tradition is not monolithic. Indeed, I suggested in chapter 6 that the Priestly חרם represented a relatively late development within the Priestly tradition. With regard to חרם, it is its Deuteronom(ist)ic conception that is determinative for good interpretation here.

Whilst Josh 6 supplies the resolution of Rahab's story, the ending retains ambiguity. Rahab and her family are placed *outside* the camp of Israel (6:23), which may simply reflect the need to undergo purification (cf. Deut 23:10-15). But Joshua's speech makes it clear that it is in accordance with *the spies'* oath that Rahab is spared (6:22-23), perhaps implying a distancing of Joshua from the decision to spare her. Joshua's only part is to uphold the oath that *has* been made, presumably reflecting positively on Joshua as one who keeps oaths (cf. Lev 5:4). There is no explicit evaluation supplied, and nothing to indicate that Rahab 'becomes' an Israelite, although the final note (6:25) is slightly more positive; Rahab's family continues to live in the midst of (בקרב) Israel. Moreover, in the light of the significance of נוח in Joshua, being the goal of the campaign, the choice of נוח rather than some other form of expression in relation to Rahab and her family in 6:23 may be significant, suggesting that Rahab and her family found rest just like the rest that Israel sought, rest that she found in the midst of Israel by confessing YHWH's greatness and 'doing חסד'. In other words, the narrator implies in every way that Rahab is, or ought to be, part of 'true Israel', and is characterized as an Israelite, although without saying so explicitly. Perhaps this is left for the reader to decide, suggesting the need for a careful re-reading of Deut 7, and of a conversion of Israel's perception of those such as Rahab.

Finally, after the destruction of Jericho a curse is placed on anyone who tries to rebuild the city. This curse was 'fulfilled' in 1 Kgs 16:34 when Hiel rebuilt Jericho's foundations during Ahab's reign. Curses following city destructions are known elsewhere, for example in the Annals of Tiglath-Pileser I:

> I overwhelmed the city Hunusu, their stronghold, (so that it looked) like a ruin hill (created by) the Deluge.
> Violently I fought with their mighty army in city and mountain. I inflicted on them a decisive defeat.
> I laid low their men-at-arms in the mountains like sheep. I cut off their heads like sheep.
> I made their blood flow into the hollows and plains of the mountains.
> (Thus) I conquered that city. I took their gods; (and)
> I carried off their booty, possessions (and) property. I burned the city.
> The three great walls which were constructed with baked bricks and the entire city I razed (and) destroyed.
> I turned (it) into a ruin hill and a heap. I strewed 'ṣipu'-stones over it.
> I made bronze lightning bolts (and)
> I inscribed on them (a description of) the conquest of the lands which by Aššur, my lord, I had conquered, (and) a warning not to occupy that city and not to rebuild its wall.
> On that (site) I built a house of baked brick.
> I put inside it those bronze lightning bolts.[73]

---

[73] Aššur Prism V.99–VI.21, in *ACA*, 80-81.

Thus as we saw in chapter 5, Joshua uses standard 'motifs' in building the story.

Turning to the Christian reception of Josh 6, Origen offers an imaginative retelling of the story in a new context, through juxtaposition with 'new myths':

> Jericho is surrounded; it must be captured. How, therefore, is Jericho captured? The sword is not drawn against it; the battering ram is not arranged, nor is the spear hurled. The priestly trumpets alone are employed, and by these the walls of Jericho are overthrown.
>
> We frequently find Jericho to be placed in Scripture as a figure of this world. ...
>
> Consequently, this Jericho (that is, this world) is about to fall; for indeed the consummation of the age has already been made known a little while ago by the sacred books. In what way, therefore, will the consummation be given to it? By what instruments? By the sound, it says, of trumpets. Of what trumpets? Let Paul make known the mystery of this secret to you. Hear what he himself says: "The trumpet will sound," he says, "and the dead who are in Christ will rise incorruptible," and, "The Lord himself with a command, with the voice of the archangel and with the trumpet of God, will descend from heaven." At that time, therefore, Jesus our Lord conquers Jericho with trumpets and overthrows it, so that out of it, only the prostitute is saved and all her house.
>
> Therefore, our Lord Jesus will come and he will come with the sound of trumpets. But just now let us pray that he may come and destroy "the world that lay in wickedness" and all things that are in the world, because "everything that is in the world is the lust of the flesh and the lust of the eyes." May he destroy that, may he dissolve it again and again, and save only this one who received his spies and who placed his apostles, received with faith and obedience, in the high places. And may he join and unite this prostitute with the house of Israel.[74]

Here, Origen interprets Josh 6 through its cultural and canonical context in which Jericho, and its inhabitants, symbolize evil that is to be overthrown (e.g. Deut 7 and 9:4-5), and develops the significance of this in a later context—his reading is an exploration of the plenitude of the symbol as appropriated in another context, drawing upon the symbolic significance of Jericho as outlined by Nelson above.

Regarding Rahab, whilst Theodoret of Cyrus offers a reading that shows more 'historical' concern than Origen does,[75] his reading of Rahab's story is similar to Origen's in which Rahab, and her house, is a type for the church.[76] Indeed, Rahab as understood as a type for the church appears to be the 'centre of

---

[74] *Hom. Josh.* 6.4, pp.71-73.

[75] *Quest. Josh.* 7, p.281.

[76] Origen, *Hom. Josh.* 3.5, pp.49-50; cf. Theodoret of Cyrus, *Quest. Josh.* 2.2 'No one should imagine that Rahab was unworthy of being a type [τὸν τύπον] of the Church', (p.267).

gravity' for Christian interpretation of the story.[77] In the New Testament however, she is a paragon of faith (Heb 11:31), and for the necessity for faith to be accompanied by works (Jas 2:25).[78] These two aspects, her 'faith' and her 'works' are differently developed and emphasized in the tradition. For Cyril of Jerusalem she is 'saved through repentance',[79] and 'saved ... when she believed'.[80] Similarly, Calvin stresses her faith; 'What seed of righteousness was in Rahab ... before she had faith?'[81] Alternatively, Gregory of Nazianzus neglects her faith and stresses her hospitality; 'Rahab the harlot was justified by one thing alone, her hospitality'.[82] In 1 Clem 12 both her faith and her hospitality are held together; 'for her faith and hospitality Rahab the harlot was saved'.[83] However, there is no indication of repentance in Josh 2, and it is her חסד that the narrative emphasizes, even though, from a later perspective 'faith' might be an appropriate way of describing her response too, reflecting a fitting development of the story. It seems that both of these aspects should be held together in the Christian interpretation of the story. I shall return to this in chapter 9.

But is the focus of Rahab's story conversion as such? A neo-structuralist reading of the Old Testament suggests that the structural system that it reflects did not allow a non-Israelite to 'convert' to, or at least become a part of, Israel, for Israel's identity was genealogically (or ethnically) constructed, something demonstrated in the patriarchal narratives.[84] Rahab, Naaman and Ruth, for example, reflect notable exceptions.[85] So Rahab's story is an instance of a

---

[77] E.g. Chrysostom (*Homilies on Repentance and Almsgiving* 7.5.16, in *ACCS*, 12); Cyprian (*Letter* 69.4 in *ACCS*, 14); Jerome (*Homily on Exodus* 91, in *ACCS*, 40).

[78] Moreover, in chapter 9 I shall consider resonances of Rahab in Matthew's gospel, e.g. Matt 15:21-28.

[79] *Catechetical Lectures* 2.9, in *ACCS*, 12.

[80] *Lecture* 10.11, in *NPNF* II.7, 201.

[81] *Inst* III.24.11, p.978. Cf. *Joshua*, 46, in which Rahab is said to 'pass by faith to a new people'. Interestingly, whilst he cites Jas 2:25 here, he uses it to emphasize only her faith, which runs against James' use of Rahab's story.

[82] *Theological Oration* 40.19, in *NPNF* II.7, 695. Cf. *Oration* 14.2—whilst Abraham is an example of faith, and justified by faith, Rahab is praised and spared for her hospitality (in B.E. Daley, *Gregory of Nazianzus* (The Early Church Fathers; Routledge, New ed.: 2000), 76).

[83] 1 Clem 12, in *ACCS*, 12,

[84] See S.D. Kunin, *We Think What We Eat: Neo-structuralist Analysis of Israelite Food Rules and Other Cultural and Textual Practices* (JSOTSup 412; London: T&T Clark, 2004), e.g. 138.

[85] Christian readers may find it strange that stories such as Ruth and Rahab's are exceptional, and that such stories would probably have been rather shocking originally. But these stories were shocking originally precisely because they sought to 'push' Israelite ideology; Christian readers might find it strange that the stories were exceptional (and one might say 'counter-cultural') originally, precisely because the stories seek to push the

'pushing' of the Israelite structure and worldview, and Deuteronomy's theology and outlook in particular, which might explain why the ending of Josh 6 retains a note of ambiguity—it is good rhetoric. Here is someone who 'looks like' the parade example of the outsider, but acts like the model Israelite. Her prostitution, and perhaps her act of deception, as deception *per se,* are simply literary features that are required at the narrative level to make the story 'work' in surprising and interesting ways. But this 'pushing' of ideology worked, in the Christian tradition as we have seen, but also in the Jewish tradition, for Rahab is a proselyte who marries Joshua (*Megilah* 14b), saves herself and those with her by her merit, attaching herself to Israel, and is an ancestor of a number of prophets, including Jeremiah, (*Ruth Rabbah* 2.1).[86]

So, in one sense Rahab's story can be understood in terms of 'conversion'. In Jewish categories, she is incorporated into Israel's genealogy, and has important descendants who are characterized as true Israelites. But in another sense the story is not about conversion at all—for Rahab's confession is not presented as deriving from a 'moment of conversion', and her character is not portrayed as changing or developing in the story. Rather, what changes is the way in which she is categorized and perceived by the community of Israel, for she does not change. It is the status that Israel accords to her that changes. In a sense it is *this community* (Israel) that undergoes conversion, in its perception of its own identity and boundaries.

Thus consideration of the dialectic between Rahab's story in terms of its sense as an act of discourse in the context of ancient Israel and its use in the church is complex and interesting. On the one hand, Rahab's story does indicate that there are those who seem hopelessly far outside the community of God's people who can, nevertheless, be joined to that community, and Rahab exhibits the sort of characteristics that are in fact essential to life in the community, characteristics which can be expressed in the Christian context in terms of faith and love. But on the other hand, her story says nothing about repentance (as it is often understood), a 'journey of faith' or a 'conversion experience' or similar. The story is not about her 'finding faith' and being changed. Her character shows no development or transformation in itself. Where the conversion in fact occurs in the story is in the perception of the community towards Rahab. So in a sense, if the story is to urge 'conversion', it is in the sense of a conversion of the perception of the church to those outside what one might think of as church. But this is not straightforward as Rahab does, nonetheless, 'confess' YHWH, and so

---

underlying ideology and structure towards what would become Christian ideology and structure, and are thus stories that sit very well in a Christian context. These stories thus gain prominence and are taken as the norm rather than the exception in Christian reading.
[86] Also see *Num. Rab.* 8.9, *Cant. Rab.* 1.22; 6.10, *Eccl. Rab.* 5.13; 8.13.

it may be unwise to push this reading of the story too far even as it encourages serious consideration of or re-engagement with difficult questions today.[87]

Joshua 7:1-8:29

Josh 7-8 develops the story of Achan through the story of an attack on Ai. The foundations of the story are laid in Josh 6 with the command to the Israelites to keep away from what was declared חרם at Jericho (6:18). Achan withheld some of the חרם, and the narrator supplies this as an 'interpretative key' at the beginning of the story (7:1), with the failure of the attack on Ai being interpreted for the reader in advance. The attack on Ai fails because Israel 'violated' (מעל) the חרם, although it is interesting that Achan's violation is interpreted as being Israel's.

The story commences with the 'literary device' of a spy mission (cf. Josh 2) in which the spies that Joshua sends out return confidently with the result that only a small force is sent to conquer Ai. Notably there is no mention of YHWH or of inquiring of his instructions here. What follows reflects a number of ironic reversals of the spy mission in Num 13. In Num 13 the spies, sent at YHWH's command, were terrified and returned pessimistically, with the result that no conquest was attempted when it could have been successfully conducted. Here, the spies go at Joshua's rather than YHWH's command and return confidently, with the result that an assault is attempted, but ends in failure. Ironic here is that Ai, if it means 'ruin', contrasts with the well-fortified, impregnable Jericho which fell so easily, for now Israel is defeated by a 'ruin'. Moreover, it is ironic that here the hearts of the Israelites 'melt' (7:5) like the hearts of the locals had previously (2:11 and 5:1), although here an extra clause,

וימס לבב־העם ויהי למים

is added for emphasis. This fear is the result of a small loss, only thirty-six troops, adding to the irony and sense of panic. Furthermore the Israelites are pursued as far as שברים (Shebarim, destruction) (7:5), suggesting that geography serves a symbolic function in the telling of the story here, and is an indicator of the nature of the text. In another ironic reversal, whilst in Josh 6 it was Israel that surrounded (סבב) Jericho, now Joshua fears that the Canaanites will סבב Israel (7:9). But the narrator also uses a 'type scene' in a rather ambiguous way - Joshua's response to the defeat (7:6-9) reflects the complaint of the Israelites wandering in the desert, a complaint that demonstrated their unfaithfulness (Exod 16:3; 17:3; Num 14:2-3). Why is Joshua, who is portrayed so positively generally, cast as responding like unfaithful, grumbling Israel? It seems to serve

---

[87] In this sense, the most straightforward appropriation of this story today would be in the context of ecumenism.

two functions. First, to add to the sense of panic and despair, and secondly, whereas previously the complaint expressed a desire to return to Egypt from the wilderness, here it expresses a desire to return *to* the wilderness, outside the promised land, symbolizing the reversal of Israel's entry into new life. Joshua's despair is thus used to indicate that Israel's new status and life hang in the balance. However, in addition to Joshua's speech suggesting that Joshua is cast as something like grumbling Israel, the introduction of his complaint uses the 'stock phrase' אהה אדני יהוה, a phrase that Ellen Davis calls the 'prophetic protest', being a phrase that is used elsewhere only by Gideon (Judg 6:22), Jeremiah (e.g. Jer 1:6) and Ezekiel (e.g. Ezek 4:14). Thus Joshua is portrayed as a prophetic leader as well as a 'grumbling Israelite', suggesting that he has the status and qualities of a liminal or mediatorial figure.[88]

As the story unfolds we see that it centres around the חרם objects that Achan withheld from Jericho. Whilst Jericho brings closure to Rahab's story, it introduces Achan's story in which he brings trouble to Israel, emphasized through the wordplay on עכר (trouble) (6:18) and the name עָכָן (Achan),[89] and indeed in the naming of the place, עָכוֹר (Achor), in the conclusion of Achan's story in 7:26. Again, the various wordplays indicate the nature and significance of the story. Achan is clearly identified as 'the sinner', confessing his sin (חטא) (7:19-20), but what is difficult to understand is the nature of Achan's response to Joshua.[90] What would be an adequate response to Joshua's command to give glory to YHWH and make confession to him (7:19)? One feels that Achan's response is inadequate. Whilst it is an adequate 'confession', there is no sense of giving YHWH glory and praise. Perhaps as Achan is already condemned to death (7:15), this inadequate response serves to *confirm* the validity of the judgment. Achan is not one who glorifies God, indicating something of his character—he acts as an outsider, even though he is set up as the paradigmatic insider through genealogy, being of the tribe of Judah, a genealogy given twice for emphasis (7:1 and 16-18). The seriousness of Achan's crime is emphasized by the repeated use of וגם in 7:11, which, rhetorically, 'piles up' and compounds the number and nature of violations that this single crime represents. Moreover, perhaps נבלה in 7:15 is an ironic pun on נחלה—rather than helping to bring Israel into her inheritance, Achan has done a 'disgraceful thing' in Israel.[91] But why is Achan's

---

[88] I am grateful to Prof. E.F. Davis for suggesting this to me.
[89] Hawk notes that the name עָכָן is meaningless, but is essentially an anagram of כנען (Canaan) (*Joshua,* 120).This might suggest that Achan is essentially a 'hidden' Canaanite.
[90] Joshua's reference to 'not hiding' here sets up a parallel with Achan's 'hiding' the חרם in 7:21, although a different root (טמן) is used here, probably to set up a parallel with Josh 2:6 to invite the reader to compare and contrast Achan with Rahab.
[91] Moreover the root נבלה is used in Gen 34, suggesting that the two stories may be mutually illuminating; this incident is compared with the trouble resulting from Dinah's rape.

crime so serious? I suggested in chapter 6 that the violation of the חרם here symbolises covenant violation. Indeed, this is how YHWH is reported as interpreting the violation (עברו את־בריתי, 7:11). Indeed, the use of גנב (steal) in 7:11 reflects the Decalogue's language (Deut 5:19), as does חמד (covet) in 7:21. Moreover, the root עבר is used here, indicating another boundary crossing, reflecting Achan's 'transition' from insider to outsider, manifested in execution.[92]

Thus Achan's story balances or contrasts with Rahab's. Rahab, the outsider, the Canaanite prostitute, gives glory to YHWH in her 'confession' and 'does חסד', symbolizing what is at the heart of the covenant, whilst Achan, the insider, the Israelite of the tribe of Judah, fails to glorify YHWH in his 'confession' and 'does חמד', symbolizing what is antithetical to the covenant. Indeed Rahab is spared because she hid (טמן, 2:6) the spies (מלאכים) whom Joshua sent (6:17), whereas Achan is executed because he hid (טמן, 7:21) the חרם (7:21), discovered by the מלאכים whom Joshua sent (7:22).[93] One is thus invited to read Achan and Rahab as two contrasting examples that have the extreme חרם of Jericho at their symbolic intersection. What happens to Achan?

Not only is Achan executed, but so are his children, representing the blotting out of his name, reflecting Deut 29:16-21. Indeed, here in Deut 29 we find the process of the singling out of the offender described, and its language reflects the process of singling the offender out through tribe and clan (29:18) found in Josh 7. Deut 29 commands that the offender's name should be blotted out (29:20), with the Deuteronomic curses falling upon the offender (29:20-21). This is reflected in Josh 7 through the execution of Achan's children. Achan is thus interpreted as being a root producing bitter poison (29:18) who is 'high handed' (29:19) and whom YHWH will *never* forgive (29:20). He is an idolater who has turned away from YHWH to worship other gods (29:16-18). Thus Achan is cast as an idolater, a true outsider, manifested in the blotting out of his name by the execution of him and his family.

Thus Achan, and his story, represent a 'limit-situation' that reflects the construction of Israel's identity. Taken together with Rahab's story, the two stories seek, as reflections of 'limit-situations' centred on the 'limit-situation' of the extreme חרם of Jericho, to probe the question of what makes a true Israelite. Recalling the discussion on the existential and amoral nature of myth in chapter 2, we may see that we are meant to be shocked by the troublesome nature of Achan's story; it is designed to call readers up short so that one can see how serious a matter the living of the covenant is. But the חרם also serves important

---

[92] Moreover, Hess detects a resonance between Achan's story and Eve in the Garden of Eden; Achan sinned when he saw (ראה) something beautiful (טוב)—the same words used in Gen 3:6 with regard to Eve and the fruit (*Joshua*, 151-2).

[93] Whilst various words are used for the hiding, the same root (טמן) is used in 7:21 and 2:6 where Rahab's action of hiding is first mentioned.

functions from a neo-structuralist perspective, creatively used as a symbol to challenge the idea of the genealogical construction of identity in the opposite way to Rahab's story.[94] The story is only a 'model to follow' for behaviour in as far as it encourages obedience to the covenant and praise of YHWH and the construction of identity in this way; it is not about the execution of innocent children, a narrative device that serves essentially structural requirements relating to the construction of Israel's identity, symbolically confirming the exclusion of Achan, the symbolic non-Israelite.

So far we have considered the story in essentially Deuteronomic terms, and seen how it is fitting to read the story from this perspective. But granted the use of the (essentially) Priestly term מעל to interpret Achan's crime, might the story thus be read well from a Priestly perspective?[95] But what would a 'Priestly perspective' on Josh 7 be? I would like to start by considering Jacob Milgrom's analysis of the theologies of P and H. He suggests that,

> The most important ideological distinction between P and H rests in their contrasting concepts of holiness. For P, spatial holiness is limited to the sanctuary; for H, it is coextensive with the promised land. Holiness of persons is restricted in P to priests and Nazirites (Num. 6:5–8); H extends it to all Israel. This expansion follows logically from H's doctrine of spatial holiness: since the land is holy, all who reside in it are to keep it that way. Every adult Israelite is enjoined to attain holiness by observing the Lord's commandments, and even the *gēr*, "resident alien," must heed the prohibitive commandments, for their violation pollutes the land (e.g., Lev. 18:26).
>
> P's doctrine of holiness is static; H's is dynamic. On the one hand, P constricts holiness to the sanctuary and its priests. P assiduously avoids the Heb term *qādôš* "holy," even in describing the Levites ... On the other hand, though H concedes that only priests are innately holy (Lev. 21:7), it repeatedly calls upon Israel to strive for holiness. The dynamic quality of H's concept is highlighted by its resort to the same participial construction Heb *mĕqaddēš*, "sanctifying," in describing the holiness of both the laity and the priesthood. Sanctification is an ongoing process for priests (Lev. 21:8, 15, 23; 22:9, 16) as well as for all Israelites (Lev. 21:8; 22:32). No different from the Israelites, the priests bear a

---

[94] One would expect חרם to consolidate a genealogical (or at least ethnic) construction of Israel's identity, as in Deut 7:1-5, since it is perhaps the paradigmatic symbolization of non-mediation and non-transformation with regard to Israel and non-Israel. I shall develop this point later.

[95] Briend notes that מעל 'followed by the noun of the same root and by an object introduced by a preposition belongs to the vocabulary of the book of Ezekiel, of P and of the Chronicler'. (J. Briend, 'The Sources of the Deuteronomistic History: Research on Joshua 1-12', in A. de Pury, *et al.*, (eds.), *Israel Constructs its History: Deuteronomistic Historiography in Recent Research* (JSOTSup 306; Sheffield: Sheffield Academic Press, 2000), 360-86, here 364).

> holiness that expands or contracts in proportion to their adherence to God's commandments.
>
> The converse doctrine of pollution also varies sharply: P holds that the sanctuary is polluted by Israel's moral and ritual violations (Lev. 4:2) committed anywhere in the camp (but not outside), and that this pollution can and must be effaced by the violator's purification offering and, if committed deliberately, by the high priest's sacrifice and confession (Lev. 16:3–22). H, however, concentrates on the polluting force of Israel's violation of the covenant (Lev. 26:15), for example, incest (Lev. 18; 20:11–24), idolatry (Lev. 2:1–6), or depriving the land of its sabbatical rest (Lev. 26:34–35). Pollution for H is nonritualistic, as shown by the metaphoric use of Heb *ṭāmēʾ* (e.g., Lev. 18:21, 24; 19:31) and by the fact that the polluted land cannot be expiated by ritual, and, hence, the expulsion of its inhabitants is inexorable (Lev. 18:24–29; 20:2).[96]

and that

> The violation of a prohibitive commandment generates impurity and, if severe enough, pollutes the sanctuary from afar. This imagery portrays the priestly theodicy. It declares that while sin may not scar the face of the sinner it does scar the face of the sanctuary ... This image graphically illustrates the priestly version of the old doctrine of collective responsibility: when the evildoers are punished they bring down the righteous with them. ...
>
> Thus, in the priestly scheme, the sanctuary is polluted (read: society is corrupted) by brazen sins (read: the rapacity of the leaders) and also by inadvertent sins (read: the acquiescence of the "silent majority"), with the result that God is driven out of his sanctuary (read: the nation is destroyed).[97]

Milgrom's discussion of H's theology is suggestive for understanding Achan's violation of a commandment as generating impurity in the camp that affects all of Israel, since Achan's crime is interpreted as Israel's, with all Israel being affected. So whilst the effects of Achan's crime on the whole Israelite camp could be construed in 'rhetorical' terms, in that the effects help construct an existentially demanding limit-situation in an imaginative way, in another sense, from a Priestly (or H) perspective, one can construe the text in terms of the impurity (resulting in the withdrawal of YHWH's presence) that disobedience to the covenant creates. Whilst I argued in chapter 6 that it is wrong to view חרם as a contagion, what Josh 7 indicates, from a Priestly perspective, is that it is the effects of disobedience to the covenant that contaminate the camp, and not חרם *per se*. Or, to put it another way, perhaps it demonstrates the communal nature of sin. Here, one need not be concerned with whether or not a 'Priestly

---

[96] J. Milgrom, 'Priestly ("P") Source' in *ABD*, 5.454-61, here, 457. However, he also notes that 'when it comes to theology, P and H mostly form a single continuum; H articulates and develops what is incipient and even latent in P' (454).

[97] Ibid., 457-8.

perspective' was 'originally' in view, for this kind of reading does, at the very least, reflect a 'fitting' exploration of the plenitude of the world of the text, granted the intersection and resonances of the concerns in view in Josh 7 and the Priestly materials.

Whilst Achan's story is now resolved, Israel's, and Ai's, are not; whilst the attack on Ai functions largely to develop Achan's story, the wider questions that it has raised must now be answered at the narrative level: Is YHWH still with Israel? Will the 'conquest' continue? Josh 8 commences with an assurance that YHWH *is* with Joshua and Israel, and that the attack of Ai will now proceed successfully, with the 'impurity of disobedience' removed so that YHWH is again 'with Israel'. YHWH's instructions differ from the suggestion of the spies in Josh 7 and from those for the taking of Jericho. The whole army is to be sent (v.1), setting an ambush (v.2).[98] Moreover, what is declared חרם, and what the Israelites are told that they may take as plunder, differs from that in Josh 6. Ironically, that which Achan took from Jericho, leading to his death and Israel's defeat at Ai, can now be taken from Ai! A successful attack follows, and thus things have returned to normal for Israel. The story of Josh 8 is essentially a captivating story to make this point, creating interest and suspense with the description of the ambush, etc.

The stories of Jericho and Ai indicate the need to obey YHWH through the covenant. It is this, rather than military tactics, that grants Israel success. If Israel obeys YHWH then impregnable walls and obstacles will fall (Jericho) and Israel will not have to worry about her enemies. But if Israel disobeys, then the simplest battle in which a ruin is attacked (Ai) will be lost.[99] Israel does not have to worry about how to possess the land or how to 'dispose' of her enemies, for YHWH will take care of this. Rather, Israel must worry about obeying YHWH, an obedience that will lead to blessing and rest. The stories of Rahab and Achan, refracted through the battles at Jericho and Ai, demonstrate the significance of Josh 5:13-15. YHWH is not 'for' ethnic Israel on her own 'national' terms, something rather unexpected in view of ideas of the favour and the election of Israel, rather, YHWH is 'for' those who confess his power and glory, who 'do חסד' and obey him, made concrete in obedience to the covenant.

Thus we see that it is in the interplay of the narrative and structural levels (in the neo-structuralist sense of the term) that one discovers the significance of Joshua as it probes questions of what it is that characterizes the insider and outsider. This is done in existential and affective terms, and *crucially* we may see that a number of elements that are present at the narrative level serve literary or structural requirements, rather than seeking to model or portray desirable

---

[98] Christian commentators have often been worried about the legitimacy of ambush in warfare, since it involves lying and deception (cf. the discussion of Rahab above), e.g. Augustine's *Questions on Joshua* 10-11 in *ACCS*, 46.

[99] Cf. Theodoret, *Quest. Josh.* 7 (p.281).

behaviour. In other words *discernment* is called for in the interpretation and use of the narrative.

Whilst the slightly ambiguous ending to Rahab's story was resolved positively in both Jewish and Christian traditions, being testimony to how one should construe the story in these contexts, Achan's seemingly unambiguous fate appears to be 'reversed' in the Jewish tradition, where he becomes a model penitent, confessing sin to gain life in the world to come.[100] The Jewish tradition thus, optimistically, tries to reinforce the centrality of the genealogical construction of Israel's identity; Achan is ethnically Israel, and so *ultimately* remains an 'insider'. So the Jewish tradition transforms his story in the context of new myths *into* a new myth itself—confession of sin brings life in the world to come. In a sense this process is not unlike the Christian transformation of Rahab's story through its juxtaposition with new 'myths'.

But, given the importance attached to the confession of sin in the Christian tradition, it is particularly interesting (and perhaps disorientating for the Christian) that the Christian tradition does not make this move that the Jewish tradition makes. Achan's 'ultimate fate' is not developed. Rather, within the Christian tradition there is more concern with punishment in the 'here and now', and with the corporate effects of Achan's crime.[101] It is interesting that Achan's story is not explicitly developed in the New Testament, unlike Rahab's, even though the idea of covetousness and greed is developed as characterizing the outsider (Col 3:5; Jas 4:2).[102] Thus Achan's story appears to find rather little Christian signifi-

---

[100] E.g. *Lev. Rab.* 9.1 (106-107): 'Another interpretation: '*Whoso offereth the sacrifice of thanksgiving* (todah), etc.' refers to Achan, who sacrificed his Evil Inclination by means of a confession (*todah*), [as it is said], *And Joshua said unto Achan: My son, give, I pray thee, glory to the Lord, the God of Israel, and make confession* (todah) *unto Him... and Achan answered Joshua and said: Of a truth I have sinned* (Josh. VII, 19 f.). *And to him who ordereth his way aright, will I show the salvation of the Lord* (Ps. *loc. cit.*), refers to the fact that he [i.e. Achan] has shown to penitents the way [to the salvation of the Lord]. This is [indicated by] what is written, And the sons of *Zerah: Zimri, and Ethan and Heman, and Calcol and Darda: five of them in all* (I Chron. II, 6).' A detailed, imaginative retelling of the story is found in *Num. Rab.* 23.6, in which Achan has a share in the world to come ('*This day*,' he implied, you are troubled, but you will not be troubled in the World to Come, and you have a share therein.' (870).

[101] E.g. Origen, *Hom. Josh.* 7.6-7 (pp.80-84); Theodoret, *Quest. Josh.* 10 (pp.283-284); *Constitutions of the Holy Apostles* 2.3.10 (*ANF* vol.7, 790) and 7.1.2 (ibid., 925). Also see various excerpts in *ACCS*, 41-5, and my 'Joshua and the Crusades' (forthcoming) for discussion of the use of Josh 7 in the mediaeval period.

[102] Some treat the story of Ananias and Sapphira (Acts 5) as a development of Achan's story. See e.g. H.D. Park, *Finding Herem? A Study of Luke-Acts in the Light of Herem* (Library of New Testament Studies 357; London: T&T Clark, 2007), 132-43. In general, I find Park's attempt to trace חרם into the New Testament unconvincing, finding 'חרם everywhere' based on rather questionable 'Greek equivalents'.

cance, perhaps because of the tension created between the narrative dynamics, in which Achan is clearly condemned like an outsider, and the later Christian importance attached to the confession of sin, which ought to suggest that Achan would be 'restored' when in fact he is not.

What is interesting then is that in neo-structuralist terms the Christian reception of Rahab's story and the Jewish reception of Achan's story both exhibit the 'clouding' of these stories as they are juxtaposed with other myths that are central to the construction of the identities within these communities. For the Christian, Rahab's 'faith' tends to be seen as bringing about her conversion or transformation, whilst for the Jew Achan's 'confession' reinforces his ultimate (genealogical) status as an Israelite. In a sense both traditions thus miss the challenge that these stories present as discourse, even if one might say that it is indeed Rahab's 'faith' that 'saves' her.[103] These stories are not concerned with conversion or restoration of individuals relative to a fixed understanding of the nature of the identity of the community of God's people.[104] Rather, these stories are concerned with the conversion of the self-understanding of the community of God's people and how the community is constituted relative to people like Rahab or Achan. The traditional reception of these stories has tended to blunt their rather demanding edge.

Joshua 8:30-35

We considered the different locations of this pericopae in the MT, LXX and 4QJosh[a] in chapter 7, and I suggested earlier that arguably 4QJosh[a] offers the 'best' location (i.e., in Josh 5), even if it is not original. It reflects the fulfilment of Deut 11:29 and 27:4ff, and demonstrates the obedience of Joshua and the people. In doing so, it characterizes Joshua and Israel as obedient to YHWH. This may help to set the rather ambiguous stories (such as Rahab, and the Gibeonites) in a more positive light, especially if the MT location is preferred; the unswervingly positive portrayal of Joshua in each unambiguous case, such as here, leads one to appraise the more ambiguous episodes in a positive light.

The ceremony emphasizes the centrality of the Mosaic Law for Israel's life in the land, being central to the construction of Israel's identity. Daniel Hawk compares Josh 8:30-35 with Deut 27, noting that in Deut 27 the focus is on writing commands on plastered stones, whereas here the focus is on altar building given that it 'receives first mention and assumes priority in the subsequent account'. He suggests that such a 'shift in focus evokes a powerful symbol', since altars throughout the Old Testament 'constitute a metaphor for social

---

[103] In this sense, the reception of Rahab's story (in both the Jewish and Christian traditions) does represent a 'crystallization' of the concerns of the story.

[104] E.g., there is no change in the characterization of Rahab in the story—there is no indication that she abandons her life of prostitution for example.

coherence and transformation ...transition in social status or configuration is marked by the construction of altars' (Gen 8:20; 12:7-8; 1 Sam 14:31-35; 2 Sam 24:25; 1 Kgs 18:30-32; 2 Kgs 16:10 and Ezra 3:2-3). The Ebal altar thus symbolically underscores the end of an old order and inaugurates a new social configuration,[105] and symbolizes the new life into which Israel is called. Having the law written onto the stones is important, for it implies that it is 'fixed', and that it will be 'remembered' in future generations, the importance of which is highlighted through the study of cultural memory. Moreover, the presence of the entire community here emphasizes the unity of Israel, and that the law is for everyone, being at the centre of the life of the community.

So this story indicates the centrality of torah for being an Israelite, and for Israel's unity and coherence. But how might the story be read in a Christian context? Origen provides us with an imaginative intertextual reading:

> I certainly think that whenever "Moses is read" to us and through the grace of the Lord "the veil of the letter is removed" [2 Cor. 3:15-16] and we begin to understand that "the law is spiritual," [Rom. 7:14] then the Lord Jesus reads that law to us. ... The law, which Paul names "spiritual," [Rom. 7:14] is thus understood and Jesus himself is the one who recites these things in the ears of all the people, admonishing us that we not follow "the letter that kills" but that we hold fast "the life-giving spirit." [2 Cor. 3:6]
>
> Therefore, Jesus reads the law to us when he reveals the secret things of the law. For we who are of the catholic church do not reject the law of Moses, but we accept it if Jesus reads it to us. For thus we shall be able to understand the law correctly, if Jesus reads it to us, so that when he reads we may grasp his mind and understanding. Therefore, should we not think that he had understood this mind who said, "And we have the mind of Christ, so that we may know those things that have been given to us by God, those things that also we speak"? [1 Cor. 2:12-13] Also, those who were saying, "Was not our heart burning within us, when he laid bare the Scriptures to us along the way?" [Lk. 24:32] when "beginning from the law of Moses up to the prophets he read all things to us and revealed those things that were written concerning him"? [Lk. 24:27][106]

Indeed, in the New Testament Jesus is portrayed as 'fulfilling' (from πληρόω) the law (Matt 5:17), or being the end or goal (τέλος) of the law (Rom 10:4).[107] Thus in the Christian context the move that the tradition, i.e. the community that uses these texts to construct their identity, clearly makes is to transpose the centrality of torah to the centrality of Jesus; obedience to the law is understood as obedience to Jesus who sums up the law, or at least, as Origen puts it, torah is accepted as 'Jesus reads it to us'.

---

[105] Hawk, *Joshua*, 133-4.
[106] Origen, *Hom. Josh.* 9.8, pp.103-104.
[107] Of course the meaning of these texts has been much disputed.

Joshua 9-10

The account of the Gibeonites, in which they trick the Israelites into making a treaty with them in order to save themselves, is a difficult and ambiguous story to interpret, and it is interesting to see how different the evaluations of it are in the commentaries. In some ways the Gibeonites are like Rahab. They respond differently from other locals, apparently motivated by the fear of Israel being given the land and of the locals being destroyed (שמד) (9:24), recognizing that resistance is futile. Hess notes that both Rahab and the Gibeonites escape annihilation through negotiation; that both stories precede an account of war against their territory, and that in both cases deliverance occurs after the 'confession' of YHWH's deeds on behalf of Israel.[108] Similarly Nelson notes that both Rahab and the Gibeonites are threatened foreigners who outwit Israel, where each appreciate YHWH's mighty acts,[109] and Creach also suggests that the Gibeonites' speech (9:9-10) is like Rahab's (2:9-11).[110] But commentators also suggest that the Gibeonites are like Achan. For instance Hess suggests that in each story Israel errs without realising it, with a successful battle occurring after the fault is identified. Moreover, Hess notes that in 9:20 the wrath (קצף) that the leaders of Israel wish to avoid is a term that occurs elsewhere in Joshua only in 22:20 where it recalls the wrath against Israel because of Achan.[111] Nelson suggests that whilst Rahab remains a positive figure, the Gibeonites are enslaved deceivers, correlating with Achan; Josh 9 is a 'problematic prelude' for Josh 10, like Josh 7 is for Josh 8, and he notes that the Gibeonites are said to be בקרב Israel (9:7, 16, 22) like the חרם was in Achan's story (7:12-13).[112]

However, Rahab was also said to be בקרב Israel (6:25). Indeed, קרב appears to be a *Leitwort* in Joshua, for lots of things or people are said to be 'in the midst' of Israel. So perhaps Joshua invites one to ponder what is, or what should be, 'in the midst' of Israel. Indeed, בקרב occurs in many of the major accounts in Joshua; the prologue, the Jordan crossing, Rahab's story, Achan's story, the Gibeonites' story, the distribution of the land and the covenant ceremonies:

1:11; 3:2	the officers (שוטר) are בקרב Israel to give instructions;
3:5	YHWH will 'do נפלאות' in Israel's midst;
3:10	the living god (אל חי) is in Israel's midst;
4:6	the collection of stones that will serve as a sign (אות) is in Israel's midst;
6:25	Rahab and her family are in Israel's midst;

---

[108] Hess, *Joshua*, 177.
[109] Nelson, *Joshua*, 131.
[110] Creach, *Joshua*, 86.
[111] Hess, *Joshua*, 177-83.
[112] Nelson, *Joshua*, 131-2.

7:12-13	חרם is in Israel's midst;
8:35	the sojourner (גר) is in Israel's midst at the covenant ceremony;
9:7, 16, 22; 10:1	the Gibeonites (Hivites) are in Israel's midst;
13:13; 16:10	peoples not driven out live in Israel's midst (Geshurites and Maacathites (13:13); Canaanites near Gezer (16:10);
18:7	the Levites are in the midst of Israel;
24:5	YHWH struck Egypt by what he did in her midst;
24:17	Israel crossed 'in the midst' of other people;
24:23	Israel is exhorted to put away the foreign gods (אלהי הנכר) that are in her midst.

So, if, as I have argued, Rahab is to be seen in a positive light, an example of an outsider who 'becomes' an insider, and Achan in a negative light, an insider who 'becomes' an outsider, then what about the Gibeonites, who are associated with both Rahab and Achan via various literary cues? The association of the Gibeonites with Achan seems rather tenuous, although comparison with Rahab is interesting, especially if one compares their 'confessions'. The 'confession' (acknowledgement of YHWH's deeds?) of the Gibeonites is less impressive than Rahab's. Rahab's 'acknowledgement' is indeed more of a 'confession', and one that is, in fact, of a superlative nature in the Old Testament, as we saw. But the Gibeonites' 'confession' *is* far less impressive (9:24), and only relates to what they fear for themselves, rather than to who YHWH *is*, which is something that Rahab's confession reflects. But the actions of both Rahab and the Gibeonites represent a realisation of the state of affairs that results in their taking action to prevent their annihilation.

However, whilst Rahab 'does חסד', the Gibeonites act with ערמה. This deception by the Gibeonites (the Hivites) seems to reflect Israel's deceitful action against Shechem the Hivite in Gen 34. Is Josh 9 thus an ironic reversal to be read alongside Gen 34? If so, then what does this indicate; that the Israelites and the Gibeonites are essentially 'one and the same'? But how is the ערמה of the Gibeonites to be interpreted? Is it to be construed positively or negatively?[113] The word resembles the term מרמה used of Jacob when he acquires Esau's birthright (Gen 27:35), and of Jacob's sons following the rape of Dinah by Shechem the Hivite (Gen 34:13), which is significant as both these stories have certain affinities with Josh 9; Israel is what she is through acts of deception, as

---

[113] ערמה is understood negatively in Exod 21:14, but positively in Prov 1:4; 8:5, 12. ערום is understood negatively in Gen 3:1; Job 5:12; 15:5, but positively in Prov 12:16, 23; 13:16; 14:8, 15, 18; 22:3; 27:12. The verb ערם is understood negatively in Job 5:13 and Ps 83:4, but positively in Prov 15:5 and 19:25. Its usage in 1 Sam 23:22 appears ambiguous.

are the Gibeonites. But מרמה is an unambiguously negative term,[114] and granted the resonances of Josh 9 with Gen 34, it seems significant that the unambiguously negative term is *avoided* here, with the more ambiguous term used instead. This cautions against viewing the Gibeonite action in an unambiguously negative way. In a modern, Western context such deceit is generally taken as unambiguously negative, as indicated in Calvin's reading of the story; he comments on 9:6 that a covenant of this nature is 'null and void' in strict law, and so the Gibeonites do not gain anything by the fraud.[115] But this misses the point; according to the text the treaty was valid, and they did gain here—their lives! Indeed, in an Oriental context, such 'cleverness' or 'wiliness' (as in Proverbs) is often seen in a positive way, as a praiseworthy trait, something that is culturally desirable.[116]

---

[114] Cf. Gen 27:35; 34:13; 2 Kgs 9:23; 1 Chr 8:10; Job 15:35; 31:5; Ps 5:7; 10:7; 17:1; 24:4; 34:14; 35:20; 36:4; 38:13; 43:1; 50:19; 52:6; 55:12, 24; 109:2; Prov 11:1; 12:5, 17, 20; 14:8, 25; 20:23; 26:24; Isa 53:9; Jer 5:27; 9:5, 7; Dan 8:25; 11:23; Hos 12:1, 8; Amos 8:5; Micah 6:11; Zeph 1:9.

[115] Calvin, *Joshua*, 139.

[116] See William Beeman's discussion of *zerængi* in Iran in which he discusses a number of stories that have resonances with the kind of behaviour exhibited by the Gibeonites in which the action was seen in positive terms (*Language, Status, and Power in Iran* (Bloomington: Indiana UP, 1986), 27-32. He gives the following example: 'One young fellow in the village where I was resident attended high school in Shiraz. He was not very bright but had nonetheless been promised the opportunity to marry his pretty cousin when he graduated from high school. The first thing he did each year was to change high schools, so that no one in the village was ever quite sure which one he was attending. He then would bring his reports home at odd or irregular times, so that his parents had no idea of when to expect his grades. In time he was able to convince his parents that he had actually graduated, when in fact he had failed his final examinations. He eventually was married to his cousin and had enlisted in the army before his parents were finally informed in a totally unexpected manner that he had in fact not graduated and indeed had not even advanced to the final class in high school, having failed his examinations the year before as well. When I had a chance to question him about this, he told me that whereas his parents were enormously irritated initially (to say nothing of his uncle, who expected a high-school graduate for a son-in-law), they were eventually convinced by their neighbors and relatives that his extraordinary *zerængi* in the whole matter more than offset his lack of filial duty, and that now he was married with a good dowry and a reasonable position in the army, they should be quite satisfied. Indeed, they had now become quite confident of his success in life. His own feeling was not that he had "put one over" on his parents, but that he had been sure that he would never be able to finish high school from the beginning and he simply wanted to arrange things so that his parents would never have to find out when he eventually was failed, to spare them pain and embarrassment.' (29-30). In other words, it is possible that the action of the Gibeonites ought to be construed in a rather more positive light than it has been traditionally. Interestingly, the action of the Gibeonites is also interpreted positively in post-colonial

But difficulties in evaluating the story are intensified by the lack of explicit interpretation or judgment by the narrator, Joshua or YHWH regarding what has transpired (perhaps reflecting the ambiguous ending of Gen 34). Joshua complains of the Gibeonite deceit, and reports that the Gibeonites are under a curse (9:23), but no further evaluation is offered. Is the story really concerned with evaluating *Israel's* actions here? Perhaps the phrase used of Israel in 9:14, 'but did not enquire of YHWH' implicitly suggests a negative appraisal of Israel, but this remains implicit and is not confirmed. Could this remark, and indeed the whole story, be deliberately ambiguous? Indeed, reading into Josh 10, the conquest of the land is reported to proceed precisely because of the faithfulness of Israel to the oath made to the Gibeonites, which might suggest a positive reading of the treaty, although it may be the Israelites' *faithfulness to the oath* that is in view in Josh 10. Finally, of course, the Gibeonites became, in at least some sense, part of Israel, even if as servants, and were not subjected to חרם.

This raises the next interesting problem; there is no mention of חרם in Josh 9, or in relation to the Gibeonites, although it returns in Josh 10 (10:1, 28, 35, 37, 39, 40) with regard to the cities that the Israelites, together with the Gibeonites, fight against. Israel enters these battles precisely as a result of faithfulness to the treaty with the Gibeonites. Indeed, in Josh 9 one might expect חרם to occur in 9:1 and 9:3, or 9:19 where נגע is used, or 9:24 where שמד is used. Moreover, in 9:24 it is the Gibeonites who say that Moses had been 'clearly told' (הגד הגד) to destroy (שמד) the inhabitants of the land (which of course includes them) but Israel does not, honouring the treaty made under oath. This seems, in an ironic sense, to *raise* the difficulty of the narrative here, rather than resolving the story. What is clear to the Gibeonites regarding what Moses had said is now unclear to the Israelites, but it is a lack of clarity that works in favour of the Gibeonites. Furthermore, when the kings 'west of the Jordan' hear (9:1-2), they do not hear of חרם, as in 2:10 and 10:1, or of the drying of the Jordan as in 5:1, but merely of 'these things', and in 9:3, the Gibeonites are said to hear only of 'what Joshua did to Jericho and Ai', *not* of their חרם, and similarly in 9:10. This is all very unusual.

However, we noted the presence of Priestly aspects to Josh 9 in chapter 4. Might one then explain the absence of חרם in Josh 9 via an appeal to its prehistory, possibly with Josh 9 being a non-Deuteronomistic insertion? Several observations tell against this. First, Josh 9 is integral with Josh 10, in which חרם repeatedly occurs. Secondly, the story of the Gibeonites is significant for the Deuteronomistic tradition (cf. 2 Sam 21). Thirdly, there is no reference to חרם in the important deueronomistic 'summaries' in Joshua (Josh 1, 21:43-45, 23-24), and so the absence of חרם in Joshua need not imply the addition of a later, non-

---

readings of Joshua in which 'the text may become a postcolonial celebration of the duping of dull colonial forces' (R. Boer, 'Green Ants and Gibeonites: B. Wongar, Joshua 9 and some Problems of Postcolonialism', in *Semeia* 75 (1996): 129-52, here 147).

Deuteronomistic passage. Finally, the term the Gibeonites employ, שמד, is rare in the Pentateuch outside Deuteronomy, (only occurring in Gen 34:40; Lev 26:30; Num 33:52) and is not used in any of these places in relation to a command to Moses to destroy the local inhabitants, but it is common in Deuteronomy (used twenty-nine times), suggesting that the story reflects Deuteronomistic shaping. Indeed, the story seems to be based upon Deut 20, as indicated in 9:7.[117] Thus, in conclusion, the absence of חרם *is* significant, suggesting that the story is more than an aetiology or a Priestly insertion for example.[118] I shall return to this point below and in chapter 9, when I develop the significance of חרם in Joshua.

Josh 9 appears to reflect the use of standard motifs from a 'submission story', reflecting a story that narrates the formation of something like an ANE vassal treaty.[119] But there are important variations from such accounts, suggesting that Josh 9 is not a story that serves the same or similar function to these, with the differences being highlighted as unusual through comparison. In particular, the failure to consult YHWH, or to make the covenant specifically with reference to his name seems irregular, perhaps illustrating folly and haste on the part of the Israelites. But maybe this absence is simply to make the story 'work' as a deliberately ambiguous narrative. Moreover, no details of the covenant are given apart from the brief note in 9:15. What is significant is simply the fact that the covenant is made, through ערמה. Similarly, it is interesting that the reference to the 'kings west of the Jordan' coming to fight Joshua (9:1-2) is not developed in Josh 9. Only the Amorites mentioned in 9:2 figure in Josh 10, and then in a different context. Thus it seems that these kings are mentioned in order to contrast them, and their hostile response, with the Gibeonites (cf. 11:19-20, discussed below), whom the story is really about. Taken together these observations suggest that there are many motifs used in this story to make it 'sound like' a standard kind of story whilst, as discourse, it is about something quite different, as sketched out above.

Origen offers a thoughtful reading of the story in a Christian context:

> [E]ven the resurrection of the dead will not exhibit an equal glory of those rising again, for "there is one flesh of birds, another of cattle, and even another of fish. There are both heavenly bodies and earthly bodies; but the glory of heavenly things is one thing, that of the earthly, another. One glory of the sun, an-

---

[117] Moreover, Hawk suggests that the story has ironic parallels with Deut 29:1-15 (*Joshua*, 141).

[118] Cf. Nelson—the story functions to bolster national identity with the story encouraging the acceptance of a troublesome status quo (*Joshua*, 132).

[119] Cf. examples in chapter 5, and also Grintz and Fensham's comparisons of Josh 9 with Hittite treaties (J.M. Grintz, 'The Treaty of Joshua with the Gibeonites' in *JAOS* 86.2 (1966): 113-26 and F.C. Fensham, 'The Treaty between Israel and the Gibeonites' in *BA* 27.3 (1964): 96-100).

other glory of the moon, another glory of the stars. Star differs from star in glory; thus also, the resurrection of the dead."

Therefore, many differences of those who come to salvation are depicted. Whence even now I think those Gibeonites, whose history has been recited, are a certain small portion of those who must be saved but in such a manner that they are not saved apart from the branding of some mark. For you see how they are condemned to become "hewers of wood" or "bearers of water" for the service of the people and for the ministry of the altar of God, because they indeed approached the sons of Israel with deceit and cunning, "clothed in old garments and shoes" and "carrying food of aged bread." Therefore, these persons come to Jesus [Joshua] with all their aged things and greatly beg of him that they may be saved.

Something such as this seems to me to be displayed in their figure. There are in the church certain ones who believe in God, have faith in God, and acquiesce in all the divine precepts. Furthermore, they are conscientious toward the servants of God and desire to serve them, for they also are fully ready and prepared for the furnishing of the church or for the ministry. But, in fact, they are completely disgusting in their actions and particular habit of life, wrapped up with vices and not wholly "putting away the old self with its actions." Indeed they are enveloped in ancient vices and offensive faults, just as those persons were covered over with old garments and shoes. Apart from the fact that they believe in God and seem to be conscientious toward the servants of God or the worship of the church, they make no attempt to correct or alter their habits. For those, therefore, our Lord Jesus certainly permits salvation, but their salvation itself, in a certain measure, does not escape a note of infamy.[120]

He continues,

Of course, it must be observed that the heretics reading this passage, those who do not accept the Old Testament, are accustomed to make a malicious charge and say, "See how Jesus [Joshua] the son of Nun showed no human kindness, so that, although permitting salvation, he inflicted a mark of infamy and a yoke of servitude upon those men who had come to him in supplication." If the soul less instructed in the divine Scriptures hears these things, it can in consequence be enfeebled and endangered, so that it may shun the catholic faith; for they do not understand their deceptions. For Jesus [Joshua] passed a fitting judgment upon them according to the measure of their own faith.

Formerly Rahab the harlot, who believed with a sound faith with all her house and received the Israelite spies with fullest devotion, was received fully into the community and society of the people; and it is written of her that "she was attached to the sons of Israel until today." But those who did not so much love the community of the Israelite clan as they were terrified by fear of their destruction approached Jesus [Joshua] with cunning and fraud. How could they de-

---

[120] *Hom Josh*. 10.1, pp.109-110.

serve the liberty of life and the community of the kingdom in their slavish deceits?

Finally, do you wish to know that the condition was dispensed toward them by Jesus [Joshua] because the inferiority of their disposition was fitting for them. They themselves say, "We have heard how many things the Lord did for you" through the midst of the Red Sea and in the desert, And although they said these things and confessed that they had both heard and known of the divine miracles, yet they produced nothing worthy in faith, nothing in admiration of such great powers. And therefore Jesus, when he sees the narrowness and smallness displayed in their faith, preserves a very just moderation towards them, so that they might merit salvation. Although they had brought a little faith, nevertheless they did not receive the highest rank of the kingdom or of freedom because their faith was not ennobled by the increase of works, since the apostle James declares, "faith without works is dead."[121]

For Origen the Gibeonites are insiders, but insiders with a problematic status.

In Josh 10 the Israelites come to the assistance of the Gibeonites who are attacked by a coalition of kings in response to what Israel has done so far, and the treaty that has been made. Following the defeat and humiliation of the kings, the Israelites proceed to capture a series of southern cities. In the battle at Gibeon YHWH's assistance is portrayed more in terms of standard 'divine warrior' motifs than is the case elsewhere in Joshua; there is המם (panic/confusion) caused by YHWH (10:10); there are 'large stones from heaven' (אבנים גדלות מן־השמים) (10:11); the assistance of the sun and moon (10:12-14),[122] and the report that YHWH fought for Israel (10:40-42). This is indicative of the use of standard motifs of ANE battle accounts.[123] Moreover, Nelson notes that the humiliation of the defeated kings in the manner indicated - placing feet on their necks (10:24) - is a symbol of unconditional surrender, and that the 'psychological impact' of this symbolism was appreciated in ANE iconography.[124] Here, however, the royal symbol is 'democratized' for it is the commanders rather than the king (or Joshua) who perform it. Moreover, hanging their bodies on trees (10:25) is a 'demonstrative act of contempt', although Deut

---

[121] *Hom. Josh.* 10.2, pp.111-2.

[122] See B. Margalit, 'The Day the Sun did not stand still: A new look at Joshua X 8-15', in *VT* 42.4 (1992): 466-91 for a study of this 'poetic fragment' and possible shifts in meaning resulting from the redaction of the text.

[123] See the texts cited in chapter 5 and cf. M. Weinfeld, 'Divine Intervention in War in Ancient Israel and in the Ancient Near East', in H. Tadmor and M. Weinfeld (eds.), *History, Historiography and Interpretation: Studies in biblical and cuneiform literatures* (Jerusalem: The Magnes Press, 1984), 121-47; P.D. Miller, *The Divine Warrior in early Israel* (Harvard Semitic Monographs 5; Cambridge: Harvard UP, 1973); S-M. Kang, *Divine War in the Old Testament and in the Ancient Near East* (BZAW 177; Berlin: Walter de Gruyter, 1989).

[124] Cf. *ANEP*, 351, 355, 393. Also cf. Deut 33:29; 1 Kgs 5:17[Heb] and Ps 110:1.

21:22-23 is obeyed (10:27, cf. 8:29).[125] Thus as in Josh 9, Josh 10 is told with reference to Deuteronomy, using a number of standard 'literary motifs', being a story based around standard building blocks of familiar motifs.

As with Josh 8, there may be little in the details of the story, *as narrative*, describing an account of a battle, that find significance in their own right at this level of description.[126] Indeed, Josh 10-11 probably reflect the most theologically and ethically difficult and troubling stories in Joshua,[127] and Christian interpreters have struggled with 10:16-28 in particular, with even Antiochene interpreters resorting to allegory, or something very close to it.[128] Likewise, the account of conquest of the southern cities that follows is difficult, with it being common to 'allegorize' the place names in the narrative to infer an existential, spiritual significance to the story.[129]

But does it help to know that reports such as in 10:41-42, in which Joshua is said to have killed everything that breathed as YHWH had commanded, and that YHWH fought for Israel, appear to reflect a pool of standard storytelling motifs, reflecting the kind of language, often described as hyperbolae, that one finds in ANE 'conquest accounts'? Initially, one might say that in Josh 1:6-9 there is a transformation of language from the military realm to the realm of torah obedience. Imagery from the military realm is developed in a metaphorical direction, used to evoke obedience to God at an existential level, as one finds in Eph 6:10-

---

[125] Nelson, *Joshua*, 146.

[126] Cf. Gregory of Nyssa's first homily on Ecclesiastes—'In all the other scriptures [i.e., other than Ecclesiastes], whether histories or prophecies, the aim of the book also includes other things not wholly of service to the Church. Why should the Church be concerned to learn precisely the circumstances of battles, or who became the rulers of nations and founders of cities, which settlers originated where, or what kingdoms will appear in time to come, and all the marriages and births which were diligently recorded, and all the details of this kind which can be learned from each book of scripture? Why should it help the Church so much in its struggle towards its goal of godliness?' (Homily 1, trans. S.G. Hall and R. Moriarty in S.G. Hall (ed.), *Gregory of Nyssa: Homilies on Ecclesiastes: An English Version with Supporting Studies* (Berlin: Walter de Gruyter, 1993), 33-4).

[127] For a recent exploration of Joshua 11 see W. Brueggemann, *Divine Presence Amid Violence: Contextualizing the Book of Joshua* (Eugene: Cascade Books/Milton Keynes: Paternoster, 2009). Brueggemann draws attention to the context of the story.

[128] Hill notes that Theodoret may be dependent on Origen here (*Quest. Josh.* 12, cf. Origen, *Hom. Josh.* 8.7), (*Quest. Josh.*, p.287).

[129] E.g. *Hom. Josh.* 13.2, pp.126-127. Whether 'allegorize' is quite the right term is unclear. Origen attempts to adapt the meanings of the names rather than impose an entirely different meaning on them, reflecting something like Stoic etymology which was sometimes considered an allegorical method and sometimes not. See D. Dawson, *Allegorical Readers and Cultural Revision in Ancient Alexandria* (Berkeley: University of California Press, 1992), 23-72.

18, a text often used to interpret Joshua in the Christian context.[130] So perhaps the language of 'God fighting for us', and the portrayal of complete conquest, finds its significance in indirect existential ways, evoking the idea that God works on one's behalf when one obeys him.[131] Indeed, the repetitive, formulaic and stylized narrative of 10:29-42 emphasises obedience resulting in the easy sweep of conquest through the land, culminating in the report that 'Joshua subdued (נכה) the land' (10:40).

But beyond this, and perhaps more significantly, it may be worth considering how, at the broader level, the various 'story blocks' in Joshua form part of an overall strategy to construct an Israelite identity that uses חרם as the central, and symbolic, theme that the stories are built around. We have 'outsiders' (the hostile kings) confirmed as such through their aggressive response to Israel in light of reports of חרם, and 'insiders' (Joshua and the Israelites) confirmed as such through obedience to YHWH manifested in obedience to חרם, an obedience that leads to success. Moreover, if Achan contrasts with Rahab, a contrast developed using חרם, then perhaps the hostile kings contrast with the Gibeonites. But if Rahab is the outsider who becomes an insider, and Achan an insider who becomes an outsider, then the five hostile kings are outsiders whose 'otherness' is manifested in their hostility, and confirmed in their deaths, whilst the Gibeonites are outsiders who form a borderline case—are they outsiders or insiders? The ambiguity of the story, and their eventual status, seems to reflect this difficulty. The story seems to be deliberately ambiguous to make the reader explore the story and their own attitudes to identity within the community. But it is noteworthy that there is no חרם mentioned in connection with the Gibeonites. In a sense then, in Joshua 'confrontation' with חרם forms a 'test' to establish identity. Rahab is shown to react 'for YHWH' when confronted with חרם, whereas the five kings react 'against YHWH' when confronted with it whilst Achan likewise reacts 'against YHWH' but in a different way when confronted with חרם. Perhaps, then, what the story of the Gibeonites is indicating by its lack of חרם is that this 'test' is too crude to establish identity near the boundary, in difficult cases. The characteristics of the Gibeonites are then typical of those around the boundary of the community.

---

[130] E.g. *Hom. Josh.* 15.1, 'In short, knowing that now we do not have to wage physical wars, but that the struggles of the soul have to be exerted against spiritual adversaries, the Apostle, just as a military leader, gives an order to the soldiers of Christ, saying, "Put on the armor of God, so that you may be able to stand firm against the cunning devices of the Devil."' (p.138).

[131] Recall the discussion of *Mekhilta Shirata* in chapter 3; God is a 'man of war', but not quite like a 'man of war' in any sense that we can easily envisage—hence the need for metaphor and symbol, and their careful use; God fights for Israel, but only when they are in need.

Thus we see how this 'probing' associated with חרם reflects the construction of identity at the *narrative level* in a way that reflects the development and 'pushing' of an underlying identity at the *structural level* (i.e. of categories of insiders and outsiders and their relationships), even if much of the story *does not* find significance at the narrative level *per se,* serving structural and literary requirements instead. In other words, these stories, whilst set in the context of a story narrating conquest, are not, as discourse, jingoistic tales, but stories that seek to probe difficult questions of Israel's identity in rather challenging ways. Perhaps one might say that the narrator skilfully uses jingoistic and 'xenophobic' discourse to challenge and qualify that very discourse, the problem being that it is often the jingoistic discourse that is appropriated, as its symbolism becomes obscured, tired and ossified. I shall return to these issues in chapter 9.

Joshua 11-12

The portrayal of the Canaanite response to Israel throughout Josh 1-11 demonstrates a progressively increasing resolve and desire to fight (5:1; 9:1; 10:1-5; 11:1-5), with 11:1-5 forming the 'literary climax' of this progression. Moreover, every military campaign since Ai is portrayed as a *defensive* reaction to Canaanite aggression,[132] with such aggression reaching a climax in Josh 11, in which Canaanite aggression is depicted with the use of 'fearful fighting machinery' (11:4).[133] Again, the Gibeonites are contrasted with other locals (11:19) and perhaps it is significant that it is the *inhabitants* of Gibeon that are contrasted with other local *kings* (cf. 9:1 and 3-4a).[134] Indeed, the cities that were fought against are depicted as royal cities, and Creach suggests that Josh 10-11 narrates 'a repudiation and defeat of royal power. The problem is ... a form of monarchy based on oppression.' He goes on to suggest that this idea is the key to the meaning of YHWH's instruction to burn chariots and hamstring horses (11:6); 'These two parts of the military machine symbolized the application of royal hegemony, gained often through brutality and abuse.'[135] Furthermore, Hawk notes that there are no details of the battles given, and that Hazor is singled out because it is the head of the kingdoms, 'exemplifying Canaanite threat', with the Anakim serving as symbols of Canaanite power.[136] So despite the wider frame of reference of the commands to take the land, Josh 11 portrays Israel's campaign

---

[132] L.G. Stone, 'Ethical and Apologetic Tendencies in the Redaction of the Book of Joshua', in *CBQ* 53.1 (1991): 25-36, here 31-3. The only two 'aggressive' campaigns (Jericho and Ai) seem mainly concerned with the stories of Rahab and Achan.
[133] Hess, *Joshua*, 211.
[134] Stone, 'Tendencies', 30.
[135] Creach, *Joshua*, 94.
[136] Hawk, *Joshua*, 170-74.

of conquest of Canaan as an essentially defensive reaction against centres of aggressive military power.[137]

Indeed, Joshua offers here a rather different perspective and interpretation of the conquest than that which is found in Deuteronomy. Stone comments that Josh 11:19 is

> the surprise of the whole account ... The text comes close to suggesting that war would not have been necessary had the Canaanite response been more cooperative. Moreover, 11:20 goes on to compare their response with Pharaoh's hard heart, completing the analogy with the exodus. ... Pharaoh's destruction is tied directly to the question of his response. Similarly, Israel's presence in Canaan presents Egypt's nominal representatives—the Canaanite kings—with the action of Yahweh, and likewise demands a response. ... Thus the destruction of the Canaanites is not because they are religiously decadent, nor is it because they have perpetrated economic oppression on the landed peasantry. They have resisted the action of Yahweh and thus have perished. [138]

Stone's last remark reinforces the line of interpretation developed above in which Josh 2-10 is construed as depicting varying responses to confrontation with YHWH's action and command, symbolized as חרם. The responses depicted are indicative of identity.

Josh 11 differs from Deuteronomy in several important ways. First, Deuteronomy 'justifies' the dispossession of the local peoples on the grounds of their 'moral wickedness' (e.g. Deut 9:4-5, although this is explicitly *not* coupled with a portrayal of Israel as righteous), which is an apologetic that we do not find in Joshua. Rather the 'apologetic' in Joshua is, generally speaking, that Israel's actions are a response to aggression. Secondly, Deuteronomy does not offer the possibility of peace treaties in the way that Josh 11:19 seems to imply that there *could* have been (cf. Deut 7, 20).

Yet in all this, Joshua is portrayed as obedient and faithful to all that YHWH commanded Moses (Josh 11:15).This note serves not to legitimate violence perhaps, but rather to legitimate the ways in which Rahab, Achan, the Gibeonites, and the aggressive kings have been dealt with, as symbolic characters who embody and exemplify different sorts of responsiveness to YHWH that relates to *structural* level concerns of Israelite identity and relationships with non-Israelites. These concerns are given content at the cultural and narrative levels through categories such as obedience and חסד, (positively), and aggression and חמד (negatively).

---

[137] Cf. Brueggemann, *Divine Presence*. Brueggemann offers a thoughtful reflection on the significance of horses and chariots in the narrative, and on the vital question of the context in which a story such as this is read. However, I think that the significance of Joshua 11 is somewhat different *in the context of Joshua as a whole* than that developed by Brueggemann.

[138] Stone, 'Tendencies', 33-4.

The motif of the hardening of the heart, in its various Hebrew forms,[139] central to the Plagues Narrative in Exodus, has occasioned considerable debate in the Christian tradition.[140] William Ford, rather than seeking to 'abstract the "hardening" as a theological issue that needs to be solved'[141] takes a 'narrative approach' to Exodus and considers the role of the reports of hardening and who it is that is reported as the agent of the hardening in the context of the person addressed, relating it to the *response* sought by YHWH in that person (or people).[142] The motif would thus appear to serve rhetorical purposes rather than being an ontological description, and perhaps it functions similarly in Joshua.

Josh 11 evokes Exodus, with the aggressive kings who stubbornly fight Israel evoking the stubborn, oppressive pharaoh who refuses to recognize and glorify YHWH. The stubborn pharaoh who will not let Israel go is balanced by the stubborn kings who will not let Israel come, and thus the reader is invited to interpret the local kings as cruel, stubborn and oppressive 'pharaohs' who fail to respond positively to YHWH just like the prototypical pharaoh. If the pharaoh of Exodus personifies evil,[143] then so do the local kings and their armies in Joshua.

However, it seems that the 'hardening' motif here in Joshua (11:19-20) serves an apologetic function—for it indicates that the 'conquest' *could* have been otherwise - even if for us it reads as strange apologetic, at least when the motif of hardening is reified into ontological description. We might find it more convincing to say that the local kings *hardened their own hearts,* rather than that YHWH hardened them. But if one may apply Ford's approach to Exodus to Joshua, this hardening note appears in the context of an address to Israel, rather than to the local kings of whom a response is called, and thus *serves as reassurance to Israel* rather than being a metaphysical description of 'what is' that can be viewed 'from nowhere'.

Do the references to the Anakim (11:21-22) suggest an apologetic concern? There are a number of groups of characters in the Old Testament who are some-

---

[139] The motif occurs with the use of one of four different verbs (כבד, חזק, קשה or אמץ), together with לב as the object in each case, appears mainly in conjunction with Pharaoh and the plagues in Exodus. Outside Exodus the hardening motif appears in Deut 2:30; Josh 11:20; 1 Sam 6:6; 2 Chr 36:13; Ps 95:8 and Isa 63:17.

[140] See e.g. Childs, *Exodus*, 170-75; D.G.C. Cox, 'The Hardening of Pharaoh's Heart in its Literary and Cultural Contexts' in *Bibliotheca Sacra* 163 (2006): 292-311; D.M. Gunn, 'The "Hardening of Pharaoh's Heart": Plot, Character and Theology in Exodus 1-14' in D.J.A. Clines, *et al.,* (eds.), *Art and Meaning: Rhetoric in Biblical Literature* (JSOTSup 19; Sheffield: JSOT Press, 1982), 72-96 and R.R. Wilson, 'The Hardening of Pharaoh's Heart' in *CBQ* 41.1 (1979): 18-36. The most recent detailed study is W.A. Ford, *God, Pharaoh and Moses: Explaining the Lord's Actions in the Exodus Plagues Narrative* (Paternoster Biblical Monographs; Milton Keynes: Paternoster, 2006).

[141] Ford, *God*, 10.

[142] Ibid., 113-24, 214-7.

[143] Cf. e.g. Ford, *God*, 120.

what 'mythical'[144] in nature; the descendants of Amalek, the Anakim, the Rephaim and the Nephilim. Moreover the Amorites, although unlike the other groups in that they are a well known 'historical' people, by being drawn into association with these other groups in the world of the text of the Old Testament take on a similar function.[145] Indeed, the Old Testament tends to draw these groups together more generally, conflating and confusing them: Num 13:33 reports that the Anakim are descendents of the Nephilim, who are giants, and the Anakim are also said to be giants (Num 13:28; Deut 9:2). But Deut 2:10-11 reports that the Anakim are considered as Rephaim, and Joshua reports that all the Anakim in the land of Israel were destroyed. But whilst Deut 3:11 suggests that Og was the last of the Rephaim, Josh 12:4 and 13:12 have Og as *one of the last* of the Rephaim. Either way, these notes restrict the existence of these figures to a distant, prototypical past. Deut 4:47 and 31:4 has Og as an Amorite (cf. Josh 2:10, etc), and so the Amorites are associated with the Rephaim, thus seeking to shape attitudes towards Amorites. Amos 2:9-10 has Amorites as giants, and Josh 10:10 has Sihon and Og as Amorite kings east of the Jordan, in addition to Amorite kings west of the Jordan (Josh 2:10; 5:1; 9:1, 10; 10:5, 6, 12: 11:3; 12:2). However, the Amalekites are not found in Joshua, and only occur in Deuteronomy in 25:17 and 19, occurring mainly in Judges and Samuel.

The rhetorical effect of this rather bewildering and disorientating set of associations is to confuse and blur the differences between these various 'prehistorical' groups to paint a picture of non-human, stereotypical, large, scary, baddies that are portrayed as the ancestors of groups hostile to Israel such as the Amorites; the Amorites and the portraits of these 'mythical beings' symbolize each other to evoke certain kinds of attitudes towards Israel's hostile neighbours

---

[144] In the traditional sense of the word.

[145] On the Anakim Mattingly comments, 'In the Egyptian Execration Texts (*ANET*, 328–29), there are references to several princes with Semitic names who are identified as rulers of *Iy-'anaq*. Many scholars regard this as a tribal name related to the Anakim, but this connection is not certain (cf. Albright 1928). Apart from these texts, which date to the 19–18th centuries B.C., there are no other extrabiblical references that shed light on the Anakim.' (G.L. Mattingly, 'Anak', in *ABD*, 1.222); The Rephaim, whilst not a historical people, are attested to in various Ugaritic texts. Their identity has been difficult to determine, but following the publication of *KTU* 1.161 (=RS 34.126) and its analysis by B.A. Levine and J-M. De Tarragon ('Dead Kings and Rephaim: The Patrons of the Ugaritic Dynasty', in *JAOS* 104.4 (1984): 649-59) it appears that they are 'long departed kings (and heroes) who dwell in the netherworld' (656); The Nephilim of Gen 6 have been compared with the *apkallu*, the semi-divine 'sages of old' in the Mesopotamian king and sage lists. They are understood to have brought civilization to humanity, but some are reported to be evil (cf. the sages (*ummiānu*) of the *Epic of Erra* I.147-153 (A.D. Kilmer, 'The Mesopotamian Counterparts of the Biblical Nephilim', in E.W Conrad and E.G. Newing (eds.) *Perspectives on Language and Text* (Winona Lake: Eisenbrauns, 1987), 39-44); For the Amorites see G.E. Mendenhall, 'Amorites', in *ABD*, 1.199-202.

such as the Amorites.[146] So by reporting in the conclusion of Josh 11:21-22 that the conquest came to completion with the extermination of the Anakim and their towns, the apologetic character of Josh 11 is reinforced; the conquest results in the elimination of shadowy, giant pre-historic warrior kings.[147] Setting these shadowy figures of the past, as attested in the Ugaritic materials, in this 'historical narrative' indicates and accentuates the mythological nature of the text, showing it to be set in a prototypical time in the distant past.

Josh 11 ends by reporting the completeness of the conquest (11:16 and 23) and the obedience of Joshua to both YHWH and Moses (11:15 and 23), something that stands in tension with what will follow in Josh 13-19, thus highlighting the rhetorical nature of the material. Moreover, the report that the land had rest from war (11:23) suggests that such rest was viewed as an important goal of the conquest, as we noted above. The text thus evokes the notion that the cessation of war is associated with obedience to YHWH. It is then a small step to develop this idea eschatologically.

Finally, Josh 12 summarizes the defeated kings, giving Joshua something of the appearance of a conquest account, perhaps in order to make the story appear to be of an apparently recognizable genre, maybe so that it will be used and not disappear into obscurity, and challenge those who most need to be challenged, i.e. those who have a penchant for jingoistic, xenophobic discourse in the construction of Israel's identity. In other words, Joshua reflects well developed, subtle and crafty rhetoric.

Joshua 13-21

In chapter 4 we considered the Priestly nature of Josh 13:1-21:42, and the absence of Deuteronomistic features here, most notably the absence of חרם. Whilst having a different origin from the remainder of the material in Joshua, it reads naturally as a second major section of Joshua, and continuation of the story, as suggested by Josh 13:1-6, narrating the settlement of the land. In particular, Josh 13-21 is concerned with the ordering of the tribes within the land

---

[146] Cf, 'The pre-Israelite residents variously called Nephilim, Rephaim, Anakites, and designated by other more elusive names such as *'Awwîm* and *'Êmîm* (the dreadful ones?), inhabited diverse regions of Canaan and Transjordan, ranging all the way from Bashan (Golan) in northern Transjordan, through Hebron in the Judean hill country and down to Seir and the southern coastal plain. What is most significant about these traditions is the consistent identification of those almost mythic creatures as non-Israelites, as having descended from other groups, some identifiable and others not, but decidedly not from Israelite ancestors. This perception differs essentially from what we find at Ugarit, for instance, where traditions about Rephaim are prominent.' (B.A. Levine, *Numbers 1-20* (AB 4A; New York: Doubleday, 1993), 378).

[147] Cf. Levine, *Numbers*, 378-9.

(Josh 13-19), cities of refuge (Josh 20), and the distribution of the Levites throughout the land (Josh 21), concerns that are central to the establishment of the society within the land. However, interwoven with the reports of allocation of land are narratives that provide reflections upon the sort of characteristics that are central to the identity of Israel, thus having affinities with the concerns of Josh 1-12. Hawk notes,

> Like the stories of Rahab, Achan, and the Gibeonites, these stories confuse concepts of territorial possession, kinship ties, and obedience to YHWH in various ways. Caleb represents the ideal Israelite, undaunted by Canaanite might and anxious to take the land promised to him. He is, however, an Israelite of questionable ancestry, a detail hinted at by his identification as a "Kenizzite" (14:14), the name of a clan which in other contexts is associated with the Edomites (Gen 36:11, 15, 42; 1 Chr 1:36, 53). The second and third stories assail the connection between land and kinship by relating land grants awarded to women. By reporting the giving of land to women, the stories of Achsah and Zelophehad's daughters challenge the patriarchal structures which reinforce both property rights and kinship relations (structures explicitly articulated in the story of pedigreed Achan [7:1]). Possession of land by women undermines the "male-territory" equation and subtly integrates the "other" gender into an Israelite community that traces the promise of the land only through those whose are marked by circumcision (Gen 17:1-14).
>
> The negative side of the program (here the failure to occupy promised land) is expressed, as it is in the story of Achan, by a story about pedigreed Israelites. In this case, the subjects are members of Joshua's own tribal group, who command the special attention of the nation's leader (17:14-18). The story sets "the tribe of Joseph" against Joshua and turns the exemplary quality of initiative on its head. The Josephites also request lands, but with less than noble motives. Because they are numerous, they want more than their share, declaring that the hill country is insufficient but rejecting the plains because Canaanites with iron chariots live there. The Josephites thus stand in stark contrast to Caleb, who requests the kind of territory that the Josephites refuse. Given prior reports that Ephraim and Manasseh failed to take many of the Canaanite cities, Joshua's command that they drive out the Canaanites concludes the episode on a note of failure. ...
>
> The resulting portrait of Israel compromises the status of all boundaries—ethnic, religious, and territorial—which construct community identity.[148]

So Josh 13-21 represents a 'charter' for constructing the life and identity of Israel, both with respect to establishing claims to land, and with respect to what it is that characterizes the Israelite as one possessing the land. Apart from the casting of the lots for the land there is no indication of any direct divine assistance in the settlement, unlike Josh 1-12, even though such assistance may be

---

[148] Hawk, *Joshua*, 192-3.

implicit (e.g. Josh 14:12). The divine allocation does, however, provide a firm warrant, set in a prototypical time, for the division of the land. But as in the other major sections of the book, the rest of the land from war is seen as a goal of settling the land (14:15, cf. 11:23; 21:44).

However, there are difficulties with the lists of towns and boundaries.[149] Nelson notes that Josh 13:1-7 reflects Num 34, but not what follows in Joshua,[150] and the boundary lists differ again from Ezek 47-48, which makes no allowance for Transjordanian territory. Hess argues for a twelfth century date for some of the references to the towns and boundaries, but notes that some are seventh or eighth century, leading him to conclude that the lists were subject to revision and updating as they continued to form an important basis for territorial claims.[151] Whether or not these dates are correct, this updating process is perhaps the most likely explanation for the differences between the lists, suggesting that this text is 'mythical' in the sense that it was 'living', shaping and reflecting the society that used it. It was continually updated to meet these needs, but by setting the boundaries in antiquity they are vested with authority. As Nelson notes, 'Traditional and administrative geography has been reutilized in a narrative and theological framework to build and bolster national identity. The communities that produced and read this literature did so in order to hold fast to their claim on the territories of their ancestors.'[152] The greater precision of the description of Judah might then be explained in terms of the use and development of the text being primarily Judean.

It is interesting that Josh 13-21 is not simply a list of territories; rather, it is a narrative that weaves listings of territories with stories of people together with 'theological' summaries. Caleb is an example of one who follows YHWH 'wholeheartedly' (מלא אחר), an expression that occurs here in Josh 14:8, 9 and 14, and only elsewhere in Num 14:24; 32:11-12; Deut 1:36 and 1 Kgs 11:6. It is a rare characteristic that exemplifies adequate response to YHWH, and it interprets and is interpreted by Caleb's actions—Caleb drives out the Anakim (14:12), and receives a blessing from Joshua (14:13). However, he is a Kenizzite (14:6), and is in one sense identified with the 'men of Judah'. But in another sense he is differentiated from them via this genealogical note (emphasized in 14:14, where there is no mention of Judah).[153] This suggests that he is of 'questionable pedigree', yet acts in an exemplary way, perhaps rather like Rahab.

---

[149] See Nelson, *Joshua*, 193, 212, 214, 229-230, 236-8; Hess, *Joshua*, 247-9, 261.
[150] Nelson, *Joshua*, 164-5.
[151] Hess, *Joshua*, 247-9, 261.
[152] Nelson, *Joshua*, 212.
[153] Hawk notes that Caleb means dog, and that given the 'low view of dogs in the Hebrew Bible' the name seems to have a negative connotation and thus 'enlarges Caleb's heroic stature through contrast' (*Joshua*, 198).

Following Caleb's anticipation of 'driving out' (ירש) the locals 'if YHWH is with me' (14:12),

אולי יהיה אותי והורשתים כאשר דבר יהוה

a 'driving out', which, by implication, occurred completely, the land had rest (שקט) from war (14:15).[154] He is portrayed as one who takes bold initiatives based upon trusting in YHWH being with him as a result of YHWH's promise, and the narrative reports the possession of Hebron as being the result of Caleb's 'wholehearted' following of YHWH. The importance of Caleb's character is reiterated in 15:13ff.

The other stories in Josh 13-19 indicate that such bold initiative taking is construed positively and is the characteristic associated with possessing the land.[155] In 15:16-19 boldness and strength is required to win Caleb's daughter, Achsah, by capturing Kiriath Sepher, which Othniel does. Following this Achsah makes a bold request of her father, which he grants.[156] Similarly, Zelophehad's request reflects a certain 'boldness', but is associated with the promise in Numbers (Num 36), and his daughters duly receive an inheritance. Whilst Ben-Barak notes that inheritance by daughters is attested elsewhere in the ANE,[157] the report of such inheritance here, and the report of Achsah's initiative, along with Rahab's story, suggests that the nature of the identity of the community that Joshua seeks to construct is not as patriarchal as one might think; indeed, as Hawk notes, these stories demonstrate that patriarchy 'does not constitute an essential element of Israelite national identity'.[158]

---

[154] שקט also occurs in 11:23.

[155] Cf. Hawk, *Joshua*, 192ff.

[156] Here, I follow Mosca's reading, that it is Achsah making a request of Caleb in 15:18 (P.G. Mosca, 'Who Seduced Whom? A Note on Joshua 15:18//Judges 1:14', in *CBQ* 46.1 (1984): 18-22)) although I understand Achsah's action more positively; she receives a blessing from Caleb, amid abundant blessings, with her action construed along similar lines to Rahab's and the Gibeonites. (The issue here is in reading וַתְּסִיתֵהוּ in 15:18. Mosca notes in a study of the usage of סות, that apart from in postexilic work where סות followed by ל + infinitive construct is used, ל + infinitive construct functions as a gerund which refers to the subject of סות. He thus proposes reading 15:18, 'When she [Achsah] arrived, she beguiled him [Caleb], asking from her father arable land.' Othniel, he notes, 'plays no role at all in the encounter described in Josh. 15:18-20 ... He is neither manipulated nor manipulating' (ibid., 21). Moreover, he notes that 'what Achsah actually demands is not property as such, but rather that ready access to water which is so essential if her future home in the Negev is to be both habitable and agriculturally productive' (ibid., 21)).

[157] Z. Ben-Barak, 'Inheritance by Daughters in the Ancient Near East', in *JSS* 25 (1980): 22-33.

[158] Hawk, *Joshua*, 209.

Moreover, these qualities of boldness and initiative taking are exemplified by the Danites (19:47-48), where they attack and settle a town outside their inheritance because they had trouble in possessing their allotted territory. The narrative creates the impression that their action is to be construed positively, although it raises the question of the role of the lot, and, arguably, their disobedience, but perhaps this is not a concern of the narrative. It is the desire to portray their bold initiative in taking possession of the land that is the main concern of the narrative.[159]

On a negative note, when the people of Joseph complain about their lack of land (17:14), Joshua's response is to suggest that they boldly take more land. But it is land that is, they complain, associated with Rephaim, and with Canaanites with iron chariots. Their complaint here contrasts them with Caleb (possibly reflecting Num 13); Caleb went up against the Anakim and the large cities, whereas the Josephites are afraid to go up against the Rephaim and iron chariots. They lack the boldness and courage that should be exercised in the light of YHWH's promise to possess the land.[160] The story ends on a rather ambiguous note; Joshua gives them reassurance that they can do it—but will they?

This theme continues to be developed in 18:1-10 where the procedure of 'treading the land' recalls 1:3 and 14:9, 'reminding both Israel and the reader that the nation will possess just as much of the gift of the land as it cares to traverse', emphasized through wordplay on dividing (והתחלקו 18:5) and wandering (והתהלכו 18:8).[161]

Thus obedience, zeal, boldness and initiative are shown to be the characteristics that exemplify response to YHWH's gift and promise. Indeed, Hawk notes with regard to Caleb that

> Judah's elaborate and coherent boundaries demonstrate the consequences of the energy and obedience that Caleb symbolizes, while the encyclopedic list of cities shows what can be accomplished by those who eagerly assault the cities of giants. In an even larger sense, Caleb represents the nation itself. The Mosaic promise that motivates him, that "the land on which your foot has trodden shall be an inheritance for you and your children forever" (v. 9), corresponds to YHWH's promise to Israel at the beginning of the book, "every place that the sole of your foot will tread upon I have given to you, as I promised to Moses" (1:3). Both promises, significantly, measure fulfillment in terms of response; the extent of territory "given" depends on how much the subject will "walk"

---

[159] If the LXX is preferred (see chapter 7), then these qualities of boldness and initiative are still exemplified, but by Judah rather than by the Danites.

[160] I.e. the boldness and initiative shown here are not autonomous, but the appropriate response resulting from trusting YHWH's promise—the land is a gift, there for the taking.

[161] Hawk, *Joshua*, 215.

(cf. Deut 11:24-25). The narrator presents Caleb as the embodiment of obedience, zeal, and initiative.[162]

Given that in the context of an ancient Israelite reading or hearing Joshua the land was not completely possessed, as emphasized in Josh 23-24, it seems that these stories are to find existential appropriation and enactment (at least in the context of ancient Israel) via the bold initiative taking of Israelites to acquire land from non-Israelites, an initiative that is taken in the context of YHWH's promise to give the land to Israel. However, whilst the narrative portrays land as being taken by force, bearing in mind that mythical material such as this does not offer models for behaviour, there is no reason to suppose, especially when this material is read in the wider Old Testament context, that it is envisaged that the narrative will be enacted through the forcible gain of land. Rather, it seems that what is encouraged is the use of initiative in acquiring land where possible.

Such characteristics of boldness and initiative taking are echoed in the Christian context, but in a different key. In Heb 4:16 Christians are encouraged to 'approach the throne of grace with boldness',[163] and bold initiative taking is exemplified in the Canaanite woman who greatly impresses Jesus with her faith (Matt 15:21-28). In other words, the New Testament and the Christian perspective of 'faith' offers an important lens through which to interpret Joshua in a new context, a context in which the symbolic connotations of the land, and its possession as inheritance are developed yet further. Perhaps Joshua can give content to what it is that characterizes such 'faith' as one juxtaposes Joshua with various new myths and interprets them in the light of each other in the Christian context. I shall return to this in chapter 9.

The portrayal of conquest here in Josh 13-21 differs from that in 1-11 in which a complete conquest is envisaged, for here there are various references to the failure to drive out (ירש) locals; Judah could not drive out the Jebusites (15:63), the Ephraimites could not drive out the Canaanites in Gezer (but did subject them to forced labour (16:10)), and likewise the Manassites were not able to occupy their towns completely, but eventually grew strong enough to subject the Canaanites to forced labour (17:13). There are several points to note here: First, forced labour seems to be regarded as a 'second best' to driving out. Secondly, together Judah, Ephraim and Manasseh seem to constitute, symbolically, all of Israel; they are the 'big three' tribes that reflect all the tribes of Israel. Indeed, apart from a slightly ambiguous note concerning the Danites (19:47) there are no other reports of failure to drive out the locals in the narratives relating to any of the other tribes. But such failure is, perhaps, to be in-

---

[162] Hawk, *Joshua*, 195-6.
[163] Cf. the closing lines of Wesley's 'And can it be?'
Bold I approach the eternal throne
And claim the crown, through Christ my own.

ferred from the three symbolic tribes. However, thirdly, it is interesting that there is no report of forced labour with regard to Judah.

Thus, as suggested above, the text evokes the need for continued action in possessing the land in the world of the readers of the text for them to find 'rest' in life with YHWH in its fullness. The land's possession and settlement is an uncompleted task, which is again suggestive of a latent eschatological picture, with rest being something for Israel to work towards in ways that are explored by the book as a whole (cf. Josh 23-24 below).

It is interesting to consider the way in which Origen develops the significance of the reference to driving out the Canaanites in 17:16-18 in a Christian context:

> For if at last we come to perfection, then the Canaanite is said to have been exterminated by us and handed over to death. But as to how this is accomplished in our flesh, hear the apostle saying, "Mortify your members that are upon the earth: fornication, impurity," and the other things that follow. And again it says, "For those who belong to Christ have crucified their flesh with its vices and lusts." Thus, therefore, in the third stage, that is, when we come to perfection and mortify our members and carry around the death of Christ in our body, the Canaanite is said to be exterminated by us.[164]

The existential nature of Origen's reading reflects the existential nature of Joshua as discourse, even though his is a 'spiritualizing' reading that develops the nature of the task that leads to 'rest' in new ways, being an *interior* struggle rather than an *exterior* one; the hindrances to finding rest in life with God are not other peoples, but vices and lusts within oneself. Whilst this is not an exegesis of Joshua *per se,* it can be said to reflect an interesting development of it as discourse in a context in which, through further reflection and 'revelation' perhaps, it is clear that the obstacles to progress in the Christian life are associated with the 'self' (cf. Mark 7:14-23). Finding the rest that Israel seeks in Joshua is interpreted in terms of coming to perfection, being a development and reading of the myth of Joshua when it is read in juxtaposition with others.

In chapter 4 we considered the significance of כבש (subdue) in the summary statement in 18:1, comparing its usage here with that in Gen 1:28, which relates to the role of humanity in creation, and Num 32:22 and 29, which finds its fulfilment in Josh 18:1. Similarly, we saw how Brueggemann compared the 'finishing' (כלה) of Gen 2:1-2 with the tabernacle's completion (Exod 39:32; 40:33) and with the 'finishing' of Josh 19:49-51.[165] Whatever the relative historical origins of these texts, we are now invited to read them in the light of each other as they interpret each other. Israel's taking possession of and settling in the land is seen as the fulfilment of the charge to humanity at creation, with God

---

[164] *Hom. Josh.* 22:2, pp.190-91.
[165] Brueggemann, *Theology,* 533.

dwelling again with humanity in the tabernacle, and later the temple. When read from a Deuteronomistic perspective, as the final form of Joshua invites, this might emphasize that the charge to humanity may be conceived in terms of avoiding idolatry and obeying *torah*. Indeed, the conclusion of this section of the book (21:43-45) is traditionally regarded as having Deuteronomistic affinities, reflecting the fulfilment of the promise of the land (cf. 1:3), and the rest as promised (21:44) (cf. e.g. Gen 12:1-7; 13:14-18 etc.).[166] The convergence of these themes is interesting, since read together from Priestly and Deuteronomistic perspectives they suggest that God promises rest and blessing for his people, but rest that is attained through obedience to torah, the avoidance of idolatry, boldness, zeal and initiative in the context of trusting responsiveness to YHWH, themes that are developed with regard to the interior life in a Christian context.[167]

Finally, I have said rather little about the establishment of the cities of refuge (Josh 20), or of the levitical cities (Josh 21). The establishment of these cities was clearly of central importance to the construction of Israel in its ancient context, as the amount of narrative space given to the establishment of these cities in this prototypical narrative indicates. But perhaps the concerns that the establishment of these cities reflects finds rather little development in the Christian context, owing to the different cultural context. Thus for the Christian reader especially, perhaps these accounts find significance only in the broad sense of cultural memory, in the sense that these stories provide the church with a narrative of the development of its own identity.

In summary then, perhaps the complete conquest of Josh 1-11 serves to indicate the fruits of obedience; that in some sense God will 'fight for us' when 'we' obey him, whilst in 13-21 the partial conquest evokes the continual eschatological nature of the task of 'possessing the land', or entering into the Christian life in its fullness. Josh 13-21 also continues to clarify what kind of 'faith' (to use a Christian category that describes human responsiveness to God) is to characterize God's people, concerns that Origen develops. The portrayal of the completeness (or otherwise) of the conquest thus serves a rhetorical function. Josh 1-11 and 13-21 represent 'testimonies' from two traditions; a Deuteronomistic and a Priestly tradition that are concerned with the construction of Israel's identity in stories set in the context of possessing and settling the land. The two testimonies, though using different language, demonstrate a remarkable convergence, complementing each other in the construction of Israel's identity.

---

[166] This note of obtaining rest stresses the fulfillment of promise, but strains the unfinished nature of the conquest. But this reflects the different rhetorical goals of the Priestly and Deuteronomistic sections of Joshua.

[167] Hence one may see how certain psychological perspectives may be helpful in developing these concerns.

Joshua 22

Josh 22 narrates the building of an altar by the Transjordanians 'near' the Jordan, a construction to which the Cisjordanians object, resulting in a dialogue which reaches an amicable resolution with the Cisjordanians accepting the legitimacy of the altar. In doing so various important issues are raised relating to land and worship, being the concerns that appear to drive the story.

We considered the Priestly character of Josh 22 in chapter 4 and saw that 21:43-22:6 (or possibly 21:43-22:8) perhaps form a Deuteronomistic (or Deuteronnomistic-like) interjection into the Priestly (or Priestly-like) material of Josh 13-22.[168] Thus Josh 22:1-6 invites one to read this Priestly, or at least 'Priestly-like' narrative also from a Deuteronomistic perspective which helps to guide its interpretation. Indeed, 22:1-6 integrates the concern with the Transjordanian tribes prevalent throughout Joshua, and indeed Numbers, with this story in such a way as to provide an interpretative key to the account. A strong concern for national unity is thus demonstrated. In 22:1-6 the reader is informed in advance of the obedience and good character of the Transjordanians; they have acted in an exemplary manner thus far, and so one would expect them to continue to do so.[169] This 'interjection' does not modify the sense of the story, for the Transjordanians emerge positively from 22:7-34 alone, but it reinforces the positive appraisal of their actions and prepares the reader for what follows.

Whilst the (essentially) Deuteronomistic Josh 1-11 is concerned with qualifying Israel's identity and self-understanding with respect to questions of ethnicity and response to YHWH developed in the world of the text around response to חרם, with similar concerns extending into the Priestly Josh 13-21 with regard to the settlement of the land, Josh 22 seeks to qualify Israel's identity construction with regard to land and geography, raising the question of what faithful response to YHWH looks like from another angle—where YHWH's people may live and how they may worship him. Hawk suggests that the 'eastern tribes appear throughout the book as implicit reminders of the ambiguities that complicate the formation of a distinctive Israelite community',[170] and that Manasseh presents in miniature the tensions within Israel's social structure, being torn in two with the issue of geography dividing, but kinship uniting.[171]

The construction of the altar forms the focus of this story which addresses three main concerns; the Transjordan land, and whether it is unclean (טמא) (22:19); the question of where legitimate offerings may be made (22:19, 23, 26,

---

[168] However, see Knauf, *Josua*, 21 for the possibility that 21:43-45 reflects Priestly theology in Deuteronomistic language.

[169] Cf. Nelson, *Joshua*, 247, and Hawk who notes that the piling up of phrases in Deuteronomistic idiom 'forcefully underscores the theme of fidelity to YHWH' (*Joshua*, 234).

[170] Hawk, *Joshua*, 228.

[171] Ibid., 234-5.

28-29) together with the associated question of the purpose of the altar constructed here; and that of the unity of Israel in future generations—are the Transjordanians part of Israel (22:24-28, 34), despite living 'across the Jordan'?

It is significant that the first concern, that of the uncleanness of the land, is raised near the beginning of the story by the Cisjordanians, but is never resolved explicitly, even if it is implicitly as we shall see below. This may indicate the extent to which this story is 'pushing' Israelite identity and theology in new directions. Nelson suggests that the notion that the Jordan marks the limit of YHWH's land 'first clearly emerges' in Ezek 47:13-48:29, and that Josh 22 implies that the 'unity of Yahweh's people is founded not on geographic proximity, but on shared faith and fidelity in worship'.[172] Butler notes that the East Jordan is impure because it is not YHWH's possession, rather it is 'your possession' (22:19); 'That means it is land where Yahweh does not live, land which his presence has not sanctified and purified (cf. Amos 7:7).'[173] However, in the story the issue of perspective is crucial, for in 22:19 it is the Cisjordanians who refer to the Transjordan as 'your land' whilst describing the Cisjordan as 'the Lord's land'. Furthermore, Hawk notes that Josh 13-21 has 'amply demonstrated' that 'a "portion" (*ḥēleq*) is precisely what situates a tribe within the established boundaries of land and community and legitimates its participation in the life of the nation.' But 22:9 indicates that YHWH *has* granted the territory to the eastern tribes, and thus in reality it is the western, Cisjordan tribes and not YHWH that has made the Jordan a boundary, pointing to a tendency for the tribes to construct boundaries not 'initiated or endorsed by YHWH'.[174]

Moreover, attention is drawn to the nature and significance of the Jordan as a boundary, or not, through the use of the verb עבר, or rather its lack of use here. We saw earlier that it symbolized transition into or out of the community of Israel and fullness of life with YHWH. But here Polzin notes that when the Israelite delegation left the Transjordan to report back to the Israelites in Canaan (22:32), although the crossing of the Jordan is indicated, in no case is the verb עבר ever used; 'The reason for this is that "the crossing over" had already taken place.' The only place where עבר is used is where one might expect it, in 22:19, in the speech of the Cisjordanian delegation, where its use demonstrates that the delegation believes that the two and a half tribes must 'cross' into Israel.[175] In other words, the narrator indicates that the Transjordanians have symbolically 'crossed' into life with YHWH, even if they have re-traversed the Jordan, whereas the Cisjordanians believe that the Transjordanians have 'crossed' out of life with YHWH by crossing the Jordan in the wrong direction. To put it another way, for the Cisjordanians the land and the river *is* the 'reality', for the narrator

---

[172] Nelson, *Joshua*, 250.
[173] Butler, *Joshua*, 247. Cf. Deut 32:8 and Ezek 48.
[174] Hawk, *Joshua*, 242.
[175] Polzin, *Deuteronomy*, 138.

and the Transjordanians it *symbolizes* that reality, of life with YHWH. Thus the geography of the land and the location of the various groups symbolize issues of identity. Indeed, the story reaches a resolution where no concessions are required on the part of the Transjordanians, indicating that ultimately the status of the land was not decisive, even if life in it with all its blessings reflected a real 'sharing in' life with YHWH. The perspective of all the parties converges as the symbolic understanding prevails. Thus the story is suggestive of a significant development of Priestly conceptions of the land.[176] Moreover, it is worth noting that the altar that is built is symbolic for the Transjordanians in a way that it was not, originally at least, for the Cisjordanians. But it is the symbolic interpretations of the land and the altar that prevail, and so in a sense perhaps here is a textually based hermeneutical key to the interpretation of Joshua—it is the symbolic dimensions that are significant. Just as anthropological approaches to myth highlight the problems with the 'tiring' or 'ossification' of symbols and myths, so does Josh 22, where the 'second order' sense, or what the symbol points to, is collapsed into the 'first order' concrete sense of the symbol in the Cisjordanian interpretation, which is shown to be defective.

The second and third issues, explicitly raised by the Transjordanians, relate to the purpose of the altar. The Cisjordanians implicitly assume that the altar is for offerings, and thus that it represents both illegitimate worship of YHWH, and a division of Israel, for a single altar for offerings serves a unifying function. But does a מזבח ('altar') imply offerings? R.D. Haak suggests that

> The term *mizbēaḥ* is also used for another type of construction which serves primarily as a "memorial" ... Several "altars" are given names, often in connection with some unusual event (cf. Gen 33:20; 35:7; Exod 17:15; Josh 22:10–34; and Judg 6:24). In none of these cases are sacrifices actually offered upon these "altars." Whether these constructions were memorials which the author calls "altars" or whether they were altars which later authors attempted to legitimize by assigning an acceptable function is not clear ... A similar case of a rock being designated as a named "memorial" is found in 1 Sam 7:12, but without the term *mizbēaḥ* being used.
>
> Altars did have other functions. Altars were built to mark the territory associated with the deity (cf. 1 Kgs 18:17–40; 2 Kgs 5:17)...
>
> There are differences among the various "authors" of the Hebrew Bible in their portrayal of altars. The Yahwist assumes Levitical distinctions for the altars even in the pre-Mosaic period. The Priestly author does not allow Levitical distinctions before Sinai. He assumes the existence of only one altar since Sinai but in some senses has reduced its sanctity compared to earlier ideas (e.g., it no

---

[176] See also J.S. Kloppenbeorg, 'Joshua 22: The Priestly editing of an Ancient Tradition', in *Biblica* 62 (1981): 347- 71 for a brief discussion on the issue of unclean-ness of the land, making reference to 1 Sam 26:19; 2 Kgs 5:15-19; Ps 137; Ezek 11:14-16; Hos 9:3-4; Amos 7:17 (359-60).

longer provides asylum ...). The Deuteronomist (Deut 12:15–24) loosens the connection between the altar and the slaughter of animals prescribed in earlier writings (Lev 17:1–7).[177]

The Transjordanians make it clear that the 'altar' is not for offerings; rather it is to function as a witness for future generations that testifies to the unity of all Israel, something that, ironically, it is in danger of undermining. Thus despite appearances, the appearance of a second altar, which is described as a copy (תבנית), is in fact intended to foster unity rather than division. Indeed, Hawk suggests that the 'crux of the story revolves around different perceptions of how the nation is to be defined and held together'. The western tribes equate identity with the possession of the land and perceive a danger in plurality if Israel should sacrifice at many sites, with her distinctive identity being lost. But the eastern tribes see bonds of kinship as more definitive for Israelite identity, and for them, the altar represents not division but an attempt to preserve unity.[178] However, it is interesting that we are not told at the beginning what the altar is built for—the reader has a Cisjordan perspective. The description of the altar (22:10);

מזבח גדול למראה

also serves to heighten the reader's concern, with attention being drawn to the imposing nature of the altar. Moreover, the altar's location is ambiguous - which side of the Jordan is it on? In 22:10 it is said to be בארץ כנען whilst in 22:11 it is

אל־מול ארץ כנען אל־גלילות הירדן אל־עבר בני ישראל

Perhaps it is significant that 22:10 reflects the Transjordanian perspective whilst 22:11 reflects the Cisjordanian perspective. Maybe, for the Transjordanians the altar signifies their presence *inside* the land (i.e., community of Israel) whereas from the Cisjordanian perspective it signifies the Transjordanian presence *outside* the land *and* community. As Hawk notes, 'With every clarifying note, the location of the altar becomes increasingly obscure!'[179] He also suggests that an altar constitutes the symbolic centre of a community, 'the place where the polarities of communal life are united and mediated ... an altar provides a place where the untidy oppositions of communal life converge', and thus an 'altar therefore constitutes the perfect symbol and setting for this story which attempts to negotiate the difficult issues of community identity.'[180] So the construction of an altar in a 'boundary region' at a disputed location is significant, for this geographical boundary ambiguity may reflect ambiguities in Israel's identity construction near the boundaries of the community.

---

[177] R.D. Haak, 'Altar', in *ABD*, 1.162-7, here 164.
[178] Hawk, *Joshua*, 229-30. In a sense then, this story presents a re-affirmation of the importance of genealogy in the construction of Israel's identity.
[179] Ibid., 237.
[180] Ibid., 228-9.

As the story unfolds the reader is shown differing possible interpretations of the altar. It is interesting that its *intention* is crucial—what is it for? As well as appealing to (presumably) established notions of purity in relation to the land, the Cisjordanians appeal to Achan's story (Josh 7) and the sin at Peor (Num 25), understanding the altar building as an act of rebellion like these acts that will bring the wrath of God on all Israel.[181] The Cisjordanian concern is considered by Phinehas, but upon hearing the Transjordanian perspective, he is satisfied with their response. The altar is built not for offerings, and not as an act of rebellion, and is not an attempt to divide (or does not risk dividing) Israel. Indeed, Phinehas ironically inverts the Cisjordanian interpretation; it is in fact the Cisjordanians that have risked divine wrath, and not the Transjordanians (22:31), who in fact avert it. Moreover, in 22:30-33, the remark that 'you have rescued the Israelites' recalls the only other instance of the identical verbal form in Joshua; Rahab's request (2:13),[182] suggesting that Rahab parallels the Transjordanians. Whilst the Cisjordanians interpreted the Transjordanians by analogy with Achan, in fact it is the Cisjordanians themselves who parallel Achan, demonstrating again ironic reversals of what is *apparently* the case.[183] Casting Phinehas as the one who pronounces the verdict grants it authority, for it is the same Phinehas who acted zealously to halt the plague against the Israelites at Peor, the incident referred to earlier by the Cisjordanians (Num 25:6-13).

Hence this story is similar to those of Rahab and Achan. Despite appearances, and conventional understanding, Rahab reflects the true Israelite, unlike Achan; despite appearances and conventional understanding, it is the Cisjordanian action that threatens God's wrath, not the Transjordanian action. Moreover, whilst Rahab and Achan's stories indicate that issues of ethnicity are not finally determinative for Israelite identity, so Josh 22 indicates that geography and land are not finally determinative either.[184] The story of Josh 22 indicates the priority of doxological response to YHWH, and Israel's unity. Together with the rest of Joshua, Josh 22 indicates that many of the expected means that might be used to define identity are qualified, and it is significant that this occurs through the juxtaposition of Priestly and Deuteronomistic witnesses here in Joshua, testify-

---

[181] The root מעל is used here (22:16, 20, 22, 31) as in Josh 7 (7:1), but not in Num 25. But in Josh 22 nothing bad has happened; it is assumed and anticipatory.

[182] Hess, *Joshua*, 293.

[183] The possible allusions to the stories of Rahab and Achan here may well suggest a complex compositional history for Josh 22, particularly as the introduction appears to be Deuteronomistic. However, the pervasiveness of Priestly themes in this text indicates that it is read well with Priestly concerns in view, even if the narrative might not be Priestly *per se*.

[184] Whilst Josh 22 might be taken to indicate that the borders of the 'clean' land where YHWH dwells have been expanded, the fact that the initial reference to issues of purity is not resolved in the story would tell against this.

ing to the fittingness of the combination of these two sets of materials since they share many of the same types of concern.

Christian reading of Josh 22 appears to be rather preoccupied with a rather atomistic kind of allegorical or typological reading of the text, discussing the significance of the altar in terms of the 'true altar' that is Christ.[185] This, it seems, reflects a rather unconvincing development of the text, being an exploration that is not really fitting and faithful to the text and to its dynamics, and what it seeks to show.[186] In this case, the contemporary interpreter is drawn toward the pole of the original act of discourse rather than to that of later reception and development.

Joshua 23

Josh 23:1 introduces a new section of Joshua; 'After many days had passed ...'. The repetition of the reference to achieving נוח (rest) here (cf. 21:44) is significant, underlining its importance as the goal of the conquest, and that to which Joshua is oriented.[187] Josh 23 is Joshua's first 'farewell speech', charging the Israelites with their ongoing task. Whatever the historical relationship between Josh 23 and the remainder of Joshua, Josh 23 offers a theological commentary on Josh 1-22, or perhaps a 'homiletic commentary', that develops something of Joshua's ongoing significance for the life of the people of Israel. Indeed, Martin Noth stated that Josh 23 'looks forward and backward in an attempt to interpret

---

[185] E.g. Origen, *Hom. Josh.* 3.2 (p.46); 23.6 (pp.218-9), and Theodoret, who concludes. 'Thus present-day Jews should know and admit that their altar was not the true one but only a prefiguration of it.' (*Quest. Josh.* 19.2, p.301).

[186] In contrast, I suggest with the Christian development of the Jordan crossing (Josh 3-4) in relation to baptism. For here, in the Christian development of Josh 3-4, it seems that the symbol of crossing into life is appropriated well in a new context that is fitting with the narrative as discourse in a way that the Christian development of Josh 22 is not. The Christian development of Josh 22 is a rather atomistic development of one aspect of the altar symbolism that does not really fit with its use in the context of the story.

[187] Hawk notes that the report that YHWH gives Israel rest (נוח) unites the three texts of Josh 1:2-8, 21:43-45 and 23:1ff, texts which taken together bring the viewpoints of YHWH, the narrator and Joshua into dialogue (*Joshua*, 247). But whereas in 21:43-45 the narrator speaks of possession of the land as something achieved, here (23:5) it is something yet to be achieved—'Joshua ... transform[s] the glorious certainties of the past into the troubling openness and incompleteness of the future' (247-8). Cf. also Von Rad, 'The odd thing was ... the promises were not regarded as having been given final effect; after the time of Joshua the promise of the land retained its character as a promise for all time—indeed, the very fulfilment of this promise in Joshua made it the source of fresh promises' (*Old Testament Theology, Volume II: The Theology of Israel's Prophetic Traditions* (London: SCM, ET: 1965), 383).

the course of events, and draws the relevant practical conclusions about what people should do.'[188]

Joshua, now old, assembles the community for a farewell address, an occasion and genre that naturally leads to an account of the book's ongoing significance. Joshua recalls in very general terms what has transpired in a two verse summary of the rest of the book (23:3-4). But here, and in what follows, there is a very interesting (re)interpretation of events. Josh 1-12 focused on *Israel's* action, and obedience, in conducting חרם against the locals. Here, the focus in relation to the 'removal' of the locals is entirely upon YHWH's action, an action that is interpreted using הדף ('push away', *HALOT*) and ירש (23:5). Moreover it is YHWH who is said to do the fighting (לחם) *for* Israel here (23:3). This idea runs through the speech, and is reiterated in 23:9-10, with Israel taking an entirely passive role with regard to warfare, apart perhaps from the rather vague rhetorical statement of 23:10a. However, Israel does not have an entirely passive role; her role is stated in 23:6-8. First, it is expressed in terms of being strong and careful to obey torah (23:6), reflecting classic Deuteronomistic idiom;

וחזקתם מאד לשמר ולעשות את כל־הכתוב בספר תורת משה לבלתי סור־ממנו ימין ושמאול

Moreover, Nelson suggests that 'the careful obedience that was laid upon Joshua as an individual at the start of the book now becomes the duty of the entire people and of their collective leadership (1:7-8; 23:6, 11). If this duty is fulfilled, then the promises made to Joshua could be continued for following generations (1:5-6, 11; 23:5, 9).'[189] In other words, Israel is 'to be' Joshua. Joshua is the paradigmatic Israelite, the hero and role model. But we saw earlier (Josh 1) that the author/redactor had transformed idioms of strength and courage from the domain of warfare into that of torah obedience, and thus the devotion and strength that Joshua exemplified evokes that which is required to obey torah for each Israelite.

However, most significantly, חרם is absent in Josh 23, even though it was so central a category for Josh 2-12. Moreover Josh 23:7-8, 12, being the charge to Israel, clearly reflects Deut 7:1-5.[190] But Josh 2-12 and Deut 7:1-5, texts in which חרם appears as a major, if not the central theme, form the 'conceptual backdrop' for Josh 23. Yet there is no mention of חרם in Josh 23, even though Josh 23 essentially provides an account of what the continued significance and

---

[188] M. Noth, *The Deuteronomistic History,* (JSOTSup 15; Sheffield: Sheffield Academic Press, ET: 1981), 5.

[189] Nelson, *Joshua,* 258. Cf. Butler who notes that no successor is appointed to Joshua; the burden is placed on the congregation (*Joshua,* 253).

[190] cf. Hawk; Deut 7:1-5 'form[s] the conceptual backdrop for the exhortations and warnings Joshua gives' (*Joshua,* 251).

practice of חרם should 'look like' through allusion to Deut 7:1-5. Perhaps then Josh 23 (and Josh 24) might be described as being 'liminal' narratives in the sense that they are aimed at merging the prototypical past of Josh 1-22 with the reader's present, sharing and mediating the 'qualities' of both eras. Josh 23-24 provide the continuity that links the reader with Joshua, showing how this prototypical past is to be constitutive of current identity and practice, and how the book of Joshua is to be 'enacted'. So here one is shown how to interpret the symbol חרם—the significance of its second-order sense of separation, particularly from idolatry, is accentuated whilst the first-order sense relating to annihilation recedes into the background. Moreover, the absence of חרם can be accounted for by the desire to avoid giving grounds to anyone to construe the contemporary significance of the concept via its first-order sense; i.e. to ensure that people do not 'take up the sword', given the rather risky way in which חרם has been used as the symbolic centre of the story of Josh 1-12 to pose challenging questions of identity and perhaps qualify the discourse that is found in Deuteronomy.

Thus as we move into Josh 23-24 we encounter material that is more readily susceptible to appropriation at the *narrative level,* rather than to what lies 'behind' it as was the case in Josh 2-12 especially. It has more 'points of contact' with the world of the reader, and serves a different illocutionary function, to use the language of speech-act theory, and guides the appropriation of the earlier material. Indeed, Nelson suggests that 'the assurances of past success, though not really denied (vv.9-10, 14), are put in perspective by the challenges of the future. Only continued obedience (vv.6-8, 11) will lead to continued success in the process of Yahweh's dispossessing of the nations (vv.5, 9, 13; *yrš* hiphil) so Israel can continue to take possession (v.5; *yrš* qal) of their land.'[191]

From a rhetorical perspective the portrayal of an incomplete conquest is almost essential if Israel is truly to be able to 'see her *current* self' in the book of Joshua; it enables the narrative to connect with experience. Had Joshua uniformly portrayed a complete conquest with Israel dwelling secure in the land, then it would be difficult for Israel to appropriate the book in an existential sense. By leaving work still to do, Israel can more readily identify with the book, and thus seek to complete the charge to Joshua, interpreted in the ways outlined; obeying torah, avoiding intermarriage, loving God and rejecting other gods.

But perhaps at another level, the faithfulness of YHWH and the fulfilment of his promise is vital too. Israel had to be able to trust in the promises of YHWH, and here the promise of possession of the land is fulfilled (23:14-15). The portrayal of God's faithfulness in the past serves as grounds for continued trust in YHWH in the present with an orientation of future hope. In other words, to achieve the desired rhetorical effect and response to YHWH, a delicate tension and balance needs to be maintained between the incompleteness of

---

[191] Nelson, *Joshua,* 259.

conquest on the one hand, and its completion on the other. Portraying a uniformly incomplete conquest would give grounds for doubting YHWH's promises and power, whereas a complete conquest would leave Israel wondering what to do in response to Joshua. Thus portraying both (contradictory) aspects can achieve the desired rhetorical effect. In structuralist perspective, Joshua is a myth that tempers these logical contradictions. In a sense then, to use later categories, one may say that Joshua reflects both latent 'realized' and 'anticipatory' eschatologies. Promised rest with YHWH is in some sense achieved and secure, whilst it is also to be worked towards.

The language of divine anger and covenant violation used here in Josh 23 recalls the fate of Achan (7:1, 15, 26).[192] Thus to violate the covenant is to place oneself into Achan's shoes, and Israel into the events that surrounded Achan's disobedience. Thus one is led to appropriate Joshua existentially. Moreover, earlier in Joshua the root עבר has repeatedly described how Israel crossed over into the land, whereas in 23:16 it is used to warn Israel not to violate the covenant, with a threat of loss of the land if it is violated; indeed עבר was used with regard to Achan's covenant violation (7:11, 15). This draws land and covenant together. Crossing into or out of the land symbolically reflects 'crossing' into or out of the covenant; life in the land, a land flowing with milk and honey enjoying YHWH's blessing *is* life in the covenant. The land is a powerful symbol for the covenant, as I suggested above.

Moreover, the assertion that YHWH will destroy (שמד) Israel (23:15) is shocking, for it is a term used previously to signify the eradication of the peoples in the land (Deut 4:26; 7:4, 23; Josh 9:24; 11:14, 20), and is used in connection with the deaths of Achan and his family (Josh 7:12).[193] Moreover, Hawk notes that the term used for perish, אבד, 'often signifies nomadic existence or aimless wandering (Lev 26:38; Deut 7:20; 8:19, 20; 11:17; 26:5; 28:20; 30:18). Its use to signify Israel's disappearance from the land thus also intimates the return to a landless and thus disintegrated existence.'[194] It appears here in 23:13 and 16, and is again used in the context of Achan's story (7:7). But the perishing and destruction here is precisely 'from the land'; transgressing (עבר) the covenant leads to a return to wandering existence outside the land, and is contrasted with the fulfilment of YHWH's promises to bring Israel into, and to establish her in the good land (23:13, 15, 16). Thus Josh 23 exhorts Israel 'to be' Joshua—obeying YHWH resulting in life and the possession of the land, and 'not to be' Achan—disobeying YHWH resulting in death and expulsion from the land. In other words, transgressing the covenant leads to an undoing, a reversal, of the conquest. So, might it be the case that the conquest setting is employed partially to be an existentially challenging *warning* to Israel? I.e., the expulsion of the

---

[192] Ibid., 257.
[193] Hawk, *Joshua*, 258.
[194] Ibid., 257.

people of the land will become Israel's fate if the Israelites transgress the covenant; the conquest will be reversed and other nations will drive Israel out of the good land, with Israelites turning themselves into 'outsiders'.

But it is interesting, as Gordon Mitchell notes, that in 23:16 serving other gods is described as breaking (עבר) the covenant, and that this 'is the first occasion that the danger of worshipping foreign gods is clearly stated. Neither has it been offered as an explanation for the extermination of the nations. The danger of their gods is not the justification for killing them, but it is a sufficient cause for retaining a social distance.'[195] This is interesting, and surprising perhaps. There is so little material in Joshua that explicitly deals with idolatry, and there is no attempt to justify killing the locals in terms of their moral evil or their idolatry, unlike Deuteronomy. Mitchell goes on to note that 'contact with the nations will itself constitute divine punishment—*they* are the trap, the scourge, etc.'[196]

Indeed, Hawk notes that '[e]thnic separation no longer finds expression through overt violence against the peoples of the land but rather through a strict admonition to maintain communal boundaries,' and that the new focus for staying within the boundaries is expressed in terms of loving (אהב) (23:11) and holding fast to (דבק) (23:8) YHWH, which is set in contrast to clinging to the nations (23:12). The usage of these terms is suggestive of the importance of marriage relationships (cf. Gen 2:24), and thus, as Hawk notes, exogamy is seen as the 'quintessential act of "joining" with the remaining nations.[197] Moreover, Nelson notes that 'in Deuteronomy intermarriage was permitted only with war captives, who had no families and could be fully integrated into the Israelite social system (Deut 21:10-14). The concern was not the modern notion of racial or ethnic purity, but the need to shield Yahwistic culture and religion from alien influences.'[198] However, Rahab's story, especially as received in the Jewish and Christian traditions in which she is incorporated into Israel's genealogy, provides an important qualification to these ethnic concerns,[199] and reflects Nelson's suggestion. In other words, Joshua does not reflect an exhortation to racial purity, but an exhortation to avoid idolatry, to avoid being tempted to turn to

---

[195] G. Mitchell, *Together in the Land: A Reading of the Book of Joshua* (JSOTSup 134; Sheffield: Sheffield Academic Press, 1993), 112-3.

[196] Ibid., 114.

[197] Hawk, *Joshua*, 255-6. He notes that marriage, 'the basic bond by which social units are connected, becomes paradigmatic for the issue of communal boundaries faced by the nation as a whole. ... Exogamy is "going to" the nations in microcosm. ... Intermarriage represents a confusion of the basic bonds of the community and will lead to pain, trouble, and eventually the disappearance of the nation itself, which will "perish from this good land that the LORD has given you."' (256-7).

[198] Nelson, *Joshua*, 261.

[199] This 'integration' is not explicit in Joshua as we saw earlier in Josh 6.

other gods, and to avoid any associations that are in danger of leading to this, which are *usually* associated with 'mingling' with the locals, because they are *usually* idolaters.[200] In practice this implies a kind of separation, and this is what is envisaged in the existential appropriation of חרם. Furthermore, Hawk notes that for the first time in Joshua the peoples of the land are 'not signified by a list but by the single term "nations"' a term which occurs here in 23:3, 4, 7, 9, 12 and 13, which corresponds to the seven-fold listings in Deut 7:1 and Josh 3:10.[201] This move suggests that a wider applicability is developed; the text speaks not only about the stereotypical 'seven nations', but about other nations more generally.

Such ideas find resonances in the New Testament in terms of not being yoked with unbelievers, (2 Cor 6:14-18), although it is worth noting that in Paul's treatment of various marriage relationships in 1 Cor 7 he does not envisage the 'putting away' of unbelieving spouses in existing relationships in the way that, for example, Ezra does (Ezra 9-10). Moreover, the qualification of this idea of separation found in 1 Cor 5:9-13—that separation is from immoral *Christians* and not immoral people outside the church, is an exhortation that has resonances with the stories of Rahab and Achan.[202]

However, taking *ACCS* as a guide, there is rather little Christian development of Josh 23. It is not covered in the extant homilies of Origen, Theodoret considers it only in 'historicizing' terms, relating it historically to Judges,[203] and Tertullian discusses it in passing with reference to the use of pagan literature.[204]

Finally, Hawk suggests that Joshua leads the reader to 'view Israel as a *people defined by choices* signified by a covenant which constitutes a metaphor for the reciprocal choosing of YHWH and the nation', and this is a theme that we see developed in Josh 24,[205] and is one that resonates well with Christianity

---

[200] Whilst I use the term 'locals' here, this reflects the portrait of a 'conquest' of the land by an external group. If in fact Israel emerged from within Canaan, then 'locals' is not the right term, although I shall use it for convenience instead of a cumbersome phrase like 'those others who do not seek to follow YHWH, or YHWH alone, as made concrete in the books that eventually emerged as the Old Testament'.

[201] Hawk, *Joshua*, 254. He notes that it is now the nations, and not their land, that is assigned to Israel as their inheritance. (Cf. Ps 2:8; 82:8). Also Nelson notes that 'Read against the background of other DH portions of Joshua, chapter 23 marks a distinct change in emphasis indicated by a new word not previously used for the population of Canaan, "nations".' (*Joshua*, 258).

[202] See my 'The Christian Significance of Deuteronomy 7', in *JTI* 3.1 (2009): 41-62 for development of these concerns, and of the concern of idolatry more generally, in relation to Deut 7.

[203] *Quest. Josh.* 19.3, p.301.

[204] *On Idolatry* 10, in *ACCS*, 93.

[205] Hawk, *Joshua*, 252.

in an existential context in which the importance of 'choice' comes to the fore. Hawk concludes,

> The themes that have configured the narrative and the sense of Israelite identity (land, separation, obedience) have steadily been dismantled by both the stories and the rhetoric of the previous episodes. Now forcefully restated, they are shown to be derivative rather than essential marks of national identity. Choosing to follow the God who has fought for the nation, and who promises to continue to fight, establishes the foundation of a distinctive Israelite identity. And if Israel chooses others, it will vanish. YHWH will not fail Israel. Will Israel hold fast to YHWH?[206]

Joshua 24[207]

Josh 24 mostly comprises Joshua's second farewell speech. It has attracted much scholarly attention, particularly in the wake of its use by Gerhard von Rad,[208] who argued that Josh 24:1-13, along with Deut 6:20-24 and 26:5-9 'constitute Israel's earliest and most characteristic theological articulation', being 'highly studied recitals, situated in contexts of worship and instruction'.[209] These texts were formative for von Rad's understanding of 'Israel's theology as a *narrative rendering* of what has happened in Israel's past, a narrative that still has decisive, defining power for subsequent generations.'[210] For von Rad, in his *Old Testament Theology*,

> The substance of Israel's theology ... consists in a recital of God's "mighty deeds" that had been worked in Israel's past. These mighty acts continued to claim Israel's imagination and to evoke Israel's trust and confidence. Israel trusted that the God who had delivered, led, and given land would continue to act in the same ways in the present and into the future.[211]

---

[206] Ibid., 252.

[207] The most recent major study of Josh 24 is W.T. Koopmans, *Joshua 24 as Poetic Narrative* (JSOTSup 93; Sheffield: JSOT Press, 1990).

[208] G. von Rad, 'The Form-critical problem of the Hexateuch', in *The Problem of the Hextateuch and other Essays* (London: SCM, ET: 1966), 1-78. It continues to attract considerable attention in the development of new paradigms for understanding the compositional history of the Pentateuch / Hexateuch. See for example the essays in T.B. Dozeman and K. Schmid, (eds.), *A Farewell to the Yahwist? The Composition of the Pentateuch in recent European Interpretation* (SBL Symposium 34; Atlanta: SBL, 2006) and J.C. Gertz, K. Schmid and M. Witte, (eds.), *Abschied vom Jahwisten: Die Komposition des Hexateuch in der jüngsten Diskussion* (BZAW 315; Berlin; Walter de Gruyter, 2002).

[209] Brueggemann, *Theology*, 32.

[210] Ibid., 32.

[211] Ibid., 34.

Significant for von Rad was the absence of the Sinai covenant in Josh 24, suggesting that there were two separate parallel historical traditions in early Israel; a Sinai tradition, and a 'redemption story' relating to settlement in the land. The absence of the covenant is therefore significant for the interpretation of this passage.

The transition from Josh 23 to 24 is awkward. Joshua had assembled Israel in Josh 23 for his farewell speech, and without any notice of dismissal the narrative moves immediately into a report of the assembling of Israel again in 24:1. Moreover, whilst Josh 23 is saturated with characteristically Deuteronomistic language and concerns, Josh 24 is not. Josh 24 has been the subject of considerable scholarly debate, with there being no consensus about its compositional history, origin, or relationship to the history and cultic life of Israel. It was first attributed to E, then later J, and although Deuteronomistic editing has been recognized, 'contradictory proposals about the text's composition have proliferated'.[212] In particular, its relationship to the DH and to Josh 23 is problematic. Nelson notes that Richter, Bonn, Fritz and Smend see Josh 24 as 'the DH conclusion for Joshua and chapter 23 as secondary to it', whereas he argues for the opposite, whilst Mayes and O'Brien 'maintain that neither chapter was part of the original DH'. But Nelson suggests that 'theorizing about this chapter has tended to outstrip the available evidence' although 'its language reflects that of Genesis-Numbers' and 'expressions also occur which are at least consistent with deuteronomistic usage'; the leadership catalogue (24:1), 'saw with your own eyes' (24:7), 'took possession of their land' (24:8), the nation list (24:11), 24:13, 'fear and serve' (24:14), 'forsake Yahweh to serve other gods' (24:16, 20) and 'serve and obey' (24:25), although, ספר תורת אלהים ('law book of God') (v.26) is a 'conspicuously non-deuteronomistic phrase (cf. Neh 8:8, 18)'.[213] Moreover, Josh 24 reflects traditions not found elsewhere in the Pentateuch or Joshua, such as the ancestors' worship of foreign gods beyond the Euphrates and Egypt (Josh 24:2, 14-15),[214] and a battle at Jericho (24:11),[215] and traces a number of allusions to stories in Genesis, Exodus and Numbers.[216] Thus there is a sense in which Josh 24 does form a fitting conclusion to what might be labelled the

---

[212] Nelson, *Joshua*, 265, with bibliography.

[213] Ibid., 266-71.

[214] Nelson, *Joshua*, 275. This tradition is found in Ezek 20:7; 23:3, 8.

[215] Ibid., 266. Nelson suggests, 'Verse 11 presents a version of the Jericho victory at odds with the one in Joshua 6, although perhaps present in some earlier form of the Rahab story. The ungainly inclusion of the nation-list in this verse widens its horizons so that the sentence can refer to the whole conquest. This suggests Jericho's paradigmatic role in the conquest tradition.' (274-5). It is difficult to know if too much is being read into the language here to produce a 'contradiction' or not. But the symbolic role of Jericho seems to be confirmed.

[216] Ibid., 274.

'Hexateuch' as well as to Joshua given that it offers a summary of much of the story of both the Pentateuch and Joshua, although not, significantly, of any of the covenants, be that of the law giving at Sinai, or the covenant with Abraham. But Josh 24 serves a rather specific rhetorical function as we shall see, so in another sense it is not a concluding summary of the 'Hextateuch'.[217] Indeed, Nelson suggests that

> The status of chapter 24 within the book of Joshua is ambivalent because it so closely parallels the function of chapter 23 in the plot structure. Without ever dismissing the assembly of chapter 23, Joshua assembles them again. His anticipated death, which prompts chapter 23 (vv.1, 14), takes place only after this second gathering (24:29), which is provided with no additional narrative motivation. There is topical overlap between the two chapters: survey of the past (23:3-5, 9-10; 24:2-13), imperative and exhortation (23:6-13; 24:14-15), and the "Yahweh alone" ideology (23:7, 12, 16; 24:2, 14-24, 27). In genre, however, they are rather different. Chapter 23 is a call for obedience to the law and separation from the nations in the form of a testament, while chapter 24 is a challenge to serve (that is, worship) Yahweh crafted in the form of a dialogue. While chapter 23 directs Israel how to worship Yahweh (exclusively, vv.7-8, 16), the question in chapter 24 is not so much how, as who ought to be worshiped, and the answer is a resounding "Yahweh." Chapter 23 works well as a summary to the book of Joshua, limiting its review to the occupation of the land. Chapter 24, in contrast, seems designed as a conclusion for the Hexateuch as a whole. It is less focused on the issue of land and operates with a wider horizon, one that includes patriarchs, exodus, and wilderness. Perhaps 23:16, which pulls together the themes of serving other gods, covenant, and the possibility of perishing from the land, served as the topical attachment point for chapter 24, which focuses on these same matters.[218]

Moreover, he suggests that the review in Josh 24 is designed to 'pilot both audience and reader to a climactic decision for Yahweh'.[219]

Whatever may be the relative origins and historical relationships of Josh 23-24 to each other and to the rest of Joshua, Josh 23 complements Josh 24 well in the final form. Together the two chapters play off and enhance each other to witness to and clarify the identity of Israel in terms of her response to YHWH. Butler suggests that Josh 24 gives 'the theological definition of the people of God' and that it is 'one of the most important chapters in the OT for biblical theologians'. Significantly, he notes that it is atemporal; 'It sets itself up as an occasion which has validity for all Israel through all time. ... It belongs to no

---

[217] Indeed, it is interesting that Knauf attributes Josh 24 to the 'book redaction' rather than to the 'Hexateuch redaction' (Knauf, *Josua*, 21).
[218] Nelson, *Joshua*, 268.
[219] Ibid., 269.

specific time and thus to all times',[220] and thus has clear existential importance. He detects several similarities between Josh 23 and 24 in that they both provide:
1. An opening survey of history leading to conclusions for present behaviour;
2. Descriptions of the consequences of disobedience;
3. Calls for total allegiance to YHWH.

He also detects several differences:
1. In Josh 23 the setting is temporal, whilst in Josh 24 it is geographical;
2. In Josh 23 past history centres on the allotment of the land, whereas in Josh 24 it centres on the victories of YHWH;
3. In Josh 23 allegiance to YHWH is expressed by obedience to the book of the law, whereas in Josh 24 it is through serving YHWH;
4. In Josh 23 disobedience is exemplified by intermarriage, whereas in Josh 24 it is exemplified by the worship of foreign gods;
5. Josh 23 is a farewell speech of a dying leader whereas Josh 24 is a ceremonial dialogue between leader and representatives.[221]

Thus Josh 23 and 24 offer two complementary perspectives of the constitution of Israel; Israel's identity is based upon the action of YHWH on her behalf, on her 'choosing' to serve YHWH, and of her serving YHWH through obedience to torah and separation from other nations and their gods. Thus the worship of foreign gods and intermarriage are drawn together, with each symbolizing the other. Likewise 'serving YHWH' is associated with obedience to the book of the law, where again each idea says something more about the other, ideas which may, furthermore, be drawn into association with the idea of worship. Together, these notions reflect what is at the heart of the significance of the decision to serve YHWH, the decision that Josh 24 encourages.

Robert Polzin stresses the importance of YHWH's first-person presentation in the narrative, with Josh 24:2-13 being 'God's autobiographical account of the significance of his previous relations with Israel'.[222] He suggests that

> The special nature of *this* interpretation [of the events that make up an account of Israel's past relationship with God], glossing over as it does not only the Mosaic covenant but also Israel's numerous past violations of that covenant, is that this is the only example of *God's direct narrative explanation of the significant aspects of his past dealings with Israel*. And *God's* explanation, in contradistinction to Moses' countless rehearsals of the events that preceded his speeches at Moab as well as Joshua's and the Deuteronomic narrator's many narrative explanations in the Book of Joshua, *gives no special status to law and covenant*

---

[220] Butler, *Joshua*, 278. Cf. Origen's comments on this passage in *Exhortation to Martyrdom* 17 (in *ACCS*, 96): 'Therefore, what Joshua said to the people when he settled them in the holy land, the Scripture might also say now to us.'
[221] Butler, *Joshua*, 265-6.
[222] Polzin, *Moses*, 142.

in the depiction of Israel's essential relationship to God. Rather, what God emphasizes here is the unmerited nature of Israel's blessings, culminating in the gift of the land (24:13).[223]

So Josh 24:2-13 emphasizes God's calling and care of Israel, and how Israel's identity is constituted by God's action on her behalf, culminating in Israel having been brought safely into the Promised Land and established there. But what follows *is not* Joshua's interpretation 'obviously go[ing] beyond what the words of God say',[224] but rather an exhortation based upon 24:2-13, an exhortation that 24:2-13 has been crafted to lead the reader toward. Indeed, ועתה (cf. Josh 24:14) is used in 'Deuteronomic orations' to move from a historical survey to a contemporary situation, or, more generally, as a 'transition from a parable to the moral lesson that is to be drawn from it'.[225] Thus recognizing the rhetorical nature of the material in Josh 24 is crucial, and so Josh 24:2-13 need not be a 'historical creed' *per se,* but a *particular* (and rhetorically selective) recital designed to evoke a *particular* response. It is good rhetoric, which may explain the absence of references to covenants, as we shall now see.

By commencing the speech in 24:2-13 with the story of Abraham who worshipped other gods, but whom YHWH led out from the land beyond the river, and concluding the speech with Israel's safe possession of the promised land, all at YHWH's initiative, it shows YHWH's favour and gracious calling of Israel; she owes her existence entirely to him. But, rhetorically speaking, precisely because of this 'grace', the possibility of a reversal is implied; this sequence of events can be 'undone' by YHWH too. Choosing YHWH and serving him (24:14ff) is the response that will be sought, a response that will lead to continued enjoyment of and blessing in the land, whereas choosing to worship idols and other gods will lead to an 'undoing', a return to the worship of other gods 'beyond the river', outside the land, where Abraham started. Indeed, Abraham is described as living 'beyond the river' (בעבר הנהר) (24:2), i.e., 'on the other side', a notion that has key symbolic significance in Joshua, as we have seen. Those 'on the other side' are the 'outsiders', whilst those living in the land symbolize the insiders, that is, those who belong to true Israel. Joshua suggests that what makes people 'outsiders' here is serving other gods, which is precisely what Joshua has warned Israel against previously (23:16). Thus in 24:2-13, YHWH brings Abraham into Canaan, in other words he bestows upon him the status of an 'insider', whilst the description of the Amorites as living 'on the other side of the Jordan' (24:8) links them with those who lived 'on the other side of the river' as outsiders.[226] Thus the characteristics of the insider and

---

[223] Ibid., 143.
[224] Cf. ibid., 143.
[225] M. Weinfeld, *Deuteronomy and the Deuteronomic School* (Oxford: Clarendon, 1972), 175.
[226] Hawk, *Joshua,* 269-70.

outsider are displayed; Abraham is the paradigmatic (or symbolic) 'insider', who chose to follow God's call, whilst the Amorites are the paradigmatic outsiders. By knowing something of the characteristics of Abraham and the Amorites one discovers what insiders and outsiders are like, and thus, positively and negatively, what Israelites ought to be like.

This rhetoric and characterization would explain why there is no interest in the law, or indeed of any covenant in 24:2-13, such as the covenant with Abraham, for what is stressed here is YHWH's gracious unilateral action on behalf of Israel. For accompanying this is the implication that YHWH can simply 'undo' what he has established and return Israel to a pre-Abrahamic existence.[227] This is powerful rhetoric that calls for Israel's response in what follows. Whatever Israel has done or failed to do before, *here, now* is the point where response and mutual commitment enters. For if Israel does not respond appropriately *now* then 'I' (YHWH) will return you to a 'pre-Abrahamic' existence.[228] So perhaps Israel is to see herself 'as Abraham' here; Israel is to respond to God as Abraham did. Moreover, with the book of Joshua set in a scenario of conquest then perhaps there is a sense in which the narrative evokes a picture in which the kind of things that happened in the conquest will happen in reverse to Israel if they forsake YHWH. Indeed,

> "Serving YHWH" signifies acceptance of the distinctive destiny articulated by YHWH's version of Israel's story. "Serving other gods," on the other hand, signifies a return to a pre-Israel state (v.2) and the rejection of all that YHWH has done for the nation. The people initially respond by endorsing YHWH's rendition of their story and proclaiming, in both negative and positive terms, their decision to serve YHWH (vv.16-18). Joshua's shocking rejoinder, however, ostensibly short-circuits the connection just forged between God and nation (vv.19-20). ... This refutation brings the forward momentum of the episode to an unexpected halt but also produces three significant rhetorical effects. First, it reminds the reader of the consequences of this decision and thus of all future decisions. The choice before Israel is a serious one, and dire consequences will follow if the people of Israel reject the God who has chosen them. Second, it establishes the genuine character of the people's response by prompting them to repeat their decision to serve YHWH (v.21). Not even their leader's rebuke will dissuade them from their decision to serve YHWH! Finally, Joshua's repudiation of the people's commitment implicitly reinforces the point of YHWH'S

---

[227] It is unclear precisely what YHWH does in sending the צרעה here (24:12). Traditionally it has been translated as hornet (cf. LXX σφηκιά), but Butler notes that most modern commentators now render צרעה as scourge, terror or discouragement (*Joshua*, 264).

[228] Moreover, Hess notes that יצב (*hithpael*) occurs in Josh 24:1 and Exod 19:17, where the people stand before Sinai (*Joshua*, 300). So perhaps there is an allusion to the giving of the law at Sinai here. But if there is, then it is evoked in relation to the response that the people are to make *now,* rather than in the context of a recital of YHWH's previous dealings with Israel.

narrative preamble (vv.2-13); ultimately Israel's existence as a people depends more on what YHWH does than on what Israel does. In choosing YHWH, the people affirm their identity as a nation formed by YHWH (vv.17-18a), but this does not mean that what they do keeps the community intact.[229]

So Joshua's 'shocking rejoinder' (24:19) accentuates the rhetorical nature of this dialogue. Perhaps a fuller and more serious realization of the character of YHWH and what serving him entails is achieved via the rather shocking 'delayed' response.[230] It serves to highlight the difficulty of the existential choice that is to be made, or rather the difficulty in following through with the positive choice for YHWH because of the demanding nature of serving YHWH, even if it is the only choice that makes sense.

Geography is symbolic, and theologically important in Josh 24. Shechem, the location of the ceremony, is a site that evokes choosing, and in particular it is the place where Israel (Jacob) 'put away' foreign gods (Gen 35:1-4).[231] Indeed, Joshua's command in Josh 24:23 is a verbatim repetition of Gen 35:2.[232] Thus Josh 24 may be interpreted in the light of Gen 35. Moreover, Hawk suggests that Shechem also recalls the rape of Dinah, a story concerned with intercourse with peoples of the land and their extermination (Gen 34:1-31).[233] But it is interesting that Gen 34 is, like Joshua, concerned with the construction of Israel's identity, where questions regarding the role of land (and how it is to be obtained), circumcision and ethnicity are raised. But the kind of answers given in Gen 34 and Joshua are rather different, highlighted when the narratives are read from a neo-structuralist perspective, for Gen 34 seeks to show that Israel's identity is constructed purely on ethnic grounds,[234] whereas Joshua has sought to qualify precisely this notion.[235] Identity in Josh 24 is constructed by *choosing* to serve YHWH, and putting away idols and foreign gods, and so here, even at the *narrative level* we find material that readily resonates with the construction of Christian identity.[236]

---

[229] Hawk, *Joshua*, 264. He adds in a footnote that 'The people declare their intention to serve and obey (v.24), but the narrator does not report that they put away the foreign gods as Joshua has (now twice) commanded. The absence of the report is noteworthy because, throughout the book, the narrator confirms obedience to Joshua's command by reporting the precise execution of the command.' (265).

[230] Perhaps cf. Exod 3:13-15.

[231] Hawk, *Joshua*, 261.

[232] Creach, *Joshua*, 119.

[233] Hawk, *Joshua*, 261.

[234] Cf. Kunin, *We Think What We Eat*, 181-5. See also my, 'Towards a Christian Hermeneutic of Old Testament Narrative: Why Genesis 34 fails to find Christian Significance' (forthcoming in *CBQ*).

[235] Moreover, Josh 9 provides a series of ironic reversals to Gen 34 as we saw previously.

[236] And this is indeed what one finds in the patristic materials, e.g. Origen, *Exhortation to Martyrdom* 17, in *ACCS*, 95-6; Athanasius, *Life of St. Anthony* 20, in *ACCS*, 96. Cf.

Josh 24 forms a fitting conclusion to Joshua. It shows that it is a book addressed to *Israel* concerned with the way that she is to relate to YHWH. It demonstrates the need for a positive choice to serve YHWH to be made, and to put away idols and foreign gods. What this means in practice has been spelled out in Josh 23 in homily, and developed in story in the rest of the book. Achan is one who fails to 'choose YHWH' whilst Rahab is one who chooses YHWH, with both stories indicating, in different ways, the demanding nature of this choice. 'True Israel' is constituted by those who gladly choose to worship and serve YHWH, expressed in living by torah and avoiding various competing, idolatrous allegiances.

Hawk: The narrative indicates that Israel is 'unique among all other peoples only because YHWH has brought it into being and shaped it through experiences of rescue and gift' and that 'By setting ... two alternatives before the nation and the reader, Joshua therefore powerfully demonstrates that *choosing YHWH* is at the heart of what it means to be "Israel" (*Joshua*, 263).

9. DRAWING IT ALL TOGETHER: READING JOSHUA AS CHRISTIAN SCRIPTURE TODAY

Joshua—Challenging and Constructing Identity

The significance of חרם *in the construction of identity*

I would like to begin by discussing the significance of חרם in Joshua, being a, if not the, major theme of the book, and indicate how it relates to the construction of identity through the interplay of the structural and narrative level concerns as identified by neo-structuralism. We saw how Josh 23-24 offered something like a 'commentary' that indicated the kinds of way in which the חרם injunctions of Deut 7:1-5 were to find continuing significance and be enacted by Israel. חרם *was* to be enacted, but in a sense of 'separation', primarily so as to remain loyal to YHWH and not be led into the worship of other gods and idolatry. Indeed, in neo-structuralist perspective, חרם in this sense indicates the denial of 'mediation'—'Israel' and 'non-Israel' are strictly distinct categories. So, whilst חרם is described 'literally' in texts such as Deut 7:1-5 and Josh 6-11—in the 'world of the text'—its significance in the 'real world' derives from its 'second-order' symbolic sense. So in Josh 23-24, a text that is more homiletic and exhortatory than symbolic, the injunction to destroy idols and altars as per Deut 7:5, let alone people, is not even mentioned.[1] Thus one might say that Joshua provides, through Josh 23-24, a 'liminal transition' that bridges the gap between the 'mythical', prototypical world of the text to the everyday world of the Israelite, indicating what it means to enact חרם via the existential contours drawn by its narration in Joshua. But I suggested in chapter 6, and we saw in chapter 8, that חרם is used in Joshua in a literary, symbolic sense that is based upon, yet differs from, its sense in Deuteronomy. It goes beyond the idea of separation, and indeed challenges and qualifies the nature of separation as it was traditionally understood in Deut 7:1-5. This is, in fact, the main locus for the significance of חרם in Joshua, a suggestion that I shall now develop.

One might say that the stories in Josh 2-11 reflect 'confrontations' with חרם—either with the command to conduct חרם, the objects declared to be חרם,

---

[1] This is not to say that Israel did not engage in warfare (this is another issue), and of course the destruction of idols and altars is something that is important in Kings. But these are questions for another day. Here, I am only concerned with Joshua.

or the effects of it. Rahab, when confronted with the threat of חרם, confessed the power of YHWH and that he was 'with Israel', and thus that she would need 'rescuing' from the חרם. Rahab demonstrated through her 'speeches' an awareness of who YHWH was in a 'confession' that matched that of Moses (Deut 4:39) and Solomon (1 Kgs 8:23). Moreover, she demonstrated in her actions of חסד that she is characterized by the very qualities that are at the heart of the covenant between YHWH and Israel (2:10-12), despite being a Canaanite prostitute. Achan is Rahab's foil. He is the model ethnic Israelite, but when confronted with חרם he coveted (חמד) it, and when asked to give glory to YHWH, whilst 'confessing his sin', he failed to glorify YHWH (7:19-21). Despite appearances, in Rahab's case the confrontation with חרם 'draws out' her nature as 'Israel', whilst in Achan's case the confrontation with חרם 'draws out' his nature as 'non-Israel'.

Similarly, when confronted with חרם various local kings react aggressively to the Israelites (9:1-2; 10:1-5; 11:1-5). This 'confirms' their status as non-Israel, being hostile towards YHWH and Israel, in contrast to Rahab. But perhaps these paradigmatic 'outsiders' who are confirmed as such through their aggression also contrast with Joshua, the 'insider' who is confirmed as a paradigmatic insider through obedience to YHWH exemplified in responding obediently to the חרם command, and in being fully obedient to torah.[2] Indeed, the portrayal of Joshua is unusual in the Old Testament as seldom are characters portrayed so unambiguously; Abraham, Moses and David have ambiguous portrayals for example. But here his 'unswervingly positive' portrayal marks Joshua out as the model Israelite, a hero and role model. But in addition to this, Joshua's positive portrayal also provides a lens through which to interpret some of the more ambiguous episodes in the book, such as the oaths with Rahab and the Gibeonites. The implication is that as Joshua is characteristically obedient to YHWH in unambiguous cases, then Joshua was obedient to YHWH in his dealings with Rahab and the Gibeonites, suggesting a positive appraisal of the way in which their stories were resolved.

But what about the Gibeonites? They do not respond aggressively, and, like Rahab, they realize the unstoppable power of YHWH, that he is with Israel, and that they need 'rescuing' from חרם, even if they do not express it as such. But they do not give the glory to YHWH as Rahab does (2:10-11); they offer no confession, and simply fear for their lives. They do not demonstrate חסד but rather ערמה, which is, I think, to be construed positively (and ironically in the light of Gen 34). But ערמה does not constitute the heart of the covenant in the way that חסד does, and so they do not exhibit the true fundamental characteris-

---

[2] G.M.H. Ratheiser, *Mitzvoth Ethics and the Jewish Bible: The End of Old Testament Theology* (Library of Hebrew Bible/Old Testament Studies 460; London: T&T Clark, 2007), 268ff who argues that Joshua is portrayed as an 'exemplary warrior'.

tics of Israelite identity.³ The Gibeonites are spared, but become servants of Israel. Thus they have a 'liminal' status; their portrayal does not characterize them as being genuinely Israelite or non-Israelite, and they remain liminal figures in their status as servants, being not quite truly 'insiders' or 'outsiders'. But it is noteworthy that חרם does not appear in Josh 9 unlike all the other stories in Josh 2-11, which might suggest that the 'test' of confrontation with חרם is unable to indicate identity in all cases—חרם is absent in the Gibeonite case because it would be unable to indicate their nature and identity.⁴ Moreover, since in neo-structuralist perspective the Gibeonites represent mediators— having the qualities of both 'Israel' and 'non-Israel', and since חרם represents the denial of the possibility of mediation, then its absence is something of a logical necessity, and helps to draw attention to the awkward liminal status of the Gibeonites.

What is interesting about these stories is the absence of explicit evaluation. But some of these stories sit uncomfortably with Deut 7 and 20, and so perhaps the evaluation is left for the reader to supply, being guided (implicitly) toward a particular conclusion by the narrator in order to qualify and challenge some of the assumptions of Deuteronomy.⁵ It is almost as if the reader or the community is confronted by the same חרם 'test' as the characters in the story; how do I/we respond to these narratives? Is it right that the stories resolve in the way that they do? The stories of Josh 2-11 set up a matrix of 'test cases' that develops the identity of Israel and her perception of and relations with outsiders, perhaps 'pushing' the conventional understanding of what it means to be Israel: The 'model outsiders' are confirmed as outsiders through their aggression (the hostile kings); the 'model outsider' who doubles as an 'insider' (Rahab); the 'model

---

³ The story reflects an ironic reversal of Gen 34 in which it was deception (ערמה) that characterized the Israelites. So the Gibeonites are in a sense 'Israel', but perhaps not Israel in their finest hour.

⁴ Such an understanding of חרם as 'test' is, I think, supported by the other main extended חרם narrative, where חרם is commanded in extreme form, 1 Sam 15. Here, Samuel brings the word of the Lord to Saul, where Saul is required to annihilate the Amalekites and all their animals. But Saul spares the best of the animals (perhaps indicating covetousness again, although the text does not spell this out), and suffers judgement accordingly. The extreme חרם serves a rhetorical function to sharpen the test; how will one tested respond in the most demanding circumstances (limit-situations), i.e., amid genocide and riches?

⁵ Or, perhaps, Joshua might indicate what they 'really meant'—myths need to be interpreted in juxtaposition with other myths. Robert Polzin argues that Joshua presents *interpretations* of the Mosaic law (R. Polzin, *Moses and the Deuteronomist: A Literary Study of the Deuteronomic History* (New York: The Seabury Press, 1980), e.g. 126, 144), whilst Daniel Hawk argues that Joshua portrays *violations* of the law (L.D. Hawk, *Every Promise Fulfilled: Contesting Plots in Joshua* (Louisville: Westminster John Knox Press, 1991), 44-7). But in canonical perspective, whatever the original intent, what Joshua represents *is now interpretation*.

insider' confirmed as the insider through torah obedience (Joshua), and the 'model insider' who is shown to be an 'outsider' (Achan). These identities are 'drawn out' through response to חרם, stories that together seek to redefine Israel, moving away from an essentially ethnic or genealogical identity to one in which character, actions, attitude, and disposition towards YHWH (qualities that were, it must be said, also to define Israel in Deuteronomy (cf. Deut 6-11) alongside ethnicity), become more important, eclipsing ethnicity. But, lest one think that identity definition is straightforward and boundary maintenance easy, the reader is confronted with the Gibeonites, whose story seems to probe ambiguous and difficult questions of identity at the boundary, refusing easy resolutions.

What these stories represent, *at the structural level*, is the probing and pushing of the underlying structure that relates to insider : outsider relationships. Is transformation from outsider to insider, or mediation between outsider and insider possible? Joshua reflects an attempt to push the underlying Israelite structure through ways that are given content at the *narrative* level, even if it is a narrative that is not to be appropriated in any straightforward sense as 'a model to follow', as Victor Turner's approach to myth highlights, as does careful consideration of how various narrative elements are actually serving structural and/or literary requirements, such as the extreme חרם of Jericho.

חרם in the world of the text in Joshua functions as the basis of a 'test' that reveals 'true' identity—not with respect to violence and genocide, but with respect to symbolizing response to YHWH. This in turn establishes the structural level concerns of the construction of 'true Israel' as against 'non-Israel' and the relationships between these categories. Using חרם as a symbol that in some senses represents divine action or command in Joshua, Joshua constructs 'true Israel' as those who respond obediently to YHWH, symbolized in terms of the nature of response to חרם. Understood in this way, חרם is employed in Joshua so as to qualify the way in which Deut 7:1-5 constructs Israel's identity, where חרם symbolized the essentially ethnic construction of Israel's identity through the separation of ethnic Israel from non-Israel. Joshua still encourages the separation of Israel from non-Israel (Josh 23-24), but redefines the nature of Israel and non-Israel, and blurs the distinction near the boundary (Josh 9). As a result, Joshua effectively 'redefines' what it means to enact Deut 7:1-5 and 'practise' חרם, reconsidering the nature of Israelite identity and her perception of others. The narratives of Joshua do then, in fact, function so as to *qualify* the accepted traditional understanding of Israelite identity, rather than simply presenting the 'fulfilment' of Deut 7:1-5.[6] They do not reinforce xenophobia or violence,

---

[6] Hence the distinction between Deuteronomic and Deuteronomistic uses of חרם developed in chapter 6.

although they use the traditional grammar of Deuteronomic discourse, with the narratives challenging what, at the surface level, one expects חרם to be about.[7]

Characteristics of Israelite identity—character traits
Having considered how חרם functions largely at the structural level to construct identity, I would now like to consider how such identity is given content through narrative level concerns. However, an appreciation of the mythical nature of Joshua, especially as construed through Victor Turner and Seth Kunin's understanding of the nature of myth, urges caution in using Joshua as a model for behaviour in a straightforward way, especially with regard to חרם. Indeed, the reading above suggests that חרם in Joshua is in some ways a symbolic literary motif serving structural requirements that is cast in the narrative as apparently the fulfilment of Deut 7:1-5 *in the prototypical world of the text*.[8] Josh 23-24 indicates in an exhortatory fashion the way in which Deut 7:1-5 is to be enacted by the reader, i.e. separation, but a form of separation whose nature is to be construed *through* Josh 2-12 which redefines the natures of Israel and non-Israel.[9] The Rahabs may be embraced by the community but the Achans expelled, with others (Gibeonites) awkwardly on the margins.

Woven in to the narrative are the portrayals of characteristics that give content to the underlying structural categories that Joshua reflects—i.e., content is given to what is meant by Israel and non-Israel. Joshua and the Israelites' obedience and Rahab's response of חסד (positively), and Achan's covetousness, lying and disobedience, together with the local kings' aggression (negatively) give content to what it means to be 'true Israel'. But the characteristics that exemplify Israelite identity are given further content in Josh 13-21 (e.g. as demonstrated in Caleb), where one discovers the importance of boldness, zeal and initiative. These stories in Josh 13-21 also challenge assumptions of patriar-

---

[7] Cf. E.F. Davis, 'Critical Traditioning: Seeking an Inner Biblical Hermeneutic', in *ATR* 82.4 (2000): 733-51, and L.G. Stone, 'Ethical and Apologetic Tendencies in the Redaction of the Book of Joshua', in *CBQ* 53:1 (2004): 25-36. I am not convinced that this is something traceable in the redaction of Joshua *per se,* rather, it is in Joshua's response to the Deuteronomic tradition. However, I think that in light of the slightly differing focus of Josh 1, 21:43-45, 23 and 24 from the rest of the material that it is possible to posit these as later additions to a relatively stable book, additions that develop and extend the significance of the remainder of the material in light of Deut 7:1-5. But these additions ought to be construed as developing the text, rather than distorting it, for, as I have indicated, they provide fitting commentary on the material in light of the juxtaposition of Joshua with the Pentateuch.

[8] I.e, whilst Joshua *presents itself* as the fulfillment of Deut 7:1-5, it is in fact doing more than this, challenging and developing the Deuteronomic assumptions of Deut 7:1-5.

[9] In other words, Joshua develops the interpretation of Deut 7 with different emphases in 2-12 and 23-24, and both are to be taken together.

chy. Land is granted to Achsah, and to Zelophehad's daughters. Like Rahab, Achsah, for example, responds well to YHWH, showing initiative and boldness, thus exhibiting core Israelite qualities. It should be noted that these character traits need not be opposed to humility, for they are not autonomous qualities exercised in a vacuum. Rather, they express action based on trust in YHWH's promises and gift. These character traits display what is required to appropriate the gift. The exercise of these qualities and characteristics is shown to lead to blessing and 'rest' in the land, whereas the exercise of covetousness, stealing, lying, disobedience and lack of trust in YHWH's promise and gift is shown to lead to expulsion and death, and to the 'contamination' of the community, highlighting the corporate effects of such sin, when read in Priestly perspective.

Characteristics of Israelite identity - land

Whilst the stories of Josh 2-21 indicate in complementary ways what is to characterize the people of Israel, often in surprising ways, Josh 22 provides a further surprise, concerning the relationship between identity and the land. Just as Josh 2-11 pushes Israel's identity *beyond genealogy*, so Josh 22 seems to push her identity *beyond geography*. Josh 22 indicates that the land is not finally central to the identity of Israel.[10] According to Josh 22 one can live outside the land and still be a true Israelite, living faithfully and obeying torah, even though the land does symbolize life with YHWH in its fullness, something that is 'made concrete' through the covenant and the blessing of a fertile land. Indeed, the Jordan river is an important boundary, and crossing it (עבר) is a powerful symbol evoking the establishment of, and entry into the life of the community of Israel. Such 'crossing' symbolizes moving into life in its fullness, enjoying life with YHWH through the covenant and enjoying the fruitfulness and blessing of the land that YHWH provides. But the symbol (life in the land) is not to be equated with the reality (life with YHWH), even as the symbol shares and partakes in the reality.

Summary

In summary then, whilst reinforcing many aspects of Israelite identity, such as the centrality of obedience to YHWH and practice of חסד, Joshua simultaneously challenges accepted views of what it is that constitutes Israelite identity. Joshua cautions against seeking to define the boundaries of the community in certain ways, and indeed of seeking to define them too precisely. Joshua thus demonstrates an openness to the 'outsider' whilst encouraging a searching exploration of the attitudes of those considered to be part of the community.

---

[10] As I argued in chapter 8, I do not think that this is an extension of the land and the bounds of its purity, but rather a qualification of the concept itself.

Joshua is thus both 'conservative' (by relating identity to torah obedience) and 'liberal' (by seeking to reshape perceptions of others and boundaries). Whilst Joshua encourages the enactment of חרם in terms of separation, it offers an unexpected perspective on the nature of such separation.

Appropriating Joshua—the Development and Use of Its Symbols and Mythemes

I will now consider how the wider symbolism of Joshua has been and *can be* appropriated and developed in the tradition of its use in ways that reflect its mythical nature, in particular via the construction of 'new myths' as Joshua is *used* in juxtaposition with other 'myths'. In this way Joshua contributes to the formation of the cultural memory of the community that values the text.[11] Here, my primary concern is the development of the symbolism of the text at the narrative level, and how this relates to the construction of identity in ways complementary with those in the previous section. In reading the text in this way here I do not wish to make metaphysical claims in the way that (especially) traditional Christian readings have tended to, but rather to indicate the kind of way in which the text, read and used as myth, provides an imaginative resource for the Christian life that, 'as testimony', ultimately 'gestures towards' the metaphysical nature of life in Christ for the Christian.

Crossing the Jordan and resting in the land

The significance of the symbolism of crossing the Jordan, and of the land, is developed in 1QS, and further in the traditional Christian typologies of baptism. The symbolism is imaginatively, constructively and, one might say, fittingly appropriated in these ways, exploring its plenitude to serve a new cultural context. It is fitting since its use in these ways reflects the concerns of Joshua as an act of discourse, i.e., that it relates to entry into new life in all its fullness with God. Both the crossing of the Jordan in Joshua and Christian baptism symbolize entry into new life. But in Joshua, having narrated the Jordan crossing, the remainder of the narrative of Joshua gives content to some aspects of what characterizes this new form of life and the community that lives this life. So if the Jordan crossing is imaginatively evoked as symbolizing baptism, reflecting entrance in to new life in the Christian community, then this symbol when understood through the context of Joshua as a whole might evoke the entrance into a community that is constituted by certain searching and demanding forms of responsiveness to God, as expressed in Christ for the Christian, a recontextu-

---

[11] That is, the use made of a text by a community is a vital aspect of its interpretation, and might be said to lead to the development of 'new myths', that, theologically speaking, can be said to be 'revelatory' in themselves.

alization that may see some aspects of the nature of the community developed whilst others recede. To go through baptism is to identify with a certain sort of community.[12]

We have seen that נוח (rest) reflects a desire and goal of the occupation of the land, although Josh 23-24 indicates that is something that one is ever moving toward, via 'choosing YHWH', obeying torah, and separating oneself from idolatry. There is thus an incipient eschatological impulse in Joshua. But the language of battle and conquest that pervades Joshua might indicate that this rest is not easily achieved; it is only reached through demanding obedience and struggle. Ironically then, the vocabulary of combat is required to evoke the demanding nature of the life that is required to lead to 'rest', and the realization of the enjoyment of life with YHWH in its fullness. Indeed, Rowan Williams remarks, in the context of feminist interpretation, that 'the importance of contemporary feminist exegesis [is] an example of disturbing scriptural reading which forces on us the 'conversion' of seeing how our own words and stories may carry sin or violence in their telling, even as they provide the resource for overcoming that sin and violence'.[13] In other words, whilst stories such as Joshua 'may carry sin or violence in their telling', as highlighted via ethical criticism, such stories may also 'provide the resource for overcoming that sin and violence'.

It is therefore natural to expect the 'spiritual' reading of Joshua to develop in the way that it did, where life in the Promised Land typifies the spiritual life, but also that the metaphors needed to describe existentially the spiritual life retain a 'militaristic' nature, such as in Eph 6:10-18. However, when reading Joshua as myth, when it is juxtaposed with other myths that arise in the Christian tradition, then the idea of desiring rest in Joshua finds resonances with

---

[12] Thus the practice of חסד and the avoidance of coveting translate well into the nature and formation of the Christian community. But problematic in the Christian context is the nature of the response of Israel to the hostile kings (Josh 11), even when read in the symbolic manner suggested as entailing separation. Should Joshua be read in a Christian context as evoking 'separation' from those hostile to the church? There appears to be something of a transformation of such a concern in the Christian context, since Christian identity is explicitly concerned with mission and the transformation of the outsider in a way that Joshua is not. Perhaps one might say that the separation from the hostile kings is taken into the Christian context in terms of the eschewal of violence as constitutive of Christian identity—the church is not to be characterized by violent action. Moreover, it is not separation from those who are violent that is the last word in a Christian response to those who are characterized by violence, but rather it is mission that constitutes essential Christian response. See my 'The Christian Significance of Deuteronomy 7', in *JTI* 3.1 (2009): 41-62 for further discussion of these issues.

[13] R. Williams, 'The Judgement of the World', in *On Christian Theology* (Oxford: Blackwell, 2000), 29-43, here 42.

Augustine's notion of the soul seeking rest in God.[14] In other words, in Joshua, as in the Christian life, one must not lose sight of the proper end and goal that is sought, the goal that the narrative moves toward—'resting' with God (cf. e.g. Josh 21:43-45). For Israel the narrative of Joshua existed precisely to help Israel to find rest with YHWH, setting out, in a narrative set in the context of conquest, ways in which the identity of the community was to be formed in response to YHWH in order to help to pursue this rest. But in a sense one needs to 'stand back' from the book to see this, and this is where certain forms of psychological approach to reading Joshua as myth are helpful.

As the Promised Land symbolizes life in relationship with God, as we have seen, the imagery of Joshua becomes a potent one for the struggle to find rest in God. But in the tradition this struggle becomes 'internalized'; the battle is no longer 'out there' with 'the righteous against the wicked', but within the 'self',[15] and how 'the self' relates to the world. In Christian terminology the struggle is worked out through crucifixion of the self with and in Christ. Traditionally, such combat is drawn in to the domain of asceticism,[16] and indeed Olivier Clément, for example, suggests that, 'Ascesis means exercise, combat. "Spiritual combat, harder than men's battles" .... Ascesis then is an awakening from the sleep-walking of daily life. It enables the Word to clear the silt away in the depth of the soul, freeing the spring of living waters.'[17] Together, Augustine and Clément point towards what constitutes rest and how one finds it in the Christian life—through (internalized) combat, with Joshua providing an imaginative symbolic resource for this difficult process. This desire—to find rest in God—is something that Joshua is expressive of, and is developed in new ways in the Christian tradition, *using* texts such as Joshua as imaginative resources which, when 'filtered' through the Christian tradition, indicate the kinds of characteristics that are central to the identity of the community, and how the community is to relate to those perceived to be outside it, in the pursuit of such 'rest'.

---

[14] Cf. Ellen Charry's comments on St. Augustine : 'Prayer and piety are the way to rest in God, and resting in God is finally the way to a wholesome self; resting in self brings at best happy moments. The goal of life is rest in God. Once the soul understands itself called to "remember its God to whose image it was made, and understand[s] and love[s] him [it is] able to share in him. . . . [It] will reign in happiness where it reigns eternal" ([*De Trinitate*] xiv:4:15)', ('Dwelling in the Dignity of God: Augustine of Hippo', in *By the Renewing of your Minds: The Pastoral Function of Christian Doctrine* (Oxford: OUP, 1997), 120-52, here 147). Augustine might then point forward to a fruitful theological development of the kind of 'rest' envisaged in Joshua for a Christian reader.

[15] Cf. Mark 7:1-23.

[16] See O. Clément, *The Roots of Christian Mysticism: Text and Commentary* (London: New City, ET 2nd ed.: 1994) in which one major section of the book is titled 'Initiation for Warfare' to describe the Christian life.

[17] Ibid., 130.

חרם, *idolatry, and conquest symbolism*

A rather demanding existential appropriation of the חרם symbolism as it is understood in rather general terms in the Christian context might be that it becomes a symbol for the conflict against idolatry that is directed against the self. Just as one might imaginatively evoke the powerful Jordan crossing symbolism in baptism, so one might imaginatively evoke the חרם symbolism in the call to the crucified life. In a sense this reflects more a development of Deut 7:1-5 rather than Joshua *per se* owing to the function of the symbol in these texts (cf. above). But reading canonically in juxtaposition with other myths and their development, חרם is used in various ways in the Old Testament. Apart from occasional anomalous usages there is a 'deuteronom(ist)ic-חרם',[18] a 'priestly-חרם', and an 'eschatological-חרם' (cf. chapter 6). Broadly speaking, the juxtaposition and fusion of these conceptions of חרם may be suggestive of the imaginative appropriation of חרם in a Christian context by way of engaging with the crucifixion, where perhaps one could say that חרם finds a 'literal' manifestation; where the eschaton breaks into history.[19] As Jesus' crucifixion is associated with the annihilation of, let us say, idolatry (construed in its broad Christian sense) in order to establish the kingdom of God so that rest may be found with God, then the crucifixion is in some ways analogous to the prototypical event of the conquest for which חרם is the category that is used to interpret it. So, might one say that by, in some sense, 'bearing the idolatry' of the world Jesus becomes an abomination to be destroyed ('My God, my God, why have you forsaken me...'), reflecting deuteronomistic-חרם, whilst simultaneously being the holy one irrevocably given over to, and set apart for God in his death, reflecting the priestly-חרם?[20] If so, then to use the traditional Christian grammar, one could say that חרם finds 'fulfilment' on the cross, even though the means of such 'fulfilment' is quite unexpected, albeit one that resonates with Isa 53.[21] However, rather than talking of 'fulfilment' in a 'typological' (or even allegorical) kind of sense, such an interpretation is better understood as an imaginative use of the symbolism of חרם.

---

[18] I shall take the Deuteronomic and Deuteronomistic uses of חרם together here—whilst they are used in different ways in the different narratives it seems that they share a common conceptuality that differs from the other conceptualities of חרם in the Old Testament.

[19] Cf. 'Christ takes upon himself the sin of the world and becomes the victim of the holy war that God wages against sin (2 Cor. 5:21).' (R.S. Hess, *Joshua* (TOTC; Leicester: IVP, 1996), 46).

[20] This kind of juxtaposition seems to lie behind the additions of Josh 6:19 and 24.

[21] As noted in chapter 7 it is interesting that early Christian reading of Joshua did not develop in this direction, probably because there was rather little interest in viewing the atonement from this kind of perspective.

But, for the Christian, a sharp reinterpretation of the nature of defilement and idolatry and the means of dealing with them is suggested in the New Testament in Mark 7:14-23 for example—it is not that which is external that defiles and leads to idolatry, but that which is within oneself.[22] Hence a sharp reinterpretation of the nature of חרם is required; it is not to be directed against that which is 'external', but to that which is 'internal', i.e. the 'self'. For the Christian, the image of destruction of the external polluting influence is replaced with that of annihilation of idolatry in the 'self', conducted in part through ascetic struggle.[23] Idolatry is overcome not by the avoidance or destruction of what is other, but by the crucifying of the self through participation in Christ.

This kind of reading in which חרם is associated with the 'crucifixion' of idolatry within the self is, however, more an imaginative appropriation of the canonical use of the חרם symbolism in the Old Testament rather than an appropriation of Joshua *per se*. Nevertheless, the symbolic use of Jericho in Joshua, a use that is developed into Jericho as symbolizing 'the world' (in its 'fallen' sense) and its destruction in the Christian tradition could be said to point towards this line of imaginative reading. Indeed, most of Joshua appears rather unconcerned with idolatry *per se*, but in Josh 23-24, the problem of idolatry is raised in terms of the response that YHWH seeks. Idolatry remains a key concern in the New Testament context, and in the subsequent Christian tradition, even if it comes to be envisaged rather differently in the tradition than in ancient Israel. Whilst the understanding of the nature of idols and idolatry would seem to have undergone transformation, the transformation is, arguably, a clarification of the 'essence' of idolatry.[24] To consider such development, it will be helpful to turn to Nicholas Lash, whose thinking

> can be organized around four key points: that idolatry essentially consists in the mistaking of creaturely for divine reality; that such mistaking is less a matter of explicit conceptual objectification and more of where the heart is set; that idolatry lives forgetful that God is no thing at all, any more than 'religion' pertains to any particular area of experience and practice; that there are significant resources intrinsic to the Christian tradition for supporting the long march from the captivating security of idolatry to the intensely challenging freedom of the

---

[22] If one reflects on Mark 7:14-23 in a post-Wittgensteinian context there is some difficulty with the language here in that it may suggest too sharp a distinction between 'external' and 'internal' factors, for the 'internal self' is partially constructed and constituted by societal and public influences and practices. It is, however, difficult to find adequate language to express the point. Perhaps one might say that the problem of defilement comes from 'oneself' rather than from purely external factors.

[23] Such asceticism may be construed broadly.

[24] See my 'The Christian Significance of Deuteronomy 7' for further treatment of the problem of idolatry in the contemporary Christian context and its relation to Deut 7 in particular.

children of God—indeed, that the Christian tradition is a school in which all are set to the slow learning of the ways of God in Christ and the Spirit.[25]

Thus, 'putting away idols' today is as much as anything an existential process that is conducted via Christian discipleship, involving a kind of ascetic struggle perhaps, being a process learned within the church, as one participates in the worship and practices of the church.[26] This call to discipleship is thus 'drawn in' to the demanding choice to follow YHWH, reflected today in following Christ.

Turning to the symbolism of the fall of Jericho, the symbolism of the conquest may be used in other ways. The fall of Jericho was often interpreted in terms of the destruction of 'the world' and the consummation of the age.[27] Alternatively, one might develop the symbolism in other directions. The well fortified, impregnable walls of Jericho collapse and the city is taken with ease after a procession around it in obedience to YHWH, but even the small 'ruin' of Ai proves too much for Israel after Achan's disobedience. In other words the stories evoke the image of YHWH 'fighting' powerfully on one's behalf when one obeys God, and thus that one need not fear apparent obstacles and difficulties in life when one is following God, but of a sense of 'leaving one to one's own devices and weaknesses' when one disobeys.[28] Achan's story indicates that disobedience 'contaminates' the community, resulting in the withdrawal of God's presence. But the rather cryptic Josh 5:13-15, which functions as something of a prologue to Josh 6-11 and the conquest, cautions against simply asking if God is on *our* side, and hence against a too 'comfortable' appropriation of Josh 6. Rather, the question asked needs to be redirected, for the correct question is that of asking whether *we* have aligned ourselves with God whose perspective transcends that of humanly constructed interests or interest groups. If we have so aligned ourselves, then one need not fear seemingly insurmountable obstacles. The narratives of Joshua then evoke the idea that YHWH is 'fighting on one's behalf', although as the *Mekhilta Shirata* indicated, YHWH fought on (Israel's) behalf *when in need*.[29]

---

[25] P.D. Murray, 'Theology 'Under the Lash': Theology as Idolatry-Critique in the Work of Nicholas Lash', in S.C. Barton (ed.), *Idolatry: False Worship in the Bible, Early Judaism and Christianity* (London: T&T Clark, 2007), 246-66, here 254-5.

[26] However, there is an important sense in which the church *as a community* is engaged in a continual ascetic struggle against idolatry given that the church has not yet reached perfection; Joshua is a book addressed to a community that challenges the community's self-understanding, whilst calling for response at the individual level too.

[27] See the various readings in *ACCS*, 35-9.

[28] Again, this can be construed in terms of the individual or the community.

[29] Cf. chapter 3 for discussion.

Joshua and 'salvation history'

I would now like to consider a very different kind of appropriation of Joshua, and one that might be problematic for a mythical reading of it. Joshua draws attention to the settlement of the land as the fulfilment of YHWH's promise (e.g. 21:44-45), a note that might add a more historical dimension to Joshua than I have sought to develop. Moreover, with the emergence of the canon in which Joshua was juxtaposed with other 'historical' or 'history-like' narratives, Joshua seems to acquire greater significance 'as history'. Indeed, it seems that Judges was redacted to be read together with Joshua via the addition of Judg 1:1-2:5 which supplies continuity and perhaps 'harmonization' of the two books so that they can be read as a continuous history, which, when read as a part of Genesis-Kings forms a larger continuous history of Israel from the creation of the world to the exile.[30] What emerges from this 'grand historical narrative' is a picture of

---

[30] The importance of 'history' in this sort of sense is something that may have arisen as a result of, or alongside a Hellenistic concern for history, in which the importance of the concept developed. See J. Van Seters, *In Search of History: Historiography in the Ancient World and the Origins of Biblical History* (Winona Lake: Eisenbrauns, 1997), 8ff in relation to Greek historiography and 209-48 in relation to Israelite historiography. In particular he discusses Mowinckel's view that Joshua and Judges filled a gap in an otherwise 'complete' history, supplementing the Yahwist account (236). Moreover, Van Seters suggests that the 'fundamental problem of the Hexateuch is, perhaps, how to view Judg. 1:1-2:5 and its relation to what comes before and after it' (337); it is an intrusion in its present context (338). The possibility that this redacting and 'harmonizing' of the materials into a continuous history occurred, and was indeed a concern, and that it occurred relatively late might find support in W.W. Hallo's observation that in Judg 1:15 Achsah 'uses the Aramaism *hāvā-lî* ('give me'), for *tēnā-lî* ('give me'), in Joshua [15:19]'. (W.W. Hallo, 'New Light on the Story of Achsah', in J. Kaltner and L. Stulman (eds.), *Inspired Speech: Prophecy in the Ancient Near East. Essays in honour of Herbert. B. Huffmon* (London: T&T Clark, 2004), 330-35, here, 330). John Strange argues that 'in view of the ingenious way that the Book of Joshua is interwoven with the rest of the story [Gen. 11–2 Kg. 25] ... the Book of Joshua is an editorial ploy, a creation by an editor who by writing it turned the whole story from Gen 11 to 2 Kings 25 into a "Hasmonean Manifesto", and at the same time made the Tetrateuch and the Deuteronomistic History into one single piece of historical literature' ('The Book of Joshua—Origin and Dating', in *SJOT* 16.1 (2002): 44-51, here 50). He argues for a very late (first century) date for this process (ibid., 44). Whilst this process may not be as late as he suggests, (and it seems very unlikely to be this late, granted that 4QJosh^a is dated on palaeographic grounds to the second half of the second century BC (M.N. Van der Meer, *Formation and Reformulation: The Redaction of the Book of Joshua in the Light of the oldest Textual Witnesses* (Leiden: Brill, 2004), 95) the possibility that a redaction of materials into a harmonized history may have taken place *relatively* late might indeed reflect the rise of Greek historiography, and concerns with history in itself, as indicated by Van Seters (*History*, 8ff).

a continuous history of God's dealing with Israel, a history that develops into the New Testament, and might rightly be termed 'salvation history'. It is a theological concept that probably developed relatively late as the community reflected on its existence and relationship to God over time, as a 'mythical' concept in its own right.

But, as I have indicated,[31] it is common for myths to 'tire' and to ossify over time, becoming objectified and indeed historicized. Does this then suggest that to try to read Joshua as such a 'history' and to see it as part of an emerging 'history of salvation' is wrong-footed? There are two issues here. First, by focusing on 'history' and 'objectifying' the text as a representation of past events it is possible (although not necessary) that the real existential significance of the text is obscured, with some of the searching and challenging ways in which Joshua seeks to shape response to God being obscured, leading to poor use of the text. In other words, when historicized, it is possible to construe the text as being 'out there in the past' rather than being concerned with the existential construction of the reader's present community and worldview. But secondly, an emerging concept of 'salvation history' is really a 'new myth' of existential significance that emerges as the result of the juxtaposition of a number of myths, being itself a 'mythical conception'[32] that says something new about God and his relationship with humanity. The world and the human race is understood as being directed, with a *telos* in view that is 'in God', an existential concern. In other words, this kind of mythical development of the text pursues a narrow and interesting dialectic between the 'tiring' of a myth and its development in new ways, as reflected in Josh 21:43-45. The emergence of the idea of 'salvation history' is a fitting exploration of the plenitude of the myth in a new context through juxtaposition with other myths and reflection on the history of the community,[33] even as it makes the interpretation and use of Joshua more ambiguous and difficult—or perhaps richer and fuller.[34]

Moreover, Axel Knauf discusses a Joshua-Judges redaction of Joshua reflected in Josh 18:2-19:48 and 23. He argues that the connection between Joshua and Judges was only made at a late stage (E.A. Knauf, *Josua* (Zürcher Bibelkommentare AT 6; Theologischer Verlag Zürich, 2008), 22).

[31] See chapters 2 and 3.

[32] This is, of course, not to say that it is not 'real', but a comment on the kind of discourse that it is and the way in which it emerged.

[33] A different sort of approach to Joshua that construes it in 'historical' categories is its use in the praise of Israel's ancestors in Sir 44-50. Joshua is referred to in Sir 46:1-6. Whilst this is clearly a 'historicizing' reading of Joshua, its use in Sirach is to serve more existential ends. Also see 2 Macc 12:15.

[34] It is interesting to note that Konrad Schmid reaches a similar conclusion from a different perspective regarding the emergence of the idea of 'salvation history', noting that 'a farewell to the Yahwist has to abandon the thesis so popular in the twentieth century that the religion of ancient Israel was based on salvation history

Perhaps, however, in our context of raised historical consciousness some difficulties do emerge. I noted in chapter 3 that there were difficulties with von Rad's *credo* and the way in which Ricoeur sought to appropriate it in his development of the idea of testimony. But I also indicated, with reference to Exodus, that *even if* there was never an exodus in anything like the form narrated, one may still regard Exodus as reflecting the discernment of a very real 'exodus experience' for Israel, and its implications. Likewise, even if there was no conquest in anything like the way that Joshua relates,[35] the establishment of the worship of YHWH and the people of Israel in the land, however this actually occurred, might be seen as a 'conquest experience'. When coupled with the 'exodus experience' and the hopes associated with it, one might discern a trajectory of hope/promise—exodus—settlement that has a historical shape and thus reflects a historical trajectory in which God engages with his people in a particular way, oriented to a particular *telos*. So even in a context with raised historical consciousness it is still possible to develop the idea of 'salvation history' with Exodus and Joshua reflecting key *symbolic* expressions of this history. These symbolic expressions form a grammar of discourse that the community agrees to and uses to talk about salvation history, even if the basis for the idea looks rather different now from what it might have done previously. One may approach the idea of 'salvation history' with a *second naiveté*.

In summary, whilst the 'historicization' of Joshua can certainly be a poor construal of the text as myth, if used well a certain form of 'historicization' may be seen as 'revelatory' in itself as Israel develops the prophetic realization of her role and of God's relationship with her and with the world. When placed in the canon Joshua *becomes* more a symbol of 'history' and helps to establish a notion of salvation history, as part of a new act of discourse that develops and expands the horizons of the original act of discourse whilst not replacing them.

(*Heilsgeschichte*). That such a view can no longer be maintained has been made clear by the numerous archaeological finds discovered and published in past years.' (K. Schmid, 'The So-called Yahwist and the Literary Gap Between Genesis and Exodus', in T.B. Dozeman and K. Schmid (eds.), *A Farewell to the Yahwist? The Composition of the Pentateuch in Recent European Interpretation* (SBL Symposium 34; Atlanta: SBL, 2006), 29-50, here 48). If P was the first to combine the traditions of the patriarchs and the exodus, with promises of the land in Genesis only arising at a late stage, then with Knauf it would make sense to regard Josh 21:43-45 as part of a 'Hexateuch Redaction' that draws upon Priestly and Deuteronomistic traditions (Knauf, *Josua*, 20-21), with the concept of salvation history arising as a new myth that *becomes* the basis of the self-understanding of the community, as I suggested above.

[35] See e.g. N.A Soggie (*Myth, God, and War: The Mythopoetic Inspiration of Joshua* (Lanham: University Press of America, 2007)), for discussion along these lines, and summary of the theories of the origins or emergence of Israel. Also see M. Weinfeld, *The Promise of the Land: The Inheritance of the Land of Canaan by the Israelites* (Berkeley: University of California Press, 1993), 99-120.

Appropriating Joshua—its Development and Use as an Act of Discourse as Myth

Some of the developments of Joshua that one finds in the Christian tradition, such as one finds exemplified in Origen for example (developments that I have sought to reconsider in the light of recent anthropological approaches to the symbolism of myth as in the previous section), whilst reflecting fitting developments of the plenitude of a number of aspects of Joshua's symbolism, may be, in a sense, rather 'atomistic', and not serious developments or readings of *Joshua per se* as a narrative, as an act of discourse, the nature of which I began to explore at the beginning of this chapter. However, some of the traditional developments of the symbolism are indeed capable of a more 'holistic' development in this regard, as I sought to show with regard to the symbolism of the Jordan crossing in the previous section. Here I attempted to consider how the evocation of this symbol in baptism might be associated with the narrative that follows (i.e., Josh 5-24) as appropriated in the sense that I developed at the beginning of the chapter. In other words, I tried to draw together the use of the symbol of the Jordan crossing with the kind of life that it portrays entry into in order to avoid an atomistic 'extraction' of motifs at the narrative level.

Moreover, I suggested in chapter 3 that it may be unhelpful to seek to construe Joshua's Christian significance *primarily* in terms of addressing questions like, 'What does it mean to practice חרם today?', or 'What does it mean to rid oneself of idols today?', even though these appear to be important questions that arise from the text. Rather, a larger frame of reference for reading is needed, a frame of reference that goes beyond the use of symbols at the narrative level, as reading the text 'as myth' would suggest. In this perspective the focus might instead be upon questions like, 'What does it mean to respond faithfully to God today in the light of Joshua and what Joshua sought to achieve and show?' This will naturally attract and involve consideration of the above questions, but such questions will not govern interpretation. Indeed, Joshua as discourse is concerned with probing difficult questions of identity and community relationships, and it is in this regard that the חרם symbolism *as found in Joshua* finds its main significance. This is not to say that it does not find significance in other ways too, as sketched above, which simply reflects the polyvalent nature of the text and symbol. Provided the explorations of the plenitude of the text are 'fitting' both with regard to the text and its tradition of use, then there is no difficulty in exploring the potential of the symbolism in various ways.

In a Christian theological sense then, read through neo-structuralist categories, Joshua may be seen as a 'preparation for the gospel' in that it pushes the structure and categories of Israelite identity away from a genealogical identity (or at least identity based on an established 'in-group') in favour of a more open identity that is constituted by character and responsiveness to God.[36] This implies the possibility of *transformation* from outsider to insider, or vice versa. The Old Testament *tended* to deny the possibility of such transformation but this is something that is central to the New Testament and the Christian gospel. Indeed, in the Old Testament חרם, certainly in its Deuteronomic sense, is perhaps the paradigmatic expression of the *denial* of mediation and transformation, whereas in the New Testament 'faith' is perhaps the paradigmatic category for *expressing* mediation and transformation, something that I shall return to below.

So in one sense Joshua could be said to find its Christian theological significance as being a 'preparation for the gospel'. It prepared ancient Israel for the possibility of 'conversion'. Its job may be regarded as having been completed in the context of ancient Israel—reaching its 'end' in the New Testament. However, even in this sense Joshua still affects us today, for Christians live in the light of its effects. Joshua might then be valued and cherished in the general sense of 'cultural memory' in that it relates to the historical roots of the Christian community, providing the community with part of a narrative for its existence.[37] So in one sense at least Joshua's significance is located in terms of pushing the perception of the identity of 'true Israel' to pave the way for the Messiah, who would transform 'outsiders' into the people of God, in a way that is described using the category of 'faith'. But does Joshua continue to find significance beyond this, and beyond being a symbolic, imaginative resource in the sorts of ways sketched in the previous section?

I think that Joshua's significance does go further. First, one way of looking at the stories in Josh 2-11 is to consider them as illustrating differing *responses* to what one might call, in the world of the text, 'divine action in the world' that is portrayed using חרם as something that symbolizes such divine action and demands a response. How one responds to divine action reflects one's identity. Such a concern is developed in John's gospel for example, in which Jesus can be said to be portrayed as the ultimate instance of 'divine action in the world', response to which/whom is an act of self-judgment, either of coming to the light or remaining in darkness, to use John's categories. In other words, perhaps in the

---

[36] This is not to say that character and responsiveness to God were not always important too (cf. Deut 6-11); rather, it is to say that there was a sense in which ethnic identity may have eclipsed these, a situation that Joshua seeks to invert.

[37] Perhaps this is rather like some Antiochene construals of the Christian significance of the Old Testament, such as in Theodore of Mopsuestia in particular. Cf. D. Zaharopoulos, *Theodore of Mopsuestia on the Bible: A Study of his Old Testament Exegesis* (New York: Paulist Press, 1989); 'Theodore's final verdict was that the Old Testament taken on its own terms does not present Christ to us; it rather prepares the way for Jesus the messiah. … [However he] was more than convinced that the Old Testament is the record which registers the initial dealings of God with his chosen people of Israel before he "spoke at the end of these days unto us in his Son." ' (183-4). Perhaps cf. Gal 3:24-25 also.

Christian context it is response to Jesus that re-expresses something of what Joshua sought to achieve in terms of response to חרם. Response to Jesus manifests one's identity in the Christian context (cf. e.g. John 3:16-21) perhaps in unsettling ways in John in which the cherished centrality of 'Jewishness' in the construction of the identity of God's people is qualified yet further than in Joshua, and perhaps rejected altogether.[38] This provides the first step toward recontextualizing Joshua as discourse by giving content to what (who) one must respond to.

Secondly, Joshua gives content to the kind of characteristics that are associated with faithful response to divine action, being חסד, obedience, initiative, zeal, boldness and trust in God.[39] Such characteristics find their trajectory developed into the New Testament and the Christian tradition, being worked out in love shown in action, faith, hope, courage and fortitude (to use the language of Christian virtue), indicated in, for example, 1 Cor 13, in the boldness of approaching God in Heb 4:16, and in the initiative, boldness and hope exemplified in the Canaanite woman who approached Jesus (Matt 15:21-28).[40] Here, of course, it is necessary to use discernment and exercise sensitivity towards the material to identify that these characteristics are, in a fairly literal sense, paradigms for behaviour that transfer to the 'real world' from the 'world of the text', unlike חרם.

Thirdly, it may be beneficial to consider the concerns that Joshua reflects in order to help read some of the stories in the gospels that relate to disturbing various ideas of the construction of Christian identity. The story about the Canaanite woman (Matt 15:21-28) has certain resonances with Rahab's story, as suggested above. But the parable of the sheep and the goats (Matt 25:31-46)

---

[38] However, the rejection of the Jews as portrayed in the world of the text in John seems to be associated with violence and evil deeds, rather than with Jewishness *per se*. For example, R.W.L. Moberly suggests, 'the portrayal of the Jews as "of the devil" in John 8 is entirely correlate with their murderous intent toward Jesus, as eventually realized in John 19. To abstract and essentialize this portrayal and to suppose on that basis that John is "anti-Semitic" is to commit a major error. It is "of the devil" to be murderous, not to be Jewish.' ('Johannine Christology and Jewish-Christian Dialogue', in M. Bockmuehl and A. Torrance (eds.), *Scripture's Doctrine and Theology's Bible* (Grand Rapids: Baker Academic, 2008), 70-93, here 90). Thus there is similarity between the characteristics of 'non-Israel' in Joshua and John in that in both cases the outsider is characterized primarily in terms of violence toward Israel (the people, in Joshua, and as Jesus in John). John introduces further categories of sight/blindness in relation to the perception of divine action in Jesus.

[39] As suggested above, this kind of responsiveness can be developed at the community as well as the individual level, being the sort of responsiveness that is to characterize the church.

[40] I.e., she responds faithfully to Jesus in the same kind of way that Rahab responds to חרם, both symbolizing divine action in the world.

offers a challenging reflection on the nature of recognizing and responding to Jesus. Matt 7:21-23 offers another demanding reflection on the nature of Christian identity, an identity that is characterized by 'doing the will of the Father' (7:21) rather than by the exercise of certain forms of more spectacular 'charismatic' ministry. One might say that Matthew's concern here is with Christlikeness of character as this is worked out in action. However, turning to Luke's gospel, we see a different kind of concern reflected in the construction of Christian identity. In the parable of the Pharisee and the tax collector (Luke 18:9-14), it is not certain kinds of action that are stressed as in Matthew's gospel, but rather a recognition of sin leading to a plea for mercy that constitutes faithful response to God. Likewise in the account of the thief on the cross, the dying thief simply asks Jesus to remember him (Luke 23:39-43). Again, for Luke this plea for mercy would seem to encapsulate faithful response to Jesus. So the gospels, like Joshua, seek to challenge certain perceptions of the fundamental characteristics of the identity of the community of God's people, as well as blurring the boundaries of the community somewhat, especially when the gospels are read in juxtaposition.

But perhaps these stories indicate that it is in some sense faith in Christ embodied in a life of Christlikeness that could be said to reflect the heart of Christian identity, as might be expressed in Jas 2:20-26. Indeed, Jas 2:20-26 does in fact represent one of the few direct appeals to Joshua in the New Testament, appealing to Rahab as a paragon of the need for faith to be accompanied by (or embodied in) works, seeking to 'flesh out' what it means to respond to God faithfully, the concern that I introduced at the beginning of this section. So Jas 2:20-26 reflects the development of Joshua as myth through its juxtaposition with other myths in which categories of 'faith' and 'works' are used to interpret response to God in Joshua. From this, principles of Christian response to God are developed. But as well as representing an important *use* of Joshua 'as myth' in the context of the New Testament, this usage, juxtaposed with certain Pauline texts in particular, itself gives rise to a plethora of treatments of conversion, justification, faith, virtue and works in the Christian tradition concerning what it means to respond to God faithfully. These developments can be said to represent a matrix of 'new myths' that shape Christian identity,[41] and define the boundaries of the Christian community, a concern that reflects what Joshua sought to achieve, albeit in rather different ways in a different context.

Rahab's story is developed as an example of faith in Heb 11:31, of faith and hospitality in 1 Clem 12, and in further similar ways in the tradition, as we saw in chapter 8, ways that essentially take Jas 2:20-26 as their point of departure.

---

[41] Here I am suggesting that much of the theological tradition is 'mythical' in the sense that it is existentially engaging, and often reflects highly 'structured' material concerned with the construction of identity (cf. chapter 2), although I do not wish to claim that it is 'myth' in the same way that Joshua is.

But several questions emerge. First, are these categories of 'faith' and 'works' fitting perspectives with which to read Rahab's story? Secondly, if these are fitting perspectives, then to what extent more generally might Rahab's story shape the construction of Christian identity in juxtaposition with other treatments of faith in the tradition, in which faith is related to virtue, conversion or salvation for example, but developed without reference to Joshua *per se*? Thirdly, given that Rahab's story is part of a matrix of stories that reflect differing responses to God in Joshua, then might some of the other stories in Joshua similarly give content (perhaps negatively) to what faith 'looks like'? Finally, can these treatments be drawn together so as to develop the significance of Joshua *as discourse* in the Christian context, i.e., seeking to integrate what one might glean from the responses to the first three questions here into a coherent attempt to re-present what Joshua represented as discourse?[42]

To address these questions it will first be necessary to consider the concepts of faith and virtue in the Christian tradition. Whilst space prevents a comprehensive treatment of the development of these concepts in the Christian tradition, I will sketch out an account by briefly considering some interesting representative figures.[43] In order to provide a renewed frame of reference for considering how 'faith' might relate to Joshua, and given that the concepts of faith, works and virtue have become problematic, it will be necessary as a ground-clearing exercise to make a slight digression.

I would like to begin with Gregory of Nyssa. Martin Laird suggests that for Gregory faith serves an epistemological function. It is, moreover, the faculty that mediates union with God after the mind has been cut off in a darkness of unknowing, resulting in divine indwelling.[44] It is a gift from God.[45] Laird suggests that 'Paul's justification by faith has become Gregory of Nyssa's union by faith'.[46] Anthony Meredith suggests that for Gregory 'faith is not a preliminary state, but that mental and spiritual condition of being perpetually open to and dependent upon the divine self-disclosure.'[47] Moreover, whilst Gregory talks of faith as uniting one with God, he also suggests that 'participation in the Beati-

---

[42] I.e., representing the culmination of reading Joshua in terms of myth in a Christian context.

[43] The kind of reading of the tradition that I wish to develop here takes the approach of Ellen Charry in her *By the Renewing of your Minds* as a point of departure.

[44] M. Laird, *Gregory of Nyssa and the Grasp of Faith: Union, Knowledge and Divine Presence* (Oxford Early Christian Studies; Oxford: OUP, 2004), 100-101.

[45] Ibid., 105.

[46] Ibid., 106. Perhaps Gregory taught universal salvation so justification is less of an issue (cf. *Life of Moses*, p.18, cf. II.82-84). However, Luther also said of faith that it 'unites the soul with Christ as a bride is united with her bridegroom' (*The Freedom of a Christian*, in *Basic Theological Writings* (ed. T.F. Lull; Minneapolis: Fortress Press, 1989), 585-629, here 603).

[47] A. Meredith, *The Cappadocians* (Crestwood: St. Vladimir's Seminary Press, 2000), 67.

tudes means nothing else but to have communion with the Godhead',[48] and Laird develops this theme through *De oratione dominica* v, commenting that,

> Gregory says that if a person imitates characteristics associated with God, that person becomes what he imitates. For Gregory forgiveness is a virtue, a characteristic of God. By imitating this virtue we become like what we imitate. Virtue, then is both a manifestation of divine life and a means of divinization, or ... 'progressive deification through virtue'.[49]

But in *The Life of Moses* Gregory speaks of those 'saved by virtue',[50] and indeed for Gregory Moses' life reflects the journey of the life of virtue,[51] even though it is impossible to attain perfection in this life.[52] However, there are 'two pursuits through which virtue is acquired, namely faith toward the divine and conscience toward life.'[53] Thus faith and virtue are intimately related in Gregory.

The eastern tradition developed a hierarchy of virtues, and Maximus the Confessor develops the hierarchy of virtues as faith, fear of God, self-mastery, patience, long-suffering, hope in God, detachment and love,[54] with love being the 'summary and summit' of the virtues.[55] But Lars Thunberg suggests that a 'striking fact in relation to Maximus' understanding of *faith* is his high evaluation of this basic theological virtue. Both Evagrius and Maximus see faith as the foundation and starting-point of Christian life as a whole,' and faith gives knowledge of God that 'can be contrasted with sensual knowledge'.[56] He suggests that the three 'theological virtues' (Thunberg's term) are related in Maximus to the progression of the Christian life in which

> faith is attached to the beginning—it lays the foundation of Christian life—while hope performs a task of mediation, since it indicates that which is believed and makes real that which is the object of love. And charity is above all related to the end, the consummation of all. ... Maximus presents charity ... as the end of man's motion toward his divine goal, an end which is able to replace

---

[48] *The Beatitudes*, Sermon 5, in H.C. Graef, *St. Gregory of Nyssa: The Lord's Prayer, The Beatitudes* (ACW 18; New York: Paulist Press, 1954), p.130.
[49] Laird, *Gregory*, 189. Cf. *Life of Moses*, I.7, p.31: '[w]hoever pursues true virtue participates in nothing other than God, because he himself is absolute virtue'.
[50] *Life of Moses*, II.9, p.57.
[51] Ibid., II.42, p.64.
[52] Ibid., II.290, pp.128-129.
[53] Ibid., II.192, p.104.
[54] L. Thunberg, *Microcosm and Mediator: The Theological Anthropology of Maximus the Confessor* (Chicago: Open Court, 2nd ed. 1995), 286.
[55] Ibid., 309.
[56] Ibid., 317-8.

both faith and hope. ... Thus it is made fully clear that charity alone, in Maximus' opinion, brings man to mystical union with God.[57]

Again, one sees the intimate relationship between faith and virtue developed, with the category of faith perhaps being drawn in to that of virtue, and how this relates to the goal of the Christian life understood as union with God.

Turning to the western tradition, Mary Clark notes that for Augustine, faith 'is the response to God's self-revelation and the only access to God as Trinity. By faith persons communicate with God',[58] whereas John Rist notes that, 'Virtue, says Augustine [*De moribus ecclesiae catholicae* I.15.25], is "nothing other" than the supreme love of God'; for Augustine all forms of virtue are 'modes of love'.[59] Likewise Bonnie Kent suggests that '[v]irtues are unified through charity' for Augustine, but also that '[v]irtue is a threshold, not the end of the road of moral development, so that we are justified in considering people virtuous if they are only moving in the right direction, are steadily *trying*'.[60] Regarding works, Gregory Lombardo notes that in *On Faith and Works* Augustine seeks to refute both 'the Pelagian heresy, which said that justification depended solely on man's efforts, and the heresy of justification by faith alone.' For Augustine, 'the only faith that justifies is that faith which is enlivened by charity'.[61] Augustine distinguishes between works before justification and those after, noting that works do not merit faith.[62]

On Faith and Works is an interesting work for it is thoroughly exegetical throughout, but is a response to a very pastoral concern, tackling the question of who should be admitted to baptism, a concern that introduces the work and remains in view throughout. In it Augustine refuses a simplistic 'proof texting', seeking a 'middle course', noting that people go astray when they do not take a middle course.[63] He argues that 'morals and faith ... are mutually connected. ... [T]he Scriptures sometimes speak of one and not of the other ... instead of both together, so that we might perceive from this procedure that the one cannot exist

---

[57] Ibid., 319-20. Here, and in the remainder of the discussion, charity should be construed more in terms of love than in the contemporary sense of charity, although contemporary understanding of love seems problematic also.

[58] M. Clark, '*de Trinitate*', in E. Stump and N. Kretzmann (eds.), *The Cambridge Companion to Augustine* (Cambridge: CUP, 2001), 91-102, here 97.

[59] J. Rist, 'Faith and Reason', in *The Cambridge Companion to Augustine*, 26-39, here 36.

[60] B. Kent, 'Augustine's Ethics', in *The Cambridge Companion to Augustine*, 205-33, here 228-9.

[61] G.J. Lombardo, 'Introduction', in *St. Augustine: On Faith and Works* (ACW 48; New York: The Newman Press, 1988), 1-6, here 3.

[62] Ibid., 4-5. Cf. *On Faith and Works* 14.21, pp.28-9; 'the works of the law are meritorious not before but after justification'.

[63] *On Faith and Works* 4.5, p.11.

apart from the other.'[64] Throughout this work Augustine repeatedly cites Gal 5:6, that 'faith works by love', although he has little to say regarding virtue *per se* in this work, even if Rist's remarks indicates that the concept is implicitly understood here.

Thus in the early period we see virtue being developed as a category that is drawn into close association with the category of faith, whilst the category of 'works' seems to be rejected.

For Thomas Aquinas faith, hope and charity are the three *theological virtues*, virtues which differ from the 'natural virtues' in that they result from a special infusion of grace,[65] and cannot be acquired by the repetition of suitable actions,[66] being 'wholly from outside'.[67] But these theological virtues are interconnected dispositions. Faith and hope can exist without charity, but do not have 'the perfect character of virtue' without it;[68] but charity cannot exist without faith and hope[69] since charity is friendship with God.[70] Terence Penelhum suggests that for Aquinas no one of the three theological virtues 'can embody, within itself, all the salient and distinctive features of the Christian life.'[71] However, he notes that acts of assent and confession that result from faith are signs that the will is disposed by charity in Aquinas; 'There is nothing odd about suggesting that a man's faith may reflect his charity, just as his charity may be a consequence of his faith.'[72] Indeed, Aquinas suggests that,

> As habits they [faith, hope and charity] are all infused together. ... Now it is by faith that the mind apprehends what it hopes for and loves. And so in the sequence of coming to be, faith has to precede hope and charity. ...
>
> In the precedence of value, however, charity comes before faith and hope, because both faith and hope come alive through charity, and receive from charity their full stature of virtues. For thus charity is the mother of all the virtues, inasmuch as it is the form of all of them.[73]

---

[64] Ibid. 13.20, pp.27-8.
[65] Cf. *ST* 1a2ae.63,1 and 51,4.
[66] *ST* 1a2ae.63,2. Cf. T. Penelhum, 'The Analysis of Faith in St. Thomas Aquinas', in *Religious Studies* 13.2 (1977): 133-54, here 134-5.
[67] *ST* 1a2ae.63,2.
[68] *ST* 1a2ae.65,4.
[69] *ST* 1a2ae.65,5.
[70] *ST* 2a2ae.23,1; Penelhum, 'Faith', 136-7.
[71] Penelhum, 'Faith', 137.
[72] Ibid., 142.
[73] *ST* 1a2ae.62, 4, vol. 23, p.147. He notes elsewhere that since 'the ultimate end is present to the will through hope and charity, to the mind through faith, it necessarily follows that faith is absolutely the first of the virtues; no natural knowledge can reach God as he is the object of beatitude, i.e. as hope and charity are fixed upon God.' (*ST* 2a2ae.4,7, vol. 31, p.139. Cf. 2a2ae.2,3; faith is beyond reason for supernatural knowl-

Elsewhere Aquinas suggests that 'the good ... the end of faith's act, is the divine good, the proper object of charity. This is why charity is called the form of faith, namely because the act of faith is completed and shaped by charity.'[74] T.C. O'Brien adds in a footnote to this text that

> There is more in the conclusion than simply an instance of a virtuous act's being shaped by charity toward the love and service of God. The primacy of end used in the argument here is meant to express the specific scriptural theme that faith is the beginning of salvation and eternal life ... Faith in its proper species and form is determined by its formal objective, God, the first truth; but he addresses the believer not as imparting information to mind alone, but as inviting to salvation ... Thus faith calls for love, self-commitment, and it is in this distinctive sense that it has its completion from charity; only in one who loves God does faith reach its fully intended meaning as the beginning of eternal life[75]

and also in a note to another text that

> 'Form' and the adjectival correlates ... were readily adopted in the medieval discussions of virtue because *forma* has the common meaning, 'perfection' or 'completion' ... Specifically with regard to faith, it is described as unformed where charity is lacking in that it empowers a person for an act of believing God without error, but not for an act that is meritorious. ... [T]he act of faith, like that of other virtues, has a further dimension, moral kind or form, by 'the diffusion, as it were, of the reign of charity over it.'[76]

Indeed, Aquinas develops a distinction between 'formed' and 'unformed' faith, suggesting that the distinction 'is grounded in something connected with the will, namely charity, and not on something connected with the intellect.'[77] He argues that formed faith is a virtue whereas formless faith is not ('Charity gives form to the act of faith').[78]

As well as distinguishing between formed and unformed faith, Aquinas also differentiates 'implicit' from 'explicit' faith, where 'implicit faith' is a faith that 'simple people' have in 'what their teachers believe'.[79] He considers whether an 'explicit faith' is necessary for all for salvation, and after noting that 'matters of

---

edge is needed (p.75).) However, he also suggests that 'certain virtues may be said to be prior to faith incidentally, i.e. as removing obstacles for the believer: courage, for example, may take away a fear inhibiting belief; humility, a pride of mind resisting submission to the truth of faith. ... [F]aith without charity is not the foundation; but this still does not require that charity exist before faith.' (*ST* 2a2ae.4,7, vol. 31, p.141).

[74] *ST* 2a2ae.4,3 vol. 31, p.125.
[75] O'Brien, in *ST*, vol. 31, p.125.
[76] Ibid., pp.123-124.
[77] *ST* 2a2ae.4,4, vol. 31, p.129.
[78] *ST* 2a2ae.4,5, vol. 31, p.133.
[79] *ST* 2a2ae.2,5-8, vol. 31, pp.79-97.

faith surpass reason', and citing Dionysius concerning hierarchies and their theological significance (*Celestial Hierarchy* 12), he concludes that it is not.[80] But what is interesting is that he continues in the next article:

> should any have been saved who had received no revelation, they were not saved without faith in the mediator. The reason: even if they did not have an explicit belief in Christ, they did have an implicit faith in God's providence, believing that God is man's deliverer in ways of his own choosing, as the Spirit would reveal this to those who know the truth.[81]

Perhaps this raises the interesting possibility that 'saving faith' may be construed and expressed as a responsiveness to Christ in ways that do not always require explicit verbal confession of Christ, however desirable and 'normative' this may and ought to be, and however central and unique Christ may be to salvation whether this is made explicit or not.

So in Aquinas we discover a development of some of the themes of the earlier material, with the importance of virtue rising to the fore. He seeks to clarify and develop the relationship between faith and virtue, particularly in the way that faith relates to love, and how this relates to God and the beatific vision. In Aquinas we find careful pastoral theology, seeking not to over-burden all (such as young children or those with learning difficulties perhaps) with an 'explicitness' of faith (however desirable this might be), whilst seeking generally to encourage faith to be formed in love as one is 'in relationship' with God.

Thus far, it is notable that this development of faith and virtue together has been conducted without it becoming 'salvation by works' (with works being a category that has been avoided). Rather the discussion has been conducted with reference to union by faith, as a response to a gracious gift to God in love, embodied in a life of virtue which *is* participation in God and the 'end' of faith.

However, this begins to change with Calvin, even though in fact the differences that develop seem to relate to emphasis, with the practical outworking of faith looking fairly similar. Over time the difference in emphasis becomes something more of a 'stand-off', with the language of virtue disappearing altogether. For Calvin faith is 'a firm and certain knowledge of God's benevolence toward us, founded upon the truth of the freely given promise in Christ, both revealed to our minds and sealed upon our hearts through the Holy Spirit.'[82] However, 'faith rests upon the knowledge of Christ. And Christ cannot be known apart from the sanctification of his Spirit. It follows that faith can in no wise be separated from a devout disposition.'[83] Thus although Calvin sets things

---

[80] *ST* 2a2ae.2,6, vol. 31, p.85.
[81] *ST* 2a2ae.2,7, vol. 31, p.93.
[82] *Inst* III.ii.7, p.551.
[83] *Inst* III.ii.8, pp.552-3.

up rather differently, he is, in fact, fairly close to Aquinas and Augustine. Indeed, later on Calvin asks,

> [H]ow can the mind be aroused to taste the divine goodness without at the same time being wholly kindled to love God in return? ... [T]he teaching of the Schoolmen, that love is prior to faith and hope, is mere madness; for it is faith alone that first engenders love in us. ... [W]herever this faith is alive, it must have along with it the hope of eternal salvation as its inseparable companion.[84]

But despite similarities, Calvin departs from the Schoolmen, and abolishes the distinctions between formed and unformed faith, and explicit and implicit faith. He suggests that 'we must refute that worthless distinction between formed and unformed faith which is tossed about in the schools. For they imagine that people who are touched by no fear of God, no sense of piety, nevertheless believe whatever it is necessary to know for salvation.'.[85] Elsewhere he discusses the problem of 'implicit faith' in the Scholastic literature, which he sees as faith based not on understanding but on ignorant obedience to the church.[86] But whilst the language of confession is accentuated in Calvin, the language of virtue drops out. He sees virtues, or 'images of virtues' as he terms them, as simply gifts from God,[87] wishing here, it seems, to emphasize the praiseworthiness of God and the fallen-ness of humanity. Indeed, he continues,

> Yet what Augustine writes is nonetheless true: that all who are estranged from religion of the one God, however admirable they may be regarded on account of their reputation for virtue, not only deserve no reward but rather punishment, because by the pollution of their hearts they defile God's good works. For even though they are God's instruments for the preservation of human society in righteousness, continence, friendship, temperance, fortitude and prudence, yet they carry out these good works of God very badly. ... Therefore, since by the very impurity of men's hearts these good works have been corrupted as from

---

[84] *Inst* III.ii.41-2, pp.589-90. This does not seem to be the view of Aquinas, although here Calvin's dialogue partner is Peter Lombard. Calvin appears to be closer in emphasis to the tradition than Luther, although Luther does suggest, for example, that, 'by faith the soul is cleansed and made to love God' (*The Freedom of a Christian*, p.611), and 'from faith ... flow forth love and joy in the Lord, and from love a joyful, willing, and free mind that serves one's neighbor willingly' (ibid., p.619), although 'the Christian who is consecrated by faith does good works, but the works do not make him holier or more Christian, for that is the work of faith alone' (ibid., pp.612-613). This, it seems, is a clear departure from the tradition in which participation (and 'ascent') in the virtues was seen as participation in, and ascent into, the life of God. It seems that in the tradition 'salvation' and 'sanctification' were construed in more holistic terms than in the Reformers. Luther is also concerned that works lead to a false confidence (ibid., pp.621-2).
[85] *Inst* III.ii.8, p.551.
[86] *Inst* III.ii.2, pp.544-5.
[87] *Inst* III.xiv.2, p.770.

their source, they ought no more to be reckoned among virtues than the vices that commonly deceive on account of their affinity and likeness to virtue.[88]

A similar account of faith is developed by Karl Barth. For Barth, 'Faith as such cannot contribute anything to our justification ... It is not a *habitus*. It is not a quality of grace which is infused into man' and it is not a virtue, which he construes as a 'power and an achievement of man' (i.e. a 'work').[89] Thus Barth develops the pessimistic theological anthropology found in Calvin, and reacts against any tendencies to reify grace and faith, with emphasis being placed on the nature of faith as trusting in the work of another (Christ) on one's behalf. He suggests that

> faith is just this and nothing but this: the confidence of sinful man in the demonstration of the undeserved faithfulness of God as given in Jesus Christ, a demonstration in which he finds that his sins are forgiven. If there is any corresponding faithfulness of sinful man to the faithful God, it consists only in this confidence. As he gives this confidence, he finds himself justified, but not otherwise. That was what the reformers maintained. ... When [faith] is a matter of recognising and apprehending of justification, it denies the competence, the relevance, the power and the value of all human action. ... Because faith is obedient humility, abnegation, it will and must exclude any co-operation of human action in the matter of man's justification.[90]

So whilst for Barth faith has 'other dimensions than that of justification',[91] 'faith of the man justified by God is opposed to all his works', although he notes that 'works' for Paul meant 'the works which the Old Testament demanded of the members of God's chosen people Israel to mark their distinction from other peoples'.[92] However,

> human works as such cannot be regarded with contempt or indifference, and rejected. They are the (in itself) inevitable and good actualisation of the (in itself) good creaturely nature of man. They can and must be done. And faith itself would not be faith if it did not work by love, if it were not as Luther put it, "a living, active, busy thing." ... Where there is faith, there are also love and works.[93]

Again, in some respects *in practice* Barth is close to Aquinas and Augustine here; for Barth faith reflects an openness to its object, that is to Jesus Christ, and

---

[88] *Inst* III.xiv.3, p.770.
[89] *CD* IV.1, p.617.
[90] *CD* IV.1, pp.626-627. The idea of faith as 'the humility of obedience' is something that is important for Barth in this section (cf. e.g. p.620, and p.628 where he describes 'faith as the humility which involves necessarily the exclusion of works').
[91] *CD* IV.1, p.618.
[92] *CD* IV.1, p.621. Perhaps Barth anticipates the 'New Perspective' on Paul here.
[93] *CD* IV.1, p.627.

'does represent an imitation of God, an analogy to His attitude and action.'[94] But Barth is concerned with the problem of absorbing the doctrine of justification into that of sanctification 'understood as the pious work of self-sanctification which man can undertake and accomplish in his own strength.'[95] He goes on to analyze the 'act of faith' using the categories of *Anerkennen, Erkennen* and *Bekennen* (acknowledgement, recognition and confession).[96] So in Barth one discovers an emphasis on the object of faith—Jesus Christ, and of the acknowledgment, recognition and confession of him. But whilst, as in Calvin, we may see a recognition of the importance of love in relation to faith, the intimate association of faith with virtue has been eclipsed, owing it seems to a theology of despair—of human depravity and the desire to avoid any hint of an idea of salvation by works; a fear of Pelagianism. Perhaps then, and rather ironically, Calvin and Barth depart from the tradition that we have considered because their theology is in fact somewhat infatuated with the human subject together with a *distrust* of the ability of God to manifest himself in and to humanity. We also see a wedge driven between justification and sanctification, something that is alien to the theologians we have considered prior to Calvin, as well as a loss of the sense of salvation as participation in the life of the Godhead.

Indeed, in the intellectual climate of modernity generally, there is a rise in concern with the cognitive dimensions of faith as belief and as a mental act, and a corresponding erosion of an epistemology based upon participation in the Godhead.[97] However, within this context, interesting accounts of faith (or belief) were developed by Rudolf Bultmann[98] and Ludwig Wittgenstein, who, in rather different ways drew attention to the existential dimensions of faith. In Bultmann's treatment, one that I will not explore in detail here, the 'object' of faith is eclipsed, but in Wittgenstein's account of religious belief he suggests,

> Suppose someone were a believer and said: "I believe in a Last Judgement," and I said: "Well, I'm not so sure. Possibly." You would say that there is an enormous gulf between us. If he said "There is a German aeroplane overhead," and I said "Possibly. I'm not so sure," you'd say we were fairly near.
>
> It isn't a question of my being anywhere near him, but on an entirely different plane, which you could express by saying: "You mean something altogether different, Wittgenstein."
>
> The difference might not show up at all in any explanation of the meaning.
>
> Why is it that in this case I seem to be missing the entire point?

---

[94] *CD* IV.1, pp.633-4.
[95] *CD* IV.1, p.768.
[96] *CD* IV.1, pp.758ff.
[97] Cf. Charry, *Renewing*, 229-36.
[98] See e.g. R. Bultmann, *Theology of the New Testament I* (London: SCM, ET: 1952), 300-302.

> Suppose somebody made this guidance for this life: believing in the Last Judgment. Whenever he does anything, this is before his mind. In a way, how are we to know whether to say he believes this will happen or not?
>
> Asking him is not enough. He will probably say he has proof.
>
> But he has what you might call an unshakeable belief. It will show, not by reasoning or by appeal to ordinary grounds for belief, but rather by regulating for all in his life.
>
> This is a very much stronger fact—foregoing pleasures, always appealing to this picture. This in one sense must be called the firmest of all beliefs, because the man risks things on account of it which he would not do on things which are by far better established for him.[99]

Thus in Wittgenstein we see the possibility, from within the context of a modernist frame of reference, for a renewal of a more 'holistic' conception of faith than that which took root in the Reformation, a conception that has subsequently affected much biblical scholarship and theology.

So, returning to Joshua, how might this study of faith in the Christian tradition relate to Joshua's Christian appropriation with reference to the use of Rahab's story in Jas 2:20-26 as a point of departure in which faith and works are categories introduced to interpret Joshua?[100] Moreover, might the category of 'faith' inform the Christian appropriation of Joshua more generally? Conversely, does Joshua inform Christian understanding of the nature of faith? Or, to situate this discussion into the context of the question of the nature of the new life entered into in Joshua as symbolized by the Jordan crossing and appropriated in the Christian context in baptism, might the narratives of Joshua be said to give content to the nature of this new life in the Christian context when read through the category of 'faith'? Working backwards from our contemporary context, starting with Wittgenstein, Wittgenstein helpfully draws attention to the way in which one uses religious language. But the 'Last Judgement', and the nature of beliefs related to it, has certain similarities with Rahab and the Gibeonites facing חרם. Rahab and the Gibeonites make this prospect of חרם the guidance for their life—they take risks and act in the light of it. Thus Joshua might be said to have certain affinities with Wittgenstein's account of belief, which draws attention to the active and existential nature of the claim to believe, or to have faith perhaps. However, perhaps Wittgenstein's account does not clearly differentiate Rahab's response from that of the Gibeonites.

---

[99] First lecture on religious belief in *Ludwig Wittgenstein: Lectures and Conversations on Aesthetics, Psychology and Religious Belief* (Oxford: Blackwell, 1966), 53-59, here 53-4.

[100] Perhaps it is important here to differentiate between the nature of 'works' in James and Paul. In the light of the 'New Perspective', 'works' in Paul might have more the sense of 'works of the law', whilst in James 'works' may carry what emerged as the notion of 'virtue'.

Turning to Barth, his analysis of the 'act of faith' in terms of *Anerkennen, Erkennen* and *Bekennen* (to recognize, to acknowledge and to confess), can certainly be applied to Rahab, but perhaps, to a lesser extent, to Achan (7:19-20), although Achan's confession appears to be confession in a rather 'thin' sense, essentially being confession of sin rather than of the glory of YHWH. However, his response does seem to reflect a recognition and acknowledgement of the true state of affairs with respect to YHWH. Furthermore, perhaps Barth's description of the act of faith may describe the Gibeonite response to some degree, but in a sense their 'confession' is more comparable to Achan's than to Rahab's, being a rather 'thin' response that does not glorify YHWH, yet they are 'saved' whereas Achan is stoned to death. So in one sense Barth's account of the 'act of faith' helpfully accentuates Rahab's response, but is a little problematic with regard to Achan and the Gibeonites.

Moreover, Achan and Rahab's stories are somewhat disorientating for those accounts of Christian response to God that stress the confession and forgiveness of sin as being 'the bottom line' of the Christian life. Indeed, unlike Achan, Rahab does not confess any sin, despite her characterization as a prostitute, and Achan is executed despite his confession of sin, a form of confession that is found everywhere in the tradition from at least 1 John 1:9-10 onwards (cf. e.g. *ST* 2a2ae.3,2), and is effective. So it is interesting that Rahab is sometimes viewed as something like a 'model convert' even though she fails to confess sin,[101] whilst Achan, whilst confessing his sin, is nowhere in the Christian tradition a model penitent, as far as I am aware.[102] Moreover Barth's account of faith as the act of the Christian life as 'obedient humility' perhaps runs into difficulty here too, for arguably it is Achan who demonstrates the most 'obedient humility' of all in the end even if not initially (7:19-20), since for Rahab and the Gibeonites, their 'faith' is expressed in bold and perhaps crafty initiative taking. Whilst 'obedient humility' does, in many senses reflect Joshua and the Israelite response to God in the story as we saw earlier, there is also a sense in which the Israelites are characterized by a greater boldness, or even assertiveness, than Barth's description might be taken to suggest.

With regard to Calvin, his rejection of the value of various scholastic notions of faith, especially as found in Aquinas, is questionable. Whilst the

---

[101] E.g., Cyril of Jerusalem suggests that she is 'saved through repentance' (*Catechetical Lectures* 2.9, in *ACCS*, 12). If this is not to do violence to the text such repentance must be construed in terms of her actions rather than a confession of sin. (Cf. chapter 8, and, e.g. Hess, *Joshua*, 96-7, 134-5).

[102] However, we saw in chapter 8 that in the Jewish tradition he was a model penitent for one finding life in the world to come, but this move does not appear to have been made in the Christian tradition. See further the discussion in chapter 8. Indeed, especially in the Middle Ages, the opposite is the case. See my 'Joshua and the Crusades' for texts and discussion.

distinction between implicit and explicit faith does not find expression in Joshua, it seems that in addition to Rahab's confession being 'fuller' than Achan's or the Gibeonites' (cf. *ST* 2a2ae.3,2), her 'faith' might be distinguished from the Gibeonite 'faith' in that it is 'formed' rather than 'unformed', being reflected in her virtue,[103] taking this to be a redescription of what the narrative interprets as חסד, being that which I have argued demonstrates her Israelite quality. This, coupled with her courage, leads to her 'salvation'. But we do not find this virtue, or 'formed-ness' of faith in the Gibeonites, although the narrative implies their 'salvation', even if, as we saw in Origen's reading of their story,[104] it is a somewhat 'thinner' salvation than Rahab's. So it seems that Joshua might lend support to the scholastic distinction between formed and unformed faith, even if it is, perhaps, to be applied in a slightly different way; the Gibeonites obtained salvation through their unformed faith, whilst Rahab obtained a 'better' or 'fuller' 'salvation' through her formed faith reflected in her virtue that constituted her response to God.

But does it make sense to speak of 'salvation' in this way—is it not part of a binary system in which one is either 'saved' or 'not saved'? It is worth developing this concept of 'salvation' here, for as Charry noted, it has become an increasingly 'thin' concept in much of the Christian tradition, with the focus of salvation being on the forgiveness of sins, rather than on participation, in some sense, in the divine life.[105] However, if salvation is construed rather more broadly and 'holistically' as conquering death *and* entering into life in its fullness, sharing in the life of God, then Rahab's and the Gibeonites' 'salvation' is intelligible in these terms—Rahab 'conquers' the death that awaits the other inhabitants of Jericho, and enters into the fullness of life with Israel, and hence YHWH, whereas the Gibeonites, whilst 'conquering death', enter into a life of servitude, albeit 'with YHWH' in some sense. The difficulties that might be raised regarding the forgiveness of the sins of Rahab's former way of life, something that the narrative does not address, are then relativized because forgiveness is not the primary focus of salvation; rather life with God is the focus. Indeed, Charry notes that for Augustine 'salvation is dwelling in the fullness of God',[106] and that one enjoys God by participating in the good— 'Augustine pressed Christians ... to taste and enjoy God. And since the "essence" of God is justice, wisdom, love and goodness, participation in these qualities *is* eternal life with God.'[107] In other words, perhaps one can construe

---

[103] I deliberately use 'virtue' in favour of 'works' here, as this is the grammar of the tradition.
[104] *Hom Josh*. 10.1-2 (cf. chapter 8).
[105] Charry, *Renewing*, 121.
[106] Ibid., 121.
[107] Ibid., 133, cf. 137 and *de Trinitate* VIII:2.5.

salvation in terms of participation in these qualities, qualities that are, in some sense, demonstrated in Rahab.

But such a construal of salvation as participation in the divine qualities (or virtues perhaps) is, it seems, suggestive of the concept of 'implicit faith' as might be developed from Aquinas. In Christian terms this might raise the *possibility* of salvation *outside* the visible church, i.e., of those who do not explicitly confess Christ *in word*, even though this is somewhere that Augustine, for example, does not go.[108] Moreover, since Rahab does confess YHWH explicitly, this would be to go beyond what the narrative of Joshua might be taken to express explicitly—but often this is the nature of Christian reading of the Old Testament, as we have seen. But if what Joshua sought to achieve as an act of discourse was to make the construction of Israelite identity a rather more problematic affair than it was traditionally perceived to be, 'blurring the boundaries' of the community, then a 'blurring of the boundaries' of those who are reckoned as 'God's people' today by making problematic the traditional criterion of explicit verbal confession of Christ (and of sin) by using the category of implicit faith seems to reflect precisely what Joshua sought to achieve. The crucial question is whether this category of 'implicit faith' developed in this way is a theologically good one to use and juxtapose with Joshua. That is, is this a faithful development of what Joshua was seeking to achieve? I do not wish to claim that it is necessarily, but rather to raise the possibility here for further discussion.

Indeed, there are patristic voices that describe the cultivation and exercise of virtue as *being* salvation and dwelling in the fullness of God. Moreover, the rather unsettling story of Matt 25:31-46 indicates the possibility that a response to Jesus *implicitly* made through actions and dispositions that reflect Christian virtue more adequately embodies that which is to characterize faithful response to God than a concern for the ability to 'name' actions or attitudes *explicitly* as being 'for Christ' or as 'Christian' perhaps.[109] In other words, cultivation and

---

[108] In *On Faith and Works* Augustine suggests that an act is 'not a morally good act unless it is done out of devotion to God' (7.11, p.17). Lombardo comments in a note that Augustine never condemns as bad virtuous acts of pagans, but suggests that for Augustine the 'defect of the virtues of the pagans ... is that ... they are not directed to God, to their supernatural end' (p.81). Since this work and *de Trinitate* were written in a similar era in Augustine's life, it may suggest that Charry's reading needs to be carefully nuanced, even if her reading opens interesting theological possibilities. The question, it seems, is one of whether a virtue needs to have an explicitly directed end that is recognized or not for it to reflect genuine participation in the Godhead. For Aquinas, it seems that it does not to the same extent that it does in Augustine.

[109] However, in the context of Matt 25 the ones to whom kindness is or is not shown would appear to be Christians (25:40, 45), which would weaken this argument in relation to implicit faith. But, particularly in the light of Prov 19:17, it would seem that this story might be developed, so that response to those in need, whether Christian or not, reflects response to Jesus, whether this is explicitly recognized as such. (Cf. D.A. Hagner,

exercise of *Christian* virtue (through grace, even if such grace is not named as grace) whether or not it is explicitly named as 'Christian' might be said to constitute dwelling in the fullness of God in Christ, and salvation. Granted, this is to go beyond and develop what the texts claim. But is it a faithful development? Even if it is, this does not, of course, imply that an explicit faith is not normative and desirable, and that it should not be encouraged and sought. Clearly, an 'explicit faith' should be seen as normative and should be encouraged in evangelism, but perhaps the notion of implicit faith offers an important pastoral resource for 'hard cases'. An explicit faith surely offers a greater 'chance of success' in cultivating Christian virtue, but the concept of implicit faith recognizes that there are those who, for various reasons, are unable to develop such an explicit faith. Conversely, it would be precisely the confidence and complacency of an explicit confession of faith that is not 'worked out' in virtue that a re-appropriation of Joshua in terms of Achan's story (and indeed Matt 25:31-46) would seek to undermine.

However, this participation in the life of God may also be viewed, according to Gregory of Nyssa, in terms of union with God through faith. Indeed, it is interesting that *Ecclesiastes Rabbah* points in a vaguely similar direction, in which it is said that Rahab is brought into 'union' with Israel.[110] Both Gregory and the *midrash* may reflect the influence of Hellenistic categories, but it is interesting that similar language may be employed in these different traditions to discuss the effects of Rahab's response. Thus one might well speak of faith as in some sense 'attaching' oneself to God, perhaps in Rahab's case demonstrating also a *detachment* from 'the world', to use a category of traditional Christian spirituality.[111] But for Gregory of Nyssa virtue seems to be a *manifestation* of the divine union too, rather than its source, although he does speak of 'salvation through virtue', which has the effect of drawing faith and virtue together. But given that in Joshua the narrative stresses Rahab's חסד as being that which leads to her 'salvation', this perspective of 'salvation through virtue' resonates with Rahab's story well. The difficulty that one encounters in the Christian context is, perhaps, the question of causality. So, for example, in Maximus faith appears to

---

Matthew 14-28 (WBC 33B; Dallas: Word, 1995), 745-6). As we have just seen, this is not somewhere that Augustine would go, but it does seem that his account might be suggestive of such a development.

[110] 'Rahab ... whom [God] brings and *attaches* to Israel' (מביאו ומדבקו בישראל) (5.13).

[111] Here, particularly as I am developing the 'mythical' nature of this material, being that which is concerned largely with existential response, I do not wish to make metaphysical claims regarding the use of such language and in what might be described as a 'Christian Neoplatonism'. Rather, such language—of union with and participation in the Godhead— offers an imaginative and existentially engaging account of the nature of the Christian life, that as symbolic language, *points toward* the metaphysical nature of the Christian life even though it may fall short of an adequate metaphysical description *per se*.

be a virtue that is always necessary, but that in some sense leads to the *development* of other virtues, whereas in Aquinas the situation appears more complex, with faith being a virtue, but one of three 'theological virtues' (faith, hope and love) that are received 'from outside' by grace, that 'raises one' above one's own nature (cf. *ST* 2a2ae.6,1). But in a sense, in Rahab's story her faith and virtue coexist, with there being no particular sense that her faith preceded her virtue or that it was graciously infused, as I suggested in chapter 8, given that the narrative does not portray any development of Rahab's character.

Indeed, Joshua is simply uninterested in these later Christian questions of causality and infusion, and the issue is how Joshua may be appropriated well in the Christian context in which these interpretative categories arise.[112] Whilst for Rahab faith and other virtues may coexist,[113] suggesting that James offers a good reading of her story, drawing attention to that which results in her 'salvation' when read in Christian terms, generally speaking, the New Testament seems to suggest that virtue or goodness (cf. 2 Pet 1:3-5) results from transformative encounter with God, which is manifested in faith as appropriate human response.[114] Indeed, Joshua is not concerned with the process or causes of 'salvation'; rather, Joshua is concerned with challenging established notions of who may 'mingle' with Israel in the practical situations in which Israelites encounter those who are not ethnically or 'visibly' Israel but behave like Israelites nonetheless, however their character and responsiveness to YHWH actually came about. Moreover, part of the difference between Joshua and the New Testament may be described in neo-structuralist categories; the New Testament is concerned with *conversion* from 'outsider to insider' in a sense that the Old Testament is not. The category of 'faith' describes at the 'narrative level' the possibility of transformation at the structural level in the New Testament, whilst perhaps the idea of the *cultivation* of virtue expresses mediation, that one is simultaneously a 'sinner and a saint',[115] a mediation that is expressed in theological language in terms of

---

[112] Cf. Clément, *Roots,* in which he notes that questions of causality become much more of a focus in the West. (81).

[113] Both faith and virtue are of course Christian categories that are used to read the story. But it seems that virtue is indeed a good way of describing her חסד, and that faith is a good way of describing her response, as we saw from Wittgenstein's analysis of faith (or at least belief).

[114] There are, I think, possible exceptions to this, e.g. John 3:19-21.

[115] Furthermore, in Paul's language of salvation, the event of 'salvation' is something generally described in the future—in the Pauline and Deutero-Pauline literature σώζω is used twenty-nine times. It is used eleven times in a future sense, three times in a present sense, and only three times in a past sense, which, it is interesting to note, all occur in the Deutero-Pauline texts (Eph 2:5, 8; 2 Tim 1:9, Tit 3:5). There are eleven occurrences that are ambiguous, with it being possible to take the sense in any of these three ways. But it seems that for Paul salvation is something that has a future rather than past dimension. In this case, if as we saw in Gregory and Maximus for example, true faith results in and is

the indwelling and transforming activity of the Holy Spirit. In the Old Testament, it was חרם that denied the possibility of transformation or mediation, although as we have seen, Joshua used this very category to undermine the distinction between Israel and non-Israel on essentially ethnic grounds. In other words, Joshua marks a very significant shift *towards* the transformation and mediation implied by the gospel that is expressed in faith and virtue.

But, as I noted in chapter 8, there has been something of a misreading of the notion of 'conversion' in Joshua in the tradition. I argued that whilst Rahab's story has been read in terms of her 'conversion', in fact the conversion that the narrative seeks to describe is the 'conversion' of Israel's perception of people such as Rahab and their relationship to the community of Israel, a concern tackled further in the stories of Achan and of the Gibeonites. Indeed, whilst in the Christian reception of Rahab's story there has been a tendency to conflate the categories of salvation and conversion (and perhaps justification) in regard to her, whilst 'salvation' is a category that may be attached to Rahab (in that she escapes death and subsequently dwells with Israel), 'conversion' is a category *attached to Israel* in the story. The story encourages the 'conversion' of Israel's perception of her identity. Rahab does not change in the story—only her status *as perceived by Israel* does, even as she and her family come to live amongst Israel. Thus it seems that good Christian use of Rahab's story would simply develop the idea that it is virtue and faith that is characteristic of Christian identity. But in addition to this, *if* Christian faith may be construed in terms of a responsiveness in 'risk' resulting from and in Christlike action and in attitudes that may or may not be explicitly 'named' as such, then the church may need conversion in her perception of her identity. Her attitudes toward those who exhibit such a 'faith' may require conversion. This may well be to go too far of course. But it is surely fair to say that contemporary Christian use of Joshua urges an ecumenical perspective on the identity of the church. In other words, the church is encouraged to understand its identity in relation to conformity to Christ.[116] This, it seems, would be one way in which Joshua as discourse could be recontextualized into the Christian context. Rahab's story in its Old Testament context has nothing to say about the process of conversion or transformation of outsiders, and nothing to say about questions of causality in relation to

---

manifested in virtue, then it seems quite possible to say that one is saved through virtue. In the sense that virtue is identified as something that one moves towards, rather than achieving in completion, then this account does still work for what has become a paradigmatic case of salvation, the thief on the cross. However, it seems that pastoral context will indeed determine whether it is the exercise of faith or of virtue that is to be emphasized.

[116] In other words, whilst it may turn out that the notion of 'implicit faith' as I have set it up is to go too far, it seems that Joshua is certainly an important resource in an ecumenical sense.

faith and virtue. Rather, the story encourages the conversion of the perception of the insiders toward others. In this sense, to introduce the category of 'justification', or the idea of 'Rahab's conversion' in relation to her story is to risk confusion in the interpretation of the story (cf. Jas 2:24-26), not being fitting with the narrative, especially as an ancient Israelite narrative, even though the introduction of such categories reflects an imaginative use and 'retelling' of the story that is fitting with the Christian gospel in the Christian context. But the use of such Christian categories for interpretation effectively creates a *new* story—a new myth is formed from the old, and *both* stories might be used to construct Christian identity. However, in terms of the interpretation of Rahab's story in its 'earlier form' it is important to stress that this conversion of perception of insiders that it urges is not to lead to a certain kind of romanticized or liberalized attitude toward 'the other', for the outsider that is to be embraced here is embraced precisely because she has certain characteristics that reflect the heart of the community's identity.

In summary then, considering the development of faith and virtue in the tradition in juxtaposition with Joshua, we see how Joshua illuminates some of the ways in which these ideas have been developed, and conversely how these categories can illuminate what is going on in Joshua. The stories of Rahab, Achan and the Gibeonites can, as we have just seen, help sketch the contours of what it means to respond to God faithfully 'in faith', and urge caution against the community of faith seeking to draw its boundaries too precisely—Joshua is certainly an ecumenical text.

However, what also emerges is a sense of the difference between Joshua and the Christian context, which prompts caution in using the material in Joshua at the narrative level to provide paradigms for faith or the Christian life even as they may challenge certain contemporary Christian assumptions. Indeed, it is important also to recognize the theological shift between the contexts of the Old and New Testaments, *and* to respect the mythical nature of the material in Joshua, which is constructed at the narrative level using 'limit-situations' which do not necessarily offer models for behaviour. So, for example, Achan's confession in Joshua does not lead to reflection on the nature of the confession of sin in the Christian context. But what Achan's story does indicate is the incompatibility of disobedience to God as expressed in covetousness with the identity of God's people. Moreover, the separation from outsiders who exhibit aggression or idolatry does not find direct continuity with the Christian context, for the Christian community is concerned with mission to and the conversion of those outside the community (expressing transformation at the structural level) in a way that Joshua is not. Some aspects of Joshua thus recede from view. In other words, the way that Joshua may be used well—how what it sought to achieve is developed today in a Christian context—needs careful treatment through a dialogue between the text as discourse and the New Testament and the Christian tradition. On the one hand, one would wish to preserve Joshua's own voice and not simply impose the New Testament on to it rather awkwardly, but on the other hand, one wishes to recognize that some aspects of Joshua's voice are truly 'old' in the sense of being obsolete. The interpretation and use of Joshua is thus a matter of discernment as Joshua is placed in dialogue with other myths.

The Context and Use of Joshua

Thus far I have said rather little about Joshua's original context and form of use. There appears to be seemingly being little need to seek to identify a precise originary context in order to make Joshua intelligible as discourse. Indeed, the identification of an originary context makes rather little difference to Joshua's theological interpretation when read as myth, as indeed myths find their significance largely in terms of use rather than origin. Whilst I argued, using the hermeneutics of Paul Ricoeur, that its good use is concerned with an exploration of its plenitude and fittingness in interpretation, with the interpreter being guided by a 'fusing of horizons' of the world of the text and the world of the reader in which the fittingness of any interpretation is guided by the public 'codes of production' with respect to which the text was created, this does not mean that the *original intention,* or perhaps 'originally intended perlocutionary response' is necessarily normative, given the 'iconic' nature of the text.[117] Indeed, I have argued that such intentions undergo transformation by the placement of texts such as Joshua in the canon as a new act of discourse, and through its later juxtaposition with other 'myths'.

However, the reading that I have been developing is one that seeks to be sympathetic to the text and one that seeks to encourage its ongoing use. This is in contrast to Robert Coote, whose reading is, however, at one level similar to the one developed here. Coote suggests that

> As an expression of Josiah's reform, the story of Joshua's conquest, patterned on Josiah's reconquest, "functions as an instrument of coercion" and intimidation, encouraging the submission of all subjects The historian wants to terrorize the populace, particularly its recalcitrant political leaders, into submission to Josiah by showing what happens to a class of people ("Canaanites") whose interests are opposed to the interests of Josiah's monarchy and of the peasantry under him. The writer also shows that obedience to Josiah can take precedence over supposed ethnic affiliation: Canaanites can submit and be saved (Rahab, the Gibeonites), and if a Judahite belonging to the Israelite in group disobeys the Commander-in-chief, he can be repudiated and killed (Achan) "The primary purpose of the conquest narrative is to send a message to internal rivals, potential Achans, that they can make themselves into outsiders very easily." Josiah's historian "uses the rhetoric of warfare and nationalism as an encouragement

---

[117] See chapters 2-3. Fittingness of interpretation for the Christian reader is also related to a criterion of fittingness to the canon.

and a threat to its own population to submit voluntarily to the central authority of a government struggling to organize itself and to [re]create its own ideological framework of inclusion. In order to justify violent action [to that end], the dynamics of the literature of warfare usually consist of a division [often outrageously overstated] between self and other," us and them.[118]

What then distinguishes Coote's reading from mine? There are two issues, that of origin, and that of use. First, I think that Coote and others, who follow Lori Rowlett for example, are rather hasty in placing Joshua in a Josianic context, and rather too hasty to interpret Josiah's reign in pejorative terms, a reign that our only witnesses to are in the books of Kings and Chronicles. But, even if Coote and Rowlett are correct on both points, I have argued that this 'original intention' (i.e., as an 'instrument of coercion') need not be normative for later usage, usage which undergoes canonical (and indeed liturgical) transformation. 'Mythically speaking', there is no reason to privilege this genetic assumption. This brings us to the second issue, that of usage. Whatever the original intention behind Joshua—whether it was an instrument of coercion or not—what matters is how one *uses* the kind of interpretation that I (and, in some ways Coote) develop. If Joshua does relate to the construction of identity and to the nature of the boundaries of the community in the ways that I have outlined, then is such identity construction implemented in a coercive manner or in a manner that allows space for disagreement and freedom in response? Coote seems to assume that Joshua *must* function as a coercive tool of intimidation. But the reading that I am presenting can be used in the sense of an invitation to *allow* oneself and the community that values the text to be shaped in particular ways, and to be called to particular ways of 'being in the world' that might depict the contours a faithful human response to God.[119]

Postcolonial approaches to Joshua and to other narratives of the Old Testament have helpfully drawn attention to the terrible ways in which some biblical narratives might be misused, such as by Puritan emigrants to America, and have helpfully forced interpreters to reengage with the texts and the frames of reference in which they are read and appropriated. But postcolonial readings in themselves often fail to be good readings of biblical texts such as Joshua inasmuch as they encourage the adoption of a readerly stance that is not fitting for the text—Joshua exists to shape and challenge identity from the perspective and context of one who is *inside* the community for whom the text is valued, and not for those outside. In other words, for the perspective of the insider, Joshua provides a searching challenge to attitudes towards outsiders such as Rahab, thus

---

[118] R.B. Coote, 'The Book of Joshua', in *The New Interpreter's Bible* (Nashville: Abingdon, 1998), 2.555-719, here 577, drawing upon L.L. Rowlett, 'Inclusion, Exclusion and Marginality in the Book of Joshua', in *JSOT* 55.1 (1992): 15-23.

[119] Of course difficult issues concerning claims to speak for God—and the issues of discourse as expressions of power that it raises—lurk beneath the surface here.

in fact encouraging openness and embrace of 'the other', as well as a searching challenge to the behaviour and attitudes of insiders (Achan). Postcolonial readings in which Joshua is read from a Canaanite perspective only seem to find in the story of Rahab the story of a colluder with imperialism, or a traitor,[120] as Dora Mbuwayesango suggested, which led her to conclude that

> the book of Joshua can help the people of God to construct its identity in a sound way, namely by acknowledging and making explicit the revulsion we have for its narratives. Precisely because these stories of relentless massacres shock us, they warn us that the construction of identities that are exclusive and religiously sanctioned—however overt or covert this religious exclusivism might be—leads to genocide and extermination of entire ethnic groups.[121]

But, as we have seen, this is to misconstrue Joshua.[122] Mbuwayesango's approach to Joshua is, perhaps, fairly typical of a number of ideological readings of Joshua that co-opt it into a 'colonial' frame of reference.[123] However, perhaps Michael Prior's analysis of biblical texts such as Joshua and their use in this regard is one of the most carefully and fully developed analyses in this frame of reference.[124] Prior calls for a 'moral critique' of the Bible and its use. How does this relate to my reading of Joshua?

There are several issues here. First, as I alluded to above, works such as Prior's helpfully provide a *theological critique* of the *use* of texts like Joshua,[125] showing how certain forms of colonial usage are not fitting with respect to the wider Christian tradition, and thus urge critical and careful re-engagement with the text. Secondly, through Victor Turner's approach to myth in particular, we have seen how it is of the nature of material such as Joshua to be amoral in character, and that such materials are not (necessarily) models for behaviour; one cannot simply read principles of Christian ethics off the Old Testament. In this sense, Prior's thesis—of the problematic moral nature of some of the narra-

---

[120] See D. Mbuwayesango, 'Joshua' in D. Patte (ed.), *Global Bible Commentary* (Nashville: Abingdon Press, 2004), 64-73, here 66 and M.W. Dube, 'Rahab says Hello to Judith: A Decolonizing Feminist Reading', in R.S. Sugirtharajah (ed.), *The Postcolonial Biblical Reader* (Oxford: Blackwell, 2006), 142-58, here 156. Cf. discussion in chapter 3.
[121] Mbuwayesango, 'Joshua', 69.
[122] Mbuwayesango also states that the 'purpose of the book of Joshua ... was to inculcate in the people of Israel an identity that was based on the land' ('Joshua', 69). But we have seen how Josh 22 runs in the opposite direction to this.
[123] Indeed, Mbuwayesango begins her commentary on Joshua, 'The book of Joshua appears to be a blueprint for the colonization of southern Africa.' ('Joshua', 64).
[124] M. Prior, *The Bible and Colonialism: A Moral Critique* (The Biblical Seminar 48; Sheffield: Sheffield Academic Press, 1997).
[125] However, I am not convinced that Joshua has been used as the warrant for various forms of 'religiously backed militarism' to anything like the extent that might be implied—see my 'Joshua and the Crusades' (forthcoming).

tives in the Bible—is well taken, but this observation, in a traditional Christian frame of reference might then lead to a desire to appropriate biblical texts in particular 'non-literal' ways, rather than to their dismissal, reflecting the approach of Origen and Gregory of Nyssa, rather than the Marcionites for example. Whilst in this sense I favour continuity with the tradition, perhaps herein lies the biggest 'break' with much traditional Christian reading, for I do not wish to identify a straightforward 'moral sense' throughout Scripture that is to be discerned and applied. But in many ways I do not depart from the way that Joshua's Christian interpretation has in fact been practised, for one finds little in the way of moral exhortation based on Joshua in Origen's homilies for example. But thirdly, there seems to be a danger that certain forms of ideological critical or postcolonial reading might in fact reinforce colonial categories and frames of reference, rather than encouraging them to be transcended, and become themselves 'new colonialisms' or hegemonies that obscure proper human response to God by doing violence to texts such as Joshua. Writing Joshua off as a 'blueprint for colonialism' mutes the text from speaking in the somewhat challenging way that it does regarding the way in which the community of God's people is to grow and develop in response to God. Indeed, it seems that just such a 'transcending' of colonial / postcolonial categories is precisely what Josh 5:13-15 might encourage. Moreover, the testimony of the tradition, broadly construed, points away from such 'colonial' frames of reference toward using Joshua as a resource with which to develop the spiritual life.

In summary then, Joshua may be read and used appropriately from *within* the community that values it, for this is the context to which it speaks, and used within this community in a non-coercive manner to urge more faithful response to God.

Conclusion

We have considered a variety of ways in which Joshua may be appropriated to become part of *my/our* story, and *my/our* community's story—it is a narrative that can be used imaginatively to interpret and develop the Christian's own, and the church's own narrative. This is, perhaps, at the heart of what it means to call Joshua myth, and is something like the perspective that Neil Soggie develops:

> Whether we like it or not, the reality is that all knowledge (especially knowledge of a sacred or religious flavoring) leads back to the mythic level of knowledge. That is, all knowledge is only meaningful when an individual incorporates it into his or her own personal narrative and worldview to give it meaning about how it relates to me. Hence, we can choose to analyze the ancient texts and great stories of our past objectively, but in the end their intent and power is in how they influence us and impact our lives. Ultimately all literature and knowledge is meaningful only when it comes back to faith, for to be human is to live, to live is to move, to move is to assume and to assume is to

have faith. Therefore everyone who is human will live by faith; the question is how do the stories of the past fill out that faith? Is it fragmentary in its mythic understanding of how the ancient source stones relate to us or does it embrace, at least on some relational level, the sacred texts?[126]

I have sought to develop a reading of the book of Joshua that is fitting with respect to the book as an act of discourse, and to the tradition of the community that uses and develops it in juxtaposition with other 'myths'. In particular, as Joshua is part of the canon of Scripture, and because the canon reflects the most significant 'moment' of the tradition to which Joshua's interpretation should be fitting, I have stressed the importance of the fittingness of interpretation to the canonical context in which Joshua is now set. But the reading developed is also an attempt to explore the plenitude of the text in dialogue with the tradition and the context of the interpreter. In this process some aspects of Joshua as an act of discourse are accentuated and developed, whilst others recede into the background.

Joshua itself is already part of a dialogue with tradition, or indeed traditions (i.e., Priestly and Deuteronomistic) as we have seen, a kind of dialogue that continues throughout Joshua's interpretation and use.[127] But this dialogue provides testimony to the fittingness of interpretation of Joshua, and gestures toward its revelatory character as the community that cherishes it 'tracks the truth' of its generation of new identity in God, and develops the 'cultural memory' of the tradition(s) of which Joshua is a part as a resource that encourages appropriate response to God by and within the community.

I have, however, said little about Joshua being a part of the specifically Jewish tradition. Joshua is a work that is concerned with the construction of the national identity of Israel before being used in the construction of the identity of the church. Joshua helps to form two 'cultural memories', cultural memories that have, however, a shared cultural memory and history in the era leading up to Christ. Whilst Joshua has been appropriated in different ways in the Jewish and Christian traditions, if the kind of reading that I have developed above is along the right lines, then perhaps it might form the basis of a fruitful conversation in Jewish-Christian dialogue. If Joshua encourages an openness and acceptance to those outside one's own community who confess the glory of YHWH and celebrate his calling of Israel and who manifest in their actions qualities such as love and faithfulness whilst eschewing covetousness for example, then it seems

---

[126] Soggie, *Myth*, xvi.

[127] Indeed, whilst the differences between the Priestly and Deuteronomistic traditions have often been emphasized, their juxtaposition in Joshua (and not just the canon) indicates an essential compatibility and harmony of these traditions, even though there are of course significant differences, which might suggest that they testify to the same reality.

that the way might be paved for the mutual edification of the Jewish and Christian communities through the reading of Joshua.

Whilst the kind of reading that I have developed here is in some ways novel, it is, I would claim, fitting with respect to Joshua as an act of discourse, and a development of the kind of careful literary reading of Joshua offered by Daniel Hawk for example. Moreover, I have sought to show that it is 'fitting' with respect to the Christian tradition,[128] especially as interpreted through the canon through texts such as Matt 15:21-28 and 25:31-46, even if I have sought to expand the traditional reading of Joshua through questions of identity construction using other parts of the tradition, concerns that were eclipsed in Joshua's earlier interpretation and use.[129]

This approach to reading Joshua is, I would claim, precisely what it means to respect its 'mythical' nature and its nature as Christian Scripture. We have seen how a neo-structuralist perspective on myth provides a perspective for reading Joshua in which one can understand much of what it is that Joshua reflects. Neo-structuralism is a tool well suited to the task of understanding Joshua as Joshua turns out, in fact, to be largely concerned with what we might call 'structural relations'. However, it is important to stress the *neo-structuralist* analysis here that recognizes the importance of *content* in the structural categories reflected in the myth. Joshua reflects the 'pushing' of an underlying structure in ways that are given content through ancient Israelite cultural categories, which are developed and transformed in the Christian context through the development of other myths, and in particular, in light of the incarnation and the gift of the Holy Spirit. Victor Turner's analysis of myth provided us with ways

---

[128] I have said little about Joshua's reception and use in the Middle Ages. The *glossa ordinaria* on Joshua is essentially a summary of earlier interpretation, suggesting that the sort of reading developed by Origen retains a certain normativity, but it is noteworthy how little used Joshua was in sermons in the Middle Ages. In the recent collation of Middle English Sermons, it is striking that there are only eight references to Joshua in the entire sermon collection (five of which concern Achan's crime, probably reflecting concerns with mediaeval piety) in comparison with over a hundred to Genesis, over a hundred to Exodus, over thirty to Leviticus, over thirty to Numbers, over fifty to Deuteronomy, eleven to Judges, over fifty to 1-2 Samuel, over fifty to 1-2 Kings (V. O'Mara and S. Paul (eds.), *A Repertorium of Middle English Prose Sermons* (SERMO: Studies on Patristic, Medieval and Reformation Sermons and Preaching; Turnhout: Brepols, 2007) (4 vols.)). See also my 'Joshua and the Crusades' (forthcoming) where I consider the mediaeval interpretation of Joshua in more detail, and in particular its use in the Crusade literature. I seek to demonstrate that it receives remarkably little use here, even in the Crusade material. Where Joshua is used, its usage tends to remain close to traditional readings of the text.

[129] For a recent study of some aspects of the reception of Joshua in certain major figures see T.R. Elssner, *Josua und seine Kriege in jüdischer und christlicher Rezeptionsgeschichte* (Theologie und Frieden 37; Stuttgart: W. Kohlhammer, 2008).

of considering what it might mean to appropriate and to enact Joshua existentially, with Paul Ricoeur's treatment of narrative and testimony providing further insight into the kind of material that Joshua is, its hermeneutics, and its significance. Finally, certain psychological approaches highlighted the significance of the *desire* for 'rest' in Joshua, which was suggestive of a latent eschatological impulse in the book which found development and expression in the Christian tradition in a number of ways, such as in Augustine's notion of resting in God as the goal of the Christian life.

Whilst I introduced the category of 'cultural memory' in chapter 1 and have said rather little about it since, it is, nonetheless, important, setting the framework for the discussion of the significance of a text such as Joshua. First, cultural memory allows the interpreter space so as not to have to find 'contemporary applicability' for every Old Testament text, or parts thereof, whilst nonetheless enabling one to claim that such texts are important in other regards, with the possibility that the contemporary significance of some text (or part of it) might be located in the fact that it simply provides the community with a sense of history and of rootedness, being part of the community's story, helping it to understand where it has come from. A text may have achieved something vital in the construction of the community's identity in the past as a foundation, and thus the community is dependent upon the effects of the text for its existence, but the enduring significance of the text might be no more than this perhaps. So, for example, one need not feel constrained to have to develop quasi-allegorical interpretations of Josh 10 in order to develop the Christian significance of the text and in some sense 'redeem' it. Moreover, I have said virtually nothing about the allocation of land in Joshua and of cities of refuge. Whilst these were important concerns in the context of ancient Israel, for the Christian interpreter perhaps there is little to say, other than to explain their significance in the story of the community. Perhaps this is precisely the move that some Antiochene exegesis of the Old Testament made. Cultural memory allows such texts to be valued, and understood as inspired, whilst not being 'used' in the sense of being 'applied' in the contemporary context. But secondly, cultural memory theory indicates the importance of the symbolic resources offered by texts such as Joshua. Texts, and their use, can become problematic for various reasons, but the perspective offered by cultural memory indicates that it is important to retain such texts as part of the tradition as a cultural resource that narrates the development of the identity of the community affected by such texts. Moreover, instead of discarding symbolism that has become problematic, an awareness of the importance of cultural memory indicates that the better long term solution to the difficulties is to find new ways of speaking about and using the symbolism, such as we saw in the *Mekhilta Shirata*. Thirdly, cultural memory forms a useful frame of reference for describing the cultural observation that important texts and symbols are collated and juxtaposed to form the identity of a community through time, often by what has been dubbed and studied as 'myth'.

It is a useful anthropological way of describing the theology of the emergence of the Christian community through Scripture and tradition.

Whilst the reading that I have developed might be criticized for being 'free ranging homily', I suggest that it is precisely the kind of reading that emerges when Joshua's mythical nature is respected, and read *and* used 'as myth' in juxtaposition with other myths and the contemporary context in which the rich symbolic resources are used to interpret and shape imaginatively one's own and the Christian community's experience and life. Moreover, it is a reading that seeks to claim a reconstrual of the very nature of Joshua as discourse, thus respecting its significance in its originary context, a reading that, based upon recent anthropological approaches to myth, seeks to show that Joshua has in fact often been misconstrued through the adoption of certain inappropriate post-enlightenment reading strategies. Because of the plenitude and richness of the symbolism, and because of the skill of the narrator of Joshua in simultaneously achieving a number of goals in the story, something that develops as Joshua is drawn into the canon, there are many ways in which Joshua can be imaginatively and constructively used as a resource to shape the response of the people of God. The reading that I have proposed represents an attempt to take seriously both the theological and anthropological ways of describing the use of cherished texts by the Christian community in ways that I hope are mutually enriching and enlightening as the community moves towards its *telos* of life resting in the goodness and love of God through Jesus Christ.

BIBLIOGRAPHY

Abizadeh, A., 'Historical Truth, National Myths and Liberal Democracy: On the Coherence of Liberal Nationalism', in *The Journal of Political Philosophy*, 12:3 (2004): 291-313.

Assmann, J., *Moses the Egyptian: The Memory of Egypt in Western Monotheism* (Cambridge MA: Harvard University Press, 1997).

_____, *Religion and Cultural Memory* (Stanford: Stanford UP, ET: 2006).

_____, 'Myth as *historia divina* and *historia sacra*', in D.A. Green and L.S. Lieber (eds.), *Scriptural Exegesis: The Shapes of Culture and the Religious Imagination: Essays in Honour of Michael Fishbane* (Oxford: OUP, 2009), 13-24.

Ateek, N.S., *Justice and only Justice: A Palestinian Theology of Liberation* (Maryknoll: Orbis Books, 1989).

Auld, A.G., *Joshua Retold: Synoptic Perspectives* (Old Testament Studies; Edinburgh: T&T Clark, 1998).

Ausloos, H., 'Deuteronom(ist)ic Elements in Exod 23,20-33? Some Methodological Remarks', in M. Vervenne (ed.), *Studies in the Book of Exodus: Redaction—Reception—Interpretation* (BETL 126; Leuven: Leuven UP, 1996), 481-500.

_____, 'Exod 23,20-33 and the "War of YHWH"', in *Biblica* 80.4 (1999): 555-563.

_____, 'The "Angel of YHWH" in Exod. xxiii 20-33 and Judg. ii 1-5. A Clue to the "Deuteronom(ist)ic" Puzzle?', in *VT* 58.1 (2008): 1-12.

Barth, K., *Church Dogmatics* (London: T&T Clark (15 vols.), paperback ed. 2004).

Barton, J., *Reading the Old Testament: Method in Biblical Study* (Louisville: WJKP, rev. ed. 1996).

Beeman, W., *Language, Status, and Power in Iran* (Bloomington: Indiana UP, 1986).

Begg, C.T., 'The Function of Josh 7,1-8,29 in the Deuteronomistic History', in *Biblica* 67 (1986): 320-33.

Ben-Barak, Z., 'Inheritance by Daughters in the Ancient Near East', in *JSS* 25 (1980): 22-33.

Bimson, J.J., *Redating the Exodus and Conquest* (Sheffield: The Almond Press, rev. ed. 1981).

Blenkinsopp, J., 'The Structure of P', in *CBQ* 38 (1976): 275-92.

_____, review of E. Blum, *Studien zur Komposition des Pentateuch* in *CBQ* 54.2 (1992): 312-3.

Blum, E., *Studien zur Komposition des Pentateuch* (BZAW 189; Berlin: Walter de Gruyter, 1990).

_____, 'Die literarische Verbindung von Erzvätern und Exodus. Ein Gespräch mit neureren Endredaktionshypothesen', in Gertz, J.C., Schmid, K., and Witte, M., (eds.), *Abschied vom Jahwisten: Die Komposition des Hexateuch in der jüngsten Diskussion* (BZAW 315; Berlin; Walter de Gruyter, 2002), 119-56.

Boer, R., 'Green Ants and Gibeonites: B. Wongar, Joshua 9 and some Problems of Postcolonialism', in *Semeia* 75 (1996): 129-52.
Boling, R.G. and Wright, G.E., *Joshua: A New Translation with Notes and Commentary* (AB 6; New York: Doubleday, 1982).
Briend, J., 'The Sources of the Deuteronomistic History: Research on Joshua 1-12', in A. de Pury, *et al.*, (eds.), *Israel Constructs its History: Deuteronomistic Historiography in Recent Research* (JSOTSup 306; Sheffield: Sheffield Academic Press, 2000), 360-86.
Brownlee, W.H., 'The Ceremony of Crossing the Jordan in the Annual Covenanting at Qumran', in W.C. Delsman, *et al.*, (eds.), *Von Kanaan bis Kerala: Festschrift für Prof. Mag. Dr. Dr. J.P.M. van der Ploeg O.P. zur Vollendung des siebzigsten Lebensjahres am 4. Juli 1979* (Verlag Butzon & Bercker, 1982), 295-302.
Brueggemann, W.A., *Theology of The Old Testament: Testimony, Dispute, Advocacy* (Minneapolis: Fortress Press, 1997).
_____, *The Land: Place as Gift, Promise and Challenge in Biblical Faith* (Overtures to Biblical Theology; Minneapolis: Fortress Press, 2nd ed. 2002).
_____, *Divine Presence Amid Violence: Contextualizing the Book of Joshua* (Eugene: Cascade Books/Milton Keynes: Paternoster, 2009).
Budd, P.J., *Numbers* (WBC 5; Dallas: Word, 1984).
Bultmann, R.,*Theology of the New Testament I* (London: SCM, ET:1952).
_____, 'New Testament and Mythology', in H-W. Bartsch (ed.), *Kerygma and Myth* (London: SPCK, ET 1953), vol. 1.
Butler, T.C., *Joshua* (WBC 7; Waco: Word Books, 1983).
Campbell, K.M., 'Rahab's Covenant: A Short Note on Joshua ii 9-21', in *VT* 22.2 (1972): 243-4.
Carroll, N., *Philosophy of Art: A Contemporary Introduction* (Routledge Contemporary Introductions to Philosophy; London: Routledge, 1999).
Cassirer, E., *The Myth of the State* (New Haven: Yale UP, 1946).
Carter, J., 'René Girard' in *Understanding Religious Sacrifice: A Reader* (London: Continuum, 2003), 239-75.
Charry, E., *By the Renewing of your Minds: The Pastoral Function of Christian Doctrine* (Oxford: OUP, 1997).
Childs, B.S., *Exodus* (OTL; London: SCM, 1974).
_____, *Introduction to the Old Testament as Scripture* (Philadelphia: Fortress Press, 1979).
Clark, M., '*De Trinitate*', in E. Stump and N. Kretzmann (eds.), *The Cambridge Companion to Augustine* (Cambridge: CUP, 2001), 91-102.
Clément, O., *The Roots of Christian Mysticism: Text and Commentary* (London: New City, ET 2nd ed.: 1994).
Coats, G.W., 'An Exposition of the Conquest Theme', in *CBQ* 47 (1985): 47-54.
_____, 'The Ark of the Covenant in Joshua: A probe into the history of a tradition', in *Hebrew Annual Review* 9 (1985),137-57.
_____, 'The Book of Joshua: Heroic Saga or Conquest Theme?', in *JSOT* 38 (1987): 15-32.
Collins, J.J., *Does the Bible Justify Violence?* (Minneapolis: Fortress Press, 2004).
_____, *The Bible after Babel: Historical Criticism in a Postmodern Age* (Grand Rapids: W.B. Eerdmans, 2005).

Coogan, M.D., 'Archaeology and Biblical Studies: The Book of Joshua', in W.H. Propp et al., (eds.), *The Hebrew Bible and its Interpreters* (Winona Lake: Eisenbrauns, 1990), 19-32.
Coote, R.B., 'The Book of Joshua', in *The New Interpreter's Bible* (Nashville: Abingdon, 1998), vol. 2, 555-719.
Coupe, L., review of *Mythography: The Study of Myths and Rituals* (Tuscaloosa: University of Alabama Press, 2nd ed. 2000), by W.G. Doty, in *Religion* 32.2 (2002): 166-8.
Cornelius, I., 'כְּנַעַן', in *NIDOTTE*, vol.2, 669.
Cox, D.G.C., 'The Hardening of Pharaoh's Heart in its Literary and Cultural Contexts', in *Bibliotheca Sacra* 163 (2006): 292-311.
Craigie, P., *The Problem of War in the Old Testament* (Grand Rapids: W.B. Eerdmans, 1978).
Creach, J.F.D., *Joshua* (Interpretation: A Bible Commentary for Teaching and Preaching) (Louisville: John Knox Press, 2003).
Cross, F.M., *Canaanite Myth and Hebrew Epic: Essays in the History of the Religion of Israel* (Cambridge MA: Harvard University Press, 1973).
Daniélou, J., *From Glory to Glory: Texts from Gregory of Nyssa's mystical writings* (London: John Murray, ET:1962).
Davies, D.J., *Anthropology and Theology* (Oxford: Berg, 2002).
Davies, G.I., review of J.C. Gertz, *Tradition und Redaktion in der Exoduserzählung* in *JTS* 53.2 (2002): 571-5.
_____, review of J.C. Gertz, K. Schmid and M. Witte (eds.), *Abschied vom Jahwisten*, in *Bib Or* 62.3-4 (2005): 315-6.
Davies, P.R., *Memories of Ancient Israel: An Introduction to Biblical History—Ancient and Modern* (Louisville: WJKP, 2008).
Davis, E.F., 'Critical Traditioning: Seeking an Inner Biblical Hermeneutic' in *ATR* 82.4 (2000): 733-51.
_____, *Scripture, Culture, and Agriculture: An Agrarian Reading of the Bible* (Cambridge: CUP, 2009).
Dawson, D., *Allegorical Readers and Cultural Revision in Ancient Alexandria* (Berkeley: University of California Press, 1992).
_____, *Christian Figural Reading and the Fashioning of Identity* (Berkeley: University of California Press, 2002).
De Troyer, K., *Rewriting the Sacred Text: What the Old Greek Texts tell us about the Literary Growth of the Bible* (Atlanta: SBL, 2003).
Dever, W.G., *What did the Biblical Writers know and when did they know it? What Archaeology can tell us about the Reality of Ancient Israel* (Grand Rapids: W.B. Eerdmans, 2002).
Doty, W.G., *Mythography: The Study of Myths and Rituals* (Tuscaloosa: University of Alabama Press, 2nd ed. 2000).
Douglas, M., *Purity and Danger* (London: Routledge & Kegan Paul, 1966).
Dozeman, T.B., and Schmid, K., (eds.), *A Farewell to the Yahwist? The Composition of the Pentateuch in recent European Interpretation* (SBL Symposium 34; Atlanta: SBL, 2006).
Driver, S.R., *A Critical and Exegetical Commentary on Deuteronomy* (ICC; Edinburgh: T&T Clark, 3rd ed. 1902).

Drucker, R., *The Book of Joshua: A New Translation with a Commentary anthologized from Talmudic, Midrashic and Rabbinic Sources* (New York: Mesorah Publications, 1982).
Dube, M.W., 'Rahab says Hello to Judith: A Decolonizing Feminist Reading', in R.S. Sugirtharajah (ed.), *The Postcolonial Biblical Reader* (Oxford: Blackwell, 2006), 142-58.
Dupré, L., *Symbols of the Sacred* (Grand Rapids: Eerdmans, 2000).
Durham, J.I., *Exodus* (WBC 3; Dallas: Word, 1987).
Earl, D.S., '"Bethany beyond the Jordan": The Significance of a Johannine Motif', in *NTS* 55.3 (2009): 279-94.
_____, 'The Christian Significance of Deuteronomy 7', in *JTI* 3.1 (2009): 41-62.
_____, 'Towards a Christian Hermeneutic of Old Testament Narrative: Why Genesis 34 fails to find Christian Significance' (forthcoming in *CBQ*).
_____, 'Joshua and the Crusades' (forthcoming).
Edinger, E., *The Bible and the Psyche: Individuation Symbolism in the Old Testament* (Toronto: Inner City Books, 1986).
Elssner, T.R., *Josua und seine Kriege in jüdischer und christlicher Rezeptionsgeschichte* (Theologie und Frieden 37; Stuttgart: W. Kohlhammer, 2008).
Evans, G.R., *The Language and Logic of the Bible: The Earlier Middle Ages* (Cambridge: CUP, 1984).
_____, *The Language and Logic of the Bible: The Road to Reformation* (Cambridge: CUP, 1985).
Faye, J-P., in 'Claude Lévi-Strauss: A Confrontation', in *New Left Review* I/62 (Jul-Aug 1970): 57-74.
Fensham, F.C., 'The Treaty between Israel and the Gibeonites' in *BA* 27.3 (1964): 96-100.
Fishbane, M., *Biblical Interpretation in Ancient Israel* (Oxford: Clarendon, corr. ed. 1985).
Fleming, C., *René Girard: Violence and Mimesis* (Cambridge: Polity Press, 2004).
Fleming, D.E., 'The Seven-Day Siege of Jericho in Holy War' in R.Chazan, *et al.*, (eds.), *Ki Baruch Hu: Ancient Near Eastern, Biblical and Judaic Studies in honour of Baruch A. Levine* (Winona Lake: Eisenbrauns, 1999), 211-28.
Ford, W.A., *God, Pharaoh and Moses: Explaining the Lord's Actions in the Exodus Plagues Narrative* (Paternoster Biblical Monographs; Bletchley: Paternoster, 2006).
Fretheim, T.E., *Exodus* (Interpretation; Louisville: John Knox Press, 1991).
Fritz, V., *Das Buch Josua* (HAT I/7; Tübingen: J.C.B. Mohr (Paul Siebeck), 1994).
Gerstenberger, E.S., *Leviticus* (Louisville: WJKP, ET: 1996).
Gertz, J.C., *Tradition und Redaktion in der Exoduserzählung: Untersuchungen zur Endredaktion des Pentateuch* (FRLANT 186; Göttingen: Vandenhoeck & Ruprecht, 2000).
_____, Schmid, K., and Witte, M., (eds.), *Abschied vom Jahwisten: Die Komposition des Hexateuch in der jüngsten Diskussion* (BZAW 315; Berlin; Walter de Gruyter, 2002).
Gevirtz, S., 'Jericho and Shechem: A Religio-literary Aspect of City Destruction', in *VT* 13 (1963): 52-62.
Goldingay, J., *Old Testament Theology* (Downers Grove: IVP, 3 vols., 2003-).

Gottwald, N.K., *The Tribes of Yahweh: A Sociology of the Religion of Liberated Israel, 1250-1050 BCE* (The Biblical Seminar 66; Sheffield: Sheffield Academic Press, 1999).
Green, W.S., 'Romancing the Tome: Rabbinic Hermeneutics and the Theory of Literature', in *Semeia* 40 (1987): 147-68.
Greer, R.A., *Theodore of Mopsuestia: Exegete and Theologian* (London: The Faith Press, 1961).
Grintz, J.M., 'The Treaty of Joshua with the Gibeonites' in *JAOS* 86/2 (1966): 113-26.
Gundry, S.N. (ed.), *Show them no Mercy: 4 Views on God and Canaanite Genocide* (Grand Rapids: Zondervan, 2003).
Gunn, D.M., 'The "Hardening of Pharaoh's Heart": Plot, Character and Theology in Exodus 1-14', in D.J.A. Clines, *et al.*, (eds.), *Art and Meaning: Rhetoric in Biblical Literature,* (JSOTSup 19; Sheffield: JSOT Press, 1982), 72-96.
Güterbock, H.G., 'The Deeds of Suppiluliuma as Told by His Son, Muršilli II', in *JCS* 10 (1956): 41-130.
Haak, R.D., 'Altar', in *ABD* vol.1, 162-7.
Habel, N.C., *The Land is Mine: Six Biblical Land Ideologies* (Overtures to Biblical Theology; Minneapolis: Fortress Press, 1995).
Hagner, D.A., *Matthew 14-28* (WBC 33B; Dallas: Word, 1995).
Halpern, B., 'Gibeon:Israelite Diplomacy in the Conquest Era', in *CBQ* 37 (1975): 303-16.
Hallo, W.W., 'New Light on the Story of Achsah', in J.Kaltner and L.Stulman (eds.), *Inspired Speech: Prophecy in the Ancient Near East. Essays in honour of Herbert. B. Huffmon* (London: T&T Clark, 2004), 330-35.
'*ḫarāmu*', in *CAD* vol.6 'ḫ', 89-90.
Hawk, L.D., *Every Promise Fulfilled: Contesting Plots in Joshua* (Louisville: Westminster John Knox Press, 1991).
_____, *Joshua* (Berit Olam: Studies in Hebrew Narrative and Poetry; Collegeville: The Liturgical Press, 2000).
Heisig, J.W., 'Symbolism' in M. Eliade (ed.), *The Encyclopedia of Religion* (New York: Simon & Schuster Macmillan), vol. 13, 198-208.
Hendy, A. von, *The Modern Construction of Myth* (Bloomington: Indiana UP, 2002).
Hervieu-Léger, D., *Religion as a Chain of Memory* (New Brunswick: Rutgers UP, ET: 2000).
Hess, R.S., *Joshua* (TOTC; Leicester: IVP, 1996).
Hoffman, Y., 'The Deuteronomistic Concept of the Herem', in *ZAW* 111.2 (1999): 196-210.
Holland, T.A., and Netzer, E., 'Jericho (place)', in *ABD*, vol. 3, 723-40.
Hurvitz, A., *A Linguistic Study of the Relationship between the Priestly Source and the Book of Ezekiel: A New Approach to an Old Problem* (Cahiers de la Revue Biblique 20; Paris: J. Gabalda, 1982).
Hyatt, J.P., *Exodus* (NCB; London: Marshall, Morgan & Scott, 1971).
James, P., *et al., (Centuries of Darkness* (London: Pimlico, 1992).
Jobling, D., '"The Jordan as a Boundary': Transjordan in Israel's Ideological Geography', in *The Sense of Biblical Narrative: Structural Analyses in the Hebrew Bible II* (JSOTSup 39; Sheffield: JSOT Press, 1986), 88-134.

Johnstone, W., 'The Use of the Reminiscences in Deuteronomy in Recovering the Two Main Literary Phases in the Production of the Pentateuch', in Gertz, J.C., Schmid, K., and Witte, M., (eds.), *Abschied vom Jahwisten: Die Komposition des Hexateuch in der jüngsten Diskussion* (BZAW 315; Berlin; Walter de Gruyter, 2002), 247-73.

Kallai, Z., 'The Land of the Perizzites and the Rephaim (Joshua 17,14-18)', in C. Brekelmans and J. Lust (eds.), *Pentateuchal and Deuteronomistic Studies: Papers read at the XIIIth IOSOT Congress Leuven 1989* (Leuven: Leuven UP, 1990), 197-205.

Kaminsky, J.S., ('Joshua 7: A Reassessment of the Israelite Conceptions of Corporate Punishment', in S.W. Holloway and L.K. Handy (eds.), *The Pitcher is Broken: Memorial Essays for Gösta W. Ahlström* (JSOTSup 190; Sheffield: Sheffield Academic Press, 1995), 315-46.

Kang, S-M., *Divine War in the Old Testament and in the Ancient Near East* (BZAW 177; Berlin: Walter de Gruyter, 1989).

Kearney, P.J., 'The Role of the Gibeonites in the Deuteronomistic History', in *CBQ* 35 (1973): 1-19.

Kent, B., 'Augustine's Ethics', in E. Stump and N. Kretzmann (eds.), *The Cambridge Companion to Augustine* (Cambridge: CUP, 2001), 205-33.

Kerr, F., *Theology after Wittgenstein* (London: SPCK, 2nd ed. 1997).

Kilmer, A.D., 'The Mesopotamian Counterparts of the Biblical Nephilim', in E.W Conrad and E.G. Newing (eds.) *Perspectives on Language and Text* (Winona Lake: Eisenbrauns, 1987), 39-44.

Kirk, A., 'Social and Cultural Memory', in A. Kirk and T. Thatcher (eds.), *Memory, Tradition, and Text: Uses of the Past in Early Christianity* (Semeia Studies 52; Atlanta: SBL, 2005), 1-24.

Kitchen, K.A., *On the Reliability of the Old Testament* (Grand Rapids: W.B. Eerdmans, 2003).

Kloppenbeorg, J.S., 'Joshua 22: The Priestly editing of an Ancient Tradition', in *Biblica* 62 (1981): 347- 71.

Knauf, E.A., *Josua* (Zürcher Bibelkommentare AT 6; Theologischer Verlag Zürich, 2008).

Koehler, L., and Baumgartner, W., *The Hebrew and Aramaic Lexicon of the Old Testament* (Leiden: Brill, rev. ed. 1994-2000).

Koopmans, W.T., *Joshua 24 as Poetic Narrative* (JSOTSup 93; Sheffield: JSOT Press, 1990).

Kratz, R.G., *The Composition of the Narrative Books of the Old Testament* (London: T & T Clark, ET: 2005).

Kunin, S.D., *We Think What We Eat: Neo-structuralist Analysis of Israelite Food Rules and Other Cultural and Textual Practices* (JSOTSup 412; London: T&T Clark, 2004).

Lacocque, A., 'The Land in D and P', in M. Augustin and K.D. Schunck (eds.), *"Dort ziehen Schiffe dahin ...": Collected Communications to the XIVth Congress of the International Organization for the Study of the Old Testament, Paris 1992* (Frankfurt: Peter Lang, 1996), 91-100.

Laird, M., *Gregory of Nyssa and the Grasp of Faith: Union, Knowledge and Divine Presence* (Oxford Early Christian Studies; Oxford: OUP, 2004).

Lash, N., 'What might Martyrdom mean?', in *Theology on the Way to Emmaus* (London: SCM, 1986), 75-92.
Lawson Younger K., Jr., *Ancient Conquest Accounts: A Study in Ancient Near Eastern and Biblical History Writing* (JSOTSup 98; Sheffield: JSOT Press, 1990).
Leach, E., 'Fishing for Men on the Edge of the Wilderness' in R. Alter and F. Kermode, *The Complete Literary Guide to the Bible* (Cambridge: Harvard UP, 1987), 579-99.
Levenson, J.D., *Creation and the Persistence of Evil* (Princeton: Princeton UP, 1988).
Levin, C., 'The Yahwist: The Earliest Editor in the Pentateuch', in *JBL* 126.2 (2007): 209-30.
Levine, B.A., and De Tarragon, J-M., ('Dead Kings and Rephaim: The Patrons of the Ugaritic Dynasty', in *JAOS* 104.4 (1984): 649-59.
Levine, B.A., *Numbers 1-20* (AB 4A: New York: Doubleday, 1993).
Lévi-Strauss, C., 'The Structural Study of Myth' in *The Journal of American Folklore* vol. 68, No. 270 (Oct.-Dec. 1955): 428-44.
—————, in 'Claude Lévi-Strauss: A Confrontation', in *New Left Review* I/62 (Jul-Aug 1970): 57-74.
—————, *From Honey to Ashes* (New York: Harper and Row, ET:1973).
Liver, J., 'The Literary History of Joshua IX', in *JSS* 8 (1963): 227-43.
Lohfink, N., '*ḥāram*' in *TDOT* V, 180-99.
Loomba, A., *Colonialism/Postcolonialism* (New Critical Idiom; London: Routledge, 2nd ed. 2005).
MacDonald, N.B., *Karl Barth and the Strange New World within the Bible: Barth, Wittgenstein, and the Metadilemmas of the Enlightenment* (Paternoster Biblical and Theological Monographs; Carlisle: Paternoster, 2000).
Maier, C.T., *Crusade Propaganda and Ideology: Model Sermons for Preaching the Cross* (Cambridge: CUP, 2000).
Malinowski, B., 'Myth in Primitive Psychology' in *Magic, Science and Religion and other Essays* (Westport: Greenwood Press, 1984), 93-148.
Margalit, B., 'The Day the Sun did not stand still: A new look at Joshua X 8-15', in *VT* 42.4 (1992): 466-91.
Marr, A., 'Violence and the Kingdom of God: Introducing the Anthropology of René Girard', in *ATR* 80.4 (1998): 590-603.
Matties, G., 'Can Girard help us to read Joshua?', in W.M. Swartley, *Violence Renounced: René Girard, Biblical Studies, and peacemaking* (Telford: Pandora Press, 2000), 85-102.
Mattingly, G.L., 'Anak', in *ABD*, vol. 1, 222.
Mbuwayesango, D., 'Joshua' in D. Patte (ed.), *Global Bible Commentary* (Nashville: Abingdon Press, 2004), 64-73.
McCarthy, D.J., 'The Theology of Leadership in Joshua 1-9', in *Biblica* 52 (1981): 165-75.
McConville, G., 'Joshua', in J. Barton and J. Muddiman (eds.), *The Oxford Bible Commentary* (Oxford: OUP, 2001).
McFague, S., *Metaphorical Theology: Models of God in Religious Language* (Philadelphia: Fortress Press, 1982).
Mendenhall, G.E., 'Amorites', in *ABD*, vol. 1, 199-202.
Meredith, A., *The Cappadocians* (Crestwood: St. Vladimir's Seminary Press, 2000).

Merling, D., Sr., *The Book of Joshua: Its Theme and Role in Archaeological Discussions* (Andrews University Seminary Doctoral Dissertation Series 23; Berrien Springs: Andrews University Press, 1997).
Milgrom, J., 'Priestly ("P") Source' in *ABD*, vol.5, 454-61.
_____, *Leviticus 23-27* (AB 3B; New York: Doubleday, 2000).
Miller, D., *On Nationality* (Oxford: OUP, 1995).
Miller, P.D., *The Divine Warrior in early Israel* (Harvard Semitic Monographs 5; Cambridge: Harvard UP, 1973).
Mitchell, G., *Together in the Land: A Reading of the Book of Joshua* (JSOTSup 134; Sheffield: Sheffield Academic Press, 1993).
Moberly, R.W.L., *The Bible, Theology and Faith* (Cambridge Studies in Christian Doctrine; Cambridge: CUP, 2000).
_____, 'Johannine Christology and Jewish-Christian Dialogue', in M. Bockmuehl and A. Torrance (eds.), *Scripture's Doctrine and Theology's Bible* (Grand Rapids: Baker Academic, 2008), 70-93.
Monroe, L.A.S., 'Israelite, Moabite and Sabaean War-ḥērem Traditions and the Forging of National Identity: Reconsidering the Sabean Text RES 3945 in Light of Biblical and Moabite Evidence', in *VT* 57.3 (2007): 318-41.
Mosca, P.G., 'Who Seduced Whom? A Note on Joshua 15:18//Judges 1:14', in *CBQ* 46 (1984): 18-22.
Murray, P.D., 'Theology 'Under the Lash': Theology as Idolatry-Critique in the Work of Nicholas Lash', in S.C. Barton (ed.), *Idolatry: False Worship in the Bible, Early Judaism and Christianity* (London: T&T Clark, 2007), 246-66.
Nelson, R.D., 'Josiah in the Book of Joshua', in *JBL* 100.4 (1981): 531-40.
_____, 'ḥerem and the Deuteronomic Social Conscience', in J. Lust and M. Vervenne (eds.), *Deuteronomy and Deuteronomic Literature: Festschrift C.H.W. Brekelmans* (Peeters, 1997), 39-54.
_____, *Joshua* (OTL; Louisville: Westminster John Knox Press, 1997).
Niditch, S., *War in the Hebrew Bible* (Oxford: OUP, 1993).
Noll, K.L, 'Deuteronomistic History or Deuteronomic Debate? (A thought experiment)', in *JSOT* 31.3 (2007): 311-45.
Northup, L.A., 'Myth-placed Priorities: Religion and the Study of Myth' in *Religious Studies Review* 32.1 (2006): 5-10.
Noth, M., *Leviticus* (Old Testament Library) (London: SCM, Rev. ET: 1977).
_____, *The Deuteronomistic History,* (JSOTSup 15; Sheffield: Sheffield Academic Press, ET: 1981).
Otto, E., 'Forschungen zur Priesterschrift', in *Th R* 62 (1997): 1-50.
Pannenberg, W., 'Dogmatic Theses on the Concept of Revelation', in W Pannenberg (ed.), *Revelation as History* (London: Sheed & Ward, 1969), 123-58.
Parry, R., *Old Testament Story and Christian Ethics: The Rape of Dinah as a Case Study* (Paternoster Biblical Monographs; Bletchley: Paternoster, 2004).
Park, H.D., *Finding Herem? A Study of Luke-Acts in the Light of Herem* (LNTS 357; London: T&T Clark, 2007).
Peckham, B., 'The Composition of Joshua 3-4', in *CBQ* 46 (1984): 413-31.
Penelhum, T., 'The Analysis of Faith in St. Thomas Aquinas', in *Religious Studies* 13.2 (1977): 133-54.

Pola, T., *Die ursprüngliche Priesterschrift: Beobachtungen zur Literarkritik und Traditionsgeschichte von P^g* (WMANT 70; Neukirchen-Vluyn: Neukirchener, 1995).
Polzin, R., *Moses and the Deuteronomist: A Literary Study of the Deuteronomistic History* (New York: Seabury Press, 1980).
Prior, M.A., *The Bible and Colonialism: A Moral Critique* (The Biblical Seminar 48; Sheffield: Sheffield Academic Press, 1997).
Ramsey, G.W., 'If Jericho was not Razed, is our Faith in Vain?' in *The Quest for the Historical Israel: Reconstructing Israel's Early History,* (London: SCM, 1982).
Rad, G. von, *Old Testament Theology, Volume II: The Theology of Israel's Prophetic Traditions* (London: SCM, ET:1965).
_____, 'The Form-critical problem of the Hexateuch', in *The Problem of the Hextateuch and other Essays* (London: SCM, ET: 1966), 1-78.
_____, *Holy War in Ancient Israel* (Grand Rapids: W.B. Eerdmans, ET: 1991).
Ratheiser, G.M.H., *Mitzvoth Ethics and the Jewish Bible: The End of Old Testament Theology* (London: T&T Clark, 2007).
Rendtorff, R., 'Two Kinds of P? Some Reflections on the Occasion of the Publishing of Jacob Milgrom's Commentary on Leviticus 1-16', in *JSOT* 60 (1993): 75-81.
Ricoeur, P., *The Symbolism of Evil* (Boston: Beacon Press, ET: 1969).
_____, in 'Claude Lévi-Strauss: A Confrontation', in *New Left Review* I/62 (Jul-Aug 1970), 57-74.
_____, 'Biblical Hermeneutics', in *Semeia* 4 (1975): 29-148.
_____, *Interpretation Theory: Discourse and the Surplus of Meaning* (Fort Worth: The Texan Christian UP, 1976).
_____, 'The Narrative Function', in *Semeia* 13 (1978), 177-202.
_____, 'The Hermeneutics of Testimony', in P. Ricoeur (ed. L.S. Mudge), *Essays on Biblical Interpretation* (London: SPCK, 1981), 119-54.
_____, 'Toward a Hermeneutic of the Idea of Revelation', in P. Ricoeur (ed. L.S. Mudge), *Essays on Biblical Interpretation* (London: SPCK, 1981), 73-118.
_____, 'Biblical Time', in *Figuring The Sacred* (Minneapolis: Fortress Press, 1995), 167-80.
_____, 'Naming God', in *Figuring the Sacred* (Minneapolis: Fortress Press, 1995), 217-35.
_____, 'Toward a Narrative Theology: Its Necessity, Its Resources, Its Difficulties', in *Figuring the Sacred* (Minneapolis: Fortress Press, 1995), 236-48.
Rist, J., 'Faith and Reason', in E. Stump and N. Kretzmann (eds.), *The Cambridge Companion to Augustine* (Cambridge: CUP, 2001), 26-39.
Rofé, A., 'The Editing of the Book of Joshua in the light of 4QJosh[a]', in G.J. Brooke (ed.), *New Qumran Texts and Studies: Proceedings of the first Meeting of the International Organization for Qumran Studies, Paris, 1992* (Leiden: E.J. Brill, 1994), 73-80.
Rogerson, J.W., *Myth in Old Testament Interpretation* (BZAW 134; New York: Walter de Gruyter, 1974).
_____, 'Towards a Communicative Theology of the Old Testament', in J.G. McConville and K. Möller (eds.), *Reading the Law: Studies in Honour of Gordon J. Wenham* (London: T&T Clark, 2007), 283-96.

Römer, T.C., and de Pury, A., 'Deuteronomistic Historiography: History of Research and related Issues', in A. de Pury, *et al.*, (eds.), *Israel Constructs its History: Deuteronomistic Historiography in Recent Research* (JSOTSup 306; Sheffield: Sheffield Academic Press, 2000), 24-141.

Römer, T.C., *The So-Called Deuteronomistic History: A Sociological, Historical and Literary Introduction* (London: T&T Clark, 2005).

Rowlett, L.L., 'Inclusion, Exclusion and Marginality in the Book of Joshua', in *JSOT* 55 (1992), 15-23.

——, *Joshua and the Rhetoric of Violence: A New Historicist Analysis* (JSOTSup 226; Sheffield: Sheffield Academic Press, 1996).

Sarna, N.M, *Exploring Exodus: The Origins of Biblical Israel* (New York: Schocken Books, 1996).

Schäfer-Lichtenberger, C., 'Bedeutung und Funktion von Ḥerem in biblisch-hebräischen Texten', in *BZ* 38 (1994): 270-75.

Schmid, K., 'The So-called Yahwist and the Literary Gap between Genesis and Exodus', in T.B. Dozeman and K. Schmid (eds.), *A Farewell to the Yahwist? The Composition of the Pentateuch in Recent European Interpretation* (SBL Symposium 34; Atlanta: SBL, 2006) 29-50.

Schneiders, S.M., *The Revelatory Text* (Collegeville: The Liturgical Press, 2nd ed. 1999).

Schwienhorst, L., *Die Eroberung Jerichos: Exegetische Untersuchung zu Josua 6* (Stuttgart: Katholisches Bibelwerk, 1986).

Segal, R.A., review of *Mythography: The Study of Myths and Rituals* (Tuscaloosa: University of Alabama Press, 1986), by W.G. Doty, in *JAAR* 56 (1988): 149-52.

——, *Theorizing about Myth* (Amherst: University of Massachusetts Press, 1999).

——, *Myth: A Very Short Introduction* (Oxford: OUP, 2004).

Seward, D., *The Monks of War: The Military Religious Orders* (London: Eyre Methuen, 1972).

Sherwood, A., 'A Leader's Misleading and a Prostitute's Profession: A Re-examination of Joshua 2', in *JSOT* 31.1 (2006): 43-61.

Smalley, B., *The Study of the Bible in the Middle Ages* (Oxford: Basil Blackwell, 3rd ed. 1983).

Smelik, K.A.D., 'Moabite Inscriptions' in *CoS* II, 137-8.

Snaith, N.H., 'The Altar at Gilgal: Joshua XXII 23-29', in *VT* 28.3 (1978): 330-35.

Soggie, N.A., *Myth, God, and War: The Mythopoetic Inspiration of Joshua* (Lanham: University Press of America, 2007).

Soggin, J.A., *Joshua* (Old Testament Library) (London: SCM Press, ET: 1972).

Southern, R.W., 'The Sovereign Textbook of the Schools: the Bible' in *Scholastic Humanism and the Unification of Europe* (Oxford: Blackwell, 1995), vol. 1.

Spina, F.A., *The Faith of the Outsider: Exclusion and Inclusion in the Biblical Story* (Grand Rapids: W.B. Eerdmans, 2005).

Stec, D.M., 'The Mantle Hidden by Achan', in *VT* 41.3 (1991): 356-9.

Stern, P.D., (*The Biblical ḥerem: A Window on Israel's Religious Experience* (Brown Judaic Studies 211; Atlanta: Scholar's Press, 1991).

Stevenson, W.T., 'History as Myth: Some Implications for History and Theology', in *Cross Currents* 20.1 (1970): 15-28.

Stone, L.G., 'Ethical and Apologetic Tendencies in the Redaction of the Book of Joshua', in *CBQ* 53 (1991): 25-36.

Strange, J., 'The Book of Joshua—Origin and Dating', in *SJOT* 16.1 (2002): 44-51.
Sutherland, R.K., 'Israelite Political Theories in Joshua 9', in *JSOT* 53 (1992): 65-74.
Szpek, H.M., 'Achsah's Story: A Metaphor for Societal Transition', in *AUSS* 40.2 (2002): 245-56.
Tamarin, G.R., *The Israeli Dilemma: Essays on a Warfare State* (Rotterdam: Rotterdam University Press, 1973).
Thompson, L.L., 'The Jordan Crossing: *ṣidqot Yahweh* and World building', in *JBL* 100.3 (1981): 343-58.
Tolkien, J.R.R., 'On Fairy Stories', in *Essays presented to Charles Williams* (London: OUP, 1947), 38-89.
Thunberg, L., *Microcosm and Mediator: The Theological Anthropology of Maximus the Confessor* (Chicago: Open Court, 2nd ed. 1995).
Tov, E., 'Midrash-type Exegesis in the LXX of Joshua', in *Revue Biblique* 85 (1978): 50-61.
Turner, V., 'Myth and Symbol', in D.L. Sills (ed.), *International Encyclopedia of the Social Sciences* (Macmillan & The Free Press, 1968), vol. 10, 576-81.
_____, *From Ritual to Theatre: The Human Seriousness of Play* (New York: PAJ, 1982).
Van der Meer, M.N., *Formation and Reformulation: The Redaction of the Book of Joshua in the Light of the Oldest Textual Witnesses* (Leiden: Brill, 2004).
Vanhoozer, K., *Biblical Narrative in the Philosophy of Paul Ricoeur* (Cambridge: CUP, 1990).
Van Seters, J., 'Joshua's Campaign of Canaan and Near Eastern Historiography', in *SJOT* 4 (1990): 1-12.
_____, review of E. Blum, *Studien zur Komposition des Pentateuch* in *JBL* 111.1 (1992): 122-4.
_____, *In Search of History: Historiography in the Ancient World and the Origins of Biblical History* (Winona Lake: Eisenbrauns, 1997).
_____, *A Law Book for the Diaspora: Revision in the Study of the Covenant Code* (Oxford: OUP, 2003).
Vervenne, M., 'The Question of "Deuteronomic" Elements in Genesis to Numbers', in F. García Martínez, et al., (eds.) *Studies in Deuteronomy in Honour of C.J. Labuschagne on the Occasion of his 65th Birthday* (VTSup 53; Leiden: E.J. Brill, 1994), 243-68.
Waardenburg, J., 'Symbolic Aspects of Myth' in A.M. Olson (ed.), *Myth, Symbol and Reality* (Notre Dame: University of Notre Dame Press, 1980), 41-68.
Wagenaar, J., 'Crossing the Sea of Reeds (Exod 13-14) and the Jordan (Josh 3-4): A Priestly Framework for the Wilderness Wandering', in M. Vervenne (ed.), *Studies in the Book of Exodus: Redaction—Reception—Interpretation* (BETL 126; Leuven: Leuven UP, 1996), 461-70.
Wallace, M.I. *The Second Naiveté: Barth, Ricoeur, and the New Yale Theology* (Studies in American Biblical Hermeneutics 6; Georgia: Mercer UP, 1990).
Walsh, R.G., *Mapping Myths of Biblical Interpretation* (Playing the Texts 4; Sheffield: Sheffield Academic Press, 2001).
Waltke, B.K., and O'Connor, M., *An Introduction to Biblical Hebrew Syntax* (Winona Lake: Eisenbrauns, 1990).

Warrior, R.A., 'Canaanites, Cowboys and Indians: Deliverance, Conquest, and Liberation Theology Today' in D. Jobling, *et al.*, (eds.), *The Postmodern Bible Reader* (Oxford: Blackwell, 2001), 188-194.
Weinfeld, M., *Deuteronomy and the Deuteronomic School* (Oxford: Clarendon, 1972).
_____, 'Divine Intervention in War in Ancient Israel and in the Ancient Near East', in H. Tadmor and M. Weinfeld (eds.), *History, Historiography and Interpretation: Studies in biblical and cuneiform literatures* (Jerusalem: The Magnes Press, 1984), 121-47.
_____, *The Promise of the Land: The Inheritance of the Land of Canaan by the Israelites* (Berkeley: University of California Press, 1993).
Weingreen, J., 'The Case of the Daughters of Zelophchad', in *VT* 16.4 (1966): 518-22.
Wenham, G.J., 'The Deuteronomic Theology of the Book of Joshua', in *JBL* 90.2 (1971): 140-48.
Williams, R., *On Christian Theology* (Oxford: Blackwell, 2000).
Williams, R.B., 'Origen's Interpretation of the Old Testament and Lévi-Strauss' Interpretation of Myth', in A.L. Merrill and T.W. Overholt (eds.), *Scripture in History & Theology: Essays in Honor of J. Coert Rylaarsdam* (*PTMS* 17; Pittsburgh: The Pickwick Press, 1977), 279-299.
Wilson, R.R., 'The Hardening of Pharaoh's Heart' in *CBQ* 41 (1979): 18-36.
Witte, M., *et al.*, (eds.), *Die deuteronomistischen Geschichtswerke: Redaktions- und religionsgeschichtliche Perspektiven zur „Deuteronomismus"-Diskussion in Tora und Vorderen Propheten* (BZAW 365; Berlin; Walter de Gruyter, 2006).
Wittgenstein, L., *Ludwig Wittgenstein: Lectures and Conversations on Aesthetics, Psychology and Religious Belief* (Oxford: Blackwell, 1966).
Woudstra, M.H., *The Book of Joshua* (NICOT; Grand Rapids: W.B. Eerdmans, 1981).
Young, F.M., *Biblical Exegesis and the Formation of Christian Culture* (Cambridge: CUP, 1997).
Zaharopoulos, D., *Theodore of Mopsuestia on the Bible: A Study of his Old Testament Exegesis* (New York: Paulist Press, 1989).

Primary texts and translations

Battles, F.L., *Calvin: Institutes of the Christian Religion*, (The Library of Christian Classics 20; Philadelphia: The Westminster Press, 2 vols., 1960).
Beveridge, H., (trans.), *Commentaries on the Book of Joshua by John Calvin*, (Grand Rapids: W.B. Eerdmans, 1949).
Bruce, B.J., (trans.), Origen, *Homilies on Joshua* (FC 105; Washington: The Catholic University of America Press, 2002).
Butterworth, G.W., (trans.), *Origen: On First Principles* (Gloucester: Peter Smith, 1973).
Daley, B.E., (trans.), *Gregory of Nazianzus* (The Early Church Fathers; Routledge, New ed.: 2000).
Elliger, K., and Rudolph, W., (eds.) *Biblia Hebraica Stuttgartensia* (Stuttgart: Deutsche Bibelgesellschaft, 4th ed. 1990).
Franke, J.R., (ed.), *Ancient Christian Commentary on Scripture, Old Testament IV: Joshua, Judges, Ruth, 1-2 Samuel* (Downers Grove: IVP, 2005).
Gilby, T., (ed.), *Summa Theologiae*, Latin text and English Translation (Blackfriars ed.) (London: Eyre & Spottiswoode, 60 vols., 1964-1974).

Graef, H.C., (trans.), *St. Gregory of Nyssa: The Lord's Prayer, The Beatitudes* (ACW 18; New York: Paulist Press, 1954).

Hall, S.G., and Moriarty, R., (trans.) 'Gregory, Bishop of Nyssa: Homilies on Ecclesiastes', in *Gregory of Nyssa: Homilies on Ecclesiastes: An English Version with Supporting Studies* (Berlin: Walter de Gruyter, 1993), 31-144.

Hill, R.C., (trans.), Theodoret of Cyrus, 'Questions on Joshua' in *The Questions on the Octateuch* (LEC 2; Washington, The Catholic University of America Press, 2007), 260-307.

Ferguson, E., and Malherbe, A.J., (trans.), Gregory of Nyssa, *The Life of Moses* (The Classics of Western Spirituality; New York: Paulist Press, 1978).

Freedman, B.A., and Simon, M., *Midrash Rabbah translated into English with notes, glossary and indices under the editorship of Rabbi Dr. H. Freedman, B.A., PH.D. and Maurice Simon, M.A.*, (London: The Soncino Press, 10 vols., 1939).

Lombardo, G.J., (trans.), *St. Augustine: On Faith and Works* (ACW 48; New York: The Newman Press, 1988).

Lull, T.F., (trans.), Luther, *The Freedom of a Christian*, in *Basic Theological Writings* (Minneapolis: Fortress Press, 1989), 585-629.

McKenna, S., (trans.), *Saint Augustine: The Trinity* (FC 45; Washington: The Catholic University of America Press, 1963).

Neusner, J., (trans.), *Mekhilta according to Rabbi Ishmael: An Analytic Translation* (Brown Judaica Studies 148; Atalanta: Scholars Press, 1988), vol. 1.

O'Mara, V., and Paul, S., (eds.), *A Repertorium of Middle English Prose Sermons* (SERMO: Studies on Patristic, Medieval and Reformation Sermons and Preaching; Turnhout: Brepols, 4 vols., 2007)

Pritchard, J.B., (ed.), *Ancient Near Eastern Texts Relating to the Old Testament* 3rd ed. with supplement (Princeton, Princeton University Press, 1969).

Roberts, A., and Donaldson, J. (eds.), *Constitutions of the Holy Apostles*, in *ANF* 7.

_____, (eds.), *Irenaeus: Against Heresies*, in *ANF* 1.

Schaff, P., (ed.), Augustine, *On Christian Doctrine*, in *NPNF* I.2.

_____, Gregory of Nazianzus: *Theological Orations*, in *NPNF* II.7.

INDEX OF SUBJECTS AND AUTHORS

Abimelech 126
Abizadeh, A. 22
Abraham 48, 193-194, 198
Achan 17, 40, 47, 87, 93, 100-103, 111, 116, 140, 143, 148-155, 157-158, 165, 167, 171, 182, 186, 188, 198-200, 208, 225-233, 235
Achsah 171, 173, 202
agency 41-43
aggression 165-167, 198, 201
Ahab 144
Ai 116, 140, 148-153, 208
Alexandrian interpretation 10, 35
allegorical interpretation / sense *see* spiritual sense
altar, altar building 47, 82, 93, 116, 177-183
Amalek, Amalekites 69, 169, 199
ambiguity 161, 181, 198
ambush 116, 153
Ammonites 105
Amorites 117, 161, 193-194
Anakim 107, 168-170, 172, 174
annihilation 95, 99, 105, 110-111, 185, 206
anthropology 14-20
anti-elect 110
Antiochene interpretation 10, 45, 50, 164, 213, 239
Aquinas, Thomas 13, 219-222
archaeology 2, 59-60
ark 32, 78, 91, 128, 141
ascesis / asceticism 205, 207
Assmann, J. 4-6, 14
Ateek, N.S., 20, 67-69
Athanasius 195
atonement 118-119
attachment 101, 229
Augustine 9, 35, 126, 153, 205, 218-219, 222, 227, 239
Auld, A.G. 76, 84, 86, 114, 117
Ausloos, H. 76, 108

authorial intention 51

Babylon 96
Balaam 86
baptism 6, 131, 203, 212
Barth, K. 2, 30-32, 37-38, 223-224, 226
beatitudes 216
Beeman, W. 159
Ben-Barak, Z. 173
Bimson, J.J. 2
Blenkinsopp, J. 74, 82
Blum, E. 73, 108
Boer, R. 160
boldness 173-175, 201-202, 214, 226
borders / boundaries 86, 121-123, 127-133, 137, 165, 178-183, 187, 200-202, 230-233
Brekelmans, C.H.W. 94, 104
bricolage 43
Briend, J. 151
Brownlee, W.H. 129, 132
Brueggemann, W.A. 54, 58, 61, 83-84, 131, 135, 164, 167, 176, 189
Budd, P.J. 104
Bultmann, R. 27, 224
Butler, T.C. 26, 122, 139, 179, 184, 192, 194

Caleb 86, 171-174, 201-202
Calvin, J. 10, 26, 35, 38, 67, 123-124, 146, 159, 221-223
Canaan 22, 135, 143, 193
Canaanite(s) 25, 35, 53, 64, 96, 111, 121, 126-127, 130, 148-150, 166-167, 174-176, 214, 233
Carol, N. 18
Carr, D. 73-74
Carter, J. 23
characterization 126-127
chariots 167, 174
Charlesworth, J. 114

Charry, E. 205, 216, 224, 227-228
Childs, B.S. 120, 139, 168
Christ *see* Jesus
Chrysostom 46, 146
circumcision 115, 133-134
Cis-jordanians 177-183
cities of refuge 171
Clark, M. 218
Clément, O. 205, 230
Coats, G.W. 128
Cohn, H.H. 94
concursus 13
confession, confessional language
  102, 121, 126-127, 130-131, 144,
  147, 149-150, 152, 157-158, 224,
  226-227
conquest 14, 22, 26, 40, 78, 82, 93,
  94, 96, 105, 107, 120, 122, 124,
  133, 135, 140, 143, 153, 170, 183,
  190, 205-208, 211, 233
  partial 40, 185
  complete 40, 177, 186
conquest account(s) 88, 89-93, 164,
  170
  Assyrian 89, 92
  Egyptian 90
  Hittite 90-92
  Sabean 92
contagion 96, 100-104, 152
conversion 30, 44-45, 144, 147, 155,
  213, 230-231
Coogan, M.D. 141
Coote, R.B. 20, 24, 54-55, 233-234
Coupe, L. 16
covenant 126, 135, 143, 151-152,
  157, 186-188, 190, 198-200, 202
  violation 102-103, 150, 186-187
coveting 97, 198-202, 232
Cox, D.G.C. 168
Craigie, P. 106
Creach, J.F.D. 54-55, 100, 125, 128,
  157, 166, 195
creation 28, 129, 132, 176, 209
  mandate 87-88, 176
crucifixion 205-208
Crusades 11, 125, 154, 235, 238

cultural memory 4-7, 13, 15, 22, 45,
  50, 62, 64, 70, 130, 156, 177, 203,
  237-240
curse 144
Cyprian 46, 146
Cyril of Jerusalem 46, 146, 226

Daniélou, J. 132
Danites 117, 174-175
David 54, 198
Davies, D.J. 136
Davies, G.I. 74
Davis, E.F. 3, 121, 135, 143, 149, 201
Dawson, J.D. 8, 63-64, 132, 164
death 136, 150, 186, 202
Decalogue 102-103, 126, 128, 150
deception 125-126, 158-160
dedication to YHWH 96
desire 25-26, 122, 239
De Troyer, K. 114, 117
Deuteronomist(ic) 54, 72-81, 85-88,
  95-97, 99-104, 116, 121-122, 128,
  151, 160-161, 170, 177-178, 182,
  190, 201, 211, 237
deuteronomistic-חרם 97, 104-112,
  206
Dinah 158, 195
discernment 153
discourse 51, 70, 123, 147, 155, 176,
  183, 185, 203, 214, 233, 240
divine action 213
divine warrior / weapon 91, 163
D-Komposition see Deuteronomistic
dogmatism 140
Doty, W.G. 16-18, 25, 27, 33, 47-48
Douglas, M. 101
Driver, S.R. 84, 108
Dube, M.W. 53, 235
Dupré, L. 27

Earl, D.S. 45, 64, 132, 188, 195, 204,
  207, 226, 235
eating 135, 143
Ebal 156
ecumenism 148, 232
Eden 131-132
Edinger, E. 22
Egypt 59-60, 115, 125, 134, 142, 149

Index of Subjects and Authors

Eleazer 82, 84, 86
election 61, 153
Eliade, M. 15, 35, 37
Elohist 72, 190
Elssner, T.R. 238
enaction 36, 48, 112, 129, 185, 203
Engels, F. 21
Ephraim 171, 175
Esau 158
eschatology / eschatologization 26, 47, 61, 96, 106, 112, 122-123, 138, 186, 206, 239
ethical criticism / ethics 2-3, 9-12, 37-38, 164, 166, 204, 233-236
Evagrius 217
Evans, G.R. 8
exile / exilic 54, 209
existential significance 35, 121-123, 164-165, 175-176, 185, 195, 204
exodus / exodus tradition 14, 59-60, 73, 107, 127, 129, 136, 211
Ezra 188

faith 46, 53, 147, 155, 162-163, 175, 177, 213-233
    explicit 220-222
    formed 220-222, 227
    implicit 220-222, 231
    unformed 220-222
faith, uncertainty of 2, 31, 37
faithful commentary / picture / reading / response 31, 49-50, 63, 109, 120, 183, 212, 215
false consciousness 21, 69
fear *see* terror
feminist interpretation 204
Fensham, F.C. 161
fiction 31
Fishbane, M. 94, 108, 121, 129, 131
'fitting' 31, 49-50, 53, 69-70, 120, 152, 203, 212, 235, 237-238
Fleming, C. 23
Fleming, D.E. 91, 141-142
Ford, W.A. 168
Frei, H. 8
Fretheim, T.E. 129
Friedman, R.I. 69
Fritz, V. 76

genealogy 149, 172, 202, 212
genocide 3, 35, 47, 69, 235
genre 51, 89-93, 170, 184
geography 148, 172, 178-183, 192, 195, 202
Gerstenberger, E.S. 104
Gertz, J.C. 73, 75
giants 169-170
Gibeonites 82, 90, 157-167, 171, 198-200, 225-233
Gilbert of Tournai 125
Gilgal 86, 116-117
Girard, R. 22-25
glossa ordinaria 238
Gottwald, N.K. 59
Gnostics 9-10
grace 216-223
Gratian 11
Green, W.S. 11
Greer, R.A. 50
Gregory of Nazianzus 146
Gregory of Nyssa 6, 35, 38, 131, 164, 216-217, 230, 236
Grintz, J.M. 161
Gunn, D.M. 168
Güterbock, H.G. 93

Haak, R.D. 181
Hagner, D.A. 228-229
(hail)stones 91, 163
Halbwachs, M 4
Hall, K.D. 119
Hallo, W.W. 209
hardening the heart 168
Hawk, L.D. 17, 26, 32-33, 100, 102, 120, 123, 125, 134, 139, 142, 149, 156, 161, 166, 171-175, 178-179, 181, 183-184, 186-188, 193, 195-196, 238, 199
Heisig, J.W. 27
Hendy, A. von 15, 21, 27-29
Hervieu-Léger, D. 4-6
Hess, R.S. 103, 118, 141, 150, 157, 166, 172, 182, 194, 206, 226
Hess, rabbi I. 69
Hexateuch 72-79, 191, 209
Hiel 144
Hill, R.C. 164

historical criticism 2
history / historiography / historical context 2, 31, 37-38, 53, 59-60, 70, 72-79, 120-121, 188, 209-211, 233-234
Hoffman, Y. 94
holiness 151-152
Holland, T.A. and Netzer, E. 2
Holy Spirit 56, 238
Holy War 95, 106, 118
hope 214
Hurvitz, A. 83
Hyatt, J.P. 108

identity, construction of 44, 47, 55, 103, 117, 126-127, 133-134, 146-147, 150-151, 155-156, 165, 167, 171, 177-179, 189, 195, 197-203, 205, 208, 214-215, 231-233, 236-240
  ethnic 44, 153-155, 172, 178, 187, 195, 200
ideology 20-22, 44, 233-236
idols / idolatry 40, 69, 88, 98, 101-102, 109, 111-112, 126, 150, 185-188, 195, 197, 206-208, 212
impurity 100-104, 178-179
Incantation Against Infertility 92, 95
insider 44, 165
intermarriage 110-111, 185, 187, 192
intertextual, intertextuality 53, 156
initiative-taking 173-175, 201-202, 214, 226
Irenaeus 11, 50
irony 127, 148-149, 198
Ishtar 139
Israel 115-116

Jacob 158
James 225
James of Vitry 125
James, P. 2
Jebusites 175
Jericho 2, 17, 20, 79, 91-92, 96-98, 111, 116, 126, 139-149, 153, 190, 200, 207-208
Jerome 146

Jesus 6, 34, 62-63, 70, 118, 123, 131, 145, 156, 175-176, 183, 206, 208, 213, 240
Jobling, D. 129
Johnstone, W. 73
jonglerie 43
Jordan 6, 17, 32-33, 82, 122, 127-133, 136-137, 157, 179, 193, 202-203, 206, 212
Josephites 171
Joshua (person) 34, 38, 63, 84, 102, 122, 127, 139-140, 147-149, 155, 162-163, 165, 167, 170, 174, 183-196, 198
Josiah, Josianic 54-55, 233-234
Jubilee 142-143
Judah 149-150, 172-175
justification 119, 215, 218, 223-224, 231

Kaminsky, J.S. 97-98, 100, 102
Kang, S-M. 163
Kenizzite 171-172
Kent, B. 218
Kenyon, K. 2
Keret Epic 142
Kilmer, A.D. 169
kings, hostile 38, 160, 165, 201
Kirk, A. 14
Kloppenbeorg, J.S. 180
Knauf, E.A. 75, 78-79, 120, 178, 191, 210-211
Koopmans, W.T. 189
Kunin, S.D. 31, 33, 40-45, 49, 146, 195, 201

Laird, M. 216-217
land 54, 120-121, 127, 133-139, 153, 157, 170-177, 178-183, 185-186, 192, 201-205, 211, 235
  promise of 6, 111, 211
  distribution of 17
  control / possession of 95, 108
  life in 107
law *see torah*
Lawson Younger Jr., K. 89-91
Lash, N. 62-63, 207-208
Leach, E. 136-137

Index of Subjects and Authors

Levenson, J.D.   60, 129
Levin, C.   73-74
Levine, B.A.   107, 170
Levine, B.A. and De Tarragon, J-M.   169
Lévi-Strauss, C.   19, 33-34, 39-40
Levitvical cities   82, 86, 93, 171, 177
liminal / liminality   36-37, 99, 127, 136-138, 143, 149, 185, 197-201
limit-situation   47-48, 103, 109, 133, 150, 152, 232
literal meaning / sense   8-12, 30, 35, 37, 105, 112, 124
Lohfink, N.   94, 104
Lombardo, G.J.   218, 228
love   214, 240
Luther, Martin   216, 222
lying   *see* deception

MacDonald, N.B   30
Maier, C.T.   125
Malinowski, B.   21, 37
manifestation   60-61, 69-70
manna   135
Marcion / Marcionites   9-12, 236
Margalit, B.   163
Margolis, M.L.   114
Mari Letters   95
Marr, A.   23
Marx, K.   21
Masoretic Text   114-119
Matties, G.   24-25
Mattingly, G.L.   169
Maximus the Confessor   217-218, 230
Mbuwayesango, D.   20, 53, 235
McFague, S.   33, 65-67
mediation   111, 151, 199, 213
Mendenhall, G.E.   169
Meredith, A.   216
Mesha Inscription   91-92, 95, 99
midrash   11-12
Milgrom, J.   94, 104, 152
Miller, D.   22
Miller, P.D.   139
miracles / miraculous   17, 127, 130
Mitchell, G.   187
Moabites   105, 125
Moberly, R.W.L.   130, 214

modern   7, 12, 31, 225
Monroe, L.A.S.   92, 95
moon   163
moral difficulty   *see* ethics
moral interpretation / sense   37, 124
Mosca, P.G.   173
Moses   120, 126, 130, 137, 140, 156, 160-161, 170, 192, 198
Murray, P.D.   207-208
myth   13, 14-48, 49-50, 59-60, 91, 93, 99, 103, 105-112, 117, 124, 145, 154, 169-170, 175, 180, 197-240
  definition of   14-20
  existential / symbolic approaches   27-39
  historicizing / objectification / tiring of   33-35, 37, 70, 110, 180, 210-211
  ideological / sociological approaches   20-22
  neo-structuralist approaches   40-46
  psychological approaches   22-26, 122, 177, 239
  structuralist approaches   39-46
mythemes   41-43, 203-211

Naaman   45, 131, 146
narrative / narrative level meaning   30, 41-46, 63, 153-155, 164-167, 175, 185, 195, 197, 200-201, 225-233
Neusner, J.   65-66
Nelson, R.D.   17, 26, 54, 77-78, 83, 86, 98-100, 102, 115-117, 120-122, 125, 129-130, 134-135, 139, 141, 143, 157, 161, 172, 178-179, 184-188, 190-191
neo-structuralism   40-48, 105, 146-147, 150, 195, 197, 238
Nephilim   169-170
New Covenant / Testament   44, 123, 154, 156, 188, 207, 210, 213, 215, 230-233
Niditch, S.   106
Noll, K.L.   77
Northup, L.A.   16
Noth, M.   77, 83, 104, 183-184

oath   144, 160
O'Brien, T.C.   220
O'Mara, V. and Paul, S.   238
offering   96-99
Og   169
Old Covenant / Testament   44-45, 62, 134, 175, 207, 213, 235, 239
Origen   7-11, 34-35, 38, 49, 66-69, 111, 119, 123-124, 136, 138, 145, 153, 156, 161-164, 176-177, 183, 188, 195, 212, 227, 236, 238
Othniel   173
Otto, E.   73
outsider   25, 44, 110, 126, 147, 149, 153-155, 165, 193, 199-203

Palestinian context   67-69
Pannenberg, W.   56
Pantycelyn, W.W.   133
Park, H.D.   97, 102, 154
Parry, R.   30
Passover   115, 133-134, 137
patriarchs / patriarchal tradition   73, 107, 146, 211
patriarchy   173
Paul   9, 34, 156, 188, 216, 223, 225, 230
Pelagianism   224
Penelhum, T.   219
Pentateuch / pentateuchal criticism   72-76, 120, 190-191, 201
Phinehas   86, 182
P-Komposition   *see* Priestly
plagues   168
plenitude   50-51, 69-70, 112, 152, 203, 212
plunder   96-98, 143
poetic discourse   57, 59
Pola, T.   73-74
pollution   152
Polzin, R.   120, 127, 140, 179, 192-193, 199
post-colonial / post-colonialism   20, 51, 53, 160, 234-236
post-modern   12
pre-modern   7

Priestly   72-79, 81-88, 96-97, 100-104, 110-112, 128, 136, 143, 151, 170, 177-180, 182, 211, 237
priestly-חרם   94, 99, 104, 112, 117, 206
projection   22-26
promised land   26, 32, 123, 129, 193, 204
Prior, M   20, 235
prototypical past / time   47, 107-108, 112, 120, 170, 177, 185, 197, 201
Puritans   2, 69, 234

rabbinic interpretation   11-12
Rad, G. von   59, 106, 183, 189-190, 211
Rahab   6, 39, 44-48, 53, 60, 87, 93, 111, 115-116, 125-127, 140, 143-147, 150-151, 153-155, 157-158, 162, 165, 167, 17-173, 182, 187-188, 198-201, 214-216, 225-233, 235
Ramsey, G.W.   2
Ratheiser, G.M.H.   94, 106, 198
reception   55
recontextualization   203-205, 214, 231
referentiality   31, 49
regula fidei   11
Rendtorff, R.   74
repentance   147
Rephaim   107, 169-170, 174
rest   26, 107, 122, 128, 131, 134, 170, 173, 183, 204-205, 239
revelation / revelatory function   12, 30, 48, 55-64, 69-70, 87, 124
Ricoeur, P.   25-31, 40, 47, 49-64, 79, 89, 211, 233, 239
Rist, J.   218
rite of passage   136-138
Rofé, A.   134
Rogerson, J.W.   4, 18, 55
Römer, T.C.   77
Rowlett, L.L.   20, 93
Ruth   45, 146

sacrifice   98-99
salvation   126, 145-146, 162, 216-233
salvation history   209-211

Index of Subjects and Authors 261

Samuel   199
Sarna, N.M.   102
Saul   199
scapegoating   22-25
Schäfer-Lichtenberger, C.   94, 97
Schmid, K.   73, 107, 210-211
Schneiders, S.M.   28, 31, 50, 56
Schweinhorst, L.   77
Scripture   2, 7, 12-13, 50-53, 114, 236-240
Segal, R.A.   15-16, 19, 21, 24, 27
Segal, rabbi M.   69
Sennacherib   105
separation   95, 99, 108-112, 187-188, 197-203
Septuagint   76, 114-119, 155, 174
Shechem   78, 117, 195
Shechem (person)   158
Shilo   78, 82, 86, 117
Shittim   125
siege   141
Sihon   169
sin   118, 121, 149, 152, 206, 226
Smalley, B.   8
Smelik, K.A.D.   99
Soggie, N.A.   17, 60, 211, 236-237
Solomon   126
Sorel, G.   21
Southern, R.W.   8, 35
spies   60-61, 124-125, 144, 148, 150, 153
Spina, F.A.   17, 125-126
spiritual life   204-205, 236
spiritual sense / spiritualizing   8-12, 26, 34, 37, 47, 63, 66-69, 121, 124, 131-132, 164, 176, 183, 204, 206, 235-236, 239
Stern, P.D.   25, 94-95, 99, 105
Stevenson, W.T.   35, 57
Stoic etymology   63
Stone, L.G.   166-167, 201
Strange, J.   209
structuralism   25
structure / structural level meaning   41-46, 153-155, 166-167, 195, 197-200, 232
sun   163

symbol   27-35, 42, 46-48, 62-70, 103, 105, 112, 122-124, 129-130, 132-133, 138, 140-141, 143, 145, 148-150, 156, 163, 169-170, 180, 193, 195, 197-213, 238-240
  affectual aspect   110
  opaque / second-order sense   28, 34, 64-69, 105, 185
  plain / manifest sense / first order sense   28, 64-69, 105
  tiring of   *see* tiring of myth

tabernacle   176
taboo   100
Tamarin, G.R.   20
terror   90-91, 127
Tertullian   188
testimony   58-64, 69-70, 87, 177, 239
Theodore of Mopsuestia   45, 50
Theodoret of Cyrus   10, 46, 145, 153, 164, 183, 188
Thunberg, L.   217-218
Torah   17, 69, 93, 120-121, 155-156, 185, 192, 196, 202
Tov, E.   116
Toynbee, A.   68
tradition / traditionality   52-53, 55, 69-70, 72-88, 153-156, 201, 207, 215, 225, 238
transformation   30, 34, 44, 213, 232
Trans-jordanians   82, 86, 93, 123, 177-183
treasury of YHWH   96, 103
trust / trustworthiness   2-3, 7, 69-70
truth / truth-claim   2, 30-31, 49-50
Turner, V.   19, 30, 36-39, 47, 49, 136, 200-201, 235, 238-239
Type, typological sense   *see* spiritual sense

Ulrich, E.   114
unclean(ness)   *see* impurity

van der Meer, M.N.   76, 114-116, 209
van Gennep, A.   36, 136-138
Vanhoozer, K.   56-57
Van Seters, J.   73-74, 108, 139, 209
Vervenne, M   74, 76

virtue   10, 214-233

Waardenburg, J.   29, 33-34
Wagenaar, J.   82, 87, 136
Wallace, M.I.   30, 50
Walsh, R.G.   17-18
Waltke, B.K. and O'Connor, M.   99
war / warfare   121-122, 139-140, 153, 158, 163-166, 197, 205
war-חרם   94
Warrior, R.A.   3, 69
Weinfeld, M.   79-82, 163, 193, 211
Wesley, John   175
wilderness   137-138, 149
Williams, R.   12-13, 57-58, 204
Williams, R.B.   40
Wilson, R.R.   168
Wittgenstein, L. / Wittgensteinian   18, 30, 207, 224-225, 230
'world of the text'   29-30, 37, 52, 55, 62, 213
works   215, 218, 221

Yahwist   72-74, 77, 180, 190, 210
Young, F.M.   10

Zaharopoulos, D.   213
Zelophehad's daughters   86, 171, 173, 202
zerængi   159

Hebrew words and phrases

אבד   186
אבנים גדלות מן־השמים   163
אהב   187
אהה אדני יהוה   149
אהל מועד   84
אחז   95
אחזה   84
אכל   135
אות   157
אל חי   157
אלהי הנכר   158
אמץ   81, 168

ארץ   130

בדל   110-111
בערב   134
בעבר הנהר   193
בערבות   134
בקרב   144, 157-158
ברית   84

גורל   83
גנב   150
גר   83, 158
גרש   95

דבק   187

הגד הגד   160
הדף   184
המם   163
הרג   95, 99

וגם   149
והתהלכו   174
והתחלקו   174
ועתה   193

זבח   98

חבל   125
חזק   81, 168
חטא   149
חמד   143, 150, 198
חסד   126-127, 143-144, 150, 153, 167, 198, 202, 204, 229-230
חרם   25, 37, 48, 61, 63, 78-81, 88, 91-93, 94-112, 117-118, 121, 125, 127, 133, 143, 148, 150-153, 157, 160-161, 167, 170, 178, 184-185, 188, 197-203, 205-208, 212-214

טהר   101
טוב   150
טמא   101, 152, 178
טמן   149-150

Index of Subjects and Authors

ידבק בידך   101
יובל   142
ירש   81, 95, 110, 173, 175, 184-185
יצא   134
יצב   194

כבד   168
כבש   83, 86, 176
כחד   61, 108, 110
כחש   103
כל   123
כלה   83, 176
כליל   98
כנען   149
כרת   84

ל   96, 98-99
לב   168

מזבח   180
מלא אחר יהוה   80-81, 172
מלאכים   150
מעבור   134
מעל   101, 103, 148, 151, 182
מקלט   83
מרמה   158-159

נבלה   149
נגע   101, 160
נוח   26, 122, 144, 183, 204
נורא עלילה   130
נחלה   149
נכה   83
נפלאות   130, 157
נקף   141
נשׂיא   84
נתן   121, 141

סבב   141, 148
סור   81
סות   173
ספר תורת אלהים   190

עבר   122, 128-129, 133-134, 150, 179, 186-187, 202

עברו את־בריתי   150
עדה   83
עבור   149
עכן   149
עכר   149
ערמה   158, 161, 198
פרשׂ   100
פשׂה   100

צרעה   194

קדשׁ   96-98, 101, 143, 151
קיא   61, 108, 110
קצף   157
קשׁה   168

ראה   150
רוח   99
רית   99

שׂר־צבא־יהוה   140

שׁבע   127
שׁברים   148
שׁבת   122
שׁוטר   157
שׁכב   125
שׁלח   110
שׁמד   99, 118, 121, 157, 160-161, 186
שׁקט   173
שׁקץ   96-98

תעב   96-97

Akkadian words

apkallu   169
assaku   95
ḫarāmu   95, 111
maqatu   91
ummiānu   169

Ugaritic words

hrg 95
ḥrm 95
rhb 125

Greek words

ἀνάθεμα 111, 118
πληρόω 156
σφηκια 194
τέλος 156

INDEX OF SCRIPTURE

Old Testament

Genesis
1:4   110
1:6   110
1:7   110
1:14   110
1:18   110
1:28   83-84, 176
2:1-2   83-84, 176
2:2-4   122
2:24   187
3:1   158
3:6   150
8:20   155
12:1-7   177
12:7   142
12:7-8   155
13:14-18   177
15:18-21   142
17:1-14   171
17:8   142
20:13   126
21:23   126
24:26   99
27:35   158-159
32:11   129
33:20   180
34   45, 64, 149, 158-160, 195, 198-199
34:1-31   195
34:13   158-159
34:40   161
35   195
35:1-2   195
35:7   180
36:11   171
36:15   171
36:42   171

Exodus
2   78
3   139
3:8   142
3:12   139
3:13-15   195
12:1-32   125
14   78
14:15-18   129
15:1-21   129
15:3   65
16:3   148
17:3   148
17:15   180
19:12   137
19:13   142
19:17   194
19:23-24   137
20:2   59
20:6   126
20:11   122
21:14   158
23:12   122
23:20-33   61, 81, 86, 108, 110
23:23   61, 108
28:31   98
33:14   122
34:6-7   126
34:10-14   108
39:22   98
39:32   84, 176
40:33   84, 176

Leviticus
2:1-6   152
3:3-4   128
4:2   152
5:4   144
6:15   98
6:16   98
12:4   101

265

Leviticus (cont.)
13-14   100
14:46-47   101
16:3-22   152
17:1-7   181
18   152
18:9-18   48
18:21   152
18:24   25, 152
18:24-29   152
18:25   61, 108, 110
18:26   151
18:28   108, 110
19:31   152
20:2   152
20:11-24   152
20:22   108, 110
20:22-26   108, 110
20:23   110
20:24   110
20:26   110
21:7   151
21:8   151
21:15   151
21:18   104
21:23   151
22:9   151
22:16   151
22:32   151
25   142-143
25:8   142
25:8-55   142
25:10   142
25:25-34   142
25:39-55   142
26   104, 143
26:15   152
26:30   161
26:31   143
26:33   143
26:34-35   152
26:38   186
27   80, 94, 96, 98, 101-102, 104, 142
27:3   104
27:21   96, 104
27:21-29   104
27:28   98

Leviticus (cont.)
27:28-29   96-97, 104

Numbers
4:6   98
6:5-8   151
10:33   122, 128
10:35-36   128
10:36   122
11:25-26   122
13   125, 141, 148, 174
13:1-33   86, 107, 124
13:21   125
13:28   140, 169
13:33   169
14:2-3   148
14:8   26
14:24   81, 172
15:15-16   83
18:14   96, 104
19:14   100
21:16   86
21:21-35   94
21:21ff   108
22-24   86
22:21-35   139
23:5-6   115
25   125, 182
25:6-13   182
25:7   86
25:11   86
26   135
26-27   82
26-36   82
26:1   86
27:1-11   86
27:2   86
32   86
32-33   81, 85
32-34   82
32:4   83
32:11-12   81, 172
32:22   83, 176
32:29   83, 176
33:50-56   86, 108
33:50-35:29   83
33:52   161
34   86, 172

Index of Scripture

Numbers (cont.)
- 34:1-12   86
- 35   82, 86
- 35:6   83
- 35:9-15   83
- 35:11   83
- 35:12   83
- 35:13   83
- 35:14   83
- 35:15   83
- 35:25   117
- 35:25ff   75
- 35:26   83
- 35:27   83
- 35:28   83
- 35:32   83
- 36   173
- 36:1ff   86
- 36:4   142

Deuteronomy
- 1:22ff   124
- 1:36   81, 86, 172
- 1:41   99
- 2-3   108
- 2:10-11   169
- 2:11   107
- 2:24-3:11   94
- 2:30   81, 168
- 3:11   107, 169
- 3:20   122
- 3:28   81
- 4   86
- 4:4   101
- 4:20   142
- 4:26   186
- 4:39   126, 198
- 4:41-43   83
- 4:47   169
- 5:10   126
- 5:14   122
- 5:19   102, 150
- 6-11   200, 213
- 6:20-24   189
- 7   87, 96, 101, 107, 110-111, 127, 144-145, 167, 199
- 7:1   188

Deuteronomy (cont.)
- 7:1-5   61, 81, 109, 112, 125-127, 151, 184-185, 197, 200-201, 206
- 7:2   84
- 7:2a   109
- 7:2b-3   109, 111
- 7:4   186
- 7:5   197
- 7:8   142
- 7:12   126
- 7:20   186
- 7:23   186
- 7:24   120
- 7:25   101
- 7:25-26   96-98, 100, 103
- 8:19   186
- 8:20   186
- 9:1ff   140
- 9:1-3   107
- 9:2   169
- 9:4-5   121, 145, 167
- 9:5   25
- 10:1-5   128
- 10:6   86
- 10:20   101
- 11:9   26
- 11:17   186
- 11:22   101
- 11:24   25   120, 175
- 11:29   155
- 12:9-10   122
- 12:15-24   181
- 13   96, 101-102, 110
- 13:5   101
- 13:13-19   96, 100-102, 109
- 13:16-17   97-98
- 13:16-18   102
- 13:17   98
- 13:18   101
- 15:7   81
- 16:1   99
- 17:18-19   120
- 19   86
- 19:1-8   83
- 19:1-13   117
- 20   101, 161, 167, 199
- 20:16-18   108

Index of Scripture

Deuteronomy (cont.)
- 20:17-18   102
- 21:10-24   187
- 21:22-23   164
- 21:23   118
- 23:10-15   144
- 25:17   169
- 25:19   122, 169
- 26:5   186
- 26:5-9   59, 189
- 27   116, 155
- 27:4ff   155
- 28:20   186
- 28:21   101
- 28:60   101
- 29   150
- 29:1-15   161
- 29:11   128-129
- 29:16-18   150
- 29:16-21   150
- 29:18   150
- 29:19   150
- 29:20   150
- 29:20-21   150
- 30:18   128-129, 186
- 30:20   101
- 31:4   169
- 31:6-7   81
- 31:14   84
- 31:23   81
- 32:8   179
- 32:49   84
- 32:51   103
- 33:10   98
- 33:29   163

Joshua
- 1   78, 81-82, 93, 120-124, 125, 128, 141, 160, 184
- 1-11   81, 166, 175, 177
- 1-12   74-75, 78, 83, 86-87, 111-112, 171, 184-185
- 1-22   183, 185
- 1:2   122
- 1:2-5   26
- 1:2-8   183
- 1:2-9   120
- 1:3   174, 177

Joshua (cont.)
- 1:5   80, 85
- 1:5-6   184
- 1:5-9   121
- 1:6   80-81, 85
- 1:6-9   164
- 1:7   80-81, 85
- 1:7-8   184
- 1:8   80, 85
- 1:9   80-81, 85
- 1:9-12   114
- 1:10-11   120
- 1:11   80, 85, 122, 157
- 1:12-15   120
- 1:12-18   123
- 1:13   26, 80, 85, 122
- 1:14   122
- 1:15   26, 80, 85, 122
- 1:16-18   120
- 1:18   80-81, 85
- 2   17, 60, 78, 93, 124-127, 133, 148
- 2-10   167
- 2-11   197, 199, 202, 213
- 2-12   184, 201
- 2-21   202
- 2:1   125, 141
- 2:2   141
- 2:4-15   114
- 2:6   149-150
- 2:7   129
- 2:9   121, 141
- 2:9-11   157
- 2:10   85, 127, 160, 169
- 2:10-11   198
- 2:10-12   198
- 2:11   80, 85, 126, 148
- 2:11-12   114
- 2:12   126-127
- 2:13   182
- 2:14   115, 121, 141
- 2:17   127
- 2:18   141
- 2:20   127
- 2:24   121, 141
- 3   78
- 3-4   17, 78, 82, 127-133, 137, 183

Joshua (cont.)
- 3-5   141
- 3:1   82, 85
- 3:1-13   32
- 3:2   157
- 3:4   78, 82, 85
- 3:5   130, 157
- 3:6   128
- 3:7   127, 130
- 3:8   82, 85, 128
- 3:9-13   130
- 3:10   127, 157, 188
- 3:13   26, 128
- 3:14   128
- 3:15   82, 85
- 3:15-4:3   114
- 4:1-3   128
- 4:3   26, 128
- 4:6   157
- 4:8   26, 128
- 4:9   82, 85, 128
- 4:12   128
- 4:14   127, 130
- 4:15-24   82, 85
- 4:16   128
- 4:19   78, 82, 141
- 4:19a   78
- 4:20   127, 128
- 4:23   127, 129, 132
- 4:24   80, 85, 127, 130, 133
- 5   115-116, 133, 142-143, 155
- 5-24   212
- 5:1   80, 85, 148, 160, 166, 169
- 5:1-12   133-139
- 5:2   116
- 5:2-6   115
- 5:2-7   114
- 5:2-9   115, 137
- 5:6   121
- 5:10   137
- 5:10-12   78, 82, 85, 115, 134-135
- 5:12   137
- 5:13   139
- 5:13-15   139-140, 153, 208
- 6   17, 76, 78-79, 93, 96-97, 137, 140-148, 153, 190, 208
- 6-7   96-97
- 6-11   197, 208

Joshua (cont.)
- 6:1   141
- 6:3b-6   116, 143
- 6:4   142
- 6:5   142
- 6:5-10   114
- 6:6   142
- 6:7-15   116
- 6:8   142
- 6:13   142
- 6:16   141
- 6:17   85, 94, 96-98, 118, 127, 150
- 6:17-18   103
- 6:18   85, 100, 102, 148-149
- 6:19   75, 80, 96- 97, 103-104, 117, 143, 206
- 6:21   85, 96
- 6:22-23   144
- 6:23   26, 144
- 6:24   75, 80, 96-97, 103-104, 117, 143, 206
- 6:25   144, 157
- 7   17, 83, 93, 97, 101-103, 150-152, 154, 157, 182
- 7-8   78
- 7:1   85, 97, 102-103, 148-149, 171, 182, 186
- 7:1-8:29   148-155
- 7:2ff   124
- 7:5   80, 85, 148
- 7:6-9   148
- 7:7   186
- 7:9   80, 85, 148
- 7:10-15   100
- 7:11   80, 85, 102-103, 149-150, 186
- 7:12   85, 97, 100, 102, 186
- 7:12-13   102, 157
- 7:12-17   114
- 7:13   85
- 7:15   80, 85, 100, 149, 186
- 7:16-18   149
- 7:19   149
- 7:19-20   149, 154, 226
- 7:19-21   198
- 7:21   97, 102-103, 149-150
- 7:22   150

Joshua (cont.)
   7:26   186
   8   96, 103, 153, 157, 164
   8:1   80, 85, 121, 153
   8:2   103, 153
   8:3-22   141
   8:9-17   116
   8:13-14   114
   8:18   26, 114
   8:22   80, 85
   8:26   85
   8:29   164
   8:30-35   17, 116, 133-134, 155-156
   8:31   80, 85
   8:32   80, 85
   8:34-35   114
   8:35   158
   9   78, 84, 157-163, 199, 200
   9-10   157-166
   9:1   160, 166, 169
   9:1-2   160-161, 198
   9:2   161
   9:3   160
   9:3-4a   166
   9:2   116
   9:6   84-85, 159
   9:7   84-85, 157-158, 161
   9:9-10   157
   9:10   160, 169
   9:11   84-85
   9:14   160
   9:14-27   40, 61
   9:15   83-85, 161
   9:15b   78
   9:15-21   82, 85
   9:16   84-85, 157-158
   9:18   83-84
   9:19   83-84, 160
   9:20   157
   9:21   83-84
   9:22   157-158
   9:23   160
   9:24   80, 85, 121, 157-158, 160, 186
   9:27   80, 83, 85
   10   78-79, 90-91, 116, 157, 160-166

Joshua (cont.)
   10-11   78, 93
   10:1   85, 158, 160
   10:1-5   166, 198
   10:2-5   114
   10:3-6   141
   10:5   169
   10:6   169
   10:8   80, 85
   10:8-11   114
   10:9-11   141
   10:10   163, 169
   10:11   26, 163-164, 166
   10:12   169
   10:12-14   163
   10:15   116
   10:16-28   164
   10:18   38
   10:24   163
   10:25   80-81, 85, 163
   10:26-28   9
   10:27   164
   10:28   40, 61, 80, 85, 160
   10:29-42   165
   10:30   80, 85
   10:33   80, 85
   10:35   160
   10:37   80, 85, 160
   10:39   80, 85, 160
   10:40   80, 85, 160, 165
   10:40-41   83
   10:40-42   163
   10:40-43   66
   10:41-42   164
   10:43   116
   11   78, 107, 166-170
   11-12   166-170
   11:1-5   141, 166, 198
   11:3   169
   11:4   166
   11:6   26, 166
   11:7-8   141
   11:8   80, 85
   11:11   80, 85
   11:12   85
   11:12-13   40, 61
   11:14   9, 80, 85, 186
   11:15   82, 85, 167, 170

Joshua (cont.)
- 11:16   170
- 11:19   121, 166-167
- 11:19-20   161, 168
- 11:20   82, 85, 167-168, 186
- 11:21   85
- 11:21-22   168, 170
- 11:21-23   107
- 11:22   40, 61
- 11:23   170, 172
- 12   120, 170
- 12:2   169
- 12:4   169
- 12:6   80, 85
- 12:7   80, 85
- 12:7-24   40, 61
- 13-19   170-171, 173
- 13-21   17, 83-84, 86, 93, 170-177, 179, 201
- 13-22   74-75, 81, 87, 178
- 13:1   84
- 13:1-6   170
- 13:1-7   81, 86, 172
- 13:1-21:42   77-78, 81, 85, 170
- 13:2-6   86
- 13:6   26
- 13:8ff   86
- 13:12   169
- 13:13   158
- 13:21   84-85
- 13:22   86
- 14   81
- 14-17   78
- 14-19   82
- 14-21   83
- 14:1   84, 86
- 14:1-5   82, 85
- 14:1-21:40   82
- 14:2   83
- 14:6   172
- 14:6-15   78
- 14:8   80-81, 85, 172
- 14:9   80-81, 172, 174
- 14:12   172-173
- 14:13   172
- 14:14   80-81, 171-172
- 14:15   172-173
- 15:1   83, 85

Joshua (cont.)
- 15:13ff   173
- 15:16-19   173
- 15:18   173
- 15:18-20   173
- 15:63   40, 61, 175
- 16:1   83, 85
- 16:10   40, 61, 158, 175
- 17:1   83, 85
- 17:1-5   114
- 17:3-4   86
- 17:4   84-86
- 17:11-12   40, 61
- 17:11-15   114
- 17:13   81, 175
- 17:14   83, 85, 174
- 17:14-18   171
- 17:16-18   176
- 17:17   83, 85
- 18-19   73-74
- 18-21   78
- 18:1   78, 82-87, 117, 176
- 18:1-10   82, 174
- 18:2-19:48   78, 210
- 18:3   80-81, 85, 121
- 18:5   174
- 18:6   83, 85
- 18:7   158
- 18:8   83, 85, 174
- 18:9   174
- 18:10   83, 85
- 18:11   83, 85
- 19:1   83, 85
- 19:10   83, 85
- 19:17   83, 85
- 19:24   83, 85
- 19:32   83, 85
- 19:40   83, 85
- 19:47   40, 61, 175
- 19:47-48   117, 174
- 19:49-51   82, 84, 87, 176
- 19:51   82-86
- 20   75, 171, 177
- 20-21   82-83, 86, 93
- 20:1-9   83
- 20:2   83, 85
- 20:3   83, 85
- 20:3-6   117

Joshua (cont.)
- 20:6   83, 85
- 20:9   83, 85
- 21   86, 171, 177
- 21:1   84, 86
- 21:1-8   82, 85
- 21:4   83
- 21:5   83
- 21:6   83
- 21:10   83, 85
- 21:12   84-85
- 21:13   83, 85
- 21:20   83, 85
- 21:21   83, 85
- 21:27   83, 85
- 21:32   83, 85
- 21:38   83, 85
- 21:40   83, 85
- 21:41   84-85
- 21:42   80, 85
- 21:43   80, 85
- 21:43-45   40, 61, 75, 78, 160, 177-178, 183, 205, 210-211
- 21:43-22:6 (8)   178
- 21:44   26, 122, 172, 177, 183
- 21:44-45   209
- 22   47, 79, 83, 86, 93, 178-183, 202
- 22:1-6   178
- 22:1-9   75
- 22:3   80, 85
- 22:4   26, 84, 121
- 22:5   80, 85, 101
- 22:7-34   178
- 22:9   84, 179
- 22:10   181
- 22:10-34   82, 85, 87, 180
- 22:11   181
- 22:12   83, 117
- 22:13   86
- 22:14   84
- 22:16   83, 103, 182
- 22:17   83
- 22:18   83
- 22:19   84, 129, 178-179
- 22:20   83, 85, 103, 157, 182
- 22:22   182
- 22:23   178

Joshua (cont.)
- 22:24-25   129
- 22:24-28   179
- 22:25   117
- 22:26   178
- 22:28-29   179
- 22:29   117
- 22:30   83-84
- 22:30-33   182
- 22:31   86, 103, 182
- 22:32   84, 86, 179
- 22:34   179
- 23   74, 78, 82, 86-87, 120, 183-189, 190-192, 196, 210
- 23-24   17, 93, 108-109, 111, 160, 175-176, 185, 197, 200-201, 204, 207
- 23:1   26, 80, 85, 122, 183, 191
- 23:1ff   183
- 23:3   80, 85, 184, 188
- 23:3-4   184
- 23:3-5   191
- 23:4   80, 85, 188
- 23:5   26, 80, 85, 183-185
- 23:6   80-81, 85, 109, 184
- 23:6-8   184-185
- 23:6-13   191
- 23:7   80, 85, 109, 188, 191
- 23:7-8   184, 191
- 23:8   80, 85, 101, 187
- 23:9   80, 85, 184-185, 188
- 23:9-10   26, 40, 61, 184-185, 191
- 23:10a   184
- 23:11   80, 85, 184-185, 187
- 23:12   80, 85, 101, 109, 184, 187-188, 191
- 23:13   80, 85, 109, 121, 185-187
- 23:14   80, 85, 185, 191
- 23:14-15   185
- 23:15   80, 85, 186
- 23:15-16   121
- 23:16   80, 85, 186-187, 191, 193
- 24   73, 78, 185, 188, 189-196
- 24:1   78, 117, 190, 194
- 24:1-13   189
- 24:2   80, 190-191, 193-194
- 24:2-13   191-195
- 24:5   158

Joshua (cont.)
- 24:7   80, 190
- 24:8   190, 193
- 24:11   130, 190
- 24:11-13   40, 61
- 24:12   194
- 24:13   121, 190, 193
- 24:14   80-81, 109, 190, 193
- 24:14ff   193
- 24:14-15   190-191
- 24:14-24   191
- 24:16   80, 190
- 24:16-18   194
- 24:17   80, 158
- 24:17-18a   195
- 24:18   80
- 24:19   195
- 24:19-20   194
- 24:20   190
- 24:21   194
- 24:23   81, 109, 158, 195
- 24:25   190
- 24:26   190
- 24:27   191
- 24:29   191
- 24:29b   78
- 24:29-33   117
- 24:31   80-81, 85
- 24:33   82, 85-86

Judges
- 1:1-2:5   209
- 1:15   209
- 1:17   105
- 1:23ff   124
- 3:3   86
- 3:28   129
- 6:22   148
- 6:24   180
- 7:15-22   141
- 8:4   129
- 10:9   129
- 12:5   129
- 18:2ff   124
- 20:40   98
- 21:11   105

1 Samuel
- 1:3   99
- 2:8   99
- 3:20   99
- 4:5-6   141
- 6:6   168
- 6:19   128
- 7:9   98
- 7:12   180
- 14:31-35   155
- 15   105, 107, 112
- 17:45   66
- 23:22   158
- 26:19   180

2 Samuel
- 5:10   141
- 6:2   128
- 14:17   122
- 17:22   129
- 21   160
- 21:6   98
- 24:25   156

1 Kings
- 5:17   164
- 6:1-2   99
- 8:23   126, 198
- 9:21   105
- 9:23   159
- 11:6   172
- 16:34   79, 144
- 18:17-40   180
- 18:30-32   156
- 19:10   99
- 20:42   105

2 Kings
- 2:15   122
- 5:15-19   180
- 5:17   180
- 6:33   99
- 16:10   156
- 19:11   105-106

1 Chronicles
- 1:36   171
- 1:53   171

1 Chronicles (cont.)
   2:6   154
   4:41   105
   6:42   83
   6:52   83
   8:10   159
   15:2   128
   21:14-16   139
   28:2   122

2 Chronicles
   14:10   66
   20:23   105
   32:14   105
   36:13   168

Ezra
   3:2-3   156
   6:21   110
   9-10   188
   9:1   110-111
   9:1ff   111
   10:8   96, 104
   10:11   110-111

Nehemiah
   8:8   190
   8:18   190

Job
   3:13   122
   3:26   122
   5:12   158
   5:13   158
   15:5   158
   15:35   159
   31:5   159

Psalms
   2:8   188
   5:7   159
   10:7   159
   17:1   159
   20:8   66
   23:2   122
   24:4   159
   34:14   159
   35:20   159

Psalms (cont.)
   36:4   159
   38:13   159
   43:1   159
   50:19   159
   51:21   98
   52:6   159
   55:12   159
   55:24   159
   66   130
   66:5   130
   66:6   130, 132
   66:16   130
   78:55   125
   82:8   188
   83:4   158
   95:8   168
   98:6   141
   109:2   159
   110:1   163
   114   17
   114:3   132
   114:5   132
   116:7   122
   132:8   122
   132:14   122
   135   106
   136   106
   137   106, 180

Proverbs
   1:4   158
   8:5   158
   8:12   158
   11:1   159
   12:5   159
   12:16   158
   12:17   159
   12:20   159
   12:23   158
   13:16   158
   14:8   158-159
   14:15   158
   14:18   158
   14:25   159
   15:5   158
   19:17   228
   19:25   158

Proverbs (cont.)
  20:23   159
  22:3   158
  26:24   159
  27:12   158
  31:10-31   125
  31:13   125
  31:21   125

Ecclesiastes 6

Isaiah
  2:18   98
  11:2   26, 122
  11:15   106
  14:3   26, 122
  14:7   26, 122
  28:12   26, 122
  32:18   26, 122
  34:2   106
  34:5   98, 106
  34:5-7   98
  37:1   105
  37:11   106
  37:18-19   106
  43:28   96, 106-107
  53   206
  53:9   159
  63:14   122
  63:17   168
  66:1   122

Jeremiah
  1:6   149
  5:27   159
  9:5   159
  9:7   159
  20:16   141
  25:9   106-107
  45:3   122
  50:21   106
  50:26   106
  51:1-3   96
  51:3   106

Lamentations
  2:15   98

Ezekiel
  4:14   149
  11:14-16   180
  16:14   98
  20:7   190
  23:3   190
  23:8   190
  27:3   98
  28:12   98
  44:29   96, 104
  47-48   172
  48   179

Daniel
  8:25   159
  11:23   159
  11:44   106
  12:13   26, 122

Hosea
  9:3-4   180
  12:1   159
  12:8   159

Amos
  2:9-10   169
  7:7   179
  7:17   180
  8:5   159

Micah
  4:13   98-99, 106
  6:4-5   130
  6:8   126
  6:11   159

Zephaniah
  1:9   159

Zechariah
  6:8   122
  14:11   106-107
  14:21   25

Deutero-canonical

Sirach
   44-50   210
   46:1-6   210

2 Maccabees
   12:15   210

New Testament

Matthew
   5:17   156
   7:21-23   215
   15:21-28   146, 175, 214
   25   228
   25:31-46   214-215, 229
   25:40   228
   25:45   228

Mark
   7:1-23   205
   7:14-23   176, 207

Luke
   18:9-14   215
   23:39-43   215
   24:32   156
   24:27   156

John
   1:28   132
   3:16-21   214
   3:19-21   230
   3:26   132
   10:40   132

Acts
   5   154
   7   17
   10-11   45

Romans
   7:14   156
   9:20-21   67
   10:4   156

1 Corinthians
   2:12-13   156
   5:9-13   188
   7   188
   10:2   132
   13   214

2 Corinthians
   3:6   156
   3:15-16   156
   5:21   118, 206
   6:14-18   188

Galatians
   3:13   118
   3:24-25   213

Ephesians
   2:5   230
   2:8   230
   6   38
   6:10-18   164-165, 204

Colossians
   3:5   154

1 Thessalonians
   2:13   13

2 Timothy
   1:9   230
   3:16   2

Titus
   3:5   230

Hebrews
   4:16   175, 214
   11:31   46, 146, 215

James
   2:20-26   17, 215
   2:24-26   232
   2:25   46, 146
   4:2   154

2 Peter
    3:1-5   230

1 John
    1:9-10   226

Apostolic Fathers

1 Clement
    12   46, 146, 215

Dead Sea Scrolls

1QS   203
    i.16f   129
    ii.19-25   129
    ii.25-iii.12   129
    iii.3-12   132

4Q379
    3 II 5-6   97

11Q19
    LV 6-12   102

4QJosh^a 114, 116, 133-134, 155, 209

4QJosh^b 114

XJoshua   114-115

Numbers Rabbah
    8.9   147
    23.6   154

Ruth Rabbah
    2.1   147

Canticles Rabbah
    1.22   147
    6.10   147

Ecclesiastes Rabbah
    5.13   147, 229
    8.13   147

Jewish

Megilah
    14b   147

Mekhilta Shirata
    IV.5-6   65-66, 165, 207, 239

Leviticus Rabbah
    9.1   154

www.ingramcontent.com/pod-product-compliance
Lightning Source LLC
Chambersburg PA
CBHW030512080526
44586CB00011B/162